ON THE ROAD TO EMMAUS

ON THE ROAD TO EMMAUS

THE CATHOLIC DIALOGUE WITH AMERICA AND MODERNITY

GLENN W. OLSEN

THE CATHOLIC UNIVERSITY OF AMERICA PRESS
WASHINGTON, D.C.

The paper used in this publication meets the minimum requirements
of American National Standards for Information Science—
Permanence of Paper for Printed Library Materials,
ANSI Z39.48-1984.
∞

Library of Congress Cataloging-in-Publication Data
Olsen, Glenn W. (Glenn Warren), 1938–
On the road to Emmaus : the Catholic dialogue with America
and modernity / Glenn W. Olsen.
p. cm.
Includes bibliographical references and index.
ISBN 978-0-8132-1954-7 (cloth : alk. paper)
1. Christianity and culture—United States—History—
21st century. 2. Church and state—United States—History—21st century.
3. Christianity and politics—United States—History—21st century.
4. Catholic Church—Doctrines.
I. Title.
BR115.C80485 2012
261′.10973—dc23
2011033549

CONTENTS

PART 3. THE ENCOUNTER WITH EUROPE, NATIVE AMERICANS, AND MODERNITY

ACKNOWLEDGMENTS

Bibliographical information on the place of original publication of each essay in this book is as follows:

1. "The 'Catholic Moment' and the Question of Inculturation," in *Catholicity and the New Evangelization*, Proceedings from the Seventeenth Convention of the Fellowship of Catholic Scholars, Corpus Christi, Texas, 1994 (Steubenville, Ohio: Franciscan University Press, 1995), 17–54.

2. "The Investiture Contest," in *Religion in the Making of Western Man*, ed. Frank J. Coppa (Jamaica, N.Y.: St. John's University Press, 1974), 79–93.

3. "Lay Spirituality *ad majorem Dei gloriam*," *Communio* 6 (1979): 405–12.

4. "Christian Faith in a Neo-Pagan Society," in *Christian Faith in a Neo-Pagan Society*, ed. Paul Williams (Scranton: Northeast Books, 1981), 16–34.

5. "Thy Kingdom Come on Earth as in Heaven: The Place of the Family in Creation," in *"And You Will Be My Witnesses,"* 2nd ed. (Irving, Tex.: University of Dallas Center for Christianity and the Common Good, 1993), 1–28.

6. "Separating Church and State," *Faith and Reason* 20 (1994): 403–25.

7. "Religion, Politics, and America at the Millennium," *Faith and Reason* 22 (1996): 285–315.

8. "America as an Enlightenment Culture," in *Actas del IV Congreso "Cultura Europea,"* Ed. Enrique Banús and Beatriz Elío (Pamplona: Arazandi, 1998), 121–28.

9. "John Rawls and the Flight from Authority: The Quest for Equality as an Exercise in Primitivism," *Interpretation: A Journal of Political Philosophy* 21 (1994): 419–36.

10. "The Quest for a Public Philosophy in Twentieth-Century American Political Thought," *Communio* 27 (2000): 340–62.

11. "Unity, Plurality, and Subsidiarity in Twentieth-Century Context," in *Actas del III Congreso "Cultura Europea,"* ed. Enrique Banús (Pamplona: Arazandi, 1996), 311–17.

12. "The Ethics of Conquest: The European Background of Spain's Mission in the New World," *Communio* 19 (1992): 619–34.

ON THE ROAD TO EMMAUS

INTRODUCTION

IN 2010 I PUBLISHED *The Turn to Transcendence: The Role of Religion in the Twenty-First Century.*[1] Though this was a large volume, there were many points touched on in it, especially in regard to politics and social thought, that I could not fully develop. Thus I formed the idea of issuing a second volume containing many of my published essays on religion, society, and politics, in which I had considered specific topics more fully than in the first book. I have decided to give this second volume a title that needs some explanation: *On the Road to Emmaus: The Catholic Dialogue with America and Modernity.* A famous bas-relief corner pier at Santo Domingo de Silos in Spain portrays Christ and two of his disciples on the road to Emmaus (Luke 24:13–35) after Christ's resurrection. According to Luke, the two disciples were walking along the road to Emmaus and talking about the events of the past week, about the meaning of Jesus' death and of women from their group finding his tomb empty and an angel declaring he was alive. Jesus joins them, but they do not recognize him. He chastises them for not believing the full message of the prophets—that is, that Christ would suffer and enter into glory. Jesus then proceeds through the (Jewish) scriptures to explain all that has been said of himself. Only at table do the disciples recognize him.

In the Middle Ages this story was taken to be about the nature of the Christian life, specifically about how, as the Christian is *in via,*

1. Glenn W. Olsen, *The Turn to Transcendence: The Role of Religion in the Twenty-First Century* (Washington, D.C.: The Catholic University of America Press, 2010).

he reflects on and more fully understands or appropriates the meaning of Christ. Some understood pilgrimage, because it is a kind of peripatetic meditation, to express this especially well. The pilgrim is to stop and meditate as he or she walks the pilgrim route. Christ, as on the road to Emmaus, gives a kind of catechism in the faith, explains its mysteries. The sculptor at Silos, a possible stop on the road to Santiago de Compostela, daringly placed the pilgrim badge of the road to Santiago (a scallop logo) on Christ's purse, as if Christ in traveling to Emmaus was anticipating the pilgrimage to Santiago. On both *caminos* the pilgrim received enlightenment from Christ.

I particularly strongly identify with this story, and thus the title of the present book. I view my life as a long "enlightenment" or education not simply by Christ, but by his disciples— that is, by those whom I have fallen among in walking my *peregrinatio.* Some of these are mentioned toward the end of this introduction. By analogy I apply the idea to the place of Catholicism in America and in the modern world. It has not been easy anyplace in the modern world for the Catholic Church to find its way. With special attention to the United States, the goal of this book is to explore the issues and options that have faced Christianity and continue to do so. The hope is first to understand better the senses in which the Christian is called to be in but not of the world, just as the pilgrim is always "on the way," and not yet "at home." But since a good deal of what I have to say at least partly involves "natural questions," I also hope that all of good will might find value in my analysis of many questions.

Naturally over the years I have been challenged on various points, and on some topics the scholarly literature has significantly developed. Occasionally my views have shifted. The purpose of this introduction is to remark on some of the challenges that have been made to positions I have embraced, to describe at least briefly where I stand now on some of the principal questions, and to take account of important developments in the scholarly literature (on this latter see also the various forewords and afterwords).

My overall political and social thought may be described as "incarnational," or as "Catholic incarnational humanism" (see especially the chapters of part 1).[2] I gather particular inspiration from the original Jesuits, with their twin beliefs that God can be found in all things, and that all should be done to the greater glory of God. I wish Christians to be "lay Jesuits." But that was also Ignatius of Loyola's original proposal: his *Spiritual Exercises* were not directed simply to Jesuits or the clergy, but to all Christians. Since the logic of an incarnational orientation is to bring the message of Christ to all, and, so far as that is possible, to reform all life, personal and social, in the light of Christ—to give it the *forma Christi*—there is potential for conflict with basic American premises, especially perhaps with the doctrine of the separation of church and state. One can understand and sympathize with the reasons that doctrine became part of the American constitutional tradition early on, but at least by one reading, its logic seems to block the formation of a Christian (or any religious) culture, or at least a culture more Christian or religious than the *de facto* one that existed from the American beginnings. Favored is religion that sees itself as private and voluntary; disfavored is religion that sees itself as intended to transform all life. Though before the American Revolution the various states had generally had established forms of Christianity, the First Amendment especially favors Protestant voluntary religion as it stood toward 1800 (see chapter 6).

In the centuries from Constantine to the American founding, Christians had thought differently, usually wishing some form of cooperation or harmony or concordance between the ecclesiastical and temporal orders. In the West, this had been expressed in the idea of Christendom—that is, not of common habitation of a single political entity, but of shared membership in the culture formed by a dominant religion.[3] American Catholics like the late Richard

2. For the background here see also my "Twelfth-Century Humanism Reconsidered: The Case of St. Bernard," *Studi Medievali,* 3a Serie, XXXI, I, 1990: 27–53; "John of Salisbury's Humanism," in *Gli Umanesimi Medievali,* ed. Claudio Leonardi (Florence: SISMEL edizioni del Galluzzo 1998), 447–68; and "Humanism: The Struggle to Possess a Word," *Logos: A Journal of Catholic Thought and Culture* 7 (2004): 97–116.

3. Christopher Dawson's books, especially *The Making of Europe: An Introduction to the History of European Unity* (New York: Sheed and Ward, 1952; repr. Washington, D.C.: The Catholic University of America Press, 2002), articulate this idea; see my "The Changing Understanding of the Making of Europe from Christopher Dawson to

John Neuhaus have tried to demote this European Catholic experience by calling it "monistic," that is, have presented it as uniting church and state, but knowledgeable historians have commonly called it "dualistic."[4] This latter term has been used to designate the assumption that the two orders, spiritual and temporal, each have their proper goals and should always exist, neither swallowing the other, but both in need of support from the other. In the Church's view the clerical order, specifically the pope, is superior in the sense that the priesthood and sacraments pursue ends intrinsically superior to temporal matters such as war and taxation, but, with the possible exception of the Papal States, the pope is to abstain from direct temporal governance. Cooperation is the ideal, not separation.

One may, as I do, indeed think that even on the belief that Christians are called to cultural conversion, the kingdom they are called to advance is eschatological. It begins in time, but is only fully realized after time. This does not lessen the point of asking whether the American separation of church and state—which of course has evolved over time—does not actually block the way to any incarnational position. If so, it seems a flawed constitutional principle, which actually serves the interests of the nation-state rather than Christian (or Jewish or Muslim) faith.

It is easy to see why the most recurring challenge to my espousal of incarnationalism has come from those who consider me insufficiently appreciative of "the American Experiment." Obviously, I think that, both historically and in principle, life has been better organized on principles other than that of the American separation of

Robert Bartlett," *Actas del V Congreso "Cultura Europea,"* ed. Enrique Banús and Beatriz Elío (Pamplona: Aranzadi, 2000), 203–10. One way of responding to the argument that Christianity is at heart a religion of empire, not of love, is found in Jonathan Riley-Smith, "Crusading as an Act of Love," *History* 65 (1980): 177–92.

4. In addition to chapters 1 and 2, see my "The Catholic Moment?" *Communio* 15 (1988): 474–87. David L. Schindler, "The Monastic *Quaere Deum:* Benedict XVI's Theology and Its Meaning for America," given in an earlier form at the annual meeting of the Fellowship of Catholic Scholars, Baltimore, Md., September 24, 2010, devoted to the theme "Catholicism in America," and to be published in the Proceedings of that meeting, edited by Elizabeth Shaw, is a splendid analysis of the issues related to John Courtney Murray's writings on the relation of church and state. I thank Professor Schindler for making a copy of this paper available to me.

church and state.[5] Therefore I cannot agree with a powerful drive in American Catholicism to approve American constitutional arrangements as not simply "best for us," but as "best for everyone"—that is, as a genuine advance on all the constitutional arrangements of the past, most specifically those of European history. A position such as mine contradicts the judgment of some of the most eminent of American Catholic thinkers, from John Carroll on. It also calls into question the conclusions of some of the most remarkable of foreign observers of the American scene, from Alexis de Tocqueville to Jacques Maritain. I have great respect for all these people. But that Tocqueville was a prescient analyst of democracy in America does not mean that at the end, and in spite of many ominous warnings he himself gave, he should have accepted its impending triumph. Somewhat similarly, having made many acute observations about America but again almost unable constitutionally to form his mind to one settled view, John Courtney Murray ended more with a credo than a position, an affirmation that does seem to me finally less worldly wise than it should have been about how rational humans are. There is a tendency in his writings to view the political process as a very large classroom, following the principles of logic and proper argument. What America has needed all along instead of such optimism is more Niebuhrs, more thinkers with a dark view of fallen human nature.[6] For serious historical thinkers, the important polarity is not that of Enlightenment contrast between pessimism and optimism, but that of Christian contrast between despair and hope.[7]

In sum, some of the things I have to say have been open to chal-

5. My point is not to enter into some inconclusive debate about exactly when and where life was better, but to note the immense achievements of some of the Catholic cultures following principles other than ours.

6. See Langdon Gilkey, *On Niebuhr: A Theological Study* (Chicago: University of Chicago Press, 2001).

7. See most recently my essay on the differences between an Enlightenment and a Catholic view of history, "History in Its Relation to Theology and the Catholic Intellectual Tradition," to be published in *Teaching the Tradition: A Disciplinary Approach to the Catholic Intellectual Tradition,* ed. John Piderit and Melanie Morey (Oxford: Oxford University Press, forthcoming).

lenge from almost any point on the American political spectrum. That said, the dialogue has been particularly with those who insist on the special genius of American political arrangements. In several of the chapters that follow, including the first, I argue for alternative ways of dealing with such questions, and that what is fundamentally at issue is our understanding of the nature of the relationship between nature and grace. Here I am, or became, a disciple of "Nouvelle Théologie," and, against a tendency of many educated American Catholics to view nature and grace as the lower and upper stories of a two-story universe, the former anterior to the latter, which perfects it, I have come to understand grace as something always there, something through which nature exists, something embracing nature. There is in this view no such thing as a "state of pure nature."[8]

I cannot say that I had this understanding in a very full form from the first, because a preparation for my conversion to Catholicism in 1964 was the embracing of a natural law position then common among Catholics—one like that of Courtney Murray. I only moved over a period of time toward the position that Henri de Lubac had been developing since the 1940s.[9] In this I had the great good fortune of living through the pontificate of John Paul II, with its development of the theology of "the gift."[10] My thought developed with my eye on John Paul's thinking, but it was only by the

8. Lawrence Feingold, *The Natural Desire to See God According to St. Thomas Aquinas and His Interpreters* (Ave Maria, Fla.: Sapientia Press, 2010), chaps. 142–15, both describes and criticizes de Lubac, and 387–92, the possibility of a state of pure nature.

9. Henri de Lubac, *The Mystery of the Supernatural,* trans. Rosemary Sheed (New York: Herder and Herder, 1967); see also Hans Urs von Balthasar, *The Theology of Henri de Lubac: An Overview,* trans. Joseph Fessio and Michael Waldstein (San Francisco: Ignatius Press, 1991), esp. 12–15, 61–73; and Serge-Thomas Bonino, ed., *Surnaturel: A Controversy at the Heart of the Twentieth-Century Thomistic Thought,* trans. Robert Williams, rev. trans. Matthew Levering (Ave Maria, Fla.: Sapientia Press, 2009).

10. See already Kenneth L. Schmitz, *The Gift: Creation* (Milwaukee: Marquette University Press, 1982), and Schmitz, *At the Center of the Human Drama: The Philosophical Anthropology of Karol Wojtyla/Pope John Paul II,* with an appendix by John M. Grondelski (Washington, D.C.: The Catholic University of America Press, 1993); cf. Holger Zaborowski, ed., *Natural Moral Law in Contemporary Society* (Washington, D.C.: The Catholic University of America Press, 2010); George Weigel, *The End and the Beginning: Pope John Paul II—The Victory of Freedom, the Last Years, the Legacy* (New York: Doubleday, 2010), continues his study of John Paul.

end that I had a fuller sense of what the great pope's life's work had been on this and other issues. Thus I was still refining my thought as late as an essay not included in the present volume, "The Natural Law: The First Grace," *Communio* 35 (2008): 354–73. In this article, whose title was a nod to a book by Russell Hittinger, I particularly insisted on the sacred cosmos that pre-Christian natural law thinkers thought of as enveloping the natural law.[11] I am pleased to note that recently the very interesting first volume of a three-volume study of *The Emergence of Western Political Thought in the Latin Middle Ages,* by Francis Oakley, insists on this sacred matrix, found around the world, from which the natural law emerged. Oakley particularly emphasizes that in the classical world, still, "nature was alive," "full of gods," a manifestation of the divine. It was not—not simply—the abstraction much of the modern scholastic tradition has taken it to be.[12] I resonate with such a view, and insist that there is no nature without grace. At the "beginning"—and this is partly an unpacking of the logic of affirming that creation is *ex nihilo*—is gift.

Oakley as a medievalist sees how exceptional the political thinking of recent centuries, often promoting some form of secularization, is.[13] In the long view human civilization has been profoundly religious, and such things even Catholics now take as part of the prescriptive given—democracy, the nation-state, individual autonomy, and human rights—were not just hardly imagined, but if imagined were thought to be the antithesis of the society humans were made for, ordered to the good, true, and beautiful. All my life I have said something similar, especially insisting on man's religious

11. Russell Hittinger, *The First Grace: Rediscovering the Natural Law in a Post-Christian World* (Wilmington, Del.: ISI Books, 2003).

12. *Francis Oakley, The Emergence of Western Political Thought in the Latin Middle Ages,* vol. 1, *Empty Bottles of Gentilism: Kingship and the Divine in Late Antiquity and the Early Middle Age (to 1050)* (New Haven: Yale University Press, 2010), 21. My review of this book is to appear in *Modern Age*; see also Jan Assmann and Harald Strohm, eds., *Herrscherkult und Heilserwartung* (Munich: Wilhelm Fink, 2010).

13. In addition to my *Turn to Transcendence,* see Joseph Ratzinger and Jürgen Habermas, *The Dialectics of Secularization: On Reason and Religion* (San Francisco: Ignatius Press, 2006), and Hans Joas and Klaus Wiegandt, eds., *Secularization and the World Religions* (Liverpool: Liverpool University Press, 2009).

nature.[14] I, too, perhaps not with Oakley but with such thinkers as Robert P. Kraynak, have come to doubt that democracy is the best form of government, and have felt a bond with those ancients such as Plato who advocated the role in society of natural and sacred hierarchies.[15] I have thought that there is something admirable found in the authority of fathers, and have wondered whether a society ordered to individuals rather than families makes human flourishing impossible.[16] These were the deeper orientations that instinctively opposed me to those who think life should be ordered to liberty, and thus that the American experiment is a good idea. I knew that its disciples always tried to save the experiment by saying it was not over, and that it was too early to judge it, but this seemed to me a deceit favoring the many social disorders that flourish in the name of freedom.

As stated, one of my basic observations has been that humans are by nature religious animals. Although capable of desacralization or secularization, this is only in the sense of being able to abandon one form of affirmation about the nature of reality or the permanently real in favor of another. This may well take the form of accommodation to the surrounding world, the *saeculum*, the root meaning of secularization. In this sense many have spoken about our now living in secularized times, and such affirmation is comprehensible, but part of my larger observation is that humans always live in secularized times, for, often slowly, they are always abandoning or modifying or marginalizing some previous understanding of reality in favor of something new. Humans simultaneously desacralize and resacralize. Therefore it is best not to speak of our own times as simply secular, but as having adopted ideas opposed to what formerly stood at the center of affirmation.

14. Cf. Nicolas Wade, *The Faith Instinct: How Religion Evolved and Why It Endures* (New York: Penguin Press, 2009).

15. I must presume that Oakley has not radically changed his views since he wrote *The Medieval Experience: Foundations of Western Cultural Singularity* (New York: Charles Scribner's Sons, 1974), which I reviewed in *The Catholic Historical Review* 64 (1978): 240–42. I treat Kraynak especially in chapter 6 of *Turn to Transcendence*.

16. See the definitions and discussions of individualism in Christopher Shannon, *Con-*

I would prefer not to follow Oakley in seeing the overall pattern of Western development as originating in a religious ancient world, passing to a differently religious medieval world, and then to a secular modern world.[17] Rather, it seems to me that at least much of the secularity of our "secular times" is just a new form of affirmation about the nature of reality, and that in any case religion is widespread in our times, albeit not necessarily in its old forms. That said, I could not agree more with Oakley that, though the ancient and medieval periods were religious, Judaism and Christianity bore with them secularizing tendencies that tended in the long run—sometimes a very long run—to desacralize kings and states. The affirmation that God was a Creator, and that creation was *ex nihilo*, meant that only God was without qualification holy, and that a kind of blasphemy was involved in seeing anything created, again without qualification, as divine. But though Judaism, Christianity, and Islam in varying degrees advocate various secularizations of the world, the things that characterize the past few secularizing centuries rather seem to me attempts to replace these religions and place life on a different basis than these religions have provided.[18]

The new things include placing the claims of individual autonomy at the center of political thought, as well as the claims of the nation-state and affirmation of its artificial nature, typically by viewing it as something contracted by the individuals that compose it (see chapter 9). Focus on liberty has expressed itself in the idea of a social contract, founding society on free individuals. Thus, though there were declensions later on, central to the founding documents and the time in which they were written already was a misunderstanding of man in society and departure from a central Aristotelian/Christian idea—that society and the family are natural.

---

spicuous Criticism: Tradition, the Individual, and Culture in American Social Thought (Baltimore: The Johns Hopkins University Press, 1996).

17. *Oakley, Empty Bottles of Gentilism,* x and throughout, on this and the following.

18. See Oakley's comments on the absence of a religious dimension to John Locke's idea of the state, and on why Locke's state would not for Aristotle be a true *polis* at all, in *Empty Bottles of Gentilism,* 10 and 118–19, on Christianity (Augustine) as intrinsically desacralizing.

Few, if pressed, would have said that the family or society are unnatural, or even have understood that that conclusion followed from affirmation of the social contract, but in the degree that the myth of the social contract was affirmed, that was the logic of their approval, only to be worked out over time. Typically humans in history are double- or multiple-minded, and their histories evolve around either clinging to incompatible notions present at the beginning, or to working out these incompatibilities. One of my main interests (see chapter 10) has been tracing the dilemmas of a people who want to build life around the individual while also aspiring to some degree of commonality and shared discourse. The forms of desacralization found in American history are not inevitable conclusions to be drawn from any of its religions. They are not natural—that is, something that follows from an analysis of what humans are, but are themselves a new form of faith, often belief in America itself.

In *The Turn to Transcendence* I argued against those who, with Churchill, hold that in spite of all its flaws, democracy is the best political system.[19] Although I am willing to discuss the question of what in principle is the best form of government—but then would come down on the side of Plato and Aristotle—I argued that what was more practically important was turning from a form of utopianism that would force democracy on everyone to develop a sense of the possible and a sense of how previous history is not likely to be overridden.[20] Thus for a number of reasons I argued that our problem was not to establish democracy everywhere, but to work within

19. I have been particularly concerned with the effect of political democracy on education: see most recently my "The Death of Liberal Education: Its Implications for the University, Democracy, and the American Polity," in *The Democratic Discourse of Liberal Education,* ed. Lee Trepanier (Cedar City, Utah: Southern Utah University Press, 2009), 1–17; and Andrew Delbanco, "Dreams of Better Schools," *New York Review of Books* (hereafter *NYRB*), November 19, 2009.

20. In addition, especially, to chapter 2 of my *Turn to Transcendence,* see Avishai Margalit, *On Compromise and Rotten Compromises* (Princeton: Princeton University Press, 2010), for the argument that avoiding evil, not seeking ideal justice, should be at the center of political effort; and the latest book of William Pfaff, *The Irony of Manifest Destiny: The Tragedy of America's Foreign Policy* (New York: Walker, 2010), against the exportation of democracy; along with Geoffrey Wheatcroft, "The Voice of Unconventional Wisdom," *NYRB,* November 11, 2010; as well as Timothy Garton Ash, "Velvet Revolution: The Prospects," *NYRB,* December 3, 2009.

the historically given to ameliorate the evils of our actual societies. I am pleased to note that scholarship on the ancient world increasingly stresses the great variation in political regimes that, say, the Greeks possessed, and warns against a kind of Golden Age view that sees in Athens all that we should be.[21]

If humans are by nature religious, it seems to me, as suggested above, that there is a certain burden of proof lying on those who would approve the American separation of church and state as an advance in political principle, as opposed to its being simply an intelligent expedient. But there is much else at issue here, not all of which I have thus far worked out in print. A reasonable query, whatever one's position, is "how religious should humans be?" Some say coercion has no place in a society ordered by Christianity. Is it indeed true that religious freedom necessitates the abandonment of all forms of coercion? Does such an idea express religious advance, or one more way in which the Enlightenment now shapes Christianity? If we try to save certain forms of coercion by calling attention to the immaturity of children, when exactly do they become mature? Ever? What of the elderly French priest who was asked what he had learned from hearing many years of confession and replied "there are no adults"? That certainly is a challenge to those among us who have been brought up to think well of themselves. If coercion is removed from society, this would seem to involve the removal of all natural hierarchies. Not only would spanking be forbidden to Christian parents, but also "time outs," which, gentler though they may be, still imply that parents are, at least vaguely, in charge. All this is implicitly involved in the argument between those who praise America's pluralism and those who wish some sharing in the truth, for certainly without any form of coercion, ever-multiplying pluralism is everyone's lot.[22]

We continue to have advocates for some form of "Christian culture." Besides myself or, say, Robert L. Wilken, Aidan Nichols has taken a very different tack from those who would make a large ac-

21. Cf. Oakley, *Empty Bottles of Gentilism,* 230 n43.

22. For how this plays out in education, see Delbanco, "Dreams of Better Schools," 28.

commodation to the world as it has become, arguing for the baptism of culture and presenting a plan to that end.[23] Nichols criticizes Jacques Maritain's optimistic "integral humanism," the naiveté of belief in the justice of pluralistic politics, and generally takes aim at any claim that the state can be religiously neutral. I think he is right on each of these issues, but the main point is that the Christian remains obligated to conversion and evangelization. From deep in the Old Testament the Psalmist still cries (Ps 71:11) "May all kings fall down before him, all nations serve him."[24] The Christian must heed the most recent popes' warnings about how this evangelization of culture should be done, and how not, and some form of "pluralism" is most certainly what we will have at the end of the day, but all that said, the Christian is to work that God be ever more glorified. As St. Ambrose held, the Church is called on to mold public life and institutions.[25]

The advocates of abundant pluralism often claim that pluralism is what we have had from the beginning. In an obvious sense this is true, for, as already noted above, the First Amendment was a response to the problem of how citizens from differing religious backgrounds could live a shared life. So also many have seen the emphasis on liberty from the time of the Declaration of Independence as at the heart of who we are. Further, some, as briefly noted above, say that neither of these things, pluralism or liberty, was deformed at the beginning—that they only became so at some later point in American history, perhaps with the development of more radical forms of democracy in the nineteenth century, or with Supreme Court decisions from the mid-twentieth century. This has seemed to me a form of primitivist thinking in which an alleged pure beginning is shielded from later aberrations by assertion that "it was not always

23. Most recently, see Aidan Nichols' *The Realm: An Unfashionable Essay on the Conversion of England* (Oxford: Family Publications, 2008). See also on the question of culture, Tracey Rowland, *Culture and the Thomist Tradition after Vatican II* (New York: Routledge, 2003). Hugh McLeod, *The Religious Crisis of the 1960s* (New York: Oxford University Press, 2007), writes of the decline of Christendom rather than of a decline of religious practice.

24. Oakley, *Empty Bottles of Gentilism,* 118.

25. Oakley, *Empty Bottles of Gentilism,* 113.

this way." As from the first a largely Protestant nation, the United States seems to me always to have been susceptible to transfer to the political order of the primitivist ideas on which Protestantism is founded (a pure Primitive Church seen as lost at some later time; a Bible alone [*Scriptura sola*], contrasted to decadent tradition).[26]

To restrict ourselves to the idea of liberty, some may hold that a position as mine does not understand the beauty of liberty, of how it flourished in proper form—"ordered liberty"—at the beginning, and only later, or even just recently, became the social disorder of the present. I read American history as does Alasdair MacIntyre, and hold that the predominant idea of liberty at the time of the Founding was already disordered. That is, if we take St. Augustine's understanding of liberty as the foundation of Christian thought, we see that it stands at 180 degrees from that often assumed by so many people in American history. For Augustine, to be free meant to give up one's own will in favor of God's, to adhere to the good, true, and beautiful, rather than doing what one wanted. This some philosophers now call "freedom for." It is a binding freedom, a freedom that exists not for itself, but as a precondition for choosing to adhere to the good, true, and beautiful, just as eyes are a precondition for seeing beauty. From the beginning there was a strong tendency to embrace the opposite, "freedom from," whether this be freedom from George III, Catholicism, or Europe.[27] It is not that the *practice*

26. See my "The Two Europes," *The European Legacy: Toward New Paradigms* 14, no. 2 (2009): 133–48. Thomas S. Kidd, *God of Liberty: A Religious History of the American Revolution* (New York: Basic Books, 2010), takes up many central themes. The latest of the specialized studies I have written on the history of the idea of the Primitive Church is "The *Ecclesia Primitiua* in John Cassian, the Ps. Jerome *Commentary* on Mark, and Bede," in *Biblical Studies in the Early Middle Ages,* ed. Claudio Leonardi and Giovanni Orlandi (Florence: SISMEL Edizione del Galluzzo, 2005), 5–27. See also on the ways Protestant habits of reading scripture have influenced the larger civilization, including Catholic education, my "Christopher Dawson and the Renewal of Catholic Education: The Proposal that Catholic Culture and History, not Philosophy, should Order the Catholic Curriculum," *Logos* 13, no. 3 (Summer 2010): 13–35.

27. Bernard Bailyn, "How England Became Modern: A Revolutionary View," *NYRB,* November 19, 2009, is on a new scholarship that stresses the radicalness of American revolutionary sentiment and sees the British radicalism of 1688 as continuing in the United States (i.e., sees a revolutionary tradition persisting in the United States). Bailyn has interesting things to say about the relation between revolution and modernization.

of freedom became distorted at some point in American history, but that, in spite of good-faith attempts to save both idea and practice by such qualification as that one was only interested in "ordered liberty," America from the first breathed the air of Protestantism and the Enlightenment, indeed of a Protestantism increasingly reshaped by Enlightenment modes of thought.

This form of Christianity, in spite of the many ways that it continued to live in its own sacred tradition and have its own forms of authority, had been founded in an attempt to be free from the immediate (Catholic) past in favor of returning to primitive or original Christianity. So, in spite of much that is worthy of approval in early American history, and many trying to advance an "ordered" idea of liberty, caught so to speak between Augustine and what we have today, it has seemed to me that to contrast a properly understood founding liberty with a later decline therefrom hides the fact that we never had it straight. I readily acknowledge that there have been particularly important moments in which some possibility there from the first has been realized, and that our understanding and practice of liberty have evolved; but in making liberty the chief political virtue from the first, and liberty in a largely modern rather than ancient sense, Americans departed radically from most of ancient pagan political thought and from early Christianity. Both had seen society and politics as ordered to the good. Liberty had never been one of the transcendentals (Good, Truth, and Beauty) that should shape all life, but, expressed as freedom of the will, "merely" a condition for embracing the transcendentals.[28] One of the tragic aspects of history is that one is often forced to live out for good and ill what was believed at the beginning. What some call a declension from our American beginnings seems to me one of the possibilities that always lay in Enlightenment, as well as Protestant, understandings of liberty. From the first, in spite of all those evangelical Protestants trying to do the will of God and bend their necks to Provi-

28. Adrian J. Walker, "Love Alone: Hans Urs von Balthasar as a Master of Theological Renewal," *Communio* 32 (2005): 517–40 at 530–36, gives an excellent presentation of Balthasar's treatment of the transcendentals.

dence, there was widespread misapprehension of what it means to stand in liberty.[29]

As stated, my goal in the present essays is to work out the implications of Catholic incarnationalism. There is a paradox in this, for, because I hold with Aristotle and Aquinas that humans are simultaneously made for politics and contemplation, part of my interest has been in fostering modes of experience relatively foreign to American life, such as the monastic and contemplative lives, whether in their ancient forms or in the patterns of the new movements. The argument is that part of our being made for God is that we are made for contemplation— not just some of us, but, in some fashion or other, all of us. This has been obscured by such things as the noisiness and busyness of our culture, and the busy and didactic liturgy of our churches. If the Eucharist is to be that point in which the immanent and transcendent come together, in which we are both sustained for our daily lives and prepared for eternal life with God, then it must be less like the surrounding American culture and more like the overarching Catholic tradition. What is at issue is whether we are to be shaped by the cult of modernity, commonly shallow and self-centered, or participate in a sacramental culture built around a Trinitarian view of Christian love, around a *communio* of persons.

I have been associated with the English-language version of *Communio: International Catholic Review* almost since the publication of its first issue. Three of the essays found here first appeared in *Communio.* At present I am a member of the journal's editorial board. "Communio theology," sharing its name with the journal, has come to designate a "school" or "style" of doing theology and cultural criticism, especially associated with Henri de Lubac, Hans Urs von Balthasar, John Paul II, and Benedict XVI. I am by training a historian rather than a theologian, and cannot claim to be a card-carrying member of *communio* or any other school of theology, but

29. Both my Introduction to Christopher Dawson, *The Crisis of Western Education* (Washington, D.C.: The Catholic University of America Press, 2010) and the book itself treat the relation in early American history of religion and the Enlightenment.

I do share many common interests with it. Over the years, I have received much helpful criticism from the *Communio* editors, especially Adrian Walker. It has been good for me to spend a life "*in communione.*"

As old as my association with *Communio* was my association with a program of Catholic studies that convened at the Escorial, in Spain, during the summer in the 1970s and 1980s. The creation of the late Brent Bozell's fertile mind, this program allowed me several times to teach a course on the history of Catholic social thought, focusing especially on the papal encyclicals. Much in the present book is a distillation of that experience, and though some of my distinguished colleagues—I think of Joseph Pieper and Fritz Wilhelmsen—have gone to their final reward, others, especially David L. Schindler, continue to provoke my thought.

A number of the following essays were originally published in such places as the *Acta* of European scholarly conferences, and are not easily accessible. I have edited or abridged a few of them to avoid repetition, while most stand essentially as first published. Although on a few stylistic matters I have modified the essays to bring them into greater conformity with the style of the Catholic University of America Press, I have generally allowed the formats used by the various journals and presses in which these essays were originally published to stand. To each I have added an "Afterword" on bibliography since its original publication.

PART I

CATHOLIC INCARNATIONAL HUMANISM

I

THE "CATHOLIC MOMENT" AND THE QUESTION OF INCULTURATION

In 1987 the then Lutheran, but soon to become Catholic, writer Richard John Neuhaus published a book, *The Catholic Moment: The Paradox of the Church in the Postmodern World* (San Francisco: Harper and Row, 1987), which received considerable discussion. I was asked to write a review article on the book, and by titling this "The Catholic Moment?" with a question mark, suggested that, though I found much useful analysis in the book, I was unpersuaded by its basic argument.[1] Of course under the heading of the theological virtue of hope, all moments are Catholic—that is, open to significant formation by Catholicism, but in life one must not simply hope.[2] One must plan and act in a worldly way, based on the best evidence and understanding one can form of one's historical situation. In this sense, I doubted that the American experience was hospitable to Catholicism in the ways and to the degree suggested by Neuhaus's book. I doubted that in America we had be-

1. Glenn W. Olsen, "The Catholic Moment?" review of *The Catholic Moment: The Paradox of the Church in the Postmodern World,* by Richard John Newhaus, *Communio* 15 (1988): 474–87, with a companion review by J. Brian Benestad, "On Richard John Neuhaus's *The Catholic Moment,*" 488–96. Neuhaus responded with "In response to Glenn W. Olsen and J. Brian Benestad," *Communio* 16 (1989): 552–57, and Olsen and Benestad each replied in the same issue with "In Reply to Richard John Neuhaus," 559–60. Among Neuhaus's many subsequent writings is *America Against Itself: Moral Vision and the Public Order* (Notre Dame, Ind.: University of Notre Dame Press, 1992).

2. See Pope John Paul II on hope, *Crossing the Threshold of Hope,* ed. Vittorio Mesori (New York: Knopf, 1994).

gun the countdown to some Catholic moment. I suppose I would have agreed more with a recent writer who, in addressing the question of whether America is a Christian country, answered "I doubt it—but I grew up in one."[3] By that I, at least, would not have meant that America ever had been "the best country there ever was," that it had ever incarnated Christianity more successfully than other countries.[4] The record, the competing traditions, here seems to me too mixed from the beginning for such judgments. But I would have meant that I grew up in a country where Protestant Christianity in the form of "Americanism," of what some have called "civil religion," had such ascendancy that in myriad ways it formed the culture and made a difference in people's lives; and that I have a strong sense that in my lifetime Protestantism, while still forming many of our cultural habits, has lost its place at the center of national life.[5]

While Neuhaus seemed to suggest that a Catholic moment might be in the offing, my best judgment as a historian was that the country was increasingly anti- or a-Catholic, the latter in the profound sense not of opposing Catholicism, but of not even under-

3. David C. Stolinsky, "America: A Christian Country?" *The New Oxford Review* 61, no. 6 (July–August 1994): 16–21, at 19. My "Cultural Dynamics: Secularization and Sacralization," in *Christianity and Western Civilization,* edited by the Wethersfield Institute (San Francisco: Ignatius Press, 1995), 97–122, argues that secularization and sacralization normally take place simultaneously in society. Thus, though the transformation taking place is not very visible, Islamic and Buddhist centers and Hindu temples increasingly dot the American landscape, sometimes otherwise described as increasingly secularized.

4. In addition to note 1 above, I pursue this in Olsen, "Separating Church and State," *Faith and Reason* 20 (1994): 403–25 (see also chapter 6 of this volume).

5. *Civil Religion and Political Theology,* ed. Leroy S. Rouner (Notre Dame, Ind.: University of Notre Dame Press, 1994), not yet published at the time of the composition of the present essay, treats the different meanings of "civil religion," with essays by Richard John Neuhaus and Matthew L. Lamb (see note 19). I have treated the question of a persisting "cultural Protestantism" in "The Meaning of Christian Culture: A Historical View," in *Catholicism and Secularization in America: Essays on Nature, Grace, and Culture,* ed. David L. Schindler (Notre Dame, Ind.: Communio, 1990), 98–130; "Deconstructing the University," the 52nd Annual Frederick William Reynolds Lecture (Salt Lake City, 1991); republished in a slightly revised version in *Communio* 19 (1992): 226–53; "John Rawls and the Flight from Authority: The Quest for Equality as an Exercise in Primitivism," *Interpretation: A Journal of Political Philosophy* 21 (1994): 419–36 (see chapter 9 of this volume); and give examples of how in America such basic aspects of life as our notions of conscience and the nature of the moral life are Protestant in "Separating Church and State" and in "1492 in the Judgment of the Nations," in *Actas del II Congreso "Cultura Europea,"* ed. Enrique Banús (Pamplona: Aranzadi, 1994), 175–81.

standing what Catholicism is about. My sense was that the larger culture aside, I live in a Church that for more than a generation has been unable or unwilling to communicate its most basic truths to the young, so that the term "Catholic" has hardly any longer a meaning for many self-described Catholics. The polls on which Neuhaus relied so much are not to be trusted.[6] Or rather, they must be read in the way Will Herberg read them, as showing that because the dominant American form of religion is a secularized Puritanism, a dualism in which the heavenly and earthly spheres are kept far apart, a high level of church attendance or religious belief is perfectly compatible with, indeed a sign of, loyalty to the American way of life—that is, to the logic of secularism. The secularism of society is not the product of some elite, as of the intellectuals, but is the way most people follow the logic of, for instance, consumerism and materialism. Secularism, a life given up to the world, is the form that most American religiosity takes, a life that most religion in America effectively baptizes. Secularism is not an aberration, but the working out of founding principles in which the Deist with his clock-maker God, the Puritan with his transcendent God, and the unbeliever with no God agreed to "articles of peace" creating a social order open to God for those who wished, but with a government defined by a claimed religious neutrality. In Herberg's words, "it is not secularism as such that is characteristic of the present religious situation in this country but secularism within a religious framework, the secularism of a religious people."[7] For a Catholic moment, I thought the presence

6. In addition to my "The Catholic Moment?" 187, and "The Meaning of Christian Culture," 99, 119–20n5, see my "Transcendental Truth and Cultural Relativism: An Historian's View," in *Historicism and Faith,* ed. Paul L. Williams (Proceedings of the Third Convention of the Fellowship of Catholic Scholars; Scranton, Pa.: Northeast Books, 1980), 49–61. Until the end, Neuhaus's writings had many references to polls, but his argument was especially developed in one of his edited books, *Unsecular America* (Grand Rapids: Eerdmans, 1986).

7. Will Herberg, *Protestant, Catholic, Jew: An Essay in American Religious Sociology,* with a new introduction by Martin G. Marty (Chicago: University of Chicago Press, 1983), 271, as quoted and interpreted in a paper of the highest importance: David L. Schindler, "Religious Freedom, Truth, and American Liberalism: Another Look at John Courtney Murray," *Communio* 21, no. 4 (1994): 696–741. Schindler works out the logic of American secularism in greater detail than I can here. The sentence quoted from Herberg is preceded, 270–71, by: "The secularism characteristic of the American mind is implicit and

of some Catholics highly desirable. Neuhaus seemed to me to have gotten long-term tendencies almost exactly wrong. There had never been much chance that America would reshape itself under the impact of Catholicism, that it would in any sustained way receive a Catholic message, but what chance for a Catholic moment there had been was increasingly slipping through the fingers.

Worse than misreading the situation, Neuhaus, by his praise of so many things American, encouraged people in the view that, outside a few anomalies like abortion, Jeffersonian separationism, racism, drugs, sex and violence at every turn, family disintegration, and an educational system with hardly the rudiments of discipline, this was a very promising place to be.[8] If only people could get the hang of "ordered liberty," the American experiment could succeed.[9] He encouraged the view that this culture was not radically separated from the Gospel. One could comfortably be both a Catholic and an American. Indeed, at times he seemed to fancy himself the defender of America against its most visible ecclesiastical critics, Joseph Cardinal Ratzinger and John Paul II.[10] He incorrectly described people with profound reservations about "the American experience," like myself, as favoring quietism and the diminishment of effort for Catholic presence in the public square.[11]

---

is not felt to be at all inconsistent with the most sincere attachment to religion. . . . Both the 'religionists' and the 'secularists' cherish the same basic values and organize their lives on the same fundamental assumption—values and assumptions defined by the American Way of Life. . . . The secularism that permeates the American consciousness is to be found within the churches themselves and is expressed through men and women who are sincerely devoted to religion. The witness to authentic Jewish-Christian faith may well prove much more difficult under these conditions than when faith has to contend with overt and avowed unbelief."

8. Using education as an example, I analyze the disintegration of community in America in "The University as Community: Community of What?" *Communio* 21 (1994): 344–62, published in a longer form in *Ideas for the University,* ed. Ed Block, Jr. (Milwaukee: Marquette University Press, 1995), 29–60.

9. Typical of his expression is Neuhaus, *America Against Itself,* 48, "The great need is to create, or recreate, a religiously informed public philosophy for the American experiment in ordered liberty." For problems with the concept of a "public philosophy," see note 47.

10. In addition to my "The Catholic Moment?" see on this criticism David L. Schindler, "Is America Bourgeois?" *Communio* 14 (1987): 263–90. Neuhaus had many good things to say about John Paul II and Benedict XVI in other contexts.

11. Neuhaus, "In response," 556, assumes that because I give a grim assessment of the facts, I acquiesce in them; Olsen, "In reply," 559.

Neuhaus, especially through his fine journal, *First Things*, continued until his death to address the question of the American historical situation. It is not my goal here to track him through the things he wrote after the publication of *The Catholic Moment.* I agree with much of this. In a significant sense the heart of our continuing disagreement could be described as lying in the area of high theology, in what implications, for instance, we see or fail to see in Trinitarian *communio* for human life in community.[12] However, to the best of my knowledge Neuhaus never pursued the discussion very far at this level.[13] We probably also conceive the relationship between grace and nature differently, though Neuhaus denied this.[14] Still, if one judges by what actually has been written, disagreement arguably centers on what is today called the question of inculturation, on how Christianity is to or could be inculturated in an American context. That is, while there is probably some theological disagreement, some disagreement about how the term "Catholic" is to be understood, specific disagreement seems to be about what "America" means, about how American culture is to be understood, and how faith is to be inculturated. This is the subject of the present chapter.

Continuing differences at this level are numerous, and involve such questions as how much a culture formed by Protestant Christianity is in fact open to Catholic Christianity—that is, to a Catholic moment—at all. The Christianity of the American founding, after all, was a reformed Christianity reared in attack on the Whore at Rome, and in many of its most prominent representatives heavily

12. The issues here have been best worked out by David L. Schindler, "The Church's 'Worldly' Mission: Neoconservatism and American Culture," *Communio* 18 (1991): 365–97; Schindler, "Towards a Eucharistic Evangelization," *Communio* 19 (1992): 549–75; Schindler, "Christology and the Church's 'Worldly' Mission: Response to Michael Novak," *Communio* 19 (1992): 164–78; and note 7 in this chapter.

13. My most extended discussions are in "Thy Kingdom Come on Earth as in Heaven: The Place of the Family in Creation," in "*And You Will Be My Witnesses,*" 2nd ed. (Irving, Tex.: University of Dallas Center for Christianity and the Common Good, 1993), 1–28 (chapter 5 of this volume), and *The Turn to Transcendence: The Role of Religion in the Twenty-First Century* (Washington, D.C.: The Catholic University of America Press, 2010), esp. chs. 5–6.

14. "In response," 552–53, which I considered unsatisfactory; "In reply," 558.

influenced by Deism and the Enlightenment. Neuhaus, almost like the Catholic immigrants of old, but also like John Courtney Murray, George Weigel, and Michael Novak, sees much more in American culture, as in a kind of connatural readiness for Catholic Christianity, than do I, and I can only guess that this is because his form of "neo-conservative" (or "neo-liberal": both systems are organized around the individual and "ordered liberty") political thought sees more in traditional American liberalism as, if not exactly Christian, working in the same direction.[15] Whereas I, for instance, have grave reservations about "democracy," and believe that a society such as ours attempts a kind of "attack on reality" by suggesting that by nature people are equal, Neuhaus wrote approvingly of things like "democratic capitalism" and "democratic governance," even verbally assimilating the American "democratic" and "republican" traditions to one another.[16] Such an approach, like that of John Courtney Murray, "tends to focus chiefly on those elements of the tradition which find ready parallels in liberalism, while largely ignoring the more distinctly Catholic elements."[17]

There seems to me to have persisted in Neuhaus's thought the odd combination of an Augustinian anthropology with a liberal social thought that one finds in so many twentieth-century writers of classical Protestant formation, Karl Barth and Reinhold Niebuhr

15. By contrast see my "'You Can't Legislate Morality': Reflections on a Bromide," *Communio* 2 (1975): 148–62, with the articles listed above in notes 5 and 12, and below in notes 17, 27, and 29, for analysis of liberalism. For orientation to the authors named, see especially the articles by George Weigel and Michael Novak in *Being Christian Today: An American Conversation*, ed. Richard John Neuhaus and George Weigel (Washington, D.C.: Ethics and Public Policy Center, 1992), 1–22, 251–84. Particularly telling in this book are the responses to Weigel by George Lindbeck, 23–26, and William Murphy, 26–32; cf. Stanley Hauerwas and Michael Baxter, "The Kingship of Christ: Why Freedom of 'Belief' is not Enough," *DePaul Law Review* 42 (1992): 107–27, which Professor Hauerwas kindly called to my attention.

16. For my views, see "The City in Christian Thought," *Thought* 66 (1991): 259–78 at 272 ff., and "John Rawls." I commented on Neuhaus' approval of the language of democracy in "The Catholic Moment?" 481–84. The discriminations largely absent from Neuhaus' discussion of American history can be made by recourse to the following reviews: Edmund S. Morgan, "Power to the People?" *NYRB,* December 2, 1991; and David Brion Davis, "The Triumph of the Country," *NYRB,* May 12, 1994.

17. William J. Gould, Jr., "The Challenge of Liberal Political Culture in the Thought of John Courtney Murray," *Communio* 19 (1992): 113–44 at 113, said of Murray.

at the forefront. Luther's idea of the two kingdoms made a certain sense when the historical situation was such that living in the earthly kingdom meant doing an actual king's will. Here there was no doubt as to where authority lay. But the persistence of this pattern of thought in a world without kings is most curious. There is in fact no command from authority to tell us, in spite of our "original sin" anthropology, to side in our politics with the Enlightenment—that is, with the individual and ordered liberty. The "people" or *vox populi* can never really replace the "king" as authority, for the people speak with many voices, and one must side with one party or another. That is, since liberalism is not the king of the earthly kingdom but only one of the pretenders to a long-empty throne, it is unclear why a Christian would ever feel an obligation to submit to it. Nobody has commanded him to do so; all logic or consistency is against it. Yet, again and again in the twentieth century, "neo-orthodox" Christians opted for a classical, somber anthropology that stressed human limitation and a politics that placed great confidence in individual liberty and the self-realized man. Indeed, one of the reasons such thinkers were so hard to pin down is that, holding fragments of two incompatible world views, shifting and feigning in argument from one to the other, they could affirm or deny almost anything. At least until late in the century, in a European context, where the politics chosen was often a socialism or Marxism with a strong subordination of the individual to the community and a strong sense of the obligation of the community for the individual, a kind of consistency was realized. But in America, the schizoid nature of living in the two kingdoms was particularly revealed in those who combined an Augustinian anthropology not with communitarian social thought, but with a stress on individual freedom and free enterprise. A little concern for internal coherency should have alerted one to the fact that, if the two kingdoms have such radically different readings of things, probably there is not much reason to believe that anyone's political experience is going connaturally to lead to a Catholic moment.

Rather than return to old disagreements in forms already discussed, my goal here is to explore the question of what sense Catholic inculturation has in an American context. We must begin with a definition and description of "inculturation." There is by no means agreement on the use of this relatively new word: Francis Cardinal George has written a first-rate book on the subject.[18] For my purposes I wish to follow an illuminating article by Matthew Lamb on "Inculturation and Western Culture: The Dialogical Experience Between Gospel and Culture."[19] In his own way, Fr. Lamb also speaks of a Catholic moment, for his argument is that, the negative aspects of post-Enlightenment culture having made themselves increasingly plain, Catholicism in America is being asked ever more insistently to make a choice. Fr. Lamb uses inculturation (126) to refer to:

> The process of how the Church, mediating the proclamation of the gospel, is involved in a mutual learning process wherein the gospel is received and, in that very reception, brings about over time transformations of the particular culture and new "incarnations" of the Church.

The distinction between Gospel and culture is one form of the distinction between the transcultural and the cultural. Inculturation involves a dialogue between the Gospel as mediated by the Church and a particular culture. This dialogue is finally between the Head and members of the whole Christ. It is a true dialogue, so that each party is open to learning from the other, "learning" in this case meaning both the possible transformation of culture and possible incarnation of Church in a new way. Many things are transcultural—mathematics and the patterns of nature, for instance. Their existence can be known across the cultures. Indeed, if I may extrapolate, it is doubtful that anyone dwells in a single culture, or indeed that cultures are stable enough clearly to mark their boundaries. As Fr.

18. Francis Cardinal George, *Inculturation and Ecclesial Communion: Culture and Church in the Teaching of Pope John Paul II* (Rome: Urbaniana University Press, 1990), esp. 136–57. I find particularly valuable the position of Cardinal Bengsch of (then) East Germany, summarized by Cardinal George, 57: "Adaptation [of Gospel to culture] might be good, but not if it leads to assimilating the Gospel to the false values of secularized societies or to the inclusion of political illusions and utopias."

19. Matthew Lamb, "Inculturation and Western Culture: The Dialogical Experience Between Gospel and Culture," *Communio* 21 (1994): 124–44. I make liberal use of my friend Fr. Lamb's essay in what follows, and perhaps should reveal that I was one of its anonymous readers.

Lamb explains the transcendental and immanent dimensions of all cultures (129), "any genuine culture is both *trans*cultural and *in*cultural." Indeed, arguably it is the transcultural that allows the great inculturations, the concrete expressions of things that are transcultural in a given culture. I am inclined to think that, especially in the contemporary world, we all simultaneously live in many cultures or subcultures, if we define culture in Fr. Lamb's way (125) "as the pattern of beliefs, meanings, and values which imply or define what the good life is." When we get on the bus in the morning, we move in one environment, when we go to Church in another, when we lecture, in a third. Each, in some degree, has its own laws. But even the most isolated person, by the very fact that he possesses a human mind, is capable of knowing transcultural truths, of knowing things known outside his own culture. Indeed almost certainly, by the very fact of being in history, every person knows things learned from more than one culture, if one can even count cultures in such fashion. This is one of the reasons the very notion of an unqualified cultural relativism is unintelligible. By the very fact that the same truths can be known across cultures, truth is not dependent on any particular culture.

This is often forgotten or overlooked by those who treat transcultural and cultural matters as somehow having equal status. It is quite common—this came out especially in the debates about the Columbian Quincentenary—to speak as if specific cultures are sacred or inviolate and should be left alone by other cultures.[20] This is to say that culture is its own justification, without reference to any other standard of judgment. At the Conference on Evangelization in the American Southwest, referred to in chapter 5 of this volume—if I may indulge in a little amateur sociology—the speakers were fairly well divided into two groups.[21] One was largely composed of Anglo lecturers with a great admiration of various so-called native cultures,

20. In addition to "1492 in the Judgment of the Nations," see my "The Ethics of Conquest: The European Background of Spain's Mission in the New World," *Communio* 19 (1992): 619–34 (chapter 12 of this volume).

21. See note 13.

who hoped for dialogue but nevertheless thought if push comes to shove the Gospel trumps culture. The other was largely composed of Hispanic lecturers who insistently argued that, since native traditions on some matters were quite different from the teaching of the Church, Church teaching should be accommodated to culture—that is, waived. For them culture trumped Gospel, or at least so it seemed to me. In such relativism, to use Fr. Lamb's words (127), "culture in fact becomes normative for the faith." The notion of dialogue—the notion that the particular should enter into dialogue with something larger than itself, which it could teach but from which it could also learn—was rejected. From the first, the idea of dialogue was foreclosed by at least the implicit assumption that particularity has the same status as universality, or indeed is higher. The obvious objection to such a line of thought is that since there are things knowable across the cultures, by definition these have a greater dignity than things actually dependent on a single culture.

There is a kind of parallel but opposite error in which the Gospel is seen as simply something with an essence that is caught in formula and creed. This error forgets that the Gospel is a Person, Himself transcending all categories. As important and necessary as creeds and propositions are, this error treats inculturation as a one-way street in which all traffic flows from Gospel to culture. The assumption is that the Gospel can briefly and stably be summarized and then merely implanted in any particular culture. Such a view ignores, if I can put it this way, the obvious fact that there are four Gospels in the Bible itself, four ways of viewing the Person of Christ. The point is that every culture will not only have its own take on how the Gospel is to be incarnated, an expression of its own cultural patterns, but that this take will in part also be the result of its discovering something unique in the transcendent richness of the Person of Christ, something "really there." If ultimately the Gospel trumps culture, this should not be taken to mean that culture does not through dialogue move the Church to new discovery.

Lamb's position, with which I agree, is that in American culture (140) "the only fully post-Enlightenment culture in the entire world," a central role of the Church is to maintain or inculturate for the first time those dimensions of reality, of being human, that either never were present or are in danger of being lost. Christianity never just enters and adjusts to a culture; it prods all cultures to become something they are not. As Bishop George summarized a 1985 International Theological Commission report, the Church must purify "human cultures so that they are apt instruments for the building of God's Kingdom."[22] Our *novus ordo saeculorum* was in its origins, as manifest in the Declaration of Independence and Constitution, very liberal indeed. Its religion was overwhelmingly Protestant. Catholicism, not so much because it is an immigrant religion as because it is a much more universal form of Christianity than Protestantism, is a stranger in this country. That is, from a Catholic point of view, what American history is about is the unresolved tensions between Catholicism and modernity, Catholicism and liberalism, Catholicism and the Enlightenment. Hopefully inculturation will involve the universal Church learning how to deal with standing human problems by attending to American experience, but most centrally the Catholic moment is the witness of the universal Church to a myriad of transcultural truths ignored by American culture, or of which American culture is ignorant. The Catholic moment is not to launch a broadside against all things American, among other reasons because we must presume that, as in the past, the average Catholic will continue deeply to desire acceptance by that culture, and can only stand a certain amount of tension between his American culture and his Catholic religion.[23] Rather, the Catholic moment is

22. Lamb, *Inculturation,* 78. George, *Inculturation and Ecclesial Communion,* 95, notes a pattern in papal visits: "He begins gradually to point out in what ways their society or culture might be evangelically deficient." See also George, *Inculturation and Ecclesial Communion,* 118, on the place of the Church "in a state of internal 'exile'" in secularized societies. George, *Inculturation and Ecclesial Communion,* 149, distinguishes between an eschatological critique, in which any society will come up sorely lacking, and an incarnational critique, in which each society will be seen to express something of the kingdom of God. Finally, 184, he reminds us "The Church's primary concern . . . is not to integrate a society but to be faithful to Christ in every cultural situation."

23. The issues involved in the choice between assimilation and retention of a distinctive cultural identity are succinctly stated by Andrew Hacker, "'Diversity' and Its Dangers," *NYRB,* October 7, 1993.

patiently to pull out deep beliefs in the culture of which Catholicism reveals the inadequacy, to try to show the relevancy of a Catholic point of view to weaknesses the average Catholic at least instinctively senses in the larger culture. If the culture sees the Church as a voluntary association, because with its decimated democratic notions of authority it sees all associations as voluntary, the Catholic moment is to assert that, with all the proper qualifications, there is no salvation outside the Catholic Church. If, because of the deleterious influence of Calvinism in America on all sacramental thought, ecclesial symbols are thought of as arbitrary signs, the Catholic moment is to assert a full sacramental theology, so that all remembrance of what it means to be a member of the Body of Christ is not lost. If even within the Church the altars have been stripped by those whose sensibilities have been more formed by American culture than by a world faith, so that they express all that is least transcendent rather than the mystery of God, the Catholic moment is to reveal a liturgical tradition infinitely richer than the banalities of liturgical "reform."[24] If in a post-Enlightenment culture with its cult of improvement, not of course something to be dismissed out of hand, the new is praised over the old, leading even in the Church to the opposing of innovation to tradition, the Catholic moment is insistently to ask where in recent history, hellish for so many, is that progress, what exactly its nature, and to suggest that the achievements of other times are literally ageless.[25] At Santiago de Compostela seven hundred years ago,

24. Eamon Duffy, *The Stripping of the Altars: Traditional Religion in England c. 1400–1580* (New Haven: Yale University Press, 1992, 2005), although about the fifteenth and sixteenth centuries, is most instructive about our own historical situation. C. John Sommerville intelligently addresses the limitations of Duffy's book in a review in *The American Historical Review* 99 (1994): 224–25. Similarly, Louis Dupré, *Passage to Modernity: An Essay in the Hermeneutics of Nature and Culture* (New Haven: Yale University Press, 1993), is most penetrating.

25. Michael Novak seems to me an example of a writer who regularly carries Enlightenment points of view into ostensibly Catholic positions. See his "Seven plus Seven—The Responsibilities of Business Corporations," *Crisis* 12, no. 7 (July-August 1994): 5–9. For a very different view, see my "Christian Philosophy, Christian History: Parallel Ideas?" in *Eternity in Time: Christopher Dawson and the Catholic Idea of History,* ed. Stratford Caldecott and John Morrill (Edinburgh: T. and T. Clark, 1997), 131–50; a slightly different version is found in *The Catholic as Historian,* ed. Donald J. D'Elia and Patrick Foley, 81–96, 225–56 (Naples, Fla.: Sapientia Press), 2006.

Master Mateo chose to portray the twenty-four elders of the Apocalypse in animated conversation, perfectly capturing a Catholic vision of the communion of saints. Here we do not have progress in the Enlightenment form of a past that is definitively left behind, but a dialogue that runs back and forth through history.

Lamb suggests three stances that characterize Enlightenment thought and are incompatible with Catholicism. These are all central to, though not exhaustive of, the American experience. The first, which we find at least as early as Machiavelli, but which, before Marx, we may associate especially with Hobbes, Locke, and Hume, is "that reality is ultimately conflictual" (141). For the Christian, although history is full of conflict, which indeed is a kind of measure of man's distance from the Gospel, ultimately reality is about service, death to self, and love—that is, the seeking of the good of others even above one's own self-interest. The great human—if always elusive—goal is peace. Man is meant for love and cooperation, not conflict.

The second Enlightenment stance is that knowledge is power. This goes back at least to Francis Bacon's promises about the usefulness of science—that the goal of science is less understanding for its own sake than as power over nature, which was caught archetypically by Goethe in the figure of Faust. It nurtures the pragmatism and utilitarianism in American life that so struck Alexis de Tocqueville, and, with Protestantism itself, largely explains both the amazing technology America has produced and the absence of much of a contemplative tradition. This stance is so closely related to the third that we may consider them together. This third, expressed in the myth of the social contract, holds that institutions, law, and the state are not natural in the Aristotelian sense, but conventional, more or less agreed to by the individuals they coerce. That is, society finds its origins not in the family, the work of nature and history, but in the individual, the expression of mathematics, of an abstract, isolated equality. Instead of an authority rooted in nature or the will of God and in the natural differences between people, which inevitably express themselves hierarchically in society, the instruments of domination are seen as conventional, receiving their legitimacy from the decision of isolated individuals to come together and abandon part of their individual freedoms to place government above themselves. No more than the state itself is law viewed as educative. Law is not an expression of reason, the result of quest for jurisprudence, patterns of life most suited to man's rational nature, but a pragmatic, problem-solving instrument with only procedural norms.

The argument is not that any of these stances rule unchallenged in American history, but that they dominate. Cicero's and Aristotle's views of law or the naturalness of the state are a minority report. The heart of American social thought to the present remains the liberal tradition of the social contract.[26] As Alasdair MacIntyre famously observed, almost all forms of political thought in America, from right to left, are but variations on the assumptions of liberalism.[27]

If I may take this as established, a brief consideration of the place of power and authority in American society may stand both as elaboration of Lamb's second and third characterizations and as an example of how, were more space available, a more ample definition of "America," and thus of the problems of Catholic inculturation, would proceed.

The American story is very complicated, and one does not have to engage in unjustified nostalgia to point back at least in some areas to an earlier time with healthier modes of life, or a healthier sense of what life is about, than we now have. Although the country has always had its Tom Paines, Protestantism by various means so spiritualized ecclesiology, or followed the laws of its own nominalism, as to eliminate all ideas of incarnate authority from life. One part of Americanism was the domination of American towns by visible structures of authority, of the two authorities of church and state, the church steeple and the courthouse or federal building. This continued ancient ideas of the expression of the order of the world through architecture. We find it in the most unexpected places. Through the gothicization of the Princeton campus, for instance, Ralph Adams

26. See especially "John Rawls."

27. Alasdair MacIntyre, *Whose Justice? Which Rationality?* (Notre Dame, Ind.: University of Notre Dame Press, 1988), 392.

Cram, against all the expectations of Calvinist theology, expressed a kind of *praeparatio evangelica*. That is, while Calvinism emphasized the infinite distance between nature and grace, Cram's buildings, especially their stained glass, spoke of wisdom, harmony, and the liberal arts, the works of nature and reason.

Whatever connaturality there earlier was, whatever piety expressed in the twinned structures of the authority of church and state, has largely disappeared, to be replaced by an urban architecture of either commerce, on the one hand, or of modernism on the other. The former communicates power, the latter emptiness—neither authority. There is very little in the architecture of the last century to communicate either a natural sense of authority or a sacramental idea of reality. On the contrary, our cities, in spite of some reaction, have been increasingly filled with especially modernist public architecture and sculpture that attack the premises of any sacramental or incarnational view of life. Instead of seeing works of art as mediating reality and a sense of the whole, the idea of a reality to be mediated is itself denied, and only the particular remains.[28]

Authority is little presented as in service to some transcendent good, truth, or beauty, and the result is a deracinated authority reduced to the category of power. Increasingly it becomes difficult to believe that any exercise of authority is for one's own good: all claims to authority are seen as cloaks for someone else's quest for power. My point is that such a world is not connatural to Catholicism, but ever more distant from it. A world in which "truth" has been reduced to "power" prepares people not for Catholicism, but for what MacIntyre has called the genealogists, for a world of feminist suspicion, in which everything is a code for obtaining power over or

28. Although as the co-creator of the Centre National d'Art et de Culture Georges-Pompidou Renzo Piano has much to answer for, the evolution of his ideas about the relation of architecture to nature and tradition since the 1970s, though unintegrated, is one of the hopeful reconsiderations of modernism now influencing America. Now technology is no longer pursued for itself, but, in the words of Peter Buchanan as quoted in Calvin Tomkins, "The Piano Principle," *The New Yorker* (August 22 and 29, 1994): 52–65 at 53 "to achieve a *gentle* accommodation not only with Man, but also with Nature and tradition."

freedom from others.[29] Freedom of the will is not understood as oriented to the good, as a capacity that exists so that we may choose or submit to the good, but on the contrary is experienced as something that allows us to do what we will. Because all institutions tend to be seen as dominative, that is, as arbitrary exercise of power, the predictable response is quest for personal freedom and autonomy.

The picture just given of church steeple and courthouse framing the American town of an earlier era should have spoken of steeples, for typically a number of religions were present, and, after the original attempt to establish specific forms of Christianity at the level of the states, pluralism of religion. This pluralism, not just in America, has undoubtedly made the Church more sensitive to the dignity of the individual, to (for instance) the limits of the state's power of coercion. It thus has been a part of the process of inculturation, and a means by which the problems of American history have helped a more general understanding of the relation of individual to community. Yet pluralism of religion also complicated the place of authority in society, for in America no single institution could mediate wisdom in the sense of being the accepted expression of the idea that wisdom is a whole that must be contemplated as a whole. Even after the Protestant Reformation, church and state had shared this task across the map of Europe. Most medieval and early modern political thought, whether Catholic or Protestant, had held to the idea that the only true authority is God's, and that kings receive their authority from God. That the Church bestowed chrism on the ruler

29. MacIntrye, *Three Rival Versions of Moral Inquiry* (Notre Dame, Ind.: University of Notre Dame Press, 1990); Lamb, "Inculturation," 132. John Horton and Susan Mendus, eds., *After MacIntyre: Critical Perspectives on the Work of Alasdair MacIntyre* (Notre Dame, Ind.: University of Notre Dame Press, 1994), continue the discussion of MacIntyre's implacable criticism of liberalism and description of the failure of modernity. Although there was a kind of reductionism at work, especially in earlier stages of the evolving thought of Michael Foucault about power, Foucault's notions about the ubiquity and productiveness of power, about the way in which every form of power creates its obverse, have, as Prof. Stanley Hauerwas pointed out to me, an Augustinian flavor about them: see Kyle A. Pasewark, *A Theology of Power: Being Beyond Domination* (Minneapolis: Fortress Press, 1993), 1, 5–55, an interesting analysis in a book that itself departs from conventional ideas about power. On feminism, see my "Marriage, Feminism, Theology, and the New Social History: Dyan Elliott's *Spiritual Marriage*," *Communio* 22 (1995): 343–56.

was a sign that, if it was not seen by all as the superior authority, it remained the repository of wisdom, the chief embodiment of the idea that life should be ordered to the transcendent. The republican, and especially the democratic, ideals in America were ambiguous. Nevertheless, Protestant American society into the twentieth century was fairly unified. Although authority was placed in the people, most did not think very intently about such matters, and also spoke of "one nation under God." Although technically the Congress could legislate what it willed, it was understood that the Ten Commandments were not in jeopardy. Similarly, the Protestantism or, after the great migrations, Catholicism preached from the pulpit was typically Americanist, and, if not of high intellectual content, did usually affirm that Christianity was to form all life.

In this sense, although implicitly the pluralism of religions in America suggested that wisdom was fractured, in practice Americanism, the common creed of Jew, Catholic, and Protestant, stood in for a more properly philosophic or religious idea of wisdom. We might say that the institutional mediation of this shared wisdom lay not in bricks, but in the flag, the Fourth of July celebration, and the national anthem. Protestantism, half comfortable with a disincarnate ecclesiology, was similarly comfortable with slightly unfocussed notions of authority and wisdom. The federalism and party systems mentioned above—particularly the latter—were probably more fracturing of the idea of wisdom. Like the habit of pragmatism, federalism and the party system fed the tendency to see life itself as not a whole. The intelligent party man was interested in the interests of his group, not in some common good, and therefore was committed to the partial view. Politics was viewed more as the compromise of interests than as the creation of harmony in acknowledgment of objective goods higher than party.

A further word needs to be said about the relation between wisdom and pragmatism just adverted to. I think we need to be careful in recommending, as certain Catholic writers have, American pragmatism or the experimentalism of capitalism to anyone. These are habits of thought and action that deal, often quite successfully, with one set of problems while creating immense new ones. Obviously we all would like free-market productiveness developed within a legal system aimed at what *Centesimus Annus* called integral human freedom, but I do not see that a writer such as Maciej Zieba, who can be very astute, has understood that the very intellectual habits that have led to capitalist success in a country like America also have blocked the development of a wisdom tradition.[30] Indeed, a kind of tragic thread running through American history is the stumbling quest for wisdom by those who hardly know how to look, a quest that has run from the orientalism of the Transcendentalists, an attempt to reassert Spirit in a culture of the machine, to the New Age.[31] It seems to me that the proposed inculturation of others with American pragmatism and experimentalism needs much further examination. With Lamb (132) I understand wisdom as "a true concern for, and contemplation of, the whole." This, by its nature, pragmatism works against. It is exactly the partial view of the pragmatist—not unlike that of Dante's hoarders and wasters—that concentrates on some limited aspect of reality without taking the larger view.

In an old classic, the romantic and very type of the Oxford don (though in fact at Bristol), H. D. F. Kitto, traced the danger of the increasing prominence of men of business in Athens after the time of Pericles—men who by nature took a limited view and could not practice a proper politics. Some things they knew very well, but by concentrating on commerce they had virtually unmanned themselves for being citizens, for looking at things in a properly political manner.[32] Disastrous decisions, if I may elaborate, such as that in favor of the Syracusan Expedition, were to be laid at their feet. If I have understood Michael Novak's comparison of professors and businessmen, a comparison in which the professors do not fare well,

30. In, for instance, Maciej Zieba, "The Monk and the Market: What Does a Priest Need Economics For?" *Crisis* 12, no. 7 (July–August 1994): 23–27.

31. Kevin P. Van Anglen, "The Latest Form of Infidelity," *Crisis* 12, no. 7 (July-August 1994): 55–57 at 57.

32. H. D. F. Kitto, *The Greeks* (Baltimore: Penguin Books, 1954).

I suppose Kitto would be the perfect target for his scorn.[33] Yet it seems to me Kitto was making an important observation, and one that was historically-minded in insisting that we not isolate developments we approve of from their larger context, from the opposite sides of their coin. Men became expert in commerce by becoming inexpert in other things. Precisely because the economists are probably right when they observe that placing a high societal value on contemplation hinders economic development, we must be very careful about the forms of economic initiative or habits of mind that we want exported from America.[34] Early on Tocqueville noticed that, if I can put it this way, something like what had happened in Athens happened in America. I am not at all uncomfortable with Novak's argument that things such as pragmatism, the openness to invention, in general the entrepreneurial spirit, partly explain America's economic productivity, but such analysis is very partial. It just as well explains why Americans are so non-philosophical, so closed to the transcendent, unifying, and sacramental dimensions of Catholicism. America is the land of "endless particularities" (Lamb, 132). I think writers like Novak and Neuhaus must consider the whole picture, both sides of each coin, before judging this American experiment especially receptive to Catholicism. Partial analysis is hardly analysis at all.

This said, well into the twentieth century, institutions like the colleges were a counterforce working in the name of wisdom and preserving the educational ideal of the Protestant academies and Jesuit colleges of an earlier age, in which the well-educated person had as his goal a view of the whole, the knowledge suitable to a free man, a liberal education.[35] This seems now to me to have been largely dissipated under the ever-fragmenting quest for, to use the most current slogans, "diversity" and "multiculturalism," but Lamb suggests that it is precisely in its institutions that Catholicism has had and likely

33. Novak, "Seven plus Seven," 5.

34. John Attarian, "Good Intentions and Bad Economics," *Crisis* 12, no. 7 (July–August 1994): 48–50 at 50.

35. See notes 5 and 8.

will have the greatest inculturating role in America. With of course church buildings themselves, Catholic hospitals, seminaries, colleges, and universities have, like yeast, been a leaven to American civilization, often embodying ideals of service or community appreciated outside the Catholic community and lovingly portrayed in movies such as "The Bells of St Mary's" and "Moonstruck." In many ways, because of their institutions, Catholics have been rightly understood to march by a different drum. Priests have been understood to be on twenty-four-hour call in ways facilitated by their celibacy; confession has been understood to embody a form of humility the opposite of the quest for freedom; and refusal to practice artificial contraception or abortion has often been understood to be an awesome form of submission to the authority of laws not made by man. All this—that is, everything that has made as much Catholic inculturation possible as has taken place—is in danger today, and Lamb suggests that if the interest really is inculturation, one of our top priorities should be moving our institutions away from being like the larger culture to being different from it. In many ways our situation continues an earlier debate between Americanists like Fr. Edward McGlynn, who wished to speed Catholic assimilation into American life by having Catholic children go to the public schools, and the proponents of a separate Catholic school system. I would argue that, then and now, if what is desired is a vibrant Catholicism, the assimilationists have been largely wrong. Theirs has always been the prescription for the disappearance of Catholicism in America. Msgr. George A. Kelly was right that one of the principal reasons American Catholics had a measure of success in instructing their own was the hard decision the bishops made for a separate school system.[36] Whereas the inculturation now being pursued by the descendants of Fr. McGlynn is really a form of secularization in which Catholic theologians and politicians facilitate the Church modifying any belief displeasing to the larger society, the inculturation we should seek is prophetic, countercultural, and instructing. Whether hospital or school, as soon as an

36. George A. Kelly, "Let's Stop Kidding Ourselves About Catholic Higher Education," *Fellowship of Catholic Scholars Newsletter* 16, no. 4 (September 1993): 15–24 at 19.

institution is known more for its private than for its Catholic character, it is worthless as an instrument of inculturation.

I know more about the schools, and would like to make one specific point here, again following Lamb. There is growing discontent in the academic world itself with many Enlightenment premises. In political thought, for instance, the communitarians nip at the heels of the politics of individualism. Here and there, there is genuine enchantment with a politics of virtue. Catholic writers such as Charles Taylor offer points of view in which the ideas of individualism and community are seen not as opposed, but mutually fructifying.[37] This is a kind of secular analogue to the thrust in Trinitarian *communio*-theology to show that the person can only be defined in relations.[38] The sciences sometimes see that a proper relativism rules out all reductionism, all claim fully to explain anything by reference to a single level of causation. Disenchantment with the war on the past that has characterized the world of art for more than a century sometimes expresses itself. The School of Architecture at the University of Notre Dame insists on a staunchly traditionalist training, and is especially a defender of continuity with the past in church architecture. Here and there, as in the music of Arvo Pärt or Henryk Górecki, we find a music or an art clearly contemporary but reasserting transcendence and connection with tradition. In philosophy and theology, writers like Andrew Louth show the limitations of all methodology rooted in Descartes and Newton and all epistemology not taking its origin in contemplation.[39] In sum, what Bernard Lonergan called the second Enlightenment, a perception of the limitations of the first Enlightenment, is not unknown.[40] One of the most important things that could advance Catholic inculturation would be for some college or university to see its mission as being Catho-

37. Charles Taylor *Sources of the Self: The Making of the Modern Identity* (Cambridge, Mass.: Harvard University Press, 1989).

38. See my "Thy Kingdom Come as on Earth" and "The University as Community."

39. See Andrew Louth, *The Origins of the Christian Mystical Tradition: From Plato to Denys* (Oxford: Clarendon Press, 1981), and Louth, *Discerning the Mystery: An Essay on the Nature of Theology* (Oxford: Clarendon Press, 1983).

40. Bernard Lonergan, *A Third Collection: Papers* (New York: Paulist Press, 1985), 63–65, with Lamb, "Inculturation," 142–43.

lic now. On the one hand, we have many ostensibly Catholic institutions so secularized, so much in step with the first Enlightenment, that there remains little distinctively Catholic about them. On the other hand, we have a few good countercultural Catholic schools that, however, tend to fight the battles of the past almost wholly with the curriculum of the past. What we need is a school both traditional and radical, traditional in giving a sufficient view of the cultural patrimony so the present can be addressed intelligently, but radical enough to leave time for consideration of the kind of authors and problems I have just listed.

To return to the larger analysis, in the degree to which Americanism itself succeeded in becoming the unifying wisdom in American life, the logic of pluralism was hidden from the view of all but the most perspicacious—Tocqueville partly saw what was at issue. By the logic of pluralism I mean the view of reality of a society, if not exactly founded on religious pluralism, one in which religious pluralism became a necessity. In many quarters, and here my differences with Neuhaus are serious, it is common to praise this American pluralism. I agree that nothing but pluralism is in the cards for Americans, as well as many other peoples. But it is one thing to say that we have no choice but pluralism, quite another that pluralism is an advance on the place of religion in human life earlier or elsewhere. Although the development of religious pluralism has, as I have suggested, helped us understand certain facets of the human person better, it does not seem to me that on balance this development has been positive. I must repeat a distinction I have made before, between cultural pluralism and moral or deep pluralism.[41] By the former I mean all the variations between cultures that fall short of logical incompatibility. Such differences normally enrich our lives, and indeed prompt the question of inculturation itself. By contrast, deep pluralism, which involves incompatible ideas of the good or the true, or incommensurable world views of the type in which Isaiah Berlin rejoiced, destroys the very idea of wisdom or of the ul-

41. See my "The Catholic Moment?" and "Deconstructing the University."

timate intelligibility of life.[42] To the degree that deep pluralism takes over a culture, the culture is literally destroyed, for it stands for opposed things.

American pluralism is of both kinds, with deep pluralism advancing daily, most clearly in the struggle over abortion. Neuhaus's praise of pluralism failed to sort out the differences between cultural and deep pluralism, and tended to underestimate how much the pluralism of America is deep pluralism. By definition this latter pluralism makes difficult not just the quest for wisdom, but the very communication of the idea that wisdom is man's highest goal. A society pluralist in this sense encourages fractured minds—people who have lost the habit of contemplation and cannot see things whole—to whom, perhaps, it does not even occur that life might be ordered. Such pluralism reinforces the mental habits of a commercial society and the tendency of pragmatism to get lost in the parts. A Catholic moment must involve a sober tracing of the logic of deep pluralism, of why on the one hand it became virtually a historical inevitability, and on the other, something that undermines wisdom. The more one understands the disadvantage of wisdom's place in a post-Enlightenment culture, the less likely one is to think of American assumptions as preparing the way for a Catholic moment in the sense of a significant cultural embodiment of Catholicism. In America the significant Catholics—the Orestes Brownsons, Flannery O'Connors, or Walker Percys—have generally been the odd ducks who knew they were in strange water; that to live in a culture significantly influenced by Catholicism, the most deeply ingrained American perceptions would have radically to be altered. Some, like Brownson, gave themselves to such an alteration, but they were not deluded as to how Heraculean this task was.

In an obvious sense, the accusation that those with a sober judgment on American life favor quietism and the diminishment of effort for Catholic presence in the public square is so misconceived

42. See esp. Isaiah Berlin, *The Crooked Timber of Humanity: Chapters in the History of Ideas* (London: J. Murray, 1990).

that it hardly merits a response. My intent is to sweep away the webs so that we can avoid investing our energies in enterprises almost certain of failure based on delusions about what humans are or can be in this world. The issue is how at this moment one is to have a Catholic impact on America. I have already made some suggestions. The argument is that what America needs is not boosters, and also not Jeremiahs, if that term be understood as prophets who declare the hopelessness of the situation. What America needs is a Catholic Church with integrity and courage, willing to explain to whoever will listen what Catholicism is. It does not need clerics so worried about being unpopular or about losing their congregations that they obfuscate the fact that a Catholic life is in many ways one set aside from the world as we find it—in but not of the world. It does need Catholic school administrators and teachers who are different from the world around them, who stress the Catholic, rather than the private, nature of their schools. The model here is the Ignatian thrust to find God in all things, to do all things to the greater glory of God.[43] Precisely because action is intended, we want this action based on realism, not optimistic or delusional projections.

I was very moved some years ago when, at the first Mass following ordination to the priesthood of one of the members of our Communio Study Circle in Salt Lake, his life story was briefly recounted.[44] In essence this was the story of a fifteen-year-old all by himself making his way to the Cathedral rectory door, having figured out "You alone have the words of everlasting life." This was a Catholic moment. It seems to me such a moment should be a point of *kairos,* of illumination of our present dilemmas by Catholic insight. The more we understand what is at issue, the less likely we are to think of imminent congruences between things American and things Catholic. The more we shed the attachment to the first Enlightenment that, in spite of so much good analysis, mars the

43. See my "Lay Spirituality *ad majorem Dei gloriam,*" *Communio* 6 (1979): 405–12 (see chapter 3 in this volume).

44. One issue a year of *Communio* gives information on and lists the study circles organized by this journal to foster local *communio.*

thought of a John Courtney Murray, the more we might appear as possessing a kind of honesty and intellectual integrity available nowhere else.[45] The need of a Catholic moment is not to justify America, to write one more paean to American exceptionalism, but to figure out where the moments are where a Catholic way of viewing things may be intruded. We need not criticize in anger, or hatred, or as a way of putting down. But we can claim that Catholicism offers a vantage point on American society available nowhere else. We need not ask for an angelism in which we expect blue-collar workers to spend their spare hours poring over the text of Aquinas, but we need to point out that if contemplation is nowhere valued, if wisdom has no incarnate expression, society from top to bottom will tend to a kind of reduction of the mind to merely calculating categories, in which no one is served. A culturally diverse society by definition possesses a certain richness of texture. Even the divisions of a society divided over religion may help one understand the truth. A society divided over such questions as abortion, however, goes far beyond what is a healthy diversity. This kind of fragmentation likely communicates to many the meaninglessness of life and the inaccessibility of truth.

What lessons in inculturation, then, does American culture have to teach the Church? From a Catholic view, America must appear as more failure than success, and stand as a warning. It teaches that if most energy is invested in commercial and material things and in problem-solving, striking successes may be had. No one can doubt the great reservoirs of generosity and good will among the American people that have, in the midst of consumerism, persisted to the present, and arguably this is the most obvious benefit of that blend of politics and religion designated Americanism. While rarely taking the specifically theological form of *caritas,* for in this country rarely does anything take a specifically theological form, it commonly has expressed itself in a philanthropy nurtured by the churches. This said, America is a warning against the pursuit of democracy, plural-

45. I try to make clear my admiration, and the limits of my admiration, for Murray in "The City in Christian Thought."

ism, and equality. The prolonged attempt, for instance, to obtain a "public philosophy," some common ground of values to achieve social cooperation in this democracy, has revealed the logical incompatibility of what I have called deep pluralism, a pluralism historically grounded in the pluralism of religions and a shared public life. This constantly appears in discussion of public education or moral education. Because the ways in which deep pluralism, by definition, makes social consensus impossible are rarely directly confronted, such discussion usually has about it a certain air of unreality.[46] The desire is for good citizens and good human beings, but actually teaching citizenship and morality is not possible without privileging someone's idea of good and disadvantaging someone else's—that is, limiting pluralism. If the good is known and can be agreed on, then alternative points of view are excluded. If, rather, freedom of expression and freedom to disagree are given priority, no consensus can ever be achieved. For a common life there must be common values, but deep pluralism marks ultimate disagreement about values. To the extent it advances, the possibility of community recedes.

Similarly, for those open to learning the lesson, the quest for a public philosophy in American life has shown the absolute necessity for a grounding of moral discussion in natural law. As I have said, the believers in the American experiment have been less than forthcoming about the fact that the very notion of a public philosophy implies the rejection of other than cultural pluralism, for what could a public philosophy be than an agreement to accept some point of view or set of values and reject others? The very notion of a public philosophy implies an attack on deep pluralism. Since a multiplicity of revealed religions could not by definition be the ground of a public philosophy—for they disagree about the nature of reality and are only open to those with the gift of faith—the ground must lie in something open in principle to all men, irrespective of revela-

46. In addition to the first group of essays in Rouner, ed., *Civil Religion,* see Barbara Darling-Smith, ed., *Can Virtue Be Taught?* (Notre Dame, Ind.: University of Notre Dame Press, 1993), which considers the problem of moral education in a pluralistic society. I have discussed these issues in "'You Can't Legislate Morality'" and "The City in Christian Thought."

tion. This could only be reason, or what historically has been called a natural-law position. This latter Neuhaus apparently saw in his judgment that, because they lacked an adequate idea of natural law, neither John Dewey nor Walter Lippmann was able successfully to create an adequate public philosophy.[47]

Inculturation is a very complicated question, and one might say that at the same time America has inculturated the world in the twentieth century, it has increasingly been inculturated especially by the Latin American world along its southern frontier. Here the North American Catholic Church, although itself largely of immigrant origins, is being taught new lessons by other styles of Catholic life found in the Hispanic world. Some of these styles of life bear the wounds of tortured historical experiences elsewhere, but on balance their presence seems to me a positive development. Just as earlier immigrants taught America much about things like social solidarity and the meaning of neighborhood, so the Hispanic peoples are helping Americans renew their commitment to family life and thus to a style of life that balances worldly advance with enjoyment of and giving joy to others. One could hope, to look for a reciprocity of influence rather different from, say, Novak's customary approach to developing nations, that while the capitalism of the North had a certain impact that will better the life of the poor in the Latin world, the richness of daily life of the South will soften the individualism, banality, and fragmentation of life in the United States.[48]

With the demise of communism and a kind of worldwide euphoria for market economies, passing as this may be, one could argue that internationally the main check on the most destructive features of capitalism is the social teaching of the Church. Clearly recent popes have taken upon themselves the task of encouraging

47. I say "apparently" because Neuhaus, *America Against Itself,* 48, muddied the waters by introducing the natural law in a discussion of how a "biblical worldview can be translated into public language" and how to create "a religiously informed public philosophy." There is thus a question of whether he understood the natural law as a philosophical or natural category or somehow associated it with revealed religion.

48. See note 23 above. Sarah Kerr, "A Tale of Two Cities," *NYRB,* December 16, 1993, considers the special situation of Mexican Americans.

the most humane, and discouraging the least humane, use of the market system.[49] Since arguably America has the most prior experience with this system, one could argue that American Catholicism has a special obligation to teach the whole Church not just about the positive aspects of capitalism, but about the entire experience, so that a sober but not disheartening view of the immediate future is possible. This was especially important a few years ago in light of the growing disillusionment with capitalism already found in territories only recently liberated, but now hankering, if not for the return to old habits, at least for liberation from the crime, greed, and opportunism the fall of the old order loosed. If capitalism is presented, not as the promise of riches overnight, but as a possible instrument to a more productive and equitable economic order for who will work and learn self-discipline, real service can be done.

To conclude, can we really believe as Catholics that the end of history is that God has been forgotten, and faith removed from life? What, then, is the point of acquiescing in America as it now is, let alone thinking of America as some advanced expression of the will of God, some especially propitious experiment? What is the point of a liberal Christianity whose essential advocacy is for the Church to embrace American cultural norms, to submit Gospel to culture? I do not know where we are in history, but it seems to me more Catholic to think of the last four hundred years as having made some terrible mistakes, as well as real advance—for instance, in human critical capacity. We now have sufficient perspective to see how serious the errors have been, and to try to amend them. The last thing we need is praise of the things that have led us from God, things at the heart of Enlightenment culture and very prominent in the American experience. What is needed now is a twenty-first century analogue to what the desert monks gave the Romans. I am not so much recalling MacIntyre's famous words about St. Benedict as saying that in the late Roman world it was that which was most transcultural, least Roman,

49. This is the argument of *Catholic Social Thought and the New World Order: Building on One Hundred Years,* edited by Oliver F. Williams and John W. Houck (Notre Dame, Ind.: University of Notre Dame Press, 1993).

that the Empire needed to know.[50] The great gift the monks gave was eschatology, understood as pointing with one's life in the direction of the race's true end. This eschatological stance was both transcendentally oriented and prophetic, for at one and the same time it pointed toward God and called those who would to live not so much as Romans but as Christians. I am too much of a layman, too committed to Ignatius' goal of restoring all things in Christ, to preach a literal return to the desert, but it might be useful to think of the Church's place in America as prophetic and eschatological.

In one sense at the end I want the same thing as did Neuhaus, a public order informed by Catholicism. I, however, see immense obstacles and stress that the Catholic moment is a teaching moment, a prophetic witness to a culture very far from God. A central part of this witness is explanation not of how much the American experience allows grace to build on nature, but of how mistaken some of our most important assumptions have been from the beginning. Usually in history one never leads a civilization very far from the assumptions of its earliest days—indeed the only partial exception I can think of is the evangelization of the Roman Empire, in which a very similar debate about inculturation took place. We want to avoid the danger of playing too Eusebian a role for America—that is, becoming propagandists for the order around us. Augustine was not less historically influential for being more critical of the order into which he was born.

AFTERWORD

I have made minor changes in the text of this chapter from its original form. Neuhaus was prolific to the end, publishing, for instance, *Catholic Matters: Confusion, Controversy, and the Splendor of Truth* and *American Babylon: Notes of a Christian Exile.* For further consideration of "the naked public square," see Christopher Wolfe, ed., *The Naked Public Square Reconsidered: Religion and Politics in the*

50. Alasdair MacIntyre, *Three Rival Versions of Moral Inquiry: Encyclopaedia, Genealogy, and Tradition,* 2nd ed. (Notre Dame, Ind.: University of Notre Dame Press, 1990), 263.

Twenty-First Century. See Joseph Bottum, "American Exceptionalism and American Religion," for a somewhat different understanding of American exceptionalism than mine. Aidan Nichols, *The Realm: An Unfashionable Essay on the Conversion of England,* takes a very different tack from Neuhaus, arguing for the baptism of culture, and presenting a plan for achieving that. Nichols criticizes Jacques Maritain's optimistic "Integral Humanism," the naiveté of belief in the justice of pluralistic politics, and generally takes aim at any claim that the state can be religiously neutral; see also Thaddeus J. Kozinski, *The Political Problem of Religious Pluralism: And Why Philosophers Can't Solve It,* foreword by James V. Schall. Harald E. Braun, *Juan de Mariana and Early Modern Spanish Political Thought,* in explicating its subject, gives an idea of the issues separating traditional European Catholic political thought and American thought. For plurality as the native American condition, see George Weigel, "Truths Still Held?" In addition to the articles mentioned in the present chapter, my analysis of liberalism has continued especially in "American Culture and Liberal Ideology in the Thought of Christopher Dawson"; "Religion, Politics, and America at the Millennium" (chapter 7 of this volume); "America as an Enlightenment Culture" (chapter 8 of this volume); "The Quest for a Public Philosophy in Twentieth-Century American Political Thought" (chapter 10 of this volume); and *The Turn to Transcendence: The Role of Religion in the Twenty-First Century,* which also expands on the limitations of the idea of progress and what I say about modernism; see also Kenneth L. Grasso, "John Paul II on Modernity, Freedom, and the Metaphysics of the Person," and in the same issue, Michael P. Krom, "Transcendence and Human Freedom: Modernity and the Right to Truth." On progress and the related "economic utopianism," see also Timothy Garton Ash, "1989!"; Tony Judt, "Ill Fares the Land"; and Benjamin M. Friedman, "Two Roads to Our Financial Catastrophe." See further on "progress," Brennan C. Pursell, "God in History: An Augustinian Approach to Narratives of Western Civilization." I have pursued the question of the stability/instability of culture and cultural boundaries further in "Why We Need Christopher Dawson"; of the problems almost universal cultural assumptions present to being Catholic today in *Beginning at Jerusalem: Five Reflections on the History of the Church;* and of the form contemporary Catholic education might take in "Christopher Dawson and the Renewal of Catholic Education: The Proposal that Catholic Culture and History, not Philosophy, should Order the Catholic Curriculum"; cf. Philippe Buc, *The Dangers of Ritual: Between Early Medieval Texts and Social Scientific Theory;* what is said of the problems German Catholics have faced in the demand to update to modernity in Walter Brandmüller, *Light and Shadows: Church History amid Faith, Fact and Legend,* trans. Michael J. Miller; the treatment of assimilation in James Davidson, *The Greeks and Greek Love;* Hilary Mantel, "Dreams and Duels of England"; Peter J. Bernardi, *Maurice Blondel, Social Catholicism, and Action Francaise: The Clash over the Church's Role in Society during the Modernist Era;* John L. Allen, Jr., *The Future Church: How Ten Trends Are Revolutionizing the Catholic Church,* who treats such subjects as secularization throughout; and Eric Metaxas, *Bonhoeffer: Pastor, Martyr, Prophet, Spy,* on Christian refusal of compromise (Bonhoeffer stressed the difference between the place of the Enlightenment in European and in American thought, the latter retaining more of the idea that all earthly power is limited). See also on the persistence of religion, David Shulman, "Living in India's Spirit World." Ben Greenberg, "The Orthodox Moment," traces the success of Orthodox Judaism in resisting assimilation, and Mark Juergensmeyer, *Global Rebellion: Religious Challenges to the Secular State, from Christian Militias to al Quaeda*, shows how religious nationalism can live with secular states. John F. Crosby, "How the Gospel Encounters the Culture in the Catholic University: Some Lessons from John Henry Newman," in *The Idea of the Catholic University,* ed.Kenneth D. Whitehead, stresses that since assimilation always goes on, the question is giving this a productive form. In this same book see Stuart W. Swetland, "Radiating Jesus in Word and Sacrament: The Role of Catholic Campus Ministry at a Non-Catholic University," on assimilation.

There is a second edition of Eamon Duffy, *The Stripping of the*

Altars: Traditional Religion in England c. 1400–1580, and wide-ranging discussion of early modern periodization in regard to the medieval/modern dichotomy in Gordon McMullan and David Matthews, eds., *Reading the Medieval in Early Modern England.* For expansion of my comments on education, see Christopher Dawson, *The Crisis of Western Education*, introduction by Glenn W. Olsen. Of course the case for allowing the forms of industrial civilization to determine the shape education takes continues to be expressed: Roderick MacFarquhar, "The Pride of Empire." John R. Searle, "Why Should You Believe It?" explores the incoherence of "multicultural democracy." See also Searle, "'Fear of Knowledge': An Exchange," and Adrian J. Walker, "Love Alone: Hans Urs von Balthasar as a Master of Theological Renewal," explaining multiculturalism as a form of monism. There are interesting essays on various American historians who have resisted "corporate liberalism" in "The Midwestern Historical Imagination." Richard A. Posner, *The Crisis of Capitalist Democracy,* gives a long view. David Novak, *Freedom for Faith, Freedom for All: In Defense of Religious Liberty,* is very useful in the definition of terms.

2

THE INVESTITURE CONTEST

THE INVESTITURE CONTEST was a struggle over what the respective positions of the royal and priestly powers should be in a Christian society. Although the most visible aspect of this contest was the struggle over lay investiture between Pope Gregory VII (1073–85) and the German emperor Henry IV (1056–1106), the attempt to determine the proper areas of competence and jurisdiction of the various ecclesiastical and civil offices occurred at all levels of society and remained a problem long after the deaths of both great protagonists.

Especially since the conversion of the Roman Emperor Constantine (312–37) to Christianity, the history of the Church had been filled with conflicts over the proper claims of the ecclesiastical and secular powers in regard to each other and to the individual Christian. However, the investiture contest of the eleventh century brought the opposed claims of the contending parties to a level of theoretical definition and actual warfare not earlier experienced in the history of the Latin West. The reasons for this seem fairly clear. By the eleventh century the continuing missionary activity of the early Middle Ages had been so successful that much of continental Europe had accepted the Christian view of the world. Although many lacked profound insight into the truths of Christianity, themselves often being only a few generations removed from paganism, most men believed in the basic teachings of Christianity. God the Creator had sent his Son to redeem fallen man, and at the end of time would judge all men. The sacraments had been given to the Catholic Church to help each man in his pilgrimage through this life, and the government of this Church had been granted to the priesthood, at the head of which stands the bishop of Rome. Since almost all men accepted this view of the world, men did not think of themselves as members of two distinct institutions, the church and the state. Rather they were all members of a single Christian society, in which there were two authorities, one ecclesiastical and one royal. Whereas the Christians of the first centuries of the history of the Church had lived in a world hostile to the Christian claims, eleventh-century man lived in a society in which there was general agreement as to the truths of Christianity. Therefore, whereas the early Christian had always been tempted to withdraw from his society in order to find Christian perfection, some men in the eleventh century came to conceive of the possibility of reforming society itself after the Christian ideal. Christians had always asked the question of what Christian perfection is for the individual—that is, of what things in life should be preferred and what things abandoned. Now in the eleventh century one could ask what the right order of society itself should be, and from one perspective the investiture contest was an attempt to order more perfectly Christendom after Christian principles.

Kings and popes had long thought that they ruled by the grace of God for the end of leading men to heaven. However, in general, from the eighth to the eleventh centuries, certain secular rulers, first the Carolingians and then the German emperors after Otto I (962–73), had been much more powerful than the papacy, and had presumed that the leadership of Christian society had been given to the royal power. These rulers conceived of themselves after the pattern of the kings of the Old Testament. They tended to look upon the Church and its properties as their own, or as a trust given by God to be managed by themselves. These theocratic monarchs were sometimes very pious men, and strove for the moral reform of the Church, but never did it occur to them that in principle the papal office was more important than their own in terms of the actual leadership of Christendom. The papacy and the priesthood were competent in matters of doctrine and the performance of the sacraments, but the theocratic monarch presumed that the royal power ought actually to lead and govern society. A theocratic monarch such as Henry III of Germany (1039–56) could even desire a pure and influential papacy without doubting that the papacy and the emperor could achieve a kind of cooperation based on the defense of the papacy by the protector and ruler of Christendom, the German emperor.

One of the results of the period of theocratic monarchy was that at all levels of Church government the clergy tended to be dependent on secular political figures. Bishops and abbots often were chosen by kings, both because they helped in the governance of the realm and because the king believed that it was the royal duty to lead the Church in his realm. From the period of the decline of the Roman Empire in the Latin West, most bishops of necessity had taken over functions that earlier would have been performed by secular officials. Throughout the earlier Middle Ages the political importance of the episcopate tended to increase, both because of the absence of strongly centralized governments, and because the clergy as a whole was the best-educated segment of society and therefore a necessary instrument of government. With the rapid development of feudalism after the death of Charlemagne (768–814), bishops and abbots as well as nobles in effect became members of the feudal hierarchy and were granted or invested with lands in the form of fiefs or benefices by kings in return for the performance of governmental and even military functions. Since all episcopates already had lands attached to them, either received from pious donors or inherited from Roman times, it was not necessary for many generations to pass before the distinctions between the various properties and functions of the bishops became blurred. All over Europe, but particularly in Germany, bishops performed both civil and ecclesiastical duties. According to the law of the Church, as religious officials they owed their episcopal offices and sacramental powers to the ecclesiastical hierarchy, but as secular office-holders they owed much of their property to lay investiture by their feudal lord, whether king or emperor. Although by origins the granting of an episcopal office was completely distinct from investiture as a vassal in a fief, with the passage of time it came to seem that the bishop received the episcopal office from the fact that he was a vassal of the royal power. This point of view was reinforced by the fact that kings naturally chose men to be bishops who were loyal to them, and excluded those men who could not be trusted unreservedly to pursue royal policy. Although the canon law always maintained that the election of bishops pertained to the clergy, it came to seem that episcopal office was received through lay investiture, especially because the sacred symbols of the ring and staff were given in the lay investiture. When the eleventh-century reformers came to reflect upon the nature of right order in a Christian society, the practice of lay investiture of bishops seemed the most obvious example of the way in which the royal power had illegitimately deprived the Church of the freedom to govern herself and to lead all men to salvation.

Just as the bishops were dependent on the secular power, so also were the lower clergy. Parish priests often were selected not by the ecclesiastical hierarchy, but by the lord of the manor in which their parish church was located. And just as the king chose bishops on the basis of their loyalty and governmental abilities, as well as sometimes their spiritual qualities, so the local lord often chose the parish priest not because of his abilities as a pastor, but because he was a good financial steward. For just as the king looked upon the church in his realm as his property, so the lord of the manor considered the parish church to be part of his property, to be a source of revenue through the collection of tithes and offerings. This arrangement, called the system of the proprietary church, of course tended to give the clergy themselves interests and points of view not very different from those of laymen, and accounts somewhat for the frequently formal and superficial practice of religion found in these centuries. However, in the hands of pious laymen the system sometimes was used to great good, and in many areas the country-dwellers first came in contact with Christianity precisely because a layman used some of his lands to found and endow a parish church or monastery.

Nevertheless, many men searching for a more meaningful Christianity found the effects of the system of theocratic monarchy and the proprietary church unsatisfactory, and throughout the eighth to eleventh centuries various movements appeared seeking more adequate forms of Christian life. Until toward the middle of the eleventh century, these movements did not usually attack the social institutions based on theocratic monarchy and the proprietary system. They rather concentrated on moral reform and the search for perfection within the existing forms of society. This attitude of seeking primarily the reform of the individual rather than the reform of society was most clearly expressed in the reform movements within monasticism, the traditional mode of the search for perfection in the early Middle Ages.

Even during periods of general decadence and chaos, many monks had never lost sight of the final end of man, reformation in the image of God, and especially from the ninth century Europe was influenced by great reform movements within monasticism. Cluny, founded in 910, was the most famous of these, and sent reformers from Burgundy throughout Europe. However, there were many other reform movements, some stimulated by Cluny, and some of independent origins. The goal of Cluny was to restore the Benedictine rule, and indeed from Cluny there spread a great enthusiasm for the religious life lived in a community centered around the liturgy of the Church.

Return to this practice of the common life was, although the most influential form of monastic reform, only one among several patterns of reform. Especially common in Italy, but found all over Europe, were small congregations that had kept alive the hermit traditions of Eastern monasticism. Peter Damian, perhaps the most important of the mid-eleventh-century reformers, had himself been the head of a small group of hermits at Fonte Avellana. With these small groups, a rather different emphasis was found than that which characterized the Cluniacs, for they were much more concerned with the practice of poverty, asceticism, and the mortification of the flesh than were most of the followers of Cluny.

In some ways the Italian eremitical movements more directly

formed the program of the Gregorian reformers than did Cluny, for such Gregorian demands as that of the absolute prohibition of all private property for all monks and regular clergy were closely related to the emphasis on poverty and purity found among the Italian reformers. But this is not to minimize the role of Cluny. Cluny had found favor with many ruling houses in Europe, and Cluniac monks had done much to form the piety that several of the German emperors were noted for, the greatest of whom was Henry III, himself the initiator of many of the changes that were to issue in the investiture contest.

The reforms of monasticism up to the mid-eleventh century give evidence of a very widespread search for a more adequate appropriation of Christianity. Not all of this religious enthusiasm was channeled into the monastic life, and in the years immediately preceding the Gregorian reform, programs for the reform of the clergy also frequently began to appear. Since patristic times the urban clergy or canons had been formed into chapters around their bishops, and certain of the fathers, such as St. Augustine and St. Gregory the Great, had encouraged their clergy to adopt a life lived in common without private property. Although this form of life was not very commonly found perfectly followed, in the ninth century a council at Aachen (817) had considered and then rejected as too severe the proposal to demand that all the cathedral and collegiate clergy give up their private property and live in common. This ideal was again taken up by the generation of reformers immediately preceding the pontificate of Gregory VII, and especially Peter Damian argued that all regular clergy should live the full common life without private property so that, not being attached to the things of this world, they would be better able to preach the Gospel. Before himself becoming pope, Hildebrand (Gregory VII) had proposed at a synod held in Rome in 1059 that where possible the clergy adopt the full common life, living in community without private property. Again this proposal was considered too radical to be made mandatory, but at this and several succeeding councils it was approved as being a more perfect form of Christian life.

The resistance to the reform of the canonical clergy was of course intense, since many of the clergy had wives or concubines, and most of them possessed private property and did not live in community. These abuses, which stemmed from the proprietary system, were not to be rooted out before the end of the Middle Ages. Although by the end of the investiture contest enthusiasm for the reformed regular canons was growing, at every stage of the reform of the clergy, popes and bishops had to fight deep-seated local opposition to any change in longstanding practices. By the time of the death of Gregory VII it was clear that although the papacy had committed itself to a policy of mandating the common life for all monks and regular clergy, the reform of the clergy had advanced little.

Not all enthusiasm for reform was directed toward the monastic and clerical vocations, and especially in the eleventh century lay reform movements became fairly frequent. These movements usually attempted to accommodate some form of the common life, based on the practice of poverty, to the laity. Perhaps the most famous of these movements during the period of the Gregorian reform itself was that of the Patarenes in Milan. Like most lay movements, the Patarenes gained much of their cohesiveness by opposition to corrupt and simonical clergy. One of the results of the period of theocratic monarchy was the common custom of giving a payment upon the reception of an ecclesiastical office, usually as a part of the practice of investiture by a layman. This practice, called simony, was against the law of the Church and of course tended to award spiritual offices to those who could pay the most, rather than to those most qualified to hold them. The laity naturally blamed much of the spiritual degeneration of the Church on the fact that this practice produced unworthy clergy, and as their own remedy for this abuse often proposed not to receive the sacraments from such clergy. Seen in context it seems fairly clear that many of these lay movements were also in part protests by the poor against the new wealth produced by the growing towns of the eleventh century. They were therefore potentially dangerous to the order of society, and indeed many of them in time adopted both religiously heretical and politically revolutionary programs. Nevertheless, the fact that Gregory VII actually encouraged the Patarenes to refuse the sacraments from unworthy clergy shows how desperately limited the means were by which reform could be advanced. Where the higher clergy could not reform themselves, as in Milan, Gregory felt he had no alternative but to support these potentially revolutionary lay movements against the corrupt clergy.

It is clear from the foregoing that by the middle of the eleventh century the need for the reform of Church and society was widely felt. Although each of the above drives to reform played its part in preparing the way for the investiture contest, from the middle of the eleventh century reform came to center on the attempt to purify and restore the papacy itself. For generations the papacy had been dominated by local Roman and Italian aristocratic factions. Not strong enough to maintain itself above Italian politics, the papacy had tended to degenerate into a political prize sought for by contending parties. Many of the popes had received and used the papal office for political advantage, and their private lives had been no purer than those of the great laymen who dominated the papacy. Without a strong secular defender, army, or territorial base, the papacy was powerless to extricate itself from this position, although especially in the early eleventh century some of the popes had made tentative attempts at reform.

Feeling this situation intolerable, in the 1040s the pious and capable German emperor Henry III began to act to restore the papacy. Himself deeply touched by the reforms of the Cluniacs, over a period of time Henry created conditions at Rome that finally permitted the capturing of the papacy by indigenous Roman reform groups led by the future Gregory VII. Although these Roman reformers eventually went far beyond the reforms envisaged by Henry, they at the beginning fully supported the German intervention in Rome. The intervention was occasioned by the scandalous conditions resulting from the reign of Benedict IX (1032–48). In 1044 one of the Roman aristocratic factions drove Benedict from Rome and installed as his successor Sylvester III (1045). When Benedict's faction returned to power, he was restored, but almost immediately he granted the papacy to a wealthy archpriest (apparently in return for the payment of a sum of money), who took the name Gregory VI (1045–46). Ironically, Gregory seems genuinely to have been interested in reform, and for this reason had committed simony in order to obtain the papacy. Benedict IX soon decided that he after all still wanted to be pope, and there followed a period of rioting and fighting in the streets of Rome as the supporters of each of the three papal claimants strove to determine the issue. Henry now intervened, and after calling three councils deposed all three claimants and nominated a reformed German bishop to become Clement II (1046–47). The following three popes, all of whom had short pontificates, were also nominated by Henry.

Henry III's third nominee to the papacy was his cousin, who took the name Leo IX (1049–54), and who refused to become pope simply because of his imperial nomination, but submitted his nomination to the clergy and people of Rome in order to follow the canon law. Hildebrand, who had gone into exile with Gregory VI, was apparently impressed with Leo from the first, and when Leo stopped at Cluny, where Hildebrand was staying, on the way to Rome, Hildebrand joined him. From this time until he himself became pope, Hildebrand was always active in the government of the Church at Rome. Leo's pontificate marks the beginning of the restoration of papal influence in the north of Europe, and Leo spent much of his reign traveling through France, Germany, and the Low Countries holding synods for the purpose of condemning and rooting out the various abuses so pervasive among the clergy. Leo also entered into negotiations with the Greek Orthodox Church for reunion with Rome, but in 1054 these negotiations led to the mutual excommunication of pope and patriarch. Leo had asserted the papal supremacy over the Greek Church, and the Patriarch of Constantinople had rejected this claim. Finally, Leo sought for some political arrangement to free the papacy from domination by Roman factions. He first tried to establish a temporal state in Southern Italy. However, in 1053 the Norman army badly defeated the papal army at Civitate, and from this time the papacy turned to the attempt to form a defensive alliance with other Italian states.

During the pontificate of Stephen IX (1057–58), Cardinal Humbert of Silva Candida composed his *Libri adversus simoniacos,* which for the first time formulated the central demands of the Hildebrandine party. In the third book of this work, centering his attack on the idea of theocratic monarchy, Humbert argued that kings are simply laymen, and should have no right to interfere in the government of the Church because of their royal office. Bishops should be elected according to the norms of canon law, and not by kings. Laymen ought not invest bishops with the sacred symbols of ring and staff, because this implies that the grace of the episcopal office comes from lay investiture, a thing in fact impossible. Humbert, certainly the most gifted theologian of the Hildebrandine Party, had penetrated to the main issues soon to be involved in the investiture contest. Whereas most of the reformers, including Hildebrand himself, were men of action rather than speculative thinkers, Humbert was both, and his book, finished in 1058, had a great influence on subsequent events. It certainly lay behind the principles involved in the decree on the election of a pope issued by Nicholas II (1059–61) the following year, and described below. And at the Lateran Synod of 1059 Hildebrand himself attacked theocratic monarchy in a fashion completely in accord with Humbert's arguments. Hildebrand stated that the Roman order, which had been corrupted since the government of the Church had passed under the government of the Germans (meaning here since the time of the Carolingians and the foundation of theocratic monarchy), must be restored by returning to the practices of the ancient Church. In sum, by 1059 the principles of the specifically Hildebrandine program of reform had become clear. The reforms that had been envisaged by Henry III were considered not to go far enough, for Henry, while desiring moral and monastic reform, as well as a purified clergy, had wanted to retain control of the Church, and indeed to use a restored papacy to strengthen his hand in Italian politics. Whereas the Cluniacs generally consented to this continuing pattern of theocratic monarchy, the ideal of the Hildebrandine party was a Church, led by a restored papacy and a reformed hierarchy, completely free from secular control. Humbert had penetrated to the root issue of what right order is in a society organized according to Catholic principles.

Nicholas II was the first pope fully in sympathy with this criticism of theocratic monarchy. Elected because the defensive alliance sought for by Leo IX finally bore fruit when Tuscany helped secure Nicholas' election free from domination by any of the Roman factions, Nicholas immediately added an alliance with the Normans to that with Tuscany. In return for the recognition of the pope as the temporal overlord of southern Italy, Robert Guiscard (1059–85) was recognized by the papacy as the duke of Apulia and Calabria and the future duke of Sicily. But the most important contribution of the reign of Nicholas to the growth of the papal power was the papal election decree, promulgated at the Lateran Synod of 1059. For the first time in the history of the Church, the decree attempted to establish a precise method for the election of a pope. Recent history had shown Nicholas that without such a method, the papacy would inevitably be dominated by either secular rulers such as Henry III or the Roman factions. And so Nicholas devised a procedure to keep the election of a pope as free from these external pressures as possible. Henceforth, popes were to be elected only by the cardinals. This decision manifests the radical advance made in the program of the reform party under Humbert's influence, for the Hildebrandine Party had now made the goal of free elections an explicit part of its program, along with the insistence that the Church should be independent of all imperial control, even if that control should be in the hands of a man as good as the lately deceased Henry III.

During the peaceful reign of Alexander II (1061–73), the gains already made by the papacy were consolidated. Henry IV of Germany was still a minor, and political conflict with the empire was unlikely unless provoked. The ideal of a restored papacy involved not only ecclesiastical freedom from secular control, but also the strengthening of the papal position within the Church, and Alexander devoted much of his energy to this later problem. Slowly the

Church became more centralized through such methods as the use of papal legates to deal with local affairs in the name of the pope, and the permission of the appeal of cases from local ecclesiastical courts to the Roman curia.

Alexander also exerted moral leadership over Christendom, several times intervening to reprimand and correct rulers whose conduct had become scandalous. The idea of the primacy of Rome had been taught in the ancient Church, and during the early Middle Ages the idea that the pope is the universal ordinary for all Christendom had occasionally been expressed. According to this teaching, the pope stands to the Church as each bishop stands to his diocese. Just as the spiritual governance of all souls within his diocese is given to each bishop, so the government of the universal Church is given to the pope. From the time of Leo IX the reformed popes had tried to give some content to this claim to be universal ordinary. Neither Alexander nor any of the other popes ever thought of replacing theocratic monarchy with some kind of papal theocracy, in which the clergy would govern the daily affairs of Christendom. All the popes presumed that there would always be a secular power, and that the respective functions of the priesthood and the royal power would be kept relatively distinct. What the popes after Leo IX tended more and more to claim was a general right of supervision over all Christians, and over all offices within Christendom. In the concrete what this meant was that the pope had the right to intervene in any serious moral or doctrinal case, because all Christians were under his supervision as universal ordinary. This should be seen as the background for the various claims of Gregory VII against Henry IV. Gregory felt he had the right and obligation to intervene in matters involving the salvation of souls, even if his intervention had political repercussions. Should the German emperor flout the canon law in regard to episcopal elections and simony, the pope, because he had the spiritual supervision of all souls, could reprimand and even depose the emperor. This power derived from the inherent superiority of the papal office to all secular offices. Although relatively autonomous within his own sphere of activity, the emperor only possessed his office on the presumption that he was a Catholic in good standing in the Church. Without this presumption, an authority that was subordinate in terms of the final end of man would be able to subvert the Church and lead men to damnation rather than aiding them to their salvation. That is, without the acknowledgement that in principle the royal office was subordinate to the papal office, right order in society could not be achieved, for the office in charge of the merely temporal aspects of man would be able to dominate the office in charge of the eternal end of man. The lower would govern the higher. The idea of right order, clearly present in the thought of Humbert, came to fruition in the reign of Alexander's successor, Gregory VII.

When Hildebrand became pope in 1073, he had been the leading protagonist of reform at the Curia for more than twenty years. A man consumed by the vision of what the Church might be if freed to perform her earthly task, Gregory was willing to use any legitimate means to further this goal. Although personally overwhelmed with the obligations laid by God on the papal office, and with a full sense of his own limitations, when pursuing the interest of the Church Gregory manifested a realism founded on the shrewdest calculation. Living in a century that would not recognize the modern separation of religious and political matters, Gregory was a man willing to use political means to achieve religious goals. If force and political manipulation should be necessary to restore right order, they would be used for a legitimate end.

Granted this point of view, the investiture contest became inevitable, for Gregory was determined to gain the freedom of the Church, and this he realized would necessitate the prohibition of simony and lay investiture. Since in large measure the empire was governed by the bishops, who held great fiefs from the emperor, to prohibit lay investiture as an illegitimate limitation on the freedom of the Church would destroy the emperor's control over his great office-holders. If the emperor could not determine that only bishops favorable to him and his policy would be elected, then the empire would disintegrate and fall prey to the territorial ambitions of the

German nobility. Since the emperor could hardly be expected to tolerate losing the loyalty of his great officers, conflict over the issue of lay investiture was implicit in the papal search for right order. The only reply that the emperor could make to the theoretical claims of the papacy was an appeal to tradition, since even the supporters of the emperor assented to the general premises on which the Gregorian idea of the papacy was built. The supporters of the emperor could, for instance, hardly deny that the final end of man was salvation, and that the purpose of the sacraments and the clergy was to lead men to that end.

The investiture contest began in 1075 when Gregory issued a decree prohibiting lay investiture. The young Henry IV, who was faced at this time with a serious rebellion in Saxony, had been docile toward the pope because of his political troubles in Germany. When in June 1075 Henry defeated the rebels, his actions toward the papacy changed. He ignored earlier promises to stop the practice of simony and lay investiture. Legates were sent to Germany to threaten Henry privately with excommunication, and in response to this Henry summoned a synod to meet at Worms early in 1076. When the German bishops met they proved their loyalty to Henry by renouncing their obedience to the pope. To this Henry added a letter deposing the pope. In response to this action Gregory excommunicated Henry and all the German bishops who had sided with him. Beyond this, Henry was deposed and all his subjects freed from their fealty to him. This caused a rebellion to break out in Germany, for the German nobles were always ready for an excuse to limit the power of the emperor, and thus to increase their own powers. Just as most of the bishops in Germany supported the emperor, most of the nobility supported the pope. The nobles declared that Henry was no longer emperor, and that a council at Augsburg the following year would elect a new emperor, with Gregory personally present and presiding. Gregory left Rome, and by January of 1077 was at Canossa in Tuscany. Henry, knowing that if the council at Augsburg was held his deposition would be enforced, left for Italy to meet the pope before he could cross the Alps. At Canossa occurred the famous confrontation between the two men, with Henry presenting himself as a simple penitent whom the pope by his priestly office was bound to absolve. By recognizing Gregory as pope and receiving his absolution, Henry had avoided his deposition.

In Germany, however, the rebellion continued, and the nobles elected a new king. Gregory now made a claim that none of his predecessors had made, namely that he had the right to judge between the two rivals for the German throne. He of course decided against Henry, and in 1080 excommunicated Henry a second time for not recognizing the papal decision. Henry proved tenacious, however, and within the year had defeated his rival, deposed Gregory for the second time, and elected an antipope. Then, to end the conflict decisively, Henry invaded Italy and in 1084 took Rome. In desperation Gregory called for aid from his Norman vassal, Robert Guiscard. Henry withdrew before the Normans, who proceeded to pillage Rome. With the Romans enraged because of this, Gregory had no choice but to retire to Salerno with the Normans when they departed. He shortly fell sick and died in exile in 1085.

For a decade following Gregory's death Henry's political fortunes improved, until his eldest son Conrad revolted and by 1097 had forced Henry to abandon Italian politics altogether in favor of restoring his position in Germany. After the death of Conrad, Henry's next eldest son, Henry, revolted in 1104, and by the death of Henry IV the imperial government had disintegrated to such a degree that Germany was never to recover a strong central government in the Middle Ages. Looked at from a political perspective, one of the continuing results of the investiture contest was that at a critical period in her constitutional development the strength of the German nobility against the German emperor was increased to such a degree that centralization became impossible, thus giving Germany a very different national development from England or France.

Henry V (1106–25) continued the struggle over investiture, which had never been resolved by his father. Paschal II (1099–1118) offered a disarmingly simple solution of the contest in proposing that in return for the emperor giving up lay investiture the Church would give up all lands that it held by feudal tenure. This proposal, which bears some similarity to the later spiritual Franciscan vision of the Church as a purely spiritual society possessing no property (although Paschal exempted the temporal possessions of the papacy from the proposal), of course raised up overwhelming opposition against itself. It would have betrayed the German nobility, who had generally supported the papacy, into the hands of the emperor, who would have received vast amounts of land. And of course it would have deprived the bishops of most of their revenues. The unsteady Paschal backed down from his proposal, only to more gravely offend the Gregorian Party by formally approving lay investiture. The Gregorian reform had obviously fallen on bad days, and some talked of deposing Paschal as a heretic. But at least Paschal's proposals had performed the function of convincing most men that any solution of the investiture contest that attempted to change radically the existing practice of episcopal election was doomed to failure. When the contest was formally resolved, the compromise achieved did little more than preserve existing practice, falling far short of the Gregorian hope for a free Church.

The resolution of the investiture contest was based on the principles already evolved in the settlement of the problem of investiture in England in 1107. According to these principles, it was necessary to recognize that the offices of bishop and abbot had a double nature. All compromise must be based on the premise that the obligations of the bishop within the ecclesiastical hierarchy must be fulfilled, and that the bishop or abbot must faithfully perform whatever duties are owed the secular authority because of the status of vassalage. The actual compromise was formed by Calixtus II (1119–24), who in 1122 negotiated the Concordat of Worms with Henry V. Although there were further settlements and negotiations after this Concordat, which suggests that the Concordat was not as decisive in ending the contest in the minds of contemporaries as it has been for some modern historians, the principles embodied in the concordat represented a compromise that could be tolerated by all parties involved. The concordat first of all satisfied the procedure of the canon law by stating that bishops and abbots were only to be elected by the clergy or the monks, respectively. However, much of the force was taken out of this concession by the provision that in Germany the elections had to take place in the presence of the emperor, who had the right to decide a disputed election. Moreover, in Germany, after election the bishop or abbot was to be invested first with the *regalia,* the temporal rights and possessions held from the emperor. Only then could he be invested with the *spiritualia* by his ecclesiastical superior, the sign of which investiture was to be for the bishop the giving of the ring and staff. In Italy and Burgundy, and this was simply a recognition of the relatively more independent position of Italy and Burgundy within the Empire, investiture with the *spiritualia* could occur immediately after election, and investiture with the *regalia* was to follow automatically within six months.

On first glance it might seem that after half a century of disturbance and warfare the procedure sanctioned by the Concordat did not differ very much from conditions before the outbreak of the investiture contest. It has often been noted that periods of revolutionary change tend merely to hasten trends already present in a society, and that after rapid change societies tend to return to previously existing patterns of life. In many ways this was true of the investiture contest, and perhaps this shows that the Gregorian search for right order implied a restructuring of society beyond that which has ever been accomplished by revolution. Christopher Dawson has remarked that even in those periods in which European society has been most unified, there has been deep-lying division between religious and temporal authority, and that in no age has the spiritual authority been able long to dominate the temporal authority. However, this is not all that can be said. The investiture contest did certainly cause some permanent changes. The period before 1050 had been dominated by theocratic monarchy, and though the secular power was far from broken, by 1122 the Church had gained a degree of independence unknown during the theocratic period. Although from the thirteenth century the old pretensions of secular rulers to dominate the Church were to be pressed with increasing vigor, it is not too much to claim that much of the vitality of the twelfth- and thirteenth-century Church was stimulated by the program of the Gregorian Reformation. From this point of view, the investiture contest must be counted a victory for the papacy. Although falling far short of the goals desired by the Gregorians—reform, for instance, had hardly touched the proprietary system and the lower offices of the Church—the contest had renewed Christendom and brought into public consideration some of the most basic issues involved in appropriating the Christian message.

The remote effects of the investiture contest are difficult to assess, but the following suggestions might be made. Within Germany, the imperial power was seriously injured, while the power of the nobility was greatly enhanced. All the monarchs of Europe for centuries to come would have to take the papal claims more seriously than they had been taken for centuries past. Beyond this, as the result of the investiture contest, in the twelfth and thirteenth centuries the papacy was to play a role in European diplomacy far greater than any influence it had had before. This role went far beyond the actual material resources of the papacy, and testifies to the presumed moral leadership that the reformed papacy had won for itself. Although the continuing struggle between the spiritual and temporal powers, which in the later period fastened on issues other than investiture, was in the long run, due to the growth of the monarchical national state, to rob the Church of most of her independence of action, in the thirteenth century the fate of nations was often influenced by the temporal ramifications of papal policy.

Within the Church itself, the investiture contest had just as striking effects. During the period of theocratic monarchy, the pope had had little influence in European life, and where effective ecclesiastical power was wielded it was at the episcopal level. The bishop of Rome had not stood above the other bishops of Europe, except in terms of the general respect paid the papal primacy. Ecclesiastical policy generally did not come from Rome, but was determined by national councils of bishops. As a result the bishops of each country tended to reflect national attitudes and the will of their kings more than devotion to the Church universal. The investiture contest made significant inroads on all these practices. More and more the pope as universal ordinary came to interfere in local matters in the name of the universal Church. Although it often appeared that the popes were trying to strengthen their own powers by reducing those of the bishops, this perspective is somewhat misleading. The popes desired to strengthen both the episcopal and papal offices, but only on the presumption that these offices would be held by men whose first interest was the common good of the whole Church. Where this was not the case, and it often was not, the papacy naturally had to attack the traditional prerogatives of the bishops as a means of removing the bishops from the influence of the theocratic patterns of life. In sum, the investiture contest engendered a struggle within the Church between the claims of the national churches and the Church universal. Although again in the later Middle Ages the old pattern of episcopalism tended to reemerge, the investiture context had brought the papal office to a position far greater than it had held before.

Beyond all these considerations, Gerd Tellenbach has argued that Gregory stands at the greatest turning point in the history of the Church. Christians had always hesitated over what their relationship should be to the world, to the culture in which they found themselves. The predominant response of the Latin Church before Gregory had been to withdraw from the world. Now from the pontificate of Gregory the papacy had committed the Church to the conversion of the world. The Church was no longer in its main emphasis to retire from the world, but rather to draw the world into itself. This did not mean simply the conversion of all men to Christianity, but rather the permeation of society with Christian principles. Implicit in this was the task of reorganizing society according to Christian priorities. This search, in a society acknowledging the Christian view of the final end of man, meant that for right order to obtain in Christendom the superiority of the papal office to all other offices in Christendom must be recognized. As Tellenbach has summarized the matter, "Gregory's real service was to leaven the earthly lump with the principles of Catholicism, and to make the latter, in a manner hitherto undreamed of, a really decisive force in politics. His aim was to bring the kingdom of God on earth, as he saw it in his mind, nearer to realization."

BIBLIOGRAPHY

The effects of the proprietary system are treated in considerable detail by Catherine Boyd, *Tithes and Parishes in Medieval Italy: The Historical Roots of a Modern Problem.* Some of the most important documents concerning the political theory of the eleventh century may be found in Brian Tierney, *The Crisis of Church and State 1050–1300.* For interpretations of the political thought of the Investiture Contest, see Ernst H. Kantorowicz, *The King's Two Bodies: A Study in Mediaeval Political Theology.* An excellent study of the legal problems involved in the investiture contest may be found in Robert L. Benson, *The Bishop-Elect: A Study in Medieval Ecclesiastical Office.* For bibliography on the continuation of reform into the twelfth century, see Glenn W. Olsen, "The Idea of the *Ecclesia Primitiva* in the Writings of the Twelfth-Century Canonists."

AFTERWORD

Minor changes have been made in this chapter, which I have included in the present book to clarify the European background of the American form of the separation of church and state. This has not always been well understood by American thinkers. Today I would qualify more some of the long-term perspectives offered toward the end of the article—for instance, Tellenbach's contrast between pre- and post-Gregorian Christianity. The original essay was presented without notes, but with an abbreviated bibliography. Some items have been dropped from this latter. Complete bibliographic references are available in the volume's bibliography at the end of this volume.

To it might be added Glenn W. Olsen, *Beginning at Jerusalem:*

Five Reflections on the History of the Church; and, on what is said in this book about the spiritual Franciscans, poverty, and proto-capitalism, Julia I. Miller and Laurie Taylor-Mitchell, "The *Ognissanti Madonna* and the Humiliati Order in Florence," in *The Cambridge Companion to Giotto,* ed. Anne Derbes and Mark Sandona. On the understanding of leadership, political or religious, before the investiture contest, see Mayke de Jong, *The Penitential State: Authority and Atonement in the Age of Louis the Pious, 814–840*, on Carolingian notions of proper political order (with index on "*correctio*"); 166–68, on the proprietary church; and on church-state theory, 176–77. Tom Holland, *The Forge of Christendom: The End of Days and the Epic Rise of the West,* argues for the centrality of the reign of Gregory VII to Western history. Constant J. Mews, *The Lost Love Letters of Heloise and Abelard: Perceptions of Dialogue in Twelfth-Century France,* 2nd ed., trans. Neville Chiavaroli and Constant J. Mews, gives recent bibliography on the rhetoric of reform. Richard W. Kaeuper, *Holy Warrior: The Religious Ideology of Chivalry,* treats lay desire for independence from the clergy and the way by which the growth of national sovereignty suffocated earlier forms of political life.

3

LAY SPIRITUALITY *AD MAJOREM DEI GLORIAM*

CONTEMPORARY CHRISTIANITY, as an expression of the contemporary world, bears some resemblance to a great carnival midway. From all sides barkers urge their goods. "Have you tried Marriage Encounter?" "Come to the Latin Mass this Sunday." "I didn't know what Christianity was about until I joined the Charismatics!" "Have you been to the First Church of Agape in the Park?" Whereas in the pre-Vatican II Church people often had relatively stable patterns of spiritual practice, people now often move in and out of new "spiritual experiences" with great rapidity, making of their lives a series of passages.[1]

Although one would, perhaps, have to be demented with charity to call all these movements and expressions "spiritualities," the existence of a variety of spiritualities in the Church is no new thing. In spite of the profound arguments by Louis Bouyer that finally all Catholic spirituality is one, even within Catholic Christianity, as Bouyer so articulately showed, there have always been schools of thought and practice.[2] Some of these have found their origin in a particular theological notion or understanding, while others have been a response to the peculiar problems and needs of a particular

1. To use analogously the term of Gail Sheehy, *Passages: Predictable Crises of Adult Life* (New York: Bantam, 1976).

2. Louis Bouyer, *Introduction to Spirituality,* trans. Mary Perkins Ryan (New York: Desclee, 1961), 1.

time and place, or of a condition or state of Christian life. It is in relation to the latter that the idea of a lay spirituality formed historically. In the present chapter I would like to consider briefly how and why a distinctive lay spirituality emerged, to present a reading of our own times, which would argue for the particular relevance of one of the historic forms of lay spirituality, and then, with the other barkers, to press this argument on my reader.

A half century ago John Courtney Murray wrote of two basic tendencies within Christianity, which he labeled "eschatological humanism" and "incarnational humanism."[3] Ancient and medieval Christianity tended to express the former, focusing on God in such a manner as to express a certain contempt for the world. From the eleventh century, "incarnational humanism," which seeks sanctification through the natural goods of this world, came more and more to carry the day. If we keep in mind that both tendencies have always been present in Christianity, Murray's perspective is useful for understanding the emergence of lay spirituality. There was a pronounced tendency in the Fathers to identify Christian perfection with celibacy and the giving up of private property, and to look upon the married state as an inferior, although legitimate, form of Christian life. Especially from the fourth century, the enthusiasm of many Christian writers was channeled into the praise of the ascetic and monastic lives, with a consequent depreciation and, in some degree, lack of interest in the lives of those left "in the world." Although many of the Fathers could and did outline the goods proper to marriage, when they urged the laity to spiritual progress the pattern of this progress was almost always implicitly ascetical and monastic in character. While some could speak of the family as a "domestic church," and of the love between husband and wife as a "communion in the same spiritual ideal," there hardly developed what might be called a theology of the family or of the lay state.[4]

3. John Courtney Murray, *We Hold These Truths: Catholic Reflections on the American Proposition* (New York: Sheed and Ward, 1960), chap. 8. The same general perspective is provided by Gerd Tellenbach, *Church, State and Christian Society at the Time of the Investiture Contest,* trans. R. F. Bennett (Oxford: Blackwell, 1959).

4. The whole ancient tradition is surveyed by Louis Bouyer, *A History of Christian*

It seems obvious to me that some form of ascetic discipline will always be necessary as a ground for progress in the spiritual life. Yet in the ancient context the pattern of discipline provided for the laity was extremely awkward, centering as it did on a "flight to the desert" away from urban civilization. Although particularly the Cappadocian fathers had some understanding of the necessity to create certain institutional and cultural supports for those who lived an active life within an urbanized culture, only the most rudimentary responses to the situation of the lay state had appeared at the end of antique civilization. This is witnessed by the fact that the problem of how the Christian young were to be educated had hardly been addressed, beyond a few experiments by men like Basil, Jerome, and John Chrysostom. Augustine had proposed a great program of studies in his *On Christian Doctrine,* but this had not been made accessible to laymen in any institutionalized form. On the contrary, both the power and a certain inappropriateness of the ascetic ideal by itself as a model for the life of the laity is evidenced by the tendency of serious married couples to undergo a conversion through which, by mutual consent, they gave up their conjugal rights, or even separated from one another to enter monastic communities. This form of ideal tended to draw people out of the lay state, rather than to guide it in the normal conditions of familial life.[5]

If late antique Christianity had tended to remake the layman into a monk, in the early Middle Ages the prestige of the monk was so great that he became a kind of representative before God of the layman. With society divided into those who work, those who fight,

---

Spirituality, vol. 1, *The Spirituality of the New Testament and the Fathers,* trans. Mary Perkins Ryan (New York: Desclee, 1963). The phrase quoted is from Jean-Paul Broudéhoux, *Mariage et Famile chez Clément d'Alexandrie,* Théologie historique 2 (Paris: Buchesne, 1970), 154; see also 188–91.

5. For the materials in this paragraph, see Werner Jaeger, *Early Christianity and Greek Paideia* (Cambridge, Mass.: Belknap Press, 1985); Henri-Irené Marrou, *Histoire de l'éducation dans l'antiquité,* 6th ed. (Paris: Éditions du Seuil, 1965), part 3, chap. 9–10; Marrou, *A History of Education in Antiquity,* 3rd ed., trans. George Lamb (London: Sheed and Ward, 1956); Marrou, *Saint Augustin et la fin de la culture antique,* 4th ed., Bibliothèque des Ecoles Francsises d'Athènes et de Rome, fasc. 145 and 146 bis (Paris: E. de Boccard, 1938, 1949), esp. 329–540; and Philip Rousseau, *Ascetics, Authority, and the Church in the Age of Jerome and Cassian* (Oxford: Oxford University Press, 1978).

and those who pray, the last *order*, that of the clergy and monks, became the intercessors before God for a sometime pious but often inactive laity. Although the idea that one class of society might represent another is not without a certain theological profundity (testifying both to the solidarity of society and the influence of Christ's representative sacrifice as an expression of the manner in which each Christian inheres in the other as a member of the body of Christ), once again this form of spirituality tended to ignore the problem of giving guidance to the layman in the concrete circumstances of life.[6]

Thus we must come to the Gregorian reform of the eleventh century before we see a concerted attempt to articulate the place of the layman within the Church and to address in a fulsome way the layman's specific needs. This attempt to provide for the laity was drawn out over many centuries, and seems to me to have received a kind of term in the *Spiritual Exercises* of St. Ignatius of Loyola, written before he had founded the Society of Jesus. The specific problem of the lay state seems to me to be that, in addition to the forms of contemplation and asceticism so well developed in monasticism, the laity needs a spirituality centered on sustaining the layman in daily activity. As Basil, Chrysostom, and Augustine had pointed out so well, every Christian needs to develop and relate the themes of contemplation and an active life of charity, but the balance between *theoria* and action is different in the life of the layman than it is in the life of the monk (the spirituality of the cleric stands halfway, so to speak, between the monk and the layman).[7] Very few people are capable of standing against the general beliefs and practices of the society in which they live for a very long time, and because the layman stands in intimate contact with these social practices and modes

6. Yves Congar, *Lay People in the Church: A Study for a Theology of Laity,* trans. Donald Attwater (Westminster, Md.: Newman Press, 1967), 405–07; André Vauchez, *La spiritualité du Moyen Age occidental: VIIIe–XIIe siécles* (Paris: Presses universitaires de France, 1975); and the stimulating review of this latter book by Caroline Bynum in *Speculum* 52 (1977): 1044–46, with which I am in part disagreeing.

7. Gerhart B. Ladner, *The Idea of Reform: Its Impact on Christian Thought and Action in the Age of the Fathers,* rev. ed. (New York: Harper and Row, 1967).

of life, he or she must be formed by a spirituality that forms activity in a manner that still allows for the reflection on and understanding of the Christian faith, above all when this faith stands in contradiction to the times.[8]

Ignatius provided an incarnational humanism for those left in the world primarily in two directions. His first great insight was that, granted the great economic and institutional developments that by his day had provided Europe with so many temptations and alternatives to a world-fleeing mode of life, the average Christian could and would elect to remain "in the world." The specific task, therefore, of such an election would be to bring to bear on worldly society the Gospel insights in such a way that average Christians would not lose their way. It could not be assumed that the general beliefs and practices of society would help people to find the kingdom of God. Rather, in many ways the practicing Christian was alienated from many aspects of his or her culture. Rather than making belief and practice easy, European culture now provided many sources for the erosion of faith. Therefore the counter-Reformation task was to continue under new circumstances the earlier Gregorian and medieval attempt by the Church to form culture in such a way that the great mass of humans who rely on culture for their directives could still live in a Christendom, a culture in which Christianity provided the leaven and the principles of right order. Because of this insight, Ignatius stressed the particular task of educating the upper classes and the leaders of society in a Christian manner that would unite the valid insights of the Renaissance with the older Christian culture it was tending to replace—hence the mission of the Jesuit colleges and of the *ratio studiorum.*[9]

Ignatius's second insight informs the *Spiritual Exercises,* which brings together the active and contemplative poles of Christian existence in a new manner. Prayer in the Middle Ages had centered

8. H. Outram Evennet, *The Spirit of the Counter-Reformation* (Notre Dame, Ind.: University of Notre Dame Press, 1970); Jean Daniélou, *Prayer as a Political Problem,* trans. J. R. Kirwan (New York: Sheed and Ward, 1967).

9. Christopher Dawson, *The Crisis of Western Education,* introduction by Glenn W. Olsen (Washington, D.C.: The Catholic University of America Press, 2010).

on contemplation, the clearing of images from the mind, and the encouraging of a passive openness of the soul before God. This form of prayer was of course particularly appropriate to the still life of the monk. Granted the new conditions of life and the "busy-ness" of a life lived in the world, Ignatius saw that the problem of forming a steadfast will was now even more acute than it had been for the contemplatives. People active in the world, and without great amounts of time to be reserved for reading and contemplation, still had to be given a firmness of the will and an intelligence in action—hence the appropriateness of meditation, the idea of prayer that is central to the *Exercises*. Meditation, as contrasted with contemplation, centers on an active mental-image forming dialogue with God, centered on the reading of the Scriptures, and reflection particularly on the passion of Christ. Realistically acknowledging that an active life rarely allows for the quiet needed for contemplation, Ignatius seized on the normal occupation of a mind living an active life, filled with images, and in the *Exercises* gave a program of development suitable to this kind of interior life. Rather than being told to clear the mind of images, the person receiving spiritual direction was to be told to take up some event from the life of Christ, to image it in all its detail, even to place oneself among those witnessing and participating in the event, and to apply the event to one's own concrete circumstances, choosing the side of Christ against the powers of Satan. In confession vague reference to such generic sins as pride or concupiscence was to be avoided in favor of picturing for oneself the full circumstances of each sin, and therefore the highly individual way in which one incarnates some evil generic to mankind. By such a method, the alternatives of fighting for or against Christ were to become clear in a way that sprang from everyday existence, and therefore could inform the will in a way relevant to this existence. Meditation could guide action, whether in the day-by-day pattern of partaking of the sacraments, Scripture, and prayer as the basis for daily activity, or in the larger pattern of a periodic retreat from normal activities to examine more longstanding tendencies toward growth or disobedience as the basis for a renewed commitment to an incarnational existence.

In *Quadragesimo Anno* 143, Pius XI (1857–1939) near our own time expressed the hope that all the laity would employ the *Spiritual Exercises,* "that most valuable means of both personal and social restoration."[10] In many ways the world we live in is like that of Ignatius, shot through with infidelity, alienation, and egotism. In some ways our conditions of life are even more precarious than his, beset as we are by the gravest problems of war and peace, natural resources, and justice. Even those open to the use of the *Spiritual Exercises* sometimes describe them as elitist, good for the few but inappropriate to the many. I am not so sure. I do not see how we can accomplish even our "secular" tasks of dealing with such things as poverty without a discipline and asceticism for the practice of which the modern world has left us sadly unprepared.[11] The tasks that face us demand not just good intentions, expressions of solidarity, and hopefulness, but immense work, exercise of the intellect, and steadfastness of the will. It seems to me that most of the spiritualities current in the Church leave people wholly unprepared for the world that is upon us. I do not deny that Marriage Encounter or the charismatic movement may touch many souls, but as I have experienced these movements I doubt that they leave even the non-leader of the world that is upon us prepared for the demands that will be placed ever more ineluctably on faithful Christians. If our only problem were to provide the bourgeoisie with a spirituality suitable to its instincts and tastes, these movements would have much to commend them, but the world as we now experience it is falling apart in large part because the instincts of the bourgeoisie have had such free reign. It is inconceivable that these values and sensibilities will determine the age to come, and the great tragedy of our own day has been the fact that the leaders of the Church, particularly in the United States, have had so little understanding of our place in

10. Terence P. McLaughlin, ed., *The Church and the Reconstruction of the Modern World: The Social Encyclicals of Pope Pius XI* (Garden City, N.Y.: Image Books, 1957), 272.

11. See the foreword and the overall argument of Friedrich Heer, *The Intellectual History of Europe,* 2 vols., trans. Jonathan Steinberg (Garden City, N.Y.: Image Books, 1968); and the powerful analysis of Romano Guardini, *The End of the Modern World,* trans. Joseph Theman and Herbert Burke, ed. Frederick Wilhelmsen (Chicago: H. Regnery, 1968).

history. Precisely at the time when asceticism is needed, most forms of discipline have been removed from the life of the Church in favor of the most amorphous conceptions of growth through charity and community. Precisely at the time when the artificial and sentimental nature of personal relationships in middle-class society is pilloried in our literature, we have been given a liturgy more contrived and pedestrian even than the Church from which it arises.[12] Precisely when the complexity of the secular problems of our society forces us to acknowledge that, indeed, one man's opinion is not as good as another's, and that if we do not respect expertise we will perish, we suspect any spirituality that treats the world as a very complicated place in which real progress of any kind comes only after the most immense and sustained exertion.

There is an obvious sense in which Ignatian spirituality is elitist and specially directed to those who lead and influence society. It should therefore be of special interest to anyone likely to read this chapter. However, my own experience suggests that, even in the attenuated form of the three-day retreat, the *Exercises* and the spirituality flowing from it have a power to form people of the most diverse backgrounds. Reforming even one life in the likeness of God is a most formidable task. I wonder if the kind of talk-sessions, even the kind of Bible group sessions, so often now passing for lay spirituality in the Church, really do much to promote serious reform. They are so easy to participate in without placing one's soul before God, without developing any sense of the soul's state before God. My own experience here is of necessity partial and biased, but in my most somber moments I think that all we now have left by way of spirituality is what remains when spirituality, like asceticism before it, has become a subject of abhorrence. The moment of such a recognition, of the taste of ashes on our mouths, may be the point from which we turn again to the great lay task of leavening the world, of doing all things to the greater glory of God, of seeking God in all things.

12. James Hitchcock, *The Recovery of the Sacred* (New York: Seabury Press, 1974), makes many useful comments on the nature of "suburban religion."

AFTERWORD

Minor changes have been made in the text of this essay, and some footnotes have been updated. André Vauchez's *La spiritualité du Moyen Age occidental: VIIIe–XIIe siécles* has been subsequently translated as *The Spirituality of the Medieval West: From the Eighth to the Twelfth Century.* Paul F. Grendler has written several books on Renaissance schooling. On Jesuit learning, see *The Jesuits: Cultures, Sciences, and the Arts, 1540–1773,* ed. John W. O'Malley, et al. Walter Brandmüller, *Light and Shadows: Church History amid Faith, Fact and Legend,* trans. Michael J. Miller, treats the baroque idea of the glory of God.

4

CHRISTIAN FAITH IN A NEO-PAGAN SOCIETY

I THINK IT WAS C. S. LEWIS who somewhere, in response to the lament of a friend over having to live surrounded by pagans, replied to the effect, "That it were so." Lewis, who liked to describe himself as a converted pagan living among apostate Puritans, meant by his exclamation that some of the pagans had had a regard for the life of the mind, a persistence in self-discipline ordered to truth, goodness, and beauty, and an openness toward the order of nature rarely found in contemporary man. Playing on the ambiguity of the word "pagan," Lewis meant to indicate that much that is loosely called pagan would most certainly have appalled the finer spirits of the pagan world, in comparison with whom modern man seems enveloped in the most profound self-will, self-deception, and hedonism. If in the present chapter an attempt is made to assess the place of Christianity in a culture that may be termed "neo-pagan," we must therefore be careful about terminology. Christianity has always had a double attitude toward paganism, which has been seen as at once the sum of all errors of life and thought of those without a correct knowledge of God, and as the measure of those human goods that may be obtained without the light of Christian revelation. I take it that when we speak of a new paganism, it is primarily the idea of a benighted paganism to which reference is made. Such reference may easily lead us into obvious, but fairly puerile, comparisons. It takes no great historical insight, for instance, to note that the lack of reverence for life, widespread in the pagan world and only in a modest degree driven from Christian civilization by the most laborious activity of men of peace, has again become a characteristic of contemporary civilization.[1] In similar fashion, we may easily note the reappearance of widespread forms of the worship of nature, or of astrology, without, I think, doing much more than indulging in a facile moralizing. Without denying some usefulness to such exercises, I would rather look at certain select patterns of thought and belief that exercised great influence in the pre-Christian world, and to the manner in which these patterns seem to be appearing in new forms in our own day. Having done this, I will make some suggestions about the implications for Christianity of these developments.

Some years ago, Peter Gay won the National Book Award for a penetrating two-volume interpretation of the Enlightenment, the title of the first volume of which was *The Rise of Modern Paganism.*[2] As an extended study of the manifold ways in which the legacy of the pagan past has been addressed and set to new purposes in the last centuries, the book can be highly recommended. Here I wish to attempt a task both more modest and bolder than that undertaken by Gay. Without giving the detail of his very substantial book, I wish to push the context of his inquiry even further, beyond what with Gay is already a very extensive engagement with almost the whole course of Western civilization. To do this, I propose that we define as "pagan" what Charles Norris Cochrane, in his splendid book on *Christianity and Classical Culture,* defined as "classical."[3] This will allow us to move beyond the positive and negative senses of the word "pagan" already noted, to encounter a very comprehensive and persis-

1. The contrast presented by Christopher Dawson, *Religion and the Rise of Western Culture* (Garden City, N.Y.: Image Books, 1958), 19 ff. and throughout, between "the war society of the barbarian kingdom with its cult of heroism and aggression and the peace society of the Christian Church with its ideals of asceticism and renunciation and its high theological culture (23)" is very illuminating.

2. Peter Gay, *The Enlightenment: An Interpretation,* vol. 1, *The Rise of Modern Paganism* (New York: Knopf, 1966).

3. Charles Norris Cochrane, *Christianity and Classical Culture: A Study of Thought and Action from Augustus to Augustine* (London: Oxford University Press, 1974).

tent view of the world, only fragments of which are expressed by the specific practices so often loosely termed pagan. It is not easy to catch Cochrane's sense of the classical in a few words. But to make a beginning, a classical view of the world embodies a manifold hostility to the material and temporal aspects of human existence. In good measure, we may therefore equate the classical with the Platonic—that is, Plato's thought represents the most consciously developed expression in the ancient world of a "time-fleeing" ontology. At the level of being itself, the real is associated with that which is permanent, unchanging, and immaterial. The more we enter the world of time and matter, the more we deal with that which is relatively unreal, and indeed, strictly speaking, change and matter are incomprehensible. True science deals with the mathematical; knowledge of physical nature, insofar as it is not mathematical, is not true science. The life of the philosopher is a learning-how-to-die, a freeing of the soul from the prison house of the body, a preparation of the mind through the study of mathematics for contact with the real, with idea.

At the level of politics, this "classical" attitude is expressed in the dream of stopping time. Thus Cochrane opens the first chapter of his book with this quotation from Suetonius (*Augustus* 28): "May it be my privilege to establish the republic safe and sound on its foundations, gathering the fruit of my desire to be known as author of the ideal constitution, and taking with me to the grave the hope that the basis which I have laid will be permanent." This prayer of Augustus expresses the hope, which had haunted the ancient world since the first Egyptians, Mesopotamians, and Greeks had given themselves to political theory, of constructing a permanent political order that could withstand the ravages of time. Such an order would permanently embody and achieve the secular values of mankind: peace, prosperity, and justice. Here again, although hints can be found even in Plato himself that the evils of the world might have something to do with a personal disorder within man, the heart of the political aspiration was to reconstruct or reorder historical human society in the light of unchanging principles, and thus to "stop history."

These kinds of attitudes had profound impact on all areas of human life, and were particularly manifest in classical literature, which we may in shorthand fashion call "exemplaristic." This term refers not merely to the purpose of forming good character to which classical letters tended to be directed, but also to the effect on the sense of human individuality of such a purpose. As Erich Auerbach pointed out in his comparison of the one pre-Christian literature of the Mediterranean world that was not classical, that of the Hebrews, with Greek literature, the one is a literature of individuals with personal histories or missions, the other of timeless ideals.[4] Abraham, Isaac, Jacob are men with highly individual histories called by God, who develop with time. The characters of Greek and Roman history and literature, on the other hand, whether Odysseus, Telemachus, or Cato, undergo very little development in terms of personal history, but rather tend to be presented as unchanging types. The "good Cato" is simply an embodiment of a fixed virtue, unchanging from childhood to old age. He has no personal or internal history, in the sense, say, of St. Augustine's interior life, but from beginning to end simply stands for a dehistoricized notion of virtue directly to be imitated at any point of time.[5] Such an attitude habitually turns from the uniqueness of historical particularity to the comfortable haven of unchanging archetypes of human character and tries to discover in human existence repetitive patterns by which historical movement may be subsumed *sub specie aeternitatis.*

The studies of people like Mircea Eliade have made us aware that what I am calling the classical vision of life is even more extensive than all the ancient civilizations of the West. Eliade has shown that the flight from time represents a kind of universal instinct of the species.[6] All the civilizations of the archaic world tend to the view

4. Erich Auerbach, *Mimesis: The Representation of Reality in Western Literature,* trans. Willard R. Trask (Princeton: Princeton University Press, 1968), esp. chaps. 1–4.

5. Peter Brown, *Augustine of Hippo: A Biography* (Berkeley and Los Angeles: University of California Press, 1969), has captured very well Augustine's sense of internal history.

6. Almost everything Eliade has written is relevant to what follows, but see first *Cosmos and History: The Myth of the Eternal Return,* trans. Willard R. Trask (New York: Harper, 1954).

that the best existed at the beginning, in the once-upon-a-time of the Golden Age or of the cosmic unity of the gods with man. Time is uniformly perceived as destructive, as removing mankind from the best time of the beginnings, the time when there was no time. Time always represents the loss of Eden, the entrance into a historical existence of suffering. The great hope is to reverse time, once again to restore the original condition of human life, whether by ritual repentance in the case of individual suffering or by the renewal of the solar year or cosmic year in terms of society. Time is not perceived as irreversible. Rather, through liturgy, one may reenter the sphere of the sacred, or through a rite like the celebration of the new year, one can wipe out the old and begin again new, full of fresh resolution.

The tendency in classical thought to try to overcome time is simply then the expression under the conditions of a historical civilization of attitudes that literally seem to be as old as the race.[7] In historical times these attitudes can take many forms of expression. Hence the perpetual Roman hope for *renovatio,* for the restoration of the Golden Age or the renewal of the empire, was as much a resistance to the idea that time is irreversible as was the desire for *otium,* a leisurely retirement from the world.[8] What Augustus, and with him Virgil, hoped for was an empire that "knows no bounds in space or time" (cf. *Aeneid* 1.278)—that is, that erases the irreversibility of time, the fact that every thing and every empire has its day.

The ideals of life thus described were in the classical vision normally united to a civic definition of life in which man was seen best achieving the good by the life of a citizen in a just constitutional or-

7. See the vast amount of materials on "primitivism" gathered by Arthur O. Lovejoy and George Boas, *Primitivism and Related Ideas in Antiquity* (Baltimore: The Johns Hopkins University Press, 1935), and by George Boas, *Essays on Primitivism and Related Ideas in the Middle Ages* (Baltimore: The Johns Hopkins University Press, 1948).

8. For *renovatio,* Johannes Straub, *Regeneratio Imperii: Aufsatze Über Roms Kaisertum und Reich im Spiegel der heidnischen und christlichen Publizistik* (Darmstadt: Wissenschaftliche Buchgesellschaft, 1972). For *otium,* Jean-Marie Andre, *L'Otium dans la vie morale et intellectuelle romaine* (Paris: Presses universitaires de France, 1966). See also the important studies of Edward D. Blodgett, "The Unquiet Heart: Time and the Poetry of Antiquity in the Middle Ages," *Filolški Pregled* 1–4 (1971): 55–83; and Blodgett, "Chaucerian Pryvetee and the Opposition to Time," *Speculum* 51 (1976): 477–93.

der. Cochrane terms this a "liberal" ideal, understanding by this the notion that the end of life is the effort through human reason and virtue to dispel those things that are "sinister and chaotic."[9] The existence of evil in the world is acknowledged in such a view, but this evil is not so much the product of some flaw in man as merely the sum of everything disordered and chaotic—that is, that has escaped human control. The task of man then is as much a task to eliminate evil as it is to eliminate history. In the world society toward which man should intend, the goal is to eliminate everything irrational, chaotic, evil, and historical. The political problem is therefore above all a structural problem, the imposition of a just and permanent form of life on all the impulsive forces of fortune and history that tend to undo human achievement.

Many hundred years of Christian reflection were necessary before the Church Fathers came to have a firm grasp on the ultimate issues separating them from this classical vision of the world. The issue was never so simple as, for instance, the replacement of the classical conception of evil with the Christian doctrine of sin, for on almost every issue there was something to be said for the classical point of view, some element to be retained and brought into Christianity after an appropriate criticism. This is nowhere clearer than in the primordial encounter between what we can call the cosmic denial of history in classical thought and the emphasis on the linear and providential development of history in Christian thought. The term here was the thought of Augustine, to which some attention must be devoted.

Whereas in archaic and classical thought prime emphasis was laid on the reassertion and defense of the unity of the cosmos, of that best order of things that time always tends to undo, for Augustine emphasis is placed on that continuing *reformatio in melius* that is to fill history. That is, a proper good is discovered for time and matter, which no longer are simply conditions to be fled, but rather are the conditions under which human maturation and sanctification are

9. Cochrane, *Christianity and Classical Culture,* 39.

possible. To try to summarize in a few words the magnificent study of *The Idea of Reform,* by Gerhart Ladner,[10] the Greek Fathers, still in large measure overwhelmed by the classical heritage, tended at critical points to adjust the distinctiveness of Pauline thought to the ancient cosmic universe. Thus Christian reform was seen as above all a recovery of the image and likeness of God once possessed by Adam, a reform achieved primarily by ascetical and mystical ascent. Adam—that is, man at the beginning—had been perfect, and reform lay in undoing the effects of the fall into history—that is, of sin. This reform was to be achieved by fleeing all that ties man to time and matter, by ascetical discipline of the body and mystical ascent above time. Although there was some recognition that Adam might be regarded as a child, and his virtue the virtue of innocence, and that therefore he had been intended to develop, so powerful was the ancient instinct for a reintegrated cosmos that the end of Christian life was widely seen as a restoration of man and the universe to its first state.

With the Latin Fathers, and above all Augustine, a relatively novel emphasis appeared. Adam was more clearly perceived as an innocent who had only begun a growth in virtue cut short by his act of disobedience. Man's task now was, so to speak, not simply to recover the Adamic state, but to take up the historical task Adam had failed. *Conversio* was not to be the return to Adam, but *reformatio* through history toward an end known only to God. That is, reform was not primarily to be ascetical or mystical, but moral. By a mysterious dispensation, the *felix culpa* had made possible a distinctively temporal and material style of reformation, in which likeness to God was achieved by moral-intellectual struggle as a united soul and body. Hence the distinctively Latin emphases are on sanctification, perseverance through time, and rest only at the end of time. The race, person by person, is intended for a perfection that goes beyond the original state to no known limit. Although what hap-

10. Gerhart Ladner, *The Idea of Reform: Its Impact on Christian Thought and Action in the Age of the Fathers,* rev. ed. (New York: Harper and Row, 1967).

pens in history may work toward the restoration of the cosmos, the fullness of this restoration is clearly placed after the end of history. History thus becomes problematic, for just as the reformed individual may become good to no known limit, so may one in self-will flee further and further from God. The ultimate notion of man and God living in harmony was as attractive to Augustine as it had been to archaic man or the Greek Fathers, but more decisively this as a human good was now seen as an end to be obtained only in part in this life, and only as a result of immense exertion. The world is perceived as more flawed by sin than classical man had dreamed, and thus no structural improvement in human life can be permanent. Time is irreversible, so that Eden can never be reentered. All is problematic: "We are the times: such as we are, such are the times."[11] Essential reform is person by person, and there is no mechanism to pass on some improvement permanently to the race, or permanently to embody some good in a political structure. The very notion of a permanent political order is a delusion, as is that of some permanently achieved historical success.

The implications of all this should be clear. Augustine and the Latins understood the nobility of the classical ideals, above all of the aspiration for a united mankind, tied by bonds of justice and perhaps even affection. In a certain sense, these ideals were indeed transferred into ecclesiology, so that the archaic vision of a harmonious cosmos became the vision of all mankind brought into one in the *corpus Christi.*[12] Rather than rejecting any of these ancient aspirations of the race, Augustine qualified each of them from a Christian point of view, specifying what reasonably could be won during the historical part of man's existence, and what not. No more was the natural world rejected than politics, but each was put in perspective. Classical man, because he had not been honest about his own flaws,

11. *Augustine, Sermo* 80, 8, *PL* 38.498, quoted in R. A. Markus, *Saeculum: History and Society in the Theology of St. Augustine* (Cambridge: Cambridge University Press, 1970), 40–41.

12. This ecclesiology is the special subject of Henri de Lubac, *Catholicism: A Study of Dogma in Relation to the Corporate Destiny of Mankind,* trans. Lancelot C. Sheppard from the 4th French ed. (New York: Sheed and Ward, 1964).

had tried to achieve more by reason and through structure than is possible, but this does not mean that the basic goods desired were other than desirable. Classical man had been blinded to the possibilities of time and matter, and thus to the hope of cooperation with Providence. Indeed, classical man had not clearly understood that man is a real union of body and soul, but nevertheless the ancients had engaged in an ennobling adherence to many permanent goods.

As the Christian Church entered the Middle Ages, one sacral universe tended to replace another. The insight achieved by Augustine was the insight of one man, not of Christians in general, or even of many theologians. Augustine himself had at most shown certain important limitations in an archaic view of the universe. He had by no means rejected the basic premise that that which is unchanging in the universe is more important than that which changes. Although asserting the relative importance of the order of time, God was still for Augustine *Deus immutabilis.* Although secular activity was seen as immensely important for a human being, even more important were those signs in time of that which transcends time, the great *symbola* that at one and the same time point to and embody the fullness of things. These mysteries and sacraments are God's way of meeting that which is in time, and are the chief indication that the Christian universe is at once sacral and historical. And this in a quite unique way. The Christian symbols do not merely point from history to that which is beyond history; they themselves embody a historical progression or revelation.[13] The brazen serpent foreshadows the cross: antitype completes type. The symbols are not mere arbitrary expressions of eternal truth; they embody the Truth. The cross is not a mere symbol fallen into history of that which is outside history, but rather is a historical event by which history itself is interpreted and redeemed. Thus the Christian lives in a sacral universe, but this is a sacral universe that is also historical, and the essential meaning of which is only given in a historical manner.

13. See Glenn W. Olsen, "Allegory, Typology and Symbol: The Sensus Spiritalis," part 1, "Definitions and Earliest History"; part 2, "Early Church through Origen," *Communio* 4 (1977): 161–79, 357–83.

But the sacral universe of the Christians was not only that of the sacraments and the saving events of salvation history. As the Church shifted into a medieval and Germanic context, another form of sacrality was experienced—namely the cosmic universe of the Germans. Tied even more than the world of the classical peoples to the time of nature, to the cycle of the seasons, this was but one expression of the agrarian forms of a-temporality that had been the most common experience of mankind since the beginnings of the race. Leaving the relatively urbanized world of classical man, the Church was almost of necessity overwhelmed by the timeless world of the peasant.[14] No amount of Augustinian sense of the irreversibility of time could overweigh the fact that for centuries to come the immediate experience of time for most people was to be that of the time of nature. Even in the classical world itself, the Church had adapted the linearity of salvation history to the cyclic time of nature in the very concept of a liturgical year—that is, of a repetitive presentation over the cycle of a year of the singular events of salvation history. Now, in being overwhelmed by the system sometimes called "theocratic monarchy," the system of Charlemagne and Otto I, the Church was threatened by a reintegration back into a purely archaic cosmos.[15]

The nature of this threat has been brilliantly, if impressionistically, characterized by the Austrian historian Friedrich Heer. Heer portrays the development of *The Intellectual History of Europe* as a continuing struggle between the representatives of high and low culture.[16] In the early Middle Ages, the representatives of high culture—that is, of the values of Latin humanism and rationalism and of Christian theology—almost disappeared. The archaic, irrational

14. See, in addition to the classic portrayal by Marc Bloch, *Feudal Society,* trans. L. A. Manyon (Chicago: University of Chicago Press, 1961), 72–75, the fine essay by A. J. Gurevich, "Time as a Problem of Cultural History," in *Cultures and Time,* ed. Louis Gardet, et al. (Paris: UNESCO Press, 1976), 229–45, at 234–40.

15. On theocratic monarchy see Gerd Tellenbach, *Church, State and Christian Society at the Time of the Investiture Contest,* translated by R. F. Bennett (Oxford: Blackwell, 1959), 26, 56–60, 69–76, 89–98.

16. Friedrich Heer, *The Intellectual History of Europe,* 2 vols., trans. Jonathan Steinberg (Garden City, N.Y.: Image Books, 1968).

(in the sense of custom-bound), and pre-Christian folkish culture of the masses showed itself almost everywhere victorious. Although set in a Christian framework in which the king is the vicar of Christ, the world of the frontispiece of the Aachen Gospels is a timeless, hieratic world centered on the ruler as the expression of power, the chief link between the people and the forces of life and death.[17] This is a fixed universe, determined by age-old custom, integrating all aspects of life into a cosmic whole. It is also a profoundly sacral universe, in which nature and authority both are the expressions of the basic life-forces. In such a world, Christianity almost was denuded of all that separates itself from the time-denying religions, of all the self-understanding won by men like Augustine. The world itself became almost purely exemplaristic, with all the visible hierarchies of being and office the expression of invisible realities. Piety became almost wholly a matter of form and formula, and the whole interior dimension discovered by men like Augustine almost disappeared.[18] Ironically even monasticism, the prime bearer of high culture in this period, in one of its aspects threatened to obliterate the whole Christian understanding of sin and grace. For while one face of monasticism preserved an almost ferocious penitential aspect, and thus a sense of how seriously flawed man and the world are, another face was little more than a prolongation, under the mask of high culture, of some of the prime attitudes we have called archaic and classical. An elaboration is necessary.

The very first biography of a saint's life, that of Antony by Athanasius, had in the fourth century already introduced a set of themes to powerfully affect the whole history of monasticism. We may call these themes paradisiacal, meaning by this that a powerful idea within monasticism was that the monastic life literally recaptures,

17. Ernst H. Kantorowicz, *The King's Two Bodies: A Study in Mediaeval Political Theology* (Princeton: Princeton University Press, 1957), 61–78 and fig. 5.

18. In spite of an omnipresent irrelevant moralizing about this state of affairs, the religion of the eighth and ninth centuries is suggestively portrayed by Heinrich Fichtenau, *The Carolingian Empire: The Age of Charlemagne,* trans. Peter Munz (New York and Evanston: Harper Torchbooks, 1964), esp. chaps. 4–7. More sympathetic is Pierre Riché, *Daily Life in the World of Charlemagne,* trans. Jo Ann McNamara (Philadelphia: University of Pennsylvania Press, 1978), esp. chaps. 5, 7, 10–11, 20–23, 26.

or tends to recapture, the life of paradise. The monks fled the societies developed by time and history into the desert, to there construct timeless communities of men living like angels. Angelic and Edenic themes were pervasive in monasticism. Thus the saints' lives speak frequently of restored right relations between the monks and the world of animals, so that all live in harmony as in Eden. The Fathers sometimes describe the monks in the desert as living like choirs of angels, and the medieval monastery is often designated simply as "Paradise."[19] I suppose it is a truism to say that the characteristic theologial temptation or aberration for monasticism has always been Pelagianism, and this is but a way of saying that all these paradisiacal themes threatened to obscure the distinctiveness of Christianity in favor of one more form of the flight from time and matter back to the original well-ordered state of the cosmos. They were yet another expression of the temptation, which we have already seen was felt especially strongly by the Greek Fathers, to conceive of Christianity along classical lines, seeing the possibility of the restoration of the Adamic state within history, indeed by a rejection of history.

That these themes did not completely overwhelm monasticism was, as I have said, due to factors like the penitential discipline, which too, however, had its characteristic danger—namely that a Christian life would be considered as no more than exile in a world containing few goods hospitable to man. In a sense, because of its lack of self-consciousness about the distinctiveness of the created order, monasticism was long to vacillate between these two forms of return to an archaic view of the world. Perhaps what saved Christianity during this period from a complete collapse before all these archaic alternatives was the simple fact that it was still an expanding

19. Helen Waddell, *Beasts and Saints* (London: Constable, 1945); Garcia Colombas, *Paraiso y vida angelica* (Montserrat: Abadía de Montserrat, 1958); George H. Williams, *Wilderness and Paradise in Christian Thought: The Biblical Experience of the Desert in the History of Christianity and the Paradise Theme in the Theological Idea of the University* (New York: Harper, 1962); Karl Suso Frank, *Aggelikos Bios, Begriffsanalytische und beriffsgeschichtliche Untersuchung zum "engelgleichen Leben,"* Beiträge zur Geschichte des alten Mönchtums und des Benediktinerordens 26 (Münster: Aschendorff, 1964).

religion, winning new peoples. Providence was still at work in the world, leading to new conquests and achievements, so that it was still possible to see that in an obvious sense history is a tale told once. Thus writers like Bede clearly saw themselves as still participating in the unfinished work of God.[20]

The Gregorian reform of the eleventh century presented the first serious challenge to the unity of the archaic Germanic world, and also, only in part intentionally, set Christianity back on the track of reflection on the distinctive purposes for which history exists. Here under the battle cry "the Lord said, 'I am the Truth,' He did not say, 'I am the custom,' but 'I am the Truth,'" there began a long drawn-out struggle, still continuing to our day, for a free Church.[21] *Libertas ecclesiae* meant that the Church was not to be dominated by any lay ruler, or by the claims of custom, no matter how longstanding. It was to be free, as was each Christian, to do the will of God, to complete the historical task of the conversion of the race. The Church was to be recommitted to the mission of being the leaven of time, and history was not to be fled but, as far as possible, redirected toward God. It was ultimately in this tradition that the Counterreformation and the Society of Jesus were to stand, committed to finding God by entering the world, finding God in all things, and, so to speak, returning the world to God. Thus it was that from the eleventh to the sixteenth centuries Christians more fully than ever before explored the "incarnational" emphasis of Christianity, appreciating more fully the created order and the possibility of a life lived in the world.[22] In the face of such a development, the archaic and classical emphasis on return to beginnings necessarily receded before the Augustinian emphasis on perseverance through time under Providence to accomplish the work of God.

20. Robert W. Hanning, *The Vision of History in Early Britain: From Gildas to Geoffrey of Monmouth* (New York: Columbia University Press, 1966), esp. chap. 3.

21. In addition to note 15 above, see Glenn W. Olsen, "The Idea of the *Ecclesia Primitiva* in the Writings of the Twelfth-Century Canonists," *Traditio* 25 (1969): 61–86; Olsen, "The Investiture Contest," in *Religion in the Making of Western Man,* ed. Frank J. Coppa (New York: St. John's University Press, 1974), 79–93 (chapter 2 of this volume).

22. Glenn W. Olsen, "Lay Spirituality *ad majorem Dei gloriam,*" *Communio* 6 (1979): 405–12 (chapter 3 of this volume).

One might have thought that the archaic and classical refusal to come to terms with time and matter had finally been shown to be a failure of the imagination and understanding. Indeed, from one point of view, modern culture seems almost to have learned its lessons too well, for instead of a devaluation of the material order and of history, there appeared now as a kind of overreaction the rampant materialism and belief in an ineluctable progress that have characterized recent centuries. From being nothing, and this is one of the messages of idealism and Marxism, history has become everything. Yet, remorselessly, the pre-Christian views have reasserted themselves. I do not have time more than to mention Heer's extraordinary suggestion that, in large perspective, Protestantism, especially Lutheranism, and various democratic movements of the last centuries have been vehicles for the reassertion of the world of low culture. At the least, in the case of Protestantism, with the elimination of a visible history for the Church, the whole function of history once again became problematic, and time came to be once again something out of which the individual is saved.

As interesting as it would be to pursue Heer's suggestion, I must restrict myself to what I take to be the point in time at which we get a full-blown reemergence of the classical view. Here we return to the Enlightenment, to which Gay correctly attributes the rise of modern paganism. My argument is simply that what Cochrane called the classical view of the world, a view that Christianity had never by any means completely replaced, reappeared in almost every respect in what we for convenience call the Enlightenment, and that, even after the reactions of the Romantic period, is today the regnant view of the world. That is, *mutatis mutandi,* we again live in a classical or pagan world. I do not want to take much time elaborating on the obvious. The political sphere is probably that in which the reappearance of classicism is most visible. Once again the fact of original sin is generally denied, and the evils of the world are considered to be essentially structural rather than personal. If only old structures can be replaced by new, all will be well. The world can be made a permanently pleasant place, and woe to the world leader who does not speak of the possibility of ending conditions endemic to the race, such as war or poverty or suffering. Many of our people have become habitually Edenic in their thinking, whether in the refusal to fight any war, or in their conceptions of how man is to relate to the world of nature. This I take to be fairly obvious. What is more interesting to me is the question of what the stance of the Church might be among such developments.

The first point to be made is that what is valid in the archaic view of life must be integrated with Christianity. We have not passed through the long course of the history of the West to any good purpose unless we learn that there are truths embodied in both the classical and Christian stances. We might even speak of the classical attitude toward time as natural to man, while the Christian attitude is an acquired taste. That is, it is natural to be afraid of time, to want to be reintegrated with nature, to stand in solidarity with one's fellows, and to cleave to permanence. It is only by an act of faith that one can be persuaded that there is more than this. But this something more, always following the principle that grace is to perfect rather than destroy nature, must integrate rather than deny our primordial instincts. The problem of achieving real integration is formidable, and is found in every sphere of our disjointed lives. A couple examples must suffice. I am no expert on matters liturgical, but some of the things James Hitchcock has been saying about *The Recovery of the Sacred* seem to me to be extremely perceptive in their diagnosis of how thoughtless we have been about a proper sacral dimension in our lives.[23] It follows from what I have already said that by nature man has a desire for the sacral. I cannot emphasize too much that the natural human condition is to wish to live in a sacral universe, and that a purely profane and historical existence, the kind of existence many today believe they are living, is a state that goes against nature. As Henri de Lubac insisted in his treatment of *The Mystery of the Supernatural*, we have by nature a desire to see God so that, as Jean Daniélou argued, religion pertains to the nature of man with-

23. James Hitchcock, *The Recovery of the Sacred* (New York: Seabury Press, 1974).

out any special revelation whatsoever.[24] Man is by nature a religious animal. Therefore we must reject the assumption almost universally found among Protestants and secularists that a religious orientation is something that must be added, as it were from the outside, to man in his natural state. I will not pursue the political implications of this observation here, important as they are in revealing the indefensibility of the principle of separation of church and state. What is of immediate importance is the need to insist that above all, in the liturgy this orientation of human life toward the divine be adequately expressed. To think that the language of the liturgy, for instance, should be taken from profane life is already to accept the notion that our lives are normally profane by nature. Even more mischievous is the notion, widespread today, that the only good liturgy is a "rational" liturgy—that is, one in which symbolization is reduced in favor of explicit unambiguous meaning. I would submit on the contrary that one of the most important functions of liturgy is to orient us into mystery, to give centrality to the idea that our lives are directed to ends that surpass rationalization, and that it is precisely symbols that express the idea of a many-sided and many-layered reality—that is, of God. It may even be that God is capable of speaking directly through the Word, without lectors warning us ahead of time of what he is about to say.

To say no more about the liturgy, I have written elsewhere about a spirituality appropriate to our time.[25] Here I will simply repeat the idea that such a spirituality must express the two poles of experience, the sacral or eternal and the historical or, in this sense, profane. In the spirit of Ignatius of Loyola, it must make room for both a reflective dimension for our daily existence and for an active life in the world. The eschatological and the incarnational must be tied together. What I have not written about elsewhere, but which per-

24. De Lubac's book, *The Mystery of the Supernatural,* was translated by Rosemary Sheed (New York: Herder and Herder, 1967). For Jean Daniélou, see *Prayer as a Political Problem,* trans. J. R. Kirwan (New York: Sheed and Ward, 1967), esp. chaps. 1–2, and my article "'You Can't Legislate Morality': Reflections on a Bromide," *Communio* 2 (1975): 148–62, at 156–58.

25. See note 22.

tains to the possibility of such a spirituality, is a problem with which I would like to close this chapter. Let me put the problem sharply: How is it possible to remain committed to a providential understanding of history? If the world has indeed in large measure returned to a pre-Christian flight from history, either in the form of a liberal abolition of history or in the Marxist form of the completion of and then abolition of history by recovery of the primordial egalitarian conditions of life, then how can the Christian remain committed to the idea of directing history toward God, of redeeming the times? This is, strictly speaking, a psychological rather than a logical problem, for we all know that the virtue of hope in God is not tied to worldly success. It is logically possible that, because of free will, at the end of a history guided by providence there might be only a handful of Christians left in a cave. Even if this is logically possible, such a possibility ravages all but the most heroic sensibility. We have had a Christendom, and indeed, as I have argued, it was precisely the existence of an observable expansion of Christianity in the world that, for whole periods of Church history, kept Christians from falling back into a purely archaic attitude toward time. What is now to keep millions of Christians from reentering the womb into which their liberal and Marxist brethren have already preceded them? I would argue that there is nothing to prevent this beyond the most radical criticism of the assumptions of our culture. This criticism can be as friendly as that of a Romano Guardini or of a John Paul II, but it also must be searing.

We are all acutely aware that the average Christian can no more over a period of years adhere to an unpopular position than can any other person. We face the frightening prospect that with time most Catholics will cave in on the most obvious questions of human morality, such as abortion, as their secular brethren have already abandoned any steady commitment to the idea that all human society must be ordered to natural goods. How is a Catholic to do anything but conform to common practice, and how can one maintain any idea of belonging to a coherent people of God being led by God, if one in fact lives in a society that does not reverence life, and in which most of the churches claiming to be led by the same God approve of the most grievous offenses against the natural order? I can only make some suggestions; foremost among them is that we seize on this idea of being the people of God, this phrase commended to us by the Second Vatican Council, in an explicit transfer of first loyalty from political society to the Church. For the criticism asked of us of our culture is one that goes to the roots of our very forms of life. The Catholic experience in America has been one of assimilation, but what is needed now is a disassociation of the people of God from the American "experiment." As an experiment founded on the incoherency of the notions of democracy and pluralism, this experiment is bound to fail. Indeed, what so ravages the Catholic community now is the fact that in a civilization in which there are no established public goods, and therefore no possibility of a shared life at any distinctively human level, assimilation has meant the reduction of shared values to the lowest common denominator. I have no idea whether the idea of defining ourselves as first members of the people of God can repair any of the temporal fortune of the Church. But I am pretty sure that unless we can psychologically separate ourselves particularly from the notion that a pluralist society is desirable, we will go down with that society. A pluralist society is by definition not one led by anything meaningful—neither a God, nor a common purpose, nor a unifying set of values. Pluralism in basic values makes almost impossible any distinctively human life. We all know the historical reasons that we have come to have such a form of life. But the time has come to say that the emperor has no clothes.

It is one thing, however, to point out embarrassing facts, and another to offer alternatives. Let me close with one suggestion. Historically, to return to Heer's thought, the Church has been the bearer of high culture, introducing whole peoples to the more sophisticated products of the human spirit. Although we must never despise those products of folkish culture that inspire many people, the Church has always felt an obligation to save full human beings, not merely disembodied souls. As a part of the incarnational emphasis of the high medieval and Baroque periods, the Church has withdrawn from whatever temptations she had earlier felt to engage merely in the archaic and neo-Platonic venture of saving simply souls. She has tried to save men, unions of body and soul, and in this has tried to offer all intellectual and material civilization back to God. It is a reaffirmation of this task that seems particularly appropriate at the present. One of the most powerful means of providing people direction in difficult times is to introduce them to their roots and to their heritage, so that they in their turn may offer back to God all the works of human culture. This seems to me to be the great task of the moment. We must reject a liturgy, a catechism, and a system of Catholic education that passes on hardly any idea of what the Catholic vision of life has been. We must rather exult in our heritage, and in enthusiasm insist that this heritage be communicated especially to the young. If we are faithful in this task, how much more will God be faithful in working all things to good.

AFTERWORD

Minor changes have been made in this chapter. Since I first published the essay I have filled in some of the details for the references to the lack of reverence for life and the struggle for a society ordered to peace in my contributions to *Christian Marriage: A Historical Study,* ed. Glenn W. Olsen. Charles Norris Cochrane's *Christianity and Classical Culture: A Study of Thought and Action from Augustus to Augustine* made a great impact on me when I first read it, and I have continued to return to some of its ideas. I will, however, have to admit that in some ways it is a dated book and that some of the criticisms of it, specifically of the degree to which Cochrane allowed intellectual history to speak for a whole culture, are justified.

I later elaborated on Augustine's sense of personal history in "St. Augustine and the Problem of the Medieval Discovery of the Individual"; see also my "A Catholic Approach to History," to be published in *Teaching the Tradition: A Disciplinary Approach to the Catholic Intellectual Tradition,* ed. John Piderit and Melanie Morey. The University of California Press published a revised version of Peter Brown's *Augustine of Hippo* in 2000. Princeton University Press published a second paperback edition of Mircea Eliade's *The Myth of the Eternal Return: Cosmos and History.* See also Brown's "A Surprise from Saint Augustine," for Augustine's disbelief in progress. My use of Eliade today would be somewhat more qualified than in this piece: see my "Problems with the Contrast between Circular and Linear Views of Time in the Interpretation of Ancient and Early Medieval History," and *The Turn to Transcendence: The Role of Religion in the Twenty-First Century.*

The distinction between high and low culture has been much discussed since the present chapter was written, and my later writings soften this distinction: "On the Frontiers of Eroticism: The Romanesque Monastery of San Pedro de Cervatos"; cf. now to the work of Marc Bloch, used in the present chapter, Thomas N. Bisson, *The Crisis of the Twelfth Century: Power, Lordship, and the Origins of European Government,* for which I have written a review to appear in *The European Legacy: Toward New Paradigms.* A number of themes broached in the present chapter, such as the nature of materialism and progress in the modern period, are developed more fully in my *Beginning at Jerusalem: Five Reflections on the History of the Church.* For the question of cultural assimilation, see Deborah Hertz, *How Jews Became Germans: A History of Conversion and Assimilation in Berlin.* John L. Allen, Jr., *The Future Church: How Ten Trends are Revolutionizing the Catholic Church,* is journalism at its best, and treats such subjects as inculturation and the Church as countercultural.

Richard Kearney, *Anatheism: Returning to God after God,* treats the return of religion to public and intellectual life.

5

THY KINGDOM COME ON EARTH AS IN HEAVEN

The Place of the Family in Creation

THE IDEA OF THE KINGDOM or reign of God was variously understood in Judaism and early Christianity. Walter Kasper has argued that Origen pierced through all this variety to see the essential point: the Kingdom is Christ and his message.[1] The kingdom is a name for doing the will of God. It announces where in history salvation and liberation from evil takes place. First, the idea of the coming Kingdom announced Christ. Then, just as he was the first of the new men, Christ was the Kingdom come on earth. Yet, as Paul and later writers such as Gregory of Nyssa insisted, even after Christ we live in a world caught between eons, caught between the old and the new.[2] The idea of progress is a great perversion or secularization of Christianity in recent centuries.[3] A true Christian

1. Walter Kasper, *Jesus the Christ,* trans. V. Green (Mahwah, N.J.: Paulist Press, 1976), 72–88, 100, with bibliography.

2. For Gregory, see Jean Daniélou, *From Glory to Glory: Texts from Gregory of Nyssa's Mystical Writings,* trans. Herbert Musurillo (New York: Scribner, 1961). See also on this and what follows, Daniélou, *The Lord of History: Reflections in the Inner Meaning of History,* trans. Nigel Abercrombie (Cleveland and New York: World Publishing, 1958), and Kasper, *Jesus the Christ,* 74–78, on the dialogical character of history.

3. Karl Löwith, *Meaning in History* (Chicago: University of Chicago Press, 1949), in a flawed book, saw the main points that "progress" is a secularized form of "providence" in which the ground of revelation has been replaced with the (unsubstantiated) claim that an overall pattern discoverable by reason alone, a universal history, is discernible in history itself; and that in turn the categories of "philosophy of history" and "universal history," if

theology of history looks more like what Augustine or Hans Urs von Balthasar suggested: a story full of surprises and unpredictability, of which we cannot read the whole.[4] It directs us to the fact that Christ is the center of history. As the Catholic Bishops of Texas said in *Mission Texas,* he is the prophet who brings knowledge of God to the world.[5] Because in him were united time and eternity, salvation history and human history, he reveals that history, like man, is open to the Father: what is ultimately significant in history comes from God and is done in obedience to the Father. Thus from a human point of view there can be nothing certain or ineluctable in history, some thread discoverable by reason alone from which we could, in the manner of Hegel, fashion the pattern of its overall interpretation. Like Christ, we are to be open to the Father, to the new and unforeseen, to the blinding moment of new insight. Because both we and God are free, and the Spirit blows where it will, no developmental or evolutionary model will fairly present history's participation in the emergence of the Kingdom.

To put a spin on von Ranke, every age is present to God, and may reveal the most extraordinary advance or regress of the Kingdom. More mysteriously, because until the end we remain caught between the eons, advance and regress occur together. In centuries full of the most cruel human outrage, a Simone Weil may be prod-

---

understood as giving a general meaning to history, are also secularizations of Judaism and Christianity, surreptitious belief systems built on unacknowledged *a prioris.* Christopher Dawson, *The Dynamics of World History,* ed. John J. Mulloy (New York: Sheed and Ward, 1956), 232, observed that there is no such thing as a Christian philosophy of history: claims to find general meaning in history should always be labeled theologies. Gerhart Ladner, *The Idea of Reform: Its Impact on Christian Thought and Action in the Age of the Fathers,* rev. ed. (New York: Harper and Row, 1967), 32–35, 153–283, discusses why Augustine allows for the progress of individuals, but not for an irreversible progress of the race.

4. On Augustine's sense of history as an unrolling tapestry, of which we cannot take the measure because we cannot judge how much of the tapestry is completed, and thence from what point of view it should be seen, see Karl F. Morrison, *The Mimetic Tradition of Reform in the West* (Princeton: Princeton University Press, 1982), chap. 3. Hans Urs von Balthasar's views about history develop throughout his writings, but see von Balthasar, *A Theology of History* (New York: Sheed and Ward, 1963). See also my "Recovering the Homeland: Acts 4:32 and the *Ecclesia Primitiva* in St. Bernard's Sermons on the Song of Songs," *Word and Spirit: A Monastic Review* 12 (1990): 92–117.

5. Catholic Bishops of Texas, *Mission Texas: A Pastoral Letter on Evangelization* (Lubbock: Catholic Bishops of Texas, 1989), 4.

ded to insights never before achieved; St. Camillus may find a new way of becoming God-like. Christ has come, but he brings the Kingdom into a foreign land. That he teaches us to pray to the Father that his Kingdom come on earth as it is in heaven implies that it has not taken sure possession of the works of man. Rather, where the Father is obeyed the reign of God begins and the end is foreshadowed. So profoundly are we to be co-creators with and do the will of the Father that in the measure we die and Christ lives in us, we continue the work of Christ in the world. The coming of Christ, his death and resurrection, are the greatest of victories, but are "only" suggestive of what, as far as history is concerned, might be. Christ, as Paul VI said in 1975 in *Evangelii Nuntiandi* 7, was the first evangelizer. He shows us the way and asks us to work for the Kingdom, but only with the assurance of the definitive defeat and passing away of the old eon on the other side of history, which remains *permixta*.

Karl Rahner helpfully identified Catholicism with one of two competing traditions in early Christianity, two ways of viewing history, which he labeled the chiliastic and the eschatological.[6] Historically, at least until what was at issue was understood, these alternative ways of looking at the world often were found intertwined in the thinking of the same person. The same irresolution evident in Christian evaluations of the empire appeared in attempts to assess one's historical position.[7] Thus the Gospel of Matthew may be understood at once to hope for the radical in-breaking into time of a new order of things in which all will be placed under the kingdom of the Heavens—that is, God: in this Matthew may be labeled "chiliastic." Yet the same Gospel, in for instance the parable of the mustard seed, may be understood to see the Kingdom as like a seed that becomes in time a great tree: that is, an "eschatological" stance may also be observed in Matthew in which human struggle in history begins to form, although more miraculously than developmentally, a King-

6. Karl Rahner, "The Hermeneutics of Eschatological Assertions," in *Theological Investigations,* vol. 4, trans. Kevin Smyth (Baltimore: Helicon Press, 1966), 323–46.

7. I have studied the parallel problem of the evaluation of time in "Problems with the Contrast between Circular and Linear Views of Time in the Interpretation of Ancient and Early Medieval History," *Fides quaerens intellectum* 1 (2001): 41–65.

dom that will be fulfilled only in heaven, when time has fallen away. Here God works not by the discontinuity of radical rupture between what we know now and what will be, but in a patient, historical, and institutional manner in which the Kingdom in one dimension takes on the shape of "Church," that is, of a visible institution working in history for the coming of the Kingdom by asking of God the fruit of the Lord's Prayer, the Kingdom come on earth as in heaven.

Because the Kingdom is the creation renewed in Christ, in history the Kingdom appears, so to speak, in the interstices. Because, just as God, the Kingdom is defined as a *communio,* it does not appear primarily in individuals, but in persons in relation, in some form of society or fellowship.[8] But also, if I may be bold to say, it does not appear primarily in what we think of as "kingdoms." Since its relations are those of charity, it is only imperfectly found in large institutions, such as the state. The individual lacks the scale, is too isolated and socially incomplete, to define *communio:* the "kingdom" lacks the intimacy to allow communion to grow. Perhaps this is why Augustine had the audacity, when he set out to describe those who do the will of God, to write not of the kingdom but of the city of God, thus supplementing the idea of the Kingdom.[9] He did not live in a kingdom, but in a vast empire, and this being the alternative, "city" more expressed for him a human scale of life. In any case my argument is that the Kingdom appears first of all in the "intermediate institutions" of human life, which stand between the individual and the state, beginning with the family. We might speak of it as caught between universality and particularity, mediating Enlightenment and Romanticism.

Created in the image and likeness of God, the human person is constituted by relations in community. John Paul II and the personalist school have shown the depth of this idea.[10] The persons of the

8. Walter Kasper, *Theology and Church,* trans. Margaret Kohl (New York: Crossroad, 1989), 148–65.

9. Ladner, *Idea of Reform,* 248–56.

10. Karol Wojtyla (John Paul II), *The Acting Person,* trans. Andrzej Potocki, *Analecta Husserliana* 10 (Boston: D. Reidel, 1979). Alistair I. McFadyen, *The Call to Personhood: A Christian Theory of the Individual in Social Relationships* (New York: Cambridge University

Trinity are not distinct in substance, but only in relation. From eternity, the Father is always father, he who sends; and the Son always son, he who is sent and is perfectly open and obedient to the will of the Father. The relations between the divine persons, their *communio,* may be conceived as prayer between the persons in complete harmony.[11] Some have gone so far as to argue that the very question of whether God is personal is at stake here: it is not clear in what sense a monad-God could from eternity, that is from "before" creation, be personal, unless the relations on which being a person depends were interior to God.[12]

A knowledge of how human personhood and individuality historically were discovered perhaps reinforces this point. It is well known how long these ideas took to develop in the Western tradition: in some other traditions they hardly exist to the present. In the West, here for better and worse the most precocious of traditions, it took a very long time for the individual to be separated from the cosmos, the polis or political life.[13] For centuries, indeed millennia, individuals could not easily be made to stand out from groups larger than themselves. They hardly thought of having personal lives or a uniqueness about themselves. Less well known is the history of how the soul came to be ordered and unified. Like small children in any age, Homeric people had a difficult time with pronouns, and more generally with discourse about themselves. They were unclear as to where the boundaries were between self and other, God and man, man and nature. For Homer people are not so much pos-

Press, 1990), introduces scholarship on the place of social relationships in the formation of personal identity, and analyzes the nature of personhood in the light of the trinity.

11. Glenn W. Olsen, "Hans Urs von Balthasar and the Rehabilitation of St. Anselm's Doctrine of the Atonement," *Scottish Journal of Theology* 34 (1981): 49–61, studies von Balthasar's arresting way of treating inter-trinitarian relations; see also Joseph Ratzinger, *Behold the Pierced One: An Approach to Spiritual Christology,* trans. Graham Harrison (San Francisco: Ignatius Press, 1986).

12. Hans Urs von Balthasar, *Theo-Drama: Theological Dramatic Theory,* vol. 1, *Prolegomena,* trans. Graham Harrison (San Francisco: Ignatius Press, 1988), as at 253–54, 264, 481–648.

13. Romano Guardini, *The End of the Modern World,* trans. Joseph Theman and Herbert Burke, ed., with an introduction by Frederick Wilhelmsen (Chicago: H. Regnery, 1968), and note 12 in this chapter.

sessed of emotions as possessed by their emotions. Sleep is less something willed than something that seizes one. Anger is less a thing of the self than a thing, doubtfully one's own, that rises in one's breast. Like our "conscience," anger is something that comes to Homeric man "from the outside." Centuries later Aristotle, in observing that in contemplation we are divine, expressed continuing uncertainty about the boundaries of *psyche* (soul).[14] The late Roman and medieval question of whether all humans share in one common intellect, which acts on us and before which we are passive, or whether we each have our own active intellect, was a discussion, already lurking in the texts of Aristotle, that illustrates how little, long after Boethius and the end of the Roman Empire, the human person stood out.[15] Ovid, at the beginning of the same empire, wonders whether we have a fixed nature or are malleable, can metamorphose, and with many other Hellenistic authors, whether we may be divinized or not—pass over to being gods. I have written elsewhere on this matter of the appearance of the individual in Western history, and cannot say more here.[16] The point is that the very history of the discovery of the individual and the person suggests that the idea of personhood cannot be conceived without a prior unifying of the soul, which is the origin of self-consciousness. When people become conscious of themselves as psychological unities, separate intellectual substances, what they discover are the relations without which "their persons" could not be. To be able to see oneself as "person" is to be able to see, become conscious of, the relations in which one already is, but now to see oneself as a unity distinguishable from one's context.

The primal human community is the family, and, not merely for Aristotle's reasons, important as they are. Indeed, modern per-

14. Dieter Georgi, *The Opponents of Paul in Second Corinthians,* trans. Harold Attridge, et al. (Philadelphia: Fortress Press, 1986), brilliantly surveys the entire Hellenistic civilization.

15. See also Arno Borst, *Medieval Worlds: Barbarians, Heretics and Artists in the Middle Ages,* trans. Eric Hansen (Chicago: University of Chicago Press, 1991), index under "*persona.*"

16. I have been summarizing my "St. Augustine and the Problem of the Medieval Discovery of the Individual," *Word and Spirit* 9 (1987): 129–56.

sonalism allows us to see a depth in Aristotle of which he apparently was not himself aware. If we cannot be persons except in relation, then by definition all conventional, individualistic, atomistic, egalitarian, and contractarian political theory is wrong. The individual cannot be the basic unit of society, as is normally the case in Anglo-American thought. By definition the basic unit must itself be social, containing the relations without which one cannot be a person.[17] This the Catholic Latin tradition has in one fashion or another always seen, and it is one of the chief reasons that the entrance of increasing numbers of Hispanics into the United States is a cause for so much hope.

Since, as Aristotle showed, by definition the family is hierarchical and complementary, parents not having the same status as children, nor mothers the same function as fathers, any politics that respects nature and is built on the primal human association of the family will replicate the hierarchy and relations found first in the family.[18] From this will be obtained the natural piety and authority that make both the family and political life stable. Passing over to revelation, we find something even more profound than Aristotle's truth: that forms of human association larger than the family exist to perfect the family. The Kingdom begins primarily in those intermediary forms of association that try to do the will of God and image the life of the Trinity. Thus the God-fearing family is one of the chief places where the kingdom of God appears in history. The family now is seen as an image of the life of the Trinity itself. Not in a political but in an ontological manner, equality of person is revealed as compatible with distinction in function. Just as in the Trinity equality of substance exists with differentiation, so in the family. In both, each person is defined in relation. Just as the Father is he who sends, and the Son he who is sent, but always in perfect equal-

17. I have worked this idea out in various publications: see "The City in Christian Thought," *Thought* 66 (1991): 259–78.

18. Cf. Leon R. Kass, "Man and Woman: An Old Story," *First Things,* no. 17 (November 1991): 14–26; Joyce A. Little, "Naming Good and Evil," *First Things,* no. 23 (May 1992): 23–30; Gilbert Meilaender, "Marriage in Counterpoint and Harmony," *First Things,* no. 24 (June–July 1992): 30–36.

ity and the harmony of prayer, mother, father, and children are seen to complement each other without anyone losing his or her inestimable worth or ontological equality. As the Spirit is the expression of the love of the Father for the Son, so children express or are the fruit of the mutual love of husband and wife. The family is revealed not merely as the first unit of politics, but as the first unit of ecclesiology. As John Chrysostom said, it is a "little church." The family's prayers lead to the prayers of the parish church, grace said in home to the Eucharistic prayer itself. In the eighth century, anonymous Irish Gospel commentators expressed the beautiful idea that the Holy Family itself was the first or primitive Church.[19]

The theme of the domestic church runs through Christian history (*Lumen Gentium* 11). It is continued in *Familiaris Consortio* and in the work of the Pontifical Council for the Family and the John Paul II Institute for Studies on Marriage and Family.[20] Like all theological ideas, it is meant for embodiment. In the mission period it was expressed in the home altar, in which the home became literally a little church. Later, although there might no longer be a home altar, many homes retained a special place for prayer, a chapel or kneeler. Today some form of embodiment is still needed, so that the practices of the home may both form children to the attitude of faith from their earliest years and lead into the life of the larger parish church. Certainly in family prayers we see the primary sense of the house being a domestic church, especially in devotions of a festive and participatory nature such as the Advent calendar, which leave their impress on young imaginations. The imagination of the young is a precious thing, and if it is to become a Christian imagination, it will likely be through the crucifixes, religious art, and books of a Christian home.

Because the relations are constituted in love, the child is the expression of the mutual love and fidelity of father and mother, as

19. Glenn W. Olsen, "Reference to the *Ecclesia Primitiva* in Eighth-Century Irish Gospel Exegesis," *Thought* 54 (1979): 303–12.

20. Richard M. Hogan and John M. LeVoir, *Covenant of Love: Pope John Paul II on Sexuality, Marriage, and Family in the Modern World* (San Francisco: Ignatius Press, 1985), esp. index under "family, as domestic church."

Aquinas said, but also is their "mission." Christ was eternally with the Father, but then was sent to save and restore all, to bring all under the reign of God. By an imperfect analogy, the child is for a while with his or her father and mother, where the Gospel is given and a mission learned. Then he or she is sent into the world. Put another way, the family cooperates in long-term projects in which the parents serve the children through sacrifice to prepare them for a life in the world "to the greater glory of God." The family thus is the first sphere of evangelization. Here the faith of mother and father most freely expresses itself. If the family is the first sphere for inculturation, it is also the first place children are prepared to deal intelligently and critically with the larger culture beyond the family.[21] God stands to the Creation as he who wishes men to mature and cooperate with him in co-creation or co-restoration in Christ: the father and mother stand to the child as they who give him life, but wish this life, while not losing its relation to themselves, to become in turn co-creating with its own appropriate autonomy and vocation (*Populorum Progressio* 34).

No more than the Church does the family, as family, merely evangelize internally. It exists with other intermediary groups in society, and thus in turn is an instrument of evangelization outside itself. This may be at the simplest level of "hospitality," of taking others into its life—especially those who do not know family life built around love of God—that is, a culture of love. This giving of hospitality is not a trivial example, for in our society many have virtually no experience of family, or at least of a healthy family. Many even who call themselves Catholic have never had explained to them, or had experience of, fidelity, of the unreserved keeping of faith that is as important between man and wife and parents and children as love itself. Many have never heard that marriage is rooted in par-

21. Kenelm Burridge, *In the Way: A Study of Christian Missionary Endeavours* (Vancouver, B.C.: University of British Columbia Press, 1991), insists on the inevitable subversion of indigenous culture involved in missionizing, and that because it is universal, Christianity is always countercultural, prodding each culture to a more universal way of looking at things. Christianity makes all cultures self-critical, at once affirming and changing each culture; cf. *Ex Corde Ecclesiae* 48.

ticipation in the great sacrament of Christ's wedding to the Church, and that human fidelity is participation in the unfailing and patient love of Christ for his spouse the Church. They more likely have picked up their ideas from TV and the movies, where marriage if present at all is often not much more than an important date, and fidelity, children, and family inhibiting of self-realization. In such a society, where many people can spend a whole life without any contact with understood and lived Christianity, something as apparently trivial as hospitality or walking into a house with crucifixes in it can have the greatest importance.

One of the most insidious things about what for shorthand I will call liberalism, one of the most serious misperceptions in some forms of liberation theology, is the belief that human beings' lives can be significantly improved by structural change in the world around them; indeed, that large-scale structural change is an intelligible idea and a controllable process. We cannot admit the truth that there is no large-scale solution to, say, the drug problem.[22] The vaster the problem, the less likely it can have a solution going beyond limited and piecemeal amelioration. The temptation here is the old power game of reconstructing the external world instead of transforming individuals.[23] Additionally, the more our final end and destiny are in question, the more changes external to the individual lie at the periphery of what is needed. There is simply no shortcut to the reformation of the individual and to holiness. In a society where a life lived to the glory of God is almost unintelligible or beyond the experience of most people, there will be no shortcut to what families are especially good at: day-after-day contact with and conversation about things that matter. There can be no substitute for the laborious and time-consuming one-on-one conversation with another human being that instructs in things outside the purview of

22. Luc Sante, "The Possessed," *NYRB,* July 16, 1992, is a sobering assessment of the drug problem; see also Christopher Jencks, *Rethinking Social Policy: Race, Poverty, and the Underclass* (Cambridge, Mass.: Harvard University Press, 1992).

23. Charles N. Cochrane, *Christianity and Classical Culture: A Study of Thought and Action from Augustus to Augustine* (London: Oxford University Press, 1974), contrasts an ideology of power with a theology of reform.

secular society. As desirable as it is that every human live a materially sufficient life, by itself this is a stone. What children need much more is the bread of a parent who is not too busy or self-absorbed to seize the teaching moment provided by a child's question. What adults who have hardly known love need much more than material goods is, if they have none, a family, a comfortable place where, perhaps around real bread, they can unburden themselves. Fellowship and evangelization here become identical. A simple act like receiving hospitality from a family that says grace may get a guest thinking about the source of the gifts he has received in this life. In a society where Christians are as cowardly as in ours, so intimidated by the liberal distinction between a claimed religiously neutral public sphere and a private sphere where even religion is licit, Catholics may think of themselves as simply sensitive never to practice any sacramental, never to say grace, in the presence of a nonbeliever. It will be a long time on such premises before the world is restored in Christ. How much better to see this as a duty owed the Creator, but also as something that witnesses to where the center of this family lies, only to be omitted if genuinely counterproductive.[24] Evangelization must be rooted in the discovery of Jesus Christ in the other and in joy for the opportunity to spread the Good News. If a stranger enters such a circle of faith, hope, and love—a Catholic family—it will rarely be out of place to be with this family when it gives thanks to the Source of all gifts—reveals, so to speak, its family secret.

One of the intermediary associations with which or in which the family exists is the ethnic group. Both the sense of ethnicity and the connection between ethnicity and religion vary greatly. I attended a vibrant Spanish Palm Sunday mass some years ago in Las Cruces, New Mexico, a community in which there clearly is a close tie between ethnicity and religion. It is not very accurate to lump Hispanics, who of course have histories as different as Cuba and Mexico, among the newer immigrants, but it is hard to put aside the suspicion

24. David Forte, 'Children No Longer Taught with 'Grace,'" *Casper Star-Tribune,* July 9, 1992, notes that in America one of the ways people have learned respect for others' religious observances has been by non-participatory presence at them.

that such religious vitality as I observed will wane with time, as it apparently has for the so-called old European immigrants.[25] Perhaps a pattern found elsewhere will repeat in which immigration initially increases religious practice, in part as a refuge from the larger, hostile culture, which practice declines with successful assimilation. Social success seems to have made deep inroads into the Catholic identity of groups such as the Irish. I wish I could say that even those many Catholics imperceptive enough fifty years ago to pair Pope John XXIII with John F. Kennedy must have figured out by now that it is quite possible to retain ethnic ties while abandoning the religion of the ethnic group. A few years ago a college professor came up to me after a lecture and asked whether JFK was not a good example of an effective synthesis of Catholicism with American culture, of how Catholicism had or could succeed in America. I could only say that this was not a synthesis, but the abandonment of one's faith, capitulation to the larger culture. If, as Kennedy could say as he did in his notorious speech to the Greater Houston Ministerial Association on September 12, 1960, that being Catholic was like being born with brown eyes, abandonment of faith, not synthesis, had taken place.

Across America we find great variation in the relations between Catholicism and ethnicity. One's suspicion is that for most, assimilation means in time the abandonment of both. There is perhaps some cruelty, but also much acuity, in the observation of a Spanish priest some years ago: "Poor Spain when Spain is no longer poor." There is a lot of evidence for the proposition that prospering in this world, especially in our day and in pluralist civilizations, means the abandonment of both one's previous ethnic identity and religion. Christ's comment about the difficulty of the rich man entering into the kingdom of God perhaps has some bearing here. Those are the options before us: capitulation or synthesis. No ethnic group or religion in America is going to be unaffected by the rest. We are all in history, and changing together. The question is whether we will sim-

25. David Arias, *Spanish Roots of America* (Huntington, Ind.: Our Sunday Visitor, 1992, provides background. Articles in the Nov./Dec., 1990 issue of *The Catholic World* analyze Hispanic cultural variety.

ply abandon traditions to obtain worldly success on someone else's terms, or, rather, in Virgilio Elizondo's phrase, have a properly *mestizo* future that will preserve the best and most essential of merging traditions in new syntheses.[26]

In the American Southwest, sense of ethnicity ranges from the very intense to the almost nonexistent. It is especially intense in the Hispanic community, which by most measures seems destined for an ever-increasing place in American Catholicism. Two of the great pastoral questions in regard to Hispanics in the immediate future will be whether internally family life can be given a sense of being ordered to God and, where this is absent, whether externally this family life can impact the larger society in such a way as to offer an alternative to all the forces of disintegration working against families. There are reasons for hope. Hispanics possess a political tradition that has usually seen that all social life is to be raised on the family, and has aimed at the flourishing of the family. Both in the organic, natural, and hierarchical traditions of political thinking carried with them, and in their living stylization of family life, Hispanics may be a lesson and example to the more individualistic traditions that prevail in American life. Polls and our everyday experience witness to the difference children make in one's life, and we all probably know many cases in which the birth of children has made parents politically more conservative, especially about free speech and moral questions, and more appreciative of the role of religion in life.[27]

Yet, there are also reasons for apprehension. As I have suggested, the record of the European immigrant ethnic minorities has been very mixed: for many the Church helped assimilation into the larger society, in turn to be rejected. Catholic schools succeeded beyond their wildest dreams in taking poor, uneducated immigrants and making them solid members of the middle class, only to find that in the process almost all effective Catholicism had been

26. Virgilio Elizondo, *The Future is Mestizo: Life where Cultures Meet* (New York: Crossroad 1988).

27. For both this and the next sentence, see "The Difference a Child Makes," *Crisis* 10, no. 7 (July-August 1992): 4–5.

lost. Liberation from poverty and social disdain also meant liberation from the restrictions of a demanding Catholicism, and these "American success stories" wanted the same freedoms that made Protestant middle-class life so easy—the right to contraception and abortion, for instance. Think of how rare among the in-some-sense Catholic governors and congressmen- and women who were the end-product of all this are those who seem to hold the faith in its fullness. Many of our once-or-hardly Catholic schools have become little more than cheerleaders for the upward mobility of the middle class, with prominent faculty or administrators who oppose anything in Church doctrine that stands in the way of an accommodated bourgeois life.[28] The question for evangelization is whether there are lessons to be learned by study of the history of assimilation that can form a Hispanic community in some sense "in America" but not completely "of America." Can we serve human needs in such a manner that the Kingdom not of this world, the norm for this world, is not lost from view? If we cannot do this, we will merely have helped the latest group of dispossessed to forget the Kingdom.

I suggest that there is not much future for an American Church that will not become more countercultural than it is.[29] My judgment is that the American Church is deeply secularized—that is, has much more adopted than critiqued the forms of the larger culture. Indeed part of the appeal of the sects for Hispanics lies in "unabashed rootedness in the Gospel," to use Bishop Roberto Gonzalez's words in *America* (October 19, 1991). Catholics know so little history, and are so determined to see themselves as good Americans that they hardly see the issue here.[30] Oblivious to the fact that

28. David W. Lutz, "Can Notre Dame be Saved," *First Things,* no. 19 (January 1992): 35–40, with the subsequent exchange in *First Things,* no. 23 (May 1992): 8–10; George A. Kelly, *The Battle for the American Church* (Garden City, N.Y.: Doubleday, 1979), index under "Hesburgh" and "McBrien."

29. Barbara Dafoe Whitehead and David Blankenhorn, "What the Bishops Don't Know About Families," *First Things,* no. 23 (May 1992): 20–22; John F. Kavanaugh, *Following Christ in a Consumer Society: The Spirituality of Cultural Resistance* (Maryknoll, N.Y.: Orbis Books, 1991).

30. John Van Engen, "The Christian Middle Ages as an Historiographical Problem," *The American Historical Review* 91 (1986): 519–52, treats one part of the story well.

the evangelization of the Roman world occurred in tandem with deep criticism of that world, or that the conversion of the Germanic world was carried out by those countercultural figures we call monks, who preached peace and gentleness to a culture built on war and the hero, many Americans do not see, for instance, that in wanting a married clergy they deprive the Church of one of the great signs that the Kingdom is not of this world. Evangelization itself is a countercultural act in which a person or culture is presented with truth coming from outside him- or itself.

The late Cardinal Archbishop of Madrid, Angel Suquía, in an address on the "new evangelization" in Europe, made observations relevant to the American situation. He contrasted the options that face us as restoration of the past or testimony to Jesus Christ. It is unfortunate that the policies of John Paul II were sometimes labeled restorationist, for while he wished continuity with the past, continuing responsibility for the present, and lay involvement in the world rather than retreat from it, the last thing he wanted was return to some moment, some specific set of institutional arrangements, found in the past. This was true despite the recognition that Christianity had been reduced from a publicly shared way of life and participation in the drama of salvation to a largely private belief system.[31] The central question today is to find a way to give testimony to Jesus Christ in an unprecedented historical circumstance. The prime goal of evangelization is not the recovery of old centers of power. Further, to blame secularization simply on factors external to the Church is to miss the greatest problem: ourselves. Certainly there are factors external to the Church that partly account for the de-Christianization we find.[32] Nietzsche observed of the churches of the nineteenth century that although they might be full, God was dead.[33] The churches were full of people who had lost almost all effective belief and acted as if God were dead. This seems to me

31. Robert W. Jenson, "Hauerwas Examined," *First Things,* no. 25 (August-September 1992): 49–51.

32. See my "The Catholic Moment?" *Communio* 15 (1988): 474–87.

33. Louis Dupré, "The Religious Crisis of our Culture," *Analecta Husselriana* 5 (1976): 205–18.

the key: the churches in America may be relatively full, but in the bourgeois religion embraced we find no "Catholic moment," but the jettisoning of almost all faith and of the testimony to Jesus Christ, which always tends toward the countercultural. We need not seek any specific political arrangement, but we ask of ourselves conversion and of all regimes the space to evangelize, "the freedom to live fully the redemption of Jesus Christ and to express publicly the light that the redemption throws on reality."[34]

Any religious person must observe with fear and quaking the sociological forces at work here. To stay with the American situation, is there some way of taking people from grinding poverty to comfortable lives without their becoming seduced and anaesthetized by their success? One tendency in liberation theology has always opposed (North) Americanizing the Hispanic cultures—has been in favor of letting each culture find its way out of poverty in its own way. Basically sympathetic to this desire as I am, the question remains: whatever route out of poverty is taken, can the result be other than some form of accommodating to the world's standards? Just as I have no faith in the Novak project, to Americanize, democratize, and capitalize the entire world, there seems to me a great naiveté in those who think they can overturn unjust social structures without an idea of what kind of non-poor Christian culture is desired.[35] If there is an answer here, I cannot imagine that it lies elsewhere than in the profoundly countercultural early Christian idea of the place of property in life. Let me give an overview. What I will argue is that we must meditate on and publicize the early Christian notion of supererogatory wealth, which has in fact been continued in the encyclical tradition beginning with *Rerum Novarum*. I want in this regard at least to bow in the direction of the idea "smaller is better," for consumerism is a great enemy of the family.

If there is no evidence that the early Christians generally aban-

34. I am working from an unpublished copy of Angel Suquía, "La Nueva Evangelizacion: Algunas Tareas Y Riesgos de la Hora Presente," the opening address of May 18, 1992, for the LVI Asamblea Plenaria de la Conferencia Episcopal Española, Madrid.

35. Charles Wilber and Laura Grimes, "On Michael Novak's Democratic Capitalism," *New Oxford Review* 59, no. 4 (May 1992): 18–25.

doned private property, Acts 2:42–47 and 4:32–35, along with Gospel texts such as Matthew 19:21, seem to be evidence of widespread early Christian esteem for a poor or modest life.[36] "We brought nothing into the world, and we can take nothing out of it; but as long as we have food and clothing, let us be content with that. People who long to be rich are a prey to temptation; they get trapped into all sorts of foolish and dangerous ambitions which eventually plunge them into ruin and destruction. 'The love of money is the root of all evils'" (1 Tim 6:7–10, Jerusalem Bible). "Poverty," as in Judaism, has always been a multivalent conception in Christian thought, and has ranged in meaning from a literal condition of helplessness, which must be defended against oppression and hopefully escaped, to the spiritual condition of "the poor in heart." Tied to the one meaning has been the Deuteronomic ideal that "there be no poor man among you"—that is, that there be a sufficiency of goods for each person. Tied to the other has been the ideal, historically from the first a part of asceticism and ultimately taking the form of monasticism, of the voluntary embracing of a poverty of goods. In the first Christian centuries some argued for literal abandonment of private property, at least for those who would be perfect, but at the turn of the third century the urbanized Clement of Alexandria initiated the way of much later theory through his idea that a Christian may have sufficient property to lead a modest life—that is, in our language, to escape poverty. Yet, since property was to be shared, to be used to build up *communio,* whatever was above that necessary for a modest existence, whatever was supererogatory, was to be given away. Christians were forever to shy away from wealth, and be content with a modest existence. Over the centuries hardly anyone held that the wealthy could not be saved, and various plausible reasons were given for tolerating differences in wealth even among Christians, but the larger point was that wealth endangered one's soul's health, and was a kind of retaining for one's own amusement and projects things that should be devot-

36. See Glenn W. Olsen, "One Heart and One Soul (Acts 4:32 and 34) in Dhuoda's *Manual*," *Church History* 61 (1992): 23–33, for the history of the understanding of the Acts verses.

ed to the building up of the Church and one's brothers and sisters.

This, at the end of the nineteenth century, was still the attitude toward property commended in *Rerum Novarum.* A qualified right to private property exists, in which private property may be possessed in forms that advance, rather than undermine, the common good. Since property does not exist as an end in itself, but to provide the necessary material basis on which all human life depends, it is only to be held privately in the degree that it supports a modest human existence. Such a position is not anti-capitalist—that is, it is not against the accumulation of capital for social goods—but it is against the large-scale accumulation of property for personal purposes, to spend on oneself. We might say that it values the creativity and human initiative favorable to capital enterprises ordered to the common good, but devalues consumptionist attitudes. This clearly is still the teaching of *Centesimus Annus.*[37]

It seems to me that our historical moment, if I have any correct understanding of it at all, cries out for this attitude toward property. Christopher Lasch showed the ways in which material abundance has weakened the family, a market system of evaluation leading women, for instance, into the workplace, to the great harm of children.[38] If there is to be a Catholic moment, it likely will be a new form of *mestizaje.* By this I mean that in Hispanic society we find an emphasis on cooperation rather than competition that already presents an alternative to the careerism and consumerism of Anglo-American society. Normally this emphasis would be lost in the course of assimilation, for it hinders success as the larger society defines it. The great question is whether against all expectations it can be retained in sufficient measure to moderate the more unbridled forms of individualism in the larger society while Latinos increasingly participate in that society. That is, can the social values of Hispanics be shown to be so attractive that a *mestizo* culture can

37. *Centesimus Annus* 42, discusses the term "capitalism" itself. Francis Canavan, "The Popes and the Economy," *First Things,* no. 16 (October 1991): 35–41, here at 39, is very useful.

38. Christopher Lasch, "Communitarianism or Populism?" *New Oxford Review* 59, no. 4 (May 1992): 5–12.

be formed in which solidarity and competition modify each other's limitations? This is to ask whether a higher standard of living for the poorest, but a lower standard of living for most, is a price that people are willing to pay for a life ordered less to competition and more to cooperation. If, as Rocco Buttiglione desires, we are able to break the linkage between libertinism and the free market and replace it by a linkage between the free market and solidarity, two things are necessary. The first is to look closer to home than Japan to find a model of a society organized around solidarity—namely, to the Hispanic societies. The second is to give pluralism a proper criticism, for the very ideas of solidarity and pluralism work against one another.[39]

If the experts are right even once in ten times about the various perils our children will face because of the lifestyles found in the developed nations, the overconsumption of most of the goods of the earth by relatively few people, we must scale down our standard of living. As the popes have said, we must be stewards (*Rerum Novarum* 14), not mere consumers. I have neither space nor expertise to work out in detail here how the insight "smaller is better" might be qualified and expressed in our historical moment.[40] My general point is that we should with the encyclical tradition in general be on the side of the flourishing of intermediate institutions according to the principle of subsidiarity (*Quadragesimo Anno* 40). Our politics should be oriented toward the defense and promotion of those institutions like the family and the Church that are "on a human scale." We must each live in a manner that makes life possible for all. I suppose I am tempted to a professorial view of things, which would allow books to be bought and symphonies and ballparks to be funded, but would make it very difficult for anyone to own two homes or the newest gas-guzzler, but the main point is clear enough. It is hard to see the justification for having more space or comfort than is

39. Rocco Buttiglione, "Christian Economics 101," *Crisis* 10, no. 7 (July–August 1992): 32–36, at 35–36, and notes 17 and 32 above.

40. James Fallows, "What Can Save the Economy?" *NYRB,* April 23, 1992, shows the limitations of "consumptionist" economics.

needed if others lack minimal space and comfort, hard to see what right there is to such excesses or supererogation. Further, Christianity teaches that charity and justice must be tied together. It is very important to address the question of the proper use of property with reference to the common good—that is, from a natural perspective. Yet Christianity seeks to transform people's attitudes about such matters. An excess of property is not something grudgingly to be given up, but something joyfully to be placed in the service of others—first of all, I would think, in service of the Church. That is, property should be seen as ordered to evangelization in all the senses that Pope John Paul II gave this word in *Redemptoris Missio* (1991).[41] We at once build up the household of faith and humankind, for, as St. Basil said, our superfluous wealth, by being directed to evangelization, increases, quantitatively and qualitatively, the house of faith that is the new humanity in formation.[42] Thus we pray with the form of our life, "thy Kingdom come on earth as it is in heaven." Because the Kingdom is love, we have been promised that, against all probability, what is done in love, and only what is done in love, will endure forever.

AFTERWORD

Minor changes have been made in this chapter from the original essay. There is a second edition of Richard M. Hogan and John M. LeVoir, *Covenant of Love: Pope John Paul II on Sexuality, Marriage, and Family in the Modern World,* and a revised edition of Virgilio P. Elizondo, *The Future Is Mestizo: Life where Cultures Meet.* James McPherson, "Lincoln Off His Pedestal," treats the place of equality in American history further, and John L. Allen, Jr., *The Future Church: How Ten Trends Are Revolutionizing the Catholic Church,* on

41. I have developed some of this in "The Ethics of Conquest: The European Background of Spain's Mission in the New World," *Communio* 19 (1992): 619–34 (chapter 12 of this volume), and in "1492 in the Judgment of the Nations," in *Actas del II Congreso "Cultura Europea,"* ed. Enrique Banús (Pamplona: Aranzadi, 1994), 175–81.

42. Paul Fedwick, *The Church and the Charisma of Leadership in Basil of Caesarea* (Toronto: Pontifical Institute of Mediaeval Studies, 1979).

immigration. On marriage and family see William May, *Marriage: The Rock on Which the Family Is Built,* rev. ed. For disagreement over the nature of world-evangelization today, see Robert Bruce Mullin, Review, *First Things,* no. 198 (December 2009): 48–50. Norman Rush, "Naipaul's Mysterious Africa," paints an implicitly darker picture of the "Southern Christian" situation than does John Allen (above).

PART 2

THE ENCOUNTER WITH AMERICAN POLITICAL CULTURE

6

SEPARATING CHURCH AND STATE

THE DISTINGUISHED Hungarian-American historian John Lukacs recounts the outcome of the poll of Catholic college women he remembers Will Herberg to have reported in the 1950s.[1] They simply were asked whether they thought of themselves first as Americans or as Catholics. Ninety-eight percent of them thought of themselves as American first. The position I would like to advance here is no one's but my own, for I would be counted with the two percent. Because I am an adult convert to Catholicism I have not directly participated in that deep yearning of the immigrant to be accepted at virtually any cost into the larger culture, to be thought a good American. This yearning, one form of which is caught in Frank Capra's movies and life, seems to me central to the history of religion in America.[2] I do not think America is the "best country there ever was," and I am not particularly enamored of the Ameri-

1. John Lukacs, "Bare Ruined Choirs (Ample Parking in Church Yard)," *Triumph* 8, no. 4 (April 1973): 22–24 at 24. Curiously, Lukacs since has written of a very similar poll, asking the same question and also set in the 1950s, but now taken by himself of his own students with all of them responding that they think of themselves as Americans who happen to be Catholics: "Christians and the Temptations of Nationalism," in *New Oxford Review* 59 (Nov. 1992): 12–18, at 12. The present chapter originated in an opening statement of position in a debate, "Separating Church and State," between myself and Kathryn D. Kendell, staff attorney of the Utah chapter of the American Civil Liberties Union, given April 20, 1993, in the McDougall Lecture Series sponsored by the Cathedral of the Madeleine, Salt Lake City.

2. Luc Sante, "American Pie," *The New York Review of Books* (hereafter *NYRB*), January 28, 1993, writes of Capra, "He had spent his life and career attempting to deny his origins and to become American in the most mainstream, unshaded way."

can legal tradition.[3] Therefore, although an American, I speak as an outsider and as someone skeptical about "the American experience." I suspect my analysis will look as strange to many of my coreligionists as their sharing of premises with the world around them—what I would call their profound secularization—seems to me.

The story is told that early in the twentieth century, George Santayana, while at Harvard, was asked about Catholicism in America. The genial nonbeliever responded that he had met no Catholics in America, only some Protestants who prayed the rosary (a dated response, that!). The position I wish to mount—this is the first step of my argument—rests on the observation that humans are by nature religious animals. I suspect that in a society in which all assimilated groups, from the framers of the Constitution to contemporary assimilated Jews, have taken into themselves the dominant Protestant world view, such an observation is, as they say, off the screen.[4] Most people in our culture take for granted the classical Protestant understanding of the separation between faith and reason and assume, for instance, that both religion itself and the moral life pertain to faith and somehow are a world apart from that of science and reason, which latter are the instruments by which a neutral public and secular sphere of life may be constructed.[5] Some such assump-

3. George F. Kennan, *Around the Cragged Hill: A Personal and Political Philosophy* (New York: W. Norton, 1993), has many wise things to say in this regard: see the review by Arthur Schlesinger, Jr., "The Radical," *NYRB,* February 11, 1993. Paul Kennedy, "The American Prospect," *NYRB,* March 4, 1993, makes suggestions about how positions asserting America's "specialness" bear on America's future, and makes an argument that because America is so large and in some degree an "escapist" culture, there is much to be said for fostering policies that are "differentiated, decentralized, and individualistic, 'muddling through' rather than a coordinated, centralized attack upon the problems." Kennedy notes that such a policy, which in some ways parallels that advocated in the present chapter, implies long-term decline, but perhaps underestimates the ways in which American political culture forecloses the alternative of "coordinated attack."

4. But see Will Herberg, *Protestant, Catholic, Jew: An Essay in American Religious Sociology,* with a new introduction by Martin G. Marty (Chicago: University of Chicago Press, 1983).

5. I have treated this question especially in "The Meaning of Christian Culture: A Historical View," in *Catholicism and Secularization in America,* ed. David L. Schindler (Notre Dame, Ind.: Communio, 1990), 98–130, and in "1492 in the Judgment of the Nations," in *Actas del II Congreso "Cultura Europea,"* ed. Enrique Banús (Pamplona: Aranzadi, 1994), 175–81. One conclusion to be drawn from the latter article and from my "The Ethics of Conquest: The European Background of Spain's Mission in the New World,"

tion must lie behind the otherwise baffling Louisiana court decision that held that an abstinence-based sex education curriculum was, as Planned Parenthood had claimed, "religiously based because it talked about abstinence but did not mention birth control."[6] Such a claim seems to take it for granted that positions on questions like abstinence come from one's religion, which they do in classical Protestantism, but completely ignores philosophical naturalism, the various natural law claims, and indeed any philosophical position that holds that reason unaided by revelation has a word to speak on such

Communio 19 (1992): 619–34, is that a strict separation of church and state would involve the state giving up such ideas as "person" and "universal human rights," which historically originated with Christianity. Jacques Maritain, *Christianity and Democracy and the Rights of Man and Natural Law,* trans. Doris C. Anson, with an introduction by Donald Arthur Gallagher (San Francisco: Ignatius Press, 1986), 47, wrote: "Under the . . . active inspiration of the Gospel, the secular conscience has understood the dignity of the human person and has understood that the person, while being a part of the State, yet transcends the State, because of the inviolable mystery of his spiritual freedom." In *Integral Humanism: Temporal and Spiritual Problems of a New Christendom,* trans. Joseph W. Evans (New York: Scribner, 1968), 95–98, Maritain also made the historically plausible argument that the very distinction between spiritual and temporal orders, the latter presupposing the former, comes from Christianity. As I argue below, groups like the ACLU of necessity use such distinctions, without realizing their Christian origins, and that the positions of the ACLU thus are not religiously neutral but express at least a "cultural Christianity"; see also Roy A. Clouser, *The Myth of Religious Neutrality: An Essay on the Hidden Role of Religious Belief in Theories* (Notre Dame, Ind.: University of Notre Dame Press, 1991); David G. Dalin, ed., *American Jews and the Separationist Faith: The New Debate on Religion in Public Life* (Washington, D.C.: Ethics and Public Policy Center, 1992); and Naomi Cohen, *Jews in Christian America: The Pursuit of Religious Equality* (New York: Oxford University Press, 1992), with the informed review of the latter by David G. Dalin, "Still Strangers," *First Things,* no. 37 (November 1993): 32–35.

6. Quoted from the description of the case in "Ban on Teaching Abstinence in Louisiana Baffles Utahns," *Deseret News,* March 28, 1993. Classical Protestantism simultaneously rejected the grounds for natural law positions and continued to make natural law arguments. Therefore we should not find surprising the reaction of one Utahn quoted in this article, "If you want to talk about abstinence being a religion, then somebody's lost their marbles." That is, in Protestant cultures it is common to find explicit rejection of natural law thinking along with *de facto* retention of scraps of such thinking. This parallels the retention of "natural rights" thinking in Protestant cultures that have largely abandoned "natural law" thinking. The former is an attenuated form of the latter. Christopher Dawson, "Natural Law in the Protestant and in the Catholic World," *The Dawson Newsletter* 10 (Fall 1992): 4–5, reprinted from *The Judgment of the Nations* (New York: Sheed and Ward, 1942), 51–56, makes more distinctions than I can here, differentiating, for instance, between the fate of natural law in Lutheran and Calvinist cultures. See also note 5 (Olsen, "1492 and the Judgment of the Nations,") and the exchange beginning with Carl E. Braaten, "Protestants and Natural Law," *First Things,* no. 19 (January 1992): 20–26 (letters in *First Things,* no. 22 [April 1992]: 4–5).

matters. They proceed as if the Protestant way of looking at such issues is the only way.

Groups like Planned Parenthood, the ACLU, indeed in good measure the courts themselves, seem to me not at all neutral in matters of religion, but in this sense profoundly Protestant, or what we might call culturally Protestant, because tacitly assuming a Protestant separation of faith from reason.[7] Thus, according to the *Deseret News,* Kathryn Kendell, in arguing that Utah officials should separate "their religious views from their public responsibilities," pointed to Mario Cuomo as doing just that on the abortion question.[8] Here Ms. Kendell, along with Gov. Cuomo, assumes a "Protestant" understanding of the nature of abortion, which she takes to be a religious question; gives no indication of understanding why the Catholic Church, if not Gov. Cuomo, considers this to be a question of natural justice; and having herself worked from Protestant premises, has the temerity to criticize Utah officials for intruding religion into the public sphere—that is, doing what she has done. One would have hoped for a glimmer of self-understanding in all this, and that it would have been seen that the lesson to be learned is that all questions of law are also questions of philosophy, and many of theology also, and that therefore a strict separation of church and state is impossible, in principle as well as in fact.

7. I have discussed aspects of "cultural Protestantism" in the articles listed in note 5 above, and in note 31 below. The approaches to the discussion of abortion taken by Ronald Dworkin, *Life's Dominion: An Argument about Abortion, Euthanasia, and Individual Freedom* (New York: Knopf, 1993), and T. M. Scanlon, "Partisan for Life," *NYRB,* July 15, 1993, are good examples of framing a question in culturally Protestant terms. Both define the question in "sanctity of life" terms, taken to be a "religious" category (i.e., a claim that, coming from revelation, can neither be established nor refuted by philosophical or natural argument), and virtually ignore natural law/Catholic approaches. Having defined abortion as a "religious" issue, Dworkin, chap. 6, is able to argue that for the government to take any position on the question would be for it to impose religious beliefs; see the critique by Damian P. Fedoryka, "'Dworking' the Abortion Issue," *Crisis* 11, no. 1 (December 1993): 50–54.

8. Mike Carter, "Prayer Debate Heightens Religious Tension in Utah," *Deseret News,* January 27, 1993. This article describes Gov. Cuomo, who was criticized for his views by the Cardinal Archbishop of New York and others, as a "staunch Catholic." Former Gov. Mike Leavitt of Utah, in his claim that his "personal [sic, apparently 'official' is meant] statements have nothing to do with the [Mormon] church," seems as naive as Kendell in thinking one can have a position on a matter such as public prayer that does not express some theological and philosophical point of view. See note 9.

The irony is that the so-called separationist position is only possible with a Protestant understanding of the separation of faith and reason, and therefore itself is a theological position.[9] This separation has made possible the very notion, central to those who would build a high wall between church and state, of a common ground, sometimes, as in Alex de Tocqueville's analysis, denominated "society," itself neither church nor state but so to speak between these two.[10] Officially this common ground, in this view, takes no religious position, and on it we live a shared political life, irrespective of our private religious notions. One's ideas about (even) moral matters are commonly taken to come, on such a view, from one's religion, and thus to be private matters that should not be intruded into the public sphere. As they say, "You can't [i.e., shouldn't] legislate morality."[11] If the stray Catholic argues that, no, his or her opposition to, say, abortion is based not on a specific religious revelation but on rational notions of justice open to any human being, the argument is met with incomprehension. If the Freedom of Choice Act in its various instaurations is opposed because hospitals ethically opposed to

9. People who have no trouble seeing that the "multiculturalists" are right in saying there is no such thing as an objective or neutral curriculum or canon, that every selection of what to teach is freighted with philosophical (and, I would say, theological) assumptions, continue to hold the naive view that legislation is different: see notes 6 and 11. When I say "only possible on a Protestant understanding," I include as "Protestant" all positions that do not recognize a natural order sufficiently distinct from revelation to be able to generate some ideas of the good. Étienne Gilson, *Reason and Revelation in the Middle Ages* (New York: Scribner, 1938) called these "Primacy of Faith" positions, and they are found in all revealed religions in the degree to which these have not articulated a distinction in principle between reason and revelation; cf. Richard H. Akeroyd, *Reason and Revelation from Paul to Pascal* (Macon, Ga.: Mercer University Press, 1991).

10. I have expressed my reservations about Tocqueville's belief that religion would flourish at the social level if disestablished at the state level more than once: for the argument that this was true in the short, but not the long, run, see note 11, and in addition "The Catholic Moment?" *Communio* 15 (1988): 474–87 at 486. John Courtney Murray shared Tocqueville's faith, as apparently does J. Leon Hooper in his review of *John Courtney Murray and the American Civil Conversation,* edited by Robert P. Hunt and Kenneth L. Grasso, *Theological Studies* 54 (1993): 184–86. This review and book will introduce the reader to current discussion.

11. See my response to such notions in "'You Can't Legislate Morality': Reflections on a Bromide," *Communio* 2 (1975): 148–62, and see further Michael J. Perry, *Love and Power: The Role of Religion and Morality in American Politics* (New York: Oxford University Press, 1991), and Robert P. George, *Making Men Moral: Civil Liberties and Public Morality* (New York: Clarendon Press, 1993).

abortions will face serious legal penalties if they refuse to perform them—that is, act against conscience—the ACLU is not likely to give support.[12] The most prestigious newspapers of record will continue to treat such questions as being about revealed religion rather than about social justice, and fail to see that their way of regarding the issue expresses the cultural Protestantism of the country—that is, a form of bigotry in which no effort is made to understand or take seriously traditions very different from Protestantism.[13]

In arguing that man is by nature a religious animal, I want to suggest a very different way of looking at the matter.[14] Aristotle, in approaching the question of how man is to be defined, saw that like anything else humans are defined by that which is unique to them. Aristotle found this in mankind's rationality, above all in the ability to examine the validity of one's own reasoning processes. Aristotle was not wrong in defining human beings as rational animals, but his definition was incomplete or narrow. For instance, without gainsaying Aristotle, one could just as well hold, with that very special meaning that Plato gave to eroticism in the *Symposium,* that humans are erotic animals. That is, the very rationality in man that Aristotle prized was in turn rooted, as Aristotle partly saw, in an erotic impulse that drives humans outside themselves in quest of truth to see the world and reduce it to understanding. One could give cultural reasons—for instance the general uneasiness of many Greek philosophers in the presence of any form of passion—for Aristotle's blind

12. Of the articles on FOCA in the *National Right to Life News,* January 1993, see especially Roger Cardinal Mahony, "*FOCA*: No 'Freedom of Choice' for Catholic Hospitals."

13. For one more example of the inability of the *New York Times* to present fairly the Catholic position, see its extended treatment of the tensions between the Catholic hierarchy and the Clinton administration in the issue of February 3, 1993. The editor of the lay Catholic *Commonweal,* Margaret O'Brien Steinfels, devoted a signed opinion piece in the March 12, 1993 issue to the anti-Catholic bias displayed by the *Times* throughout the controversy over Joseph Fernandez, the former chancellor of the New York public schools. The *Times,* as in its treatment of abortion, continues to single out Catholics for religious identification and refuses to portray accurately their objections to Fernandez' policies. The controversy is described in "Commonweal Editor Accuses *New York Times* of Anti-Catholic Bias," *Intermountain Catholic,* March 26, 1993. To the present hardly a week goes by without the *Times* indulging in such bias.

14. Cf. Ernest Becker, *The Denial of Death* (New York: Free Press, 1973), as at 174–75, 178, 190, 200.

spot here. The point is that, in the spirit of the observation in the *Poetics* 4 that man is the most imitative of animals, Aristotle could have enlarged his definition of man as rational to see him as also clearly possessing *eros* to drive himself out of himself in a way that no other animal can. In a similar fashion, while showing in the *Metaphysics* that the rational man concludes to the existence of God, and while with Plato recognizing the origins in religion of everything from drama to philosophy itself, Aristotle had another blind spot in not seeing clearly that contemplation, the highest act of reason for him, and that which is closest to the divine in us, is very closely related to worship and prayer. By the very fact that man is a rational animal he is a praying or religious animal. Undoubtedly this second blind spot resulted from Aristotle's failure to realize that if God is rational—what he called self-thinking thought—he must also be personal. His inferior in so many ways, Cicero saw more clearly here.

I cannot linger over the meaning of either "religion" or "natural." My observation is that an unprejudiced view of man sees that, both across the cultures and in himself, one of the things distinctive to man, without any specific religious revelation as understood by the religions of the Book, is that he is a praying, worshipping, pious kind of being. I am not claiming that each member of the species is religious, or that each culture or period is religious in the same measure—although I am inclined to think of a so-called secular age like our own as simply having transmuted its forms of religious expression.[15] No, I would no more make that argument than hold that, because human beings have the capacity for mathematics, any given person or culture knows that 2 and 2 are 4. Self-described irreligious people are no counter-evidence to what I am proposing. A person or an age may have its form of blindness or incapacity. I am simply saying that, just as humans as a species have the capacity for mathematics, they have the capacity for religion. It is part of their nature, of what they might become.

15. In addition to my "Meaning of Christian Culture," I develop this idea in "Cultural Dynamics: Secularization and Sacralization," in *Christianity and Western Civilization,* ed. the Wethersfield Institute (San Francisco: Ignatius Press, 1995), 97–122.

My next observation is that the nature of religion, if its full development is allowed, is to be public, because finally religion is about the cosmos, our attitude and response to being. By "public" I do not simply mean visible, but with a standing in the law, what a separationist would call some degree of establishment, although I am not talking here of revealed religion, and believe what I intend is compatible with the First Amendment. We are—as again Aristotle saw—social animals and naturally wish to make common affirmations and live in a shared public space. We are made to communicate the truth to one another, and to want to affirm it in common, which includes in legislation. Here I will not linger over the privatizing of religion in recent centuries, one form of which is the already mentioned American distinction between state and society. This privatizing makes it difficult to understand our essential nature, and strict separation of church and state attempts to make the distinction between state and society permanent. My point is that religion, because it is about our understanding of our place in being, naturally fills the life of the religious person. Left to its own devices, it creates a public sphere of shared perceptions of God and the world, and issues in public art, architecture, music, liturgy, and law. One wishes to share one's deepest understanding and appreciation with others, above all to create a public order in which the forms of culture themselves will communicate truth about the world to those around oneself, above all to one's children.[16] A Roman public cult, a Christendom, a Confucian public order, is the working out in history of the logic of man's being religious.[17]

The second step of my argument can be briefly stated. Because

16. Michael Medved, *Hollywood vs. America: Popular Culture and the War on Traditional Values* (New York: HarperCollins, 1992), counters the "big lie" that "if you don't like it, you can turn it off," which seems an argument developed by those with no experience of children. In a lecture at the University of Utah, Medved commented, "To say to people that if you don't like the popular culture, just turn it off, is like saying if you don't like the smog, stop breathing"; Jeffrey D. Jonsson and Sean McBride, "Critic's Book Exposes Hollywood's Three Big Lies," the *Utah Daily Chronicle,* March 5, 1993).

17. Louis L. Hammann and Harry M. Buck, eds., *Religious Traditions and the Limits of Tolerance,* with Michael McTighe (Chambersburg, Pa.: publisher unknown, 1988), presents a variety of approaches.

the function of government is to foster the common good, all governments have the natural obligation to foster religion.[18] I intend here the common good as the classical philosophers understood it, as the sum of all those goods needed for human natural development. This is very far removed from what the expression "the common good" has come to mean in Anglo-Saxon thought, in which habitually this idea is associated with the will of the majority. Only a pragmatist—that is, someone in despair of truth—could think that what the majority wants is what is good for them.[19] The classical common good of which I speak is that good that is good even for the person who refuses to recognize it as good. No more than the truth is the common good determined by a show of hands. Using this definition, my claim then is simply that because man is of his nature religious, and government is obliged to seek all the goods that pertain to man's natural development, government must foster, rather than separate itself from, religion. Prayer, to put it in the words of Jean Cardinal Daniélou, will always be a political problem because prayer is a part of the political properly understood.[20]

What can this mean in a pluralistic society? Even those who

18. Cf. the argument for teaching religion in public schools and state universities in John Courtney Murray, *Religious Liberty: Catholic Struggles with Pluralism,* ed. J. Leon Hooper (Louisville, Ky: Westminster/John Knox Press, 1993).

19. The tradition of pragmatism, specifically John Dewey, is considered in the article listed in note 11 above. Robert B. Westbrook, *John Dewey and American Democracy* (Ithaca, N.Y.: Cornell University Press, 1991), attempts a defense of Dewey. Christopher Dawson, *Christianity and the New Age* (Manchester, N.H.: Sophia Institute Press, 1985), 66, provocatively analyzes "that moral pragmatism which is the essence of modern Protestantism," commenting on Harnack's famous *dictum* that "the Reformation is only completed when *faith cancels dogma.*" David Bromwich, *Politics by Other Means: Higher Education and Group Thinking* (New Haven, Conn.: Yale University Press, 1992), follows David Hume in arguing, in the words of one reviewer, "that we can have common standards without a foundation beyond the common features of human life": Alan Ryan, "Invasion of the Mind Snatchers," *NYRB,* February 11, 1993. How silly of Socrates to think, metaphysically speaking, that the unexamined life was not worth living!

20. I refer to Daniélou's great *Prayer as a Political Problem,* trans. J. R. Kirwan (New York: Sheed and Ward, 1967). Douglas G. Jacobsen, *An Unprov'd Experiment: Religious Pluralism in Colonial New Jersey* (Brooklyn: publisher unknown, 1991), attempts to show how a vague "public piety" was constructed from the "private pluralisms" of the denominations, and how this prefigured the future. For the developments to the passage of the First Amendment, see Thomas J. Curry, *The First Freedoms: Church and State in America to the Passage of the First Amendment* (New York: Oxford University Press, 1986).

would agree that the argument thus far has not in principle gone astray will have trouble understanding what its practical implications could be for today's world. If even in Daniélou's France, divided for centuries between a Catholic majority and a Calvinist minority, the now huge party of the areligious vies with voices that once expressed the Other, such as Islam, what are we to make of American pluralism? Here we come to the third step of the argument. It seems to me a simple point of logic that the more pluralistic a society is, the more difficult it will be to specify the manner in which its government is to fulfill its natural obligation to foster religion. Indeed, every other natural good will be in the same position, for one of the things "pluralism," what I have elsewhere called pluralism of world-views or "deep pluralism," designates is lack of agreement about the good.[21] It would take us too far afield to consider here in depth whether such pluralism is not simply another name for hell—that is, for "all coherence gone," but it should give even those most optimistic about the American experiment long pause. In a brilliant series of talks in my diocese, Owen F. Cummings showed that in a society such as ours people do not know how to stylize the most central points of their lives, because there is no consensus about the meaning of life or its stages.[22] There is no social consensus to tell us when we are old, or how we should die; indeed, rather than dealing with death in a human way, looking it in the face, talking about it, and preparing our souls, we hope death will be quick and painless—that is, subhuman—and the last thing we want to acknowledge with a dying person is his or her impending death. Not for us

21. See note 5, and my "Deconstructing the University," *Communio* 19 (1992): 226–53. George Kateb, *The Inner Ocean: Individualism and Democratic Culture* (Ithaca, N.Y.: Cornell University Press, 1992), is part of a growing literature that attempts to defend democratic individualism against the communitarian critique, but that hardly engages the point made here.

22. Especially Owen F. Cummings, "The Mystery of Evil and Suffering: the Contribution of Stanley Hauerwas," given March 22, 1993, at the Cathedral of the Madeleine, Salt Lake City, with special reference here to the thought of Daniel Callahan, *Setting Limits: Medical Goals in an Aging Society* (New York: Simon and Schuster, 1987); cf. Becker, *Denial of Death*, 159–60; and the account of the development of Philippe Ariès' study of death by Philippe Carrard, *Poetics of the New History: French Historical Discourse from Braudel to Chartier* (Baltimore: Johns Hopkins University Press, 1992), 47–48, 51, 201.

those early warning signals of pain and faltering that make the *ars moriendi,* dying well, possible. As I have said elsewhere, pluralism is more than piñatas and espresso; deep pluralism means that beings made for society must live in the atomized horror a liberalism centered on the autonomous individual confuses with a human life.[23] Still, the point that we must focus on here is that for us deep pluralism is part of the given: it is not likely to disappear, and so all analyses must come to terms with it.

But here is the rub. My earlier list of the Roman public order, Christendom, and the Confucian public order as examples of religion given public expression gave, in spite of a myriad of possible objections, relatively benign examples of embodied religion compared to other examples that could have been chosen. What if instead I had chosen the triad Bosnia, Sudan, and India? Even if we set aside the question of pluralism in its American form, we must admit that religion's role in forming corporate life also has led to grave evils, to various forms of clash, internal and external. It may well be true, as George F. Kennan has observed in comparing the Balkan crises of 1913 and 1993, that aggressive nationalism has in many cases been more directly the cause of war than religion, but religion nevertheless has been set to unworthy causes.[24] This obvious fact has fed the development of the liberal tradition, especially since that great sign of the breakdown of cultural identity in the West, the wars of religion in the seventeenth century.[25] I presume that it lies both instinctively and explicitly behind attempts to construct a high wall between church and state. Such responses to our obviously flawed human natures, to the ways our highest instincts often result in our greatest moral failure, must earn deep sympathy. Yet I think as they are found today in the attempt to construct a high wall between church and state they are profoundly misguided, and only exacerbate the problem of an adequately human public life.

23. Olsen, "Deconstructing the University," 237.

24. George F. Kennan, "The Balkan Crisis: 1913 and 1993," *NYRB,* July 15, 1993.

25. See the argument of Jeffrey Stout, *The Flight from Authority: Religion, Morality, and the Quest for Autonomy* (Notre Dame, Ind.: University of Notre Dame Press, 1981), used in the article listed in note 30.

Yet, I repeat, such responses earn my respect, for on a reading of the facts pretty close to my own, they are correct. That is, Booth Fowler and the "existential communitarians" seem rightly to hold that our sinful nature and the tragic dimensions of life make community an ever desirable and ever elusive goal, more something for which we forever strive than something possessed in any very full way. I would only add that the quest for even a modestly shared life is made especially difficult for us in the United States by the lack of a natural law tradition. In such conditions it becomes plausible to view the churches as a refuge from the larger society. Further, in the light, say, of Islamic fundamentalism, we need worry in turn about the churches' potential destructiveness if allowed into the political order. The proper response to both threats seems the construction of as high a wall as possible for the protection of both society and the churches themselves.[26] I am pretty close to sharing this reading of our public life, but only with two provisos that make high separationism an improper conclusion.[27] First, because we are political animals, it is better to struggle to exercise this capacity and fail than not to struggle. More importantly, especially in a media-dominated world, there is no refuge from public life.[28] Inevitably what the world is the churches largely become. Therefore to the end we must remain involved in the public order as, for instance, we must in matters of the environment.

There seems to me a great lack of imagination across the American political spectrum in these matters. First, the politics of many, right and left, see the goal of government as the maximization of human freedom. Granted that goal, those on the left with a "thin"

26. See note 32, and Robert Booth Fowler, *The Dance with Community: The Contemporary Debate in American Political Thought* (Lawrence, Kan.: University Press of Kansas, 1991), esp. chap. 9, with 154–61 on existential community. I am deeply grateful to Prof. Fowler for a very thoughtful letter he sent me about the matters following his illuminating participation in a church-state conference sponsored by the Humanities Center of the University of Utah in February, 1993.

27. I note how close Fowler's reading of the situation is to my conclusions in the article listed in note 32.

28. The media receive a ferociously funny treatment by Robert Hughes, *Culture of Complaint: The Fraying of America* (New York: Oxford University Press, 1993).

notion of the common good—that is, who largely abandon the notion of a shared public life built on cultural consensus—seem to have logic on their side both in wishing to expand the rights of individuals and in seeing government as essentially an arbitrator of rights between individuals. Those on the right, in reaction to a certain diminishment of all that is communitarian in life by the program of the left, often try to have their cake and eat it too—that is to say that they are for both liberty and community. The program of the libertarian left is in fact a prescription for society's dissolution in a kind of unending pluralism that tends as a limit to reduce society to autobiography, to largely solitary lives linked only to the select few. I do not mean that society is about to collapse, though, in the words of Alfred Kazin some years ago, there are many attempts "to impose the spirit of Yugoslavia on us."[29] Elsewhere I have shown that under the guise of neutrality that form of liberalism espoused by John Rawls in fact attempts to construct a new orthodoxy.[30] A recent triumvirate on the Supreme Court (Souter, Kennedy, and O'Connor) indeed insisted in *Planned Parenthood v. Casey* that social peace in the matter of abortion was such an overriding consideration that *Roe* is to stand simply because it has been in place for decades.[31] Clearly prudential considerations—the old Constantinian

29. Alfred Kazin, "The Way We Live Now," *NYRB,* April 22, 1993, reviewing the book by Robert Hughes listed in note 28.

30. In addition to "Deconstructing," see my "John Rawls and the Flight from Authority: The Quest for Equality as an Exercise in Primitivism," *Interpretation: A Journal of Political Philosophy* 21 (1994): 419–36 (see chapter 9 of this volume).

31. See the splendid editorial "Abortion and a Nation at War," *First Things,* no. 26 (October, 1992): 9–13. The potential of a legal tradition based on precedent rather than jurisprudence for the exercise of "raw judicial power" is particularly clear in *Casey,* which hardly attempts a justification going beyond the quest for social harmony. The triumvirate seemed to think that national division can be ended without facing the issues, and their stance revealed the intrinsic tendency to irrationalism of a precedent-based legal system not held in check by a natural-law theory. In effect they said that what is crucial is not truth, but submission—that is, categories of power. Similarly, the refusal of the Democratic National Convention of 1992 even to allow Governor Robert Casey to present his views about abortion, and President Clinton's subsequent statement that having a pro-choice position would be a litmus test for any new Supreme Court Justice, continue the attempt to achieve a new orthodoxy by force. Robert S. Alley, *The Supreme Court on Church and State* (New York: Oxford University Press, 1988), and Terry Eastland, ed., *Religious Liberty in the Supreme Court: The Cases That Define the Debate Over Church and State* (Washington,

"above all, resolve the problem"—here outweigh all else in the mind of the Court majority.

For all I know we can go on for a very long time caught, as on a New York City street, between the delights and dangers of pluralism (I would want to attribute most of the delights to cultural pluralism, the dangers to deep pluralism). But we cannot avoid and have not avoided the trivialization of the life of the mind and spirit in such circumstances, in which, because there are few shared notions about even how to mount a valid argument, human interchange is reduced to talk of baseball, movies, and food. Churches become a refuge from a dehumanizing public space inhabited by antagonistic ideological positions facing one another with few principles of mediation—but a refuge only different in degree from the public space because, as suggested above, in a media-dominated society there is no refuge.[32] The program of the communitarian right is a healthy but ineffective reaction against this dissolution of the public order, a reaction in the name of social solidarity, perhaps of a nostalgic quest for the return of neighborhoods or of community standards. The left will want a high wall separating church and state; the right, if its goal is the fostering of intermediary social institutions, including churches, a low wall, but neither sees the way actually to foster religion, what is the heart of being human, in a pluralistic environment.

To suggest opportunities missed in the above dialectic, we must turn from this ping-pong game in which especially the libertarian right and left end up emphasizing the maximization of liberty as the goal of government to a reconsideration of the classical under-

D.C.: Ethics and Public Policy Center, 1993), give helpful introductions to the constitutional cases.

32. As I argued in "The City in Christian Thought," *Thought* 66 (1991): 259–78, the Church inevitably takes on the shape of the surrounding "city." Therefore, it is always shortsighted for the Church or for Christians to abandon the attempt to influence the city. There are of course degrees here, but even monastic movements have inevitably been shaped by their surroundings. Distinction should be made between the clash of opinion in society, which is often healthy, and the clash of opinion in a society of deep pluralism, where by definition there are no agreed-on rules for mediation. The great question is whether some form of limited democracy is possible; otherwise the clash of opinion seems to lead to deep pluralism.

standing of the common good.[33] Here government exists to advance, irrespective of class, race, sex, or the advantages or disadvantages of historical accident, all the natural goods of human beings, one of which is the life of religion. In a sense there is no answer to the American objection to this project—that is, to the objection coming from the pluralism of a society in dissolution: "who determines what is natural to man and good for him?" The obvious answer is the same as to the question "who determines that 2 and 2 are 4," namely anyone who reasons aright. But this will have small impact in a society that has lost its grip on rules of evidence and logic—that decreasingly believes that one can actually establish the truth by an argument. For a historically Protestant society that commonly sees notions of the good coming from religion, or in Lawrence Tribe's secularized form of Protestantism centered on the autonomous self and without a natural law tradition, there is little notion that the unaided reason might really be able to discover those goods that the state should then foster.[34] Nor is there much idea that a public life is in part a great debate about the truth. Two generations ago Walter Lippmann could hope for such a public philosophy, not realizing that such a hope was, like that of Arthur Schlesinger, Jr., a hope that pluralism could be limited.[35] I would be the last to deny that such

33. Kenneth Pennington, *The Prince and the Law, 1200–1600: Sovereignty and Rights in the Western Legal Tradition* (Berkeley: University of California Press, 1993), dramatically recasts parts of the history of these subjects, showing that the origin of ideas central to due process, such as the presumption of innocence of the accused, is not, as commonly believed, in the English common law, but older and Continental.

34. Tribe has argued that the authors of the joint opinion in *Planned Parenthood v. Casey* have finally acknowledged the intellectual dead-end of the attempt, so central to Supreme Court decisions from *Griswold v. Connecticut* through and beyond *Roe v. Wade,* to ground such rights as the right to contraception and to abortion in an ever-expanding privacy doctrine. Tribe approves of this acknowledgment, and believes the three justices set out on a new path to a more principled rights doctrine built on the autonomous individual who chooses his or her form of life, the good for him or her. The right to abortion is necessary "to define one's own concept of existence, of meaning, of the universe, and of the mystery of human life" (quoted from *Casey* in the analysis in "Abortion and a Nation at War [see note 31]," 9). "Liberty" replaces "privacy" as the controlling idea. The triumvirate and Tribe seem to me merely to be replicating the logic of the historical development of liberalism.

35. See the bibliography above note 11 for expansion on Lippmann. Critics have noted that Schlesinger never really understood how much his form of liberalism was the cause of many of the problems he criticized in Schlesinger, *The Disuniting of America* (New York: Norton, 1992).

a project appears increasingly quixotic, but would argue for an accommodationist position on the church-state question in the following way.

Obviously the classical project, whether in its pagan, Catholic, or Islamic historical expressions, was at once the product of and a source of social unity, the feeling of the obligation to live according to what seemed shared public truths, a shared view of the world. This seems largely closed to us, and the establishment clause of the First Amendment seems necessary for self-protection. Obviously I do not consider this a social advance, but a necessity. Still, and this is the last step of my argument, I would argue that not all is lost if we see that our current situation is not an inevitable development of some constitutional logic, but a doctrinaire imposition. It is important here to remember that it was only in 1947 with *Everson v. Board of Education* that strict separationism established itself as a dominating tradition. Before *Everson* there had indeed been a growing tendency to reconceive the prohibition of establishment to include any giving of aid to "church." Still, an earlier hope for active cooperation between church and state in the promotion of social goods lingered. Only the establishment of a state-church was absolutely prohibited: this left much ground for cooperation between church and state short of favoring any one religion in particular. Then, according to *Everson,* religion was to be separated from public life.[36]

For a more than a half-century we have been developing a constitutional tradition in which the friendly separation and accommodation of church and state widely hoped for from the First Amendment has become a dim memory, even granted the second thoughts here of some thinkers.[37] Originally no more than any of the other rights was separation understood absolutely, but now an earlier cooperation of state with church in fostering social goods has been

36. John Courtney Murray, "A Common Enemy, A Common Cause," *First Things,* no. 26 (October 1992): 29–37, a previously unpublished address in response to *Everson* and *McCollum* (1948), is incisive and prescient. I am barely alluding to Justice Reed's important distinction, appropriated by Murray, between the original and developed meaning of the First Amendment.

37. See on all this Murray, "Common Enemy."

severely limited. Yet, more generous arrangements still exist elsewhere, and, as Mary Ann Glendon continues to point out, we may fuel our imaginations as to the road not taken by looking at other Western societies that have less opted for our current path.[38] I am interested in an imitation of, a learning from, how other countries have dealt with this problem in ways more generous to religion than the high-separationist tradition. I have already mentioned France: let me here simply allude to the German or Canadian pattern of public funding of a higher educational system composed of church-related faculties or institutions. Each of the colleges of the public University of Toronto, for instance, is church-related, and though in recent years the ties between the colleges and their churches have been increasingly attenuated, I sometimes wonder whether the wonderful cultural diversity of Toronto, tied to a very low rate of crime in comparison to the United States, is not partly accounted for by the historic Canadian notion of letting various religious groups share the public space.[39] If you let groups, religion and all, share in the public space, there seems some likelihood that they will not be alienated from this space, but will have a sense of proprietorship toward it. In America we tend to set the groups against one another.

The principle here is that it is good that as many subgroups in the population as possible be able to educate their children and young people by their own best lights, and that each religion be treated in accord with its position in the population. This was one goal of nineteenth-century Catholic liberalism as represented by Charles le

38. See most recently Mary Ann Glendon, *Rights Talk: The Impoverishment of Political Discourse* (New York: Free Press, 1991), and Glendon, "Religion and the Court: A New Beginning?" *First Things,* no. 21 (March 1992): 21–26.

39. For studying a parallel question, John D. Blum, "Ontario Health Care: A Model to Be Emulated or Avoided?" *National Forum: The Phi Kappa Phi Journal* 73, no. 3 (Summer 1993): 41–44 at 43, traces differences in health care to different conceptions of community. Articles making adverse comparisons between American and other societies are standard fare in the daily press: see in the wake of the slaying of a German tourist in Miami the syndicated article by Rheta Grimsley Johnson, "Is America Spinning Out of Control?" *Deseret News,* April 18, 1993. The range of constitutional possibilities is very large: see Gary Jacobsohn, *Apple of Gold: Constitutionalism in Israel and the United States* (Princeton: Princeton University Press, 1993).

Comte de Montalembert (1810–1870). Freedom of religion did not exist for him simply to protect the individual, but groups, associations, and churches. Obviously lines have to be drawn somewhere for practical reasons, and groups that are small minorities will probably have no claim to public monies. And obviously such a system will be easier to administer in a relatively homogenous society as Germany than in the more diverse Canada, and again be easier to administer in Canada than in the United States. But if religion is a part of man's natural constitution, it is wrong to solve the problem of the place of religion in a pluralist society prematurely by simply constructing the wall of separation as high as we can. Our lives are in principle humanized in the degree in which we can find ways for religion, not just to influence the public order in the ways we each can as individuals, but to express itself in that order institutionally, for instance in the form of church-related schools.

There is a lot in the matter of attitude here. In regard to public prayer, for instance, if our basic attitude is gratefulness for the embodiment of truth we find in the lives of others, why not take turns in the offering or non-offering of public prayer? It has always seemed to me an ungrounded argument to assert that some right is violated if I must be present at the prayer or non-prayer of someone of another or of no religion. I would much rather hear an explicitly Mormon prayer at one graduation, and—to pursue a *reductio ad absurdum*—have no prayer at all at another because it was the atheists' turn, than hear the lowest-common-denominator prayers that are the result of trying to find the impossible: something acceptable to all on each occasion. At one level I have some trouble giving the atheist here his or her due. If the existence of God can be proved by reason alone, which it seems to me it can, giving atheists their turn in the matter of (abstention from) prayer is a bit like celebrating the failure of someone to learn math. In addition, to return to an earlier theme, to abstain from having public prayer is as much a theological statement as praying: both portray how we conceive our nature and destiny, how we define our humanity. Still, it is clear that in our civilization a fair number of people become atheists because of the way in which God or some specific religion has been presented to them. Their atheism may express their own sense of the truth, and thus is worthy of some respect.

My argument is that government is to encourage all forms of religion compatible with its other natural goals. This means not simply that the state has no competence to judge between the truth claims of revealed religions, but that it has more power to outlaw certain religious practices than is generally accorded it in American thought—but only if we abandon the notion that all morality is rooted in revelation. From a natural law point of view, it is quite possible for the state to condemn certain religious practices as against right reason. Our justice system is so ignorant of and antagonistic toward what it is ignorant of—natural law positions—that an obvious candidate for the application of such reasoning, the *Church of the Lukumi Babalu Aye v. City of Hialeah* or Santería case, was in fact resolved on quite other criteria.[40] Nevertheless, if, for instance, a religion claimed to have received the revelation that some group in the population was to be murdered by them, it certainly seems to me that the state has the right to outlaw this religion on the grounds that *prima facie* it (at least on this point) is false. This is not simply because for reasons of public order homicide trumps freedom of religion, but because the state has the responsibility of pursuing natural justice. It therefore must stop any person or group that claims the right to take away the lives of people who have done nothing to forfeit their lives. The state has the right to declare a religious practice illegal, not when the religion makes claims that go beyond the order of natural justice, but when it makes claims that violate the order of justice. For now such a proposal is made simply to provoke the imagination, not with the hope that such a way of looking at things will be invoked in the near future.

Others have shown just how tendentious the reading of Ameri-

40. Still, as David G. Savage of the *Los Angeles Times* pointed out in analyzing three of the 1993 rulings on religion in "Supreme Court Taking 'Neutral' Tack on Religion," *Deseret News,* June 20, 1993, there is some suggestion of a drawing back from strict separationism interpreted as discrimination against religion; see on this Raul F. Yanes and Mary Ann Glendon, "Religion and the Court 1993," *First Things,* no. 37 (Nov. 1993): 28–30.

can history by the high separationists is.[41] The argument here has been that their positions, especially that of the ACLU, express not a disinterested reading of the Constitution, First Amendment, and constitutional tradition, but a *parti pris* that effectively is a form of religious intolerance. Without reformulation of the problem of church and state along a line something like that given here, it is not likely that such an intolerance can be abated, nor a healthier common life in society pursued.

AFTERWORD

I have made minor revisions in the text of this chapter from the original essay. In *The Turn to Transcendence: The Role of Religion in the Twenty-First Century,* I explore further claims about America's uniqueness and the separation of church and state; I analyze the natuoral law further in "The Natural Law: The First Grace." On humans as naturally religious, see Anthony Grafton, "'A Jewel of a Thousand Facets.'" See also Terry Eagleton, *Reason, Faith, and Revolution: Reflections on the God Debate;* David Novak, *In Defense of Religious Liberty;* and Kenneth R. Craycraft, Jr., *The American Myth of Religious Freedom.* Bernard Bailyn, "How England Became Modern: A Revolutionary View," has interesting things to say about the nation-state and nationalism. On the ongoing debate about democracy, see Joseph S. Lucas, "Montesquieu, the Modern West, and Democracy's Drift: An Interview with Paul A. Rahe." On some new forms religion is taking today, see Robert H. Nelson, *The New Holy Wars: Economic Religion versus Environmental Religion in America Today.*

41. See Ellis Sandoz, *A Government of Laws: Political Theory, Religion, and the American Founding* (Baton Rouge: Louisiana State University Press, 1990).

7

RELIGION, POLITICS, AND AMERICA AT THE MILLENNIUM

IN THIS CHAPTER I would like to reflect on the role of pluralism, especially religious pluralism, in what I take to be the failure of the American experiment in ordered liberty. My argument is that, examined from the vantage point of the turn of the millennium, American claims to exceptionalism and superiority, clustered around the idea of ordered liberty, have proven unjustified. Enough American history has passed to see how the instability, internal incoherence, and inadequacy of the founding American assumptions about God, man, and society daily make the dream of ordered liberty ever more remote. The evidence of profound social disorder, of disordered liberty, lies all around. The jibes against Europe, that in America a fresh historical beginning, freed from Europe's burdens and mistakes, would sustain something better than Europe had known, a *novus ordo seclorum,* seem now premature and naïve.[1]

In America it is most uncommon to admit this. Awareness of the manifold signs of disorder that mark one's daily life rarely results in acknowledgment that there might be something wrong with the experiment itself. Indeed, the pseudo-scientific language

1. Glenn W. Olsen, "The Meaning of Christian Culture: A Historical View," in *Catholicism and Secularization in America: Essays on Nature, Grace, and Culture,* ed. David L. Schindler (Notre Dame, Ind.: Communio, 1990), 98–130. The present chapter originated in a paper given at an American-German Colloquium on Pluralism sponsored by the School of Philosophy, The Catholic University of America, September 18–20, 1995.

of "experiment," especially William Penn's sacralized language of "holy experiment," puts off indefinitely any day of reckoning, for one can always say not enough evidence is in on whether the American experiment "works."[2]

In the past fifty years the logic of older forms of liberalism, both French and Anglo-American, central to the American founding has been revealed in a radical liberalism unafraid to embrace what always had lain in liberalism's premises. I use "liberalism" in an etymological way to describe any politics to which the quest for liberty in its evolved modern sense of "freedom from" is central. As Alasdair MacIntyre pointed out, liberalism, although originating historically in attack on tradition and aiming at a social order founded on "universal, tradition-independent norms," has itself become a tradition.[3] In it an initially deficient idea of human autonomy, in which insufficient attention was paid to the relations between the individual and both other human beings and the cosmos generally, has worked itself out in an arbitrary freedom that takes the form of moral relativism and utilitarian and hedonistic domination of others. Similarly, an initially deficient idea of man, endemic to Protestantism but much exacerbated by the Newtonian idea of *techne,* in which man is not recognized as first of all a contemplative being, has unrolled itself in an almost completely mechanistic view of life in which man is interiorly empty and exteriorly manipulative.[4]

Even were somehow the developments of more than a half century to be rolled back, we would be left with the earlier liberalisms, which continue to exist, and their flawed view of the nature of human autonomy and man's relation to God. This would give us as little warrant for hope as were we spectators at a rerun of Daedalus' experiment. José Casanova may well be right that a worldwide re-

2. Gordon S. Wood, "Not So Poor Richard," *New York Review of Books* (hereafter *NYRB,* June 6, 1996.

3. Alasdair MacIntyre, *Whose Justice? Which Rationality?* (Notre Dame, Ind.: University of Notre Dame Press, 1988), 335. MacIntyre has observed that virtually all thought in America is one of three forms of liberalism: conservative, liberal, or radical.

4. Cf. David L. Schindler, "Christological Aesthetics and *Evangelium Vitae:* Toward a Definition of Liberalism," *Communio: International Catholic Review* 22 (1995): 193–224.

bellion is taking place against the privatization or marginalization of religion that accompanied modernization and secularization.[5] Still, wherever it has occurred, such rebellion has hardly done other than to reassert older cultural forms without engaging the historical quandries that helped generate modernity in the first place. Thus the public reemergence of Evangelical Protestantism in the United States beginning in the 1980s seems aimed at something like recovery of the hegemonic status of nineteenth-century Protestant civil religion. Nineteenth-century civil religion feared (and contemporary Evangelicalism fears) unabated pluralism—especially religious pluralism—and, while unable to eliminate a primary *datum* on which America was founded, attempted to reduce its most deleterious effects. In America, a country in which the need to facilitate the coexistence of differing religious views has been primordial to all constitutional arrangement from the beginning, the worthy goal of "deprivatization" of religion, which is really a name for attack on or restriction of deep pluralism, can only develop in quite constricted limits.

I have written elsewhere on the distinction between cultural pluralism and deep pluralism, the latter of which might also, following John Gray's brilliant critique of Isaiah Berlin, be called "value pluralism."[6] Although these two shapes of pluralism constantly invade each other's territory, I have suggested that at least in principle we can distinguish between a cultural pluralism that enriches life together and a deep pluralism that, because embodying irreconcilable views of the good, true, and beautiful, undermines the possibility of a shared life. I have suggested that Americans have not been very open, indeed probably not very self-conscious, about the logic of their experiment, insofar as it involves pluralism. Some writ-

5. José Casanova, *Public Religions in the Modern World* (Chicago: University of Chicago Press, 1994), 5, 8, on this and the following, with the intelligent review by Joseph A. Varacalli in *The Catholic Historical Review* 81 (1995): 407–08.

6. Olsen, "The Catholic Moment?" *Communio* 15 (1988): 474–87, at 478–79. Michael Walzer, "Are There Limits to Liberalism?" *NYRB*, October 19, 1995, by giving essentially pragmatic arguments in defense of Berlin against Gray, acknowledges how telling Gray's criticism is.

ers have, for instance, written as if the various religions in America could indefinitely share in public life while retaining their distinctive identities. This seems to me a religious form of the national myth, *e pluribus unum:* that a meaningful *unum* is possible that allows the *pluribus* from which it was constructed to live on. Such an idea is not fully historical. It seems to me, rather, that to the degree a shared life is achieved, deep pluralism, here including the pluralism of real religious differences, recedes.[7] To the degree that deep pluralism advances, the *unum* recedes. Perhaps this is not obvious to many Americans because they do not see how profoundly the American experience has remolded the historical religions. That is, to the extent that an *unum* has been achieved, it falls under the categories of civil religion, the flag, the Fourth of July, the American way of life. In America—and of course not only America—classical Calvinism, classical Lutheranism, dogmatic Catholicism, hardly exist: what has replaced them for most is American civil religion, the religion of the American way of life itself. This is not deep pluralism, but an emptying of an earlier real variation between religions into a kind of suburban religion of sameness.

Always ways are found to limit deep pluralism. At the center of American history lies the attempt, while praising various pluralist phenomena, especially religious freedom, to do everything possible to tame, constrict, or domesticate these. A Catholicism loyal first to the pope is feared, a Catholicism loyal first to America is praised. Americans have had as many apprehensions about deep pluralism as have had other societies, but, as in so much else, have deceived themselves about their defensive strategies against that which they praise.

I have no structural reformation to propose that if followed would let the American experiment proceed. It seems to me that,

7. Thus far I agree with Michael Lind, *The Next American Nation: The New Nationalism and the Fourth American Revolution* (New York: Free Press, 1995), but as a liberal populist who largely thinks in economic categories, above all seeking the prosperity of every citizen, Lind sees religion and religious and cultural variation as happily disappearing in the melting pot of national culture. The generally intelligent review of this book by Alan Ryan notes that Lind places religious and cultural questions on the periphery: "It Takes All Kinds," *NYRB,* October 5, 1995.

for both good and ill, peoples generally live out the logic of their basic assumptions about life to the end. "Honor," for instance, is at the center of all that is most glorious and most sad in Spanish history, playing the role that "liberty" does in American history. The goals of cultural criticism must be more modest, to examine assumptions, to show how these assumptions have affected history, and by the very discussion of such matters, to give people some power to brake, accelerate, or redirect the tendencies of their times. My point of view is that of the Spanish social analyst, Juan Donoso Cortés (1809–53), who in his mature, post–1848 thought saw that every great political question is wrapped up in a theological question.[8] Cortés did not mean by this that one could ignore economic or political analysis, but that such analysis was most incomplete until one had grasped how the great questions of theology repeat themselves in the political order. This was the approach of John Paul II when he looked at the evidence of disordered liberty strewn across the social order and described it as a "culture of death." For a culture of death to form, individual evil choices must be made, but there must be more than this. *Pace* liberalism, which is congenitally dishonest on such matters, personal sin comes, in the shape of badly ordered ideas, to shape the life of the mind in general, and institutions take on a "structure of sin."[9]

If there is a sense in which the American experiment was doomed from the first as a form of "magic-thinking," that does not mean that America is doomed in some near future: one goal of cultural criticism should be sober assessment of what a future shorn of belief in exceptionalism might realistically be. It is extremely difficult to separate the good from the bad effects of any set of ideas so that the one may be encouraged, the other discouraged, but this is our goal. Even now, in America as elsewhere, mingled with the "culture of death" is another culture, that of "love and life," that

8. Juan Donoso Cortés, *Ensayo Sobre el Catolicismo, el Liberalismo y el Socialismo,* 2nd ed. (Buenos Aires: Espasa-Carpe Argentina, 1949), esp. chap. 1.

9. *Evangelium vitae* no. 12, trans. *The Gospel of Life,* Special Supplement to *Inside the Vatican,* April 1995 (New Hope, Ky.: New Hope Publications, 1995).

crosses most party labels and is in some measure willed by virtually every camp, giving reasons for hope.[10] It is becoming a commonplace that in the Church itself a long generation of priests and bishops—in which there were many who were, in matters sexual, disciplinary, or doctrinal, accommodated to the world and unwilling to teach or themselves live by the full Gospel—has aged and is being replaced with younger priests formed by the pontificates of John Paul II and Benedict XVI and willing, for instance in the matter of celibacy, to live counterculturally as signs to the age.[11]

While attacking liberalism's evil fruits, we encourage the good things it has promoted, among them certain forms of medical and technological advance, the search for alternatives to war as a means of conflict resolution, and economic and political institutions capable of resisting the more overt forms of tyranny. Still, when all is said and done, because we cannot deny that much has the smell of death about it, Catholicism should impart a deep sense of the limitations of the American experiment. American Catholics need to spend less time underwriting that experiment and more time helping Americans understand the predicaments in which it has placed them. Possibly on the other side of such criticism, for those with hearts to understand, lies development of some of the things American culture has undervalued from the beginning.

Because it has been the religion of immigrants who have longed above all for acceptance, Catholicism in America has not lived up to its potential as an instrument for raising Americans to self-consciousness about the true nature of the dilemmas that face them. Like Jews, Catholics in America have had to work especially hard for social acceptance, and have in the process come to be among the prime boosters of what since the 1930s has been called "the American way of life."[12] The greatest political gift Catholic criticism can

10. The contrast between the two cultures is integral to *Evangelium vitae,* as at no. 27; nos. 26–28 spell out the signs of hope in liberal society.

11. See the Associated Press article by David Briggs, "A New Generation Is Heeding Pope's Call to Serve the Lord," *Deseret News,* October 7, 1995.

12. David L. Schindler, *Heart of the World, Center of the Church: "Communio" Eccle-*

give to America is critique of its Enlightenment, Protestant, and democratic assumptions. A sense of the limitations of received views of the world is not a bad thing. It can liberate from tasks not worth pursuing in favor of effort well expended.

America has been called a melting pot of peoples. American historians quarrel among themselves as to whether this is an appropriate metaphor, noting the tenacity of some American subcultures, continuing regional variation, and the persistence of ethnic boundaries in many large American cities.[13] This quarrel is partly a debate about, often a taking of sides over, the outcome of choosing one or the other of two paths open to every immigrant: assimilation to the mainstream or conscious retention of a distinctive cultural identity. Probably most immigrants have wanted it both ways, to be accepted by American society and successful by American standards, while retaining some degree of cultural distinctiveness, often founded in religion. As long as we view the surface and the middle depths, they seem often to have gotten their way, and America may be described as a cultural mosaic bonded by very widely shared common beliefs originating in the years surrounding 1776. Yet, if we leave aside those brought to America as slaves and view the story of immigration over as short a period as a century, we see that it overwhelmingly has been about assimilation.

Immigrants such as Irish Americans commonly have passed in no more than three generations from being despised to being, with Catholics generally, among the best educated (by the conventions of American society) and financially most successful of Americans. As assimilation proceeded, most either shed their religion or radically adjusted it to the larger culture. John F. Kennedy may be taken as a symbol of a late stage of this process, of a sentimental attachment to ethnic ways loosened from religion and subordinated to making

siology, Liberalism, and Liberation (Grand Rapids, Mich.: Eerdmans, 1996), 70, 106, more generally chaps. 1–2, considers this expression and much else related to the present essay.

13. Cf. Lind, *Next American Nation;* Fox Butterfield, *All God's Children: The Bosket Family and the American Tradition of Violence* (New York: Knopf, 1995); and David Hackett Fischer, *Albion's Seed: Four British Folkways in America* (New York: Oxford University Press, 1989).

one's way in the world. He was the hero of a generation of Catholics who saw in his success their acceptance.

Those groups who have stood or been pushed aside, say the Amish or some Native Americans, in a real sense are hardly part of the American story: they simply have a different story to tell, one infringed at every point by the dominating story. At one level this is but to say that America is not exempt from larger patterns. All religions and ways of life adapt to the cultures they enter by some degree of assimilation or what today is called inculturation.[14] Consciously to try to avoid all syncretism is with the Amish to opt for social isolation. A full-bodied pluralism, were that possible for very long, would depend on the isolation and marginalization of each of society's components—the lack of a syncretic spirit. Otherwise, a deep pluralism in which there are not shared core beliefs among the various social groups must tear society apart. If there is to be a shared life in society, deep pluralism must by definition give way to a pluralism more of the surface, to the relative homogenization attendant on assimilation. Deep pluralism on the one side is the enemy of any religion or morality taken seriously, and on the other of shared life in society. In a society of relative homogenization, "civility" becomes not just a prime social virtue naming the ability to negotiate between common belief and whatever remains distinctive to one's own group, but acceptance of some such distinction as likely permanent. The agreement not to discuss religion or politics at parties must be enforced as "good manners" in the degree that one's religion or politics is genuinely of the depths. Always the truly pluralistic must be marginalized. Let me reiterate: many Americans have not been very honest about this process, claiming in effect that the American experiment is about both a common faith and a vibrant pluralism, without observing the ways in which the one necessarily works against the other.

14. Glenn W. Olsen, "The 'Catholic Moment' and the Question of Inculturation," in *Catholicity and the New Evangelization,* Proceedings from the Seventeenth Convention of the Fellowship of Catholic Scholars, Corpus Christi, Texas, 1994 (Steubenville, Ohio: Franciscan University Press, 1995), 17–54 (chapter 1 of this volume).

Of course Americans are not alone in their lack of candor here: witness the thought of Jürgen Habermas. Indeed, in some ways America presents an advanced case of Habermas' "communicative interaction" and "discourse ethics" at work.[15] The goal is social integration achieved by discussion and struggle between points of view. This integration, however, is not through a "common good" suited to all human beings, universally true, and deserving obedience, but through assent to the momentary configuration of the ever-shifting normative structures of an unending debate. This sounds very much like the American notion that the common good is the will of the majority. We might call it democratic fascism, for, in the degree it lacks a transcendental standard for judging truth, social integration is by the "soft fascism" of majority rule. *Evangelium Vitae* (nos. 20, 23) observes that a "supremacy of the strong" can lead democracy "toward a form of totalitarianism." As in all positions that lack or are deficient in an idea of natural law, agreement is for its own sake rather than for the sake of truth. If I may draw out the tautology, to the degree pluralism is present in a society, agreement about unchanging moral principles is impossible and non-philosophical categories such as civility and force—physical or procedural—must provide whatever level of social cohesion is achieved. Conversely, if there is an objective good to be known and adhered to, to the degree a society does this it will abandon deep pluralism. In American history the phrase "we hold these truths" initially marked the point beyond which pluralism was rejected, and every society will have such a point or it cannot survive. Even a liberalism that reduces all social questions to matters of procedure still must insist that all play by the same rules—its rules.

In a sense the quarrel over which metaphor best describes America, melting pot or stew, is more an argument about the surface than about the depths. Because especially the democratic and Enlightenment beliefs on which America is founded are intrinsically unstable, each calls forth its counter. As much as Pericles in his "Funeral Ora-

15. See on this and the following chapter text the discussion of Casanova, *Public Religions,* 230–31 in the review noted in note 5.

tion," trying to justify Athenian bids to exceptionalism and superiority, had in fact to scurry from one unbalanced claim to its rhetorical counterweight, from the claim of equality to the claim of merit, from advocacy of free circulation of ideas to respect for "unwritten laws," so does virtually all American political rhetoric. Since freedom is at the center of what is sought, the anxiety is that agreement and cooperation between individuals will be impossible. Thus, as night the day, the principle of freedom calls forth its counter in the myth and aspiration *e pluribus unum*. This is but to say that from the beginning, Americans at least instinctively realized that centering political life on the Enlightenment principle of liberty exacerbated the problems of pluralism with which all political regimes must come to terms.

The expression "ordered liberty" itself linked ideas tugging in different directions. All but the most despotic regimes, regimes that suppress one of the terms, must seek to link order and liberty. To do so is one of the great, worthy tasks of politics. But in America, because so much weight was laid on "freedom from" and the possibility of a dissolving pluralism was so real, special emphasis had to be placed on a counterbalancing consensus formed around the principles expressed in the founding documents, raised virtually to the status of inspired scripture. Precisely because Americans had so many religions and cultures, they had to have one faith, and that in America itself. The American faith demanded the loyalties that elsewhere—except where establishment also ruled (for in America there is an established religion, the cult of liberty or liberalism)—were reserved to religion. In time the First Amendment insured that no faith could be established in America but the American faith. That is, despite the pervasive role of religion in American life from the beginning, the problem of pluralism was dealt with by placing the Declaration of Independence, Constitution, and Bill of Rights at the center of national life and increasingly marginalizing all religious institutions *qua* institutions as threats to the *unum*.[16]

16. See my "Separating Church and State," *Faith and Reason* 20 (1994): 403–25 (chapter 6 of this volume).

The various forms of Christianity, which normally supported the national faith, were useful bulwarks of society, and religious practice indeed one of the chief ways by which one manifested loyalty to the American way of life.

The great question was whether this kind of common faith could sustain the "order" that liberty, if it were to be more than untrammeled license, needed—i.e., the ordering of liberty to truth. Although America was founded in rebellion and has always been marked also by the selective "flight from authority" of Protestantism, the Founding Fathers generally understood freedom not simply as "freedom from" or as an end in itself.[17] Freedom generally for them was a condition for pursuit of goods rooted in the natural order of things. These goods might have a distinctly commercial flavor—"life, liberty, and the pursuit of happiness"—but they were not for that completely closed to transcendence, to the idea of a life ordered to truth and to God. The constitutional documents assumed that liberty had ontological roots in universal rights of man above and beyond the touch of any government. It followed that the order to which liberty aspired was not one of force, simple negation, or a merely worldly flourishing. In some measure, a true way of life was the goal.

Such an idea had its historical roots in natural law thought, of which the doctrine of natural rights was at once a development and, in some respects, diminution. Protestantism in all its forms was raised on the rejection of natural theology and natural law, but especially Calvinism, the most influential form of Christianity in America, reintroduced with one hand what the other had withdrawn. Calvin himself, in defiance of his own epistemology, had retained certain Stoic understandings of the natural and natural law, of a "general revelation" that enlightened those who had never received the "specific revelation" of Christianity. The question, in the United States as elsewhere, was whether Protestantism, with its antinomi-

17. Glenn W. Olsen, "John Rawls and the Flight from Authority: The Quest for Equality as an Exercise in Primitivism," *Interpretation: A Journal of Political Philosophy* 21 (1994): 419–36 (chapter 9 of this volume).

anism and radically diminished notions of the natural, could in the long run in any form sustain an ontological ordering of liberty to truth. The radical liberalism of the last half century or so, with its notion, now esconced in a number of Supreme Court decisions, of the unencumbered individual who fosters her own morality, seems only one of the most distasteful of the answers to that question. In America the so-called mainline Protestant churches themselves have now largely been captured and destroyed by their complicity in the denial of universal moral norms, and place very few limits on freedom. What ontology there was in the American founding documents and in Protestantism into the twentieth century has been insufficient to sustain an objective order at which freedom aims. One must be very glad for those who instinctively react against such developments, such as many Evangelical Christians; but, in spite of the acute analyses occasionally coming from such circles, one can expect little help dealing with philosophical questions from traditions so markedly aphilosophical.[18]

Seen over time, the American story as almost all historians and the general populace have conceived it has centered on those who have assimilated, those who have abated the problems of pluralism by adhering to a shared set of beliefs. True, recent historians have increasingly placed their scholarship in service of an agenda that stresses and promotes (a not usually very clearly defined) cultural diversity, and one can reasonably doubt whether the historic road to assimilation is as open to Muslims as it has been to most others. However, there is little reason to believe that the advocacy of diversity will have any effect on the already socially marginalized other than to keep them marginalized, slowing or stopping assimilation. For most the story will continue to be about assimilation. In spite of certain advantages of geography that will presumably indefinitely feed Hispanic immigration and lengthen the period needed for any given genera-

18. Keith J. Pavlischek, *John Courtney Murray and the Dilemma of Religious Toleration* (Kirksville, Mo.: Thomas Jefferson University Press, 1994), is an example. There is a review of this book by Kenneth R. Craycraft, Jr.: "Church-State Problems," *Crisis* 13, no. 6 (June, 1995): 47–48.

tion to assimilate, it is unlikely that the story of the assimilation of recent Hispanic immigrants will have a very different outcome from that of earlier immigrants from Europe. They will come to have as their first loyalty the *unum* of "the American way of life." If they are Catholic, they will, like an overwhelming proportion of earlier immigrants, come to think of themselves as "Americans who happen to be Catholics" rather than "Catholics who happen to be Americans." In spite of an initial culture shock that will continue to lead a certain proportion into the evangelical or charismatic camp, and in spite of regional variations related to the relative density of Latino population, to judge by the years since Vatican II, their Catholicism will be, like themselves, increasingly suburban, middle class, and innocuous, at no great distance from the generic Protestantism that has long stood at the heart of the American way of life.

What is this "American way of life," this common set of beliefs that has tied most Americans together, in spite of all their apparent diversity? It is what Christopher Dawson described as a national faith founded on widely shared belief in the principles of the Enlightenment.[19] Whereas in Europe the Enlightenment fostered vicious attack on religion and the old order, in America it began the age of faith that has given America the soul of a church. In this blend of religiosity and nationalism, the language of faith and of Enlightenment constantly interpenetrate one another. This is not grace perfecting nature in any Catholic sense, extrinsic or intrinsic, for the centrality of Protestantism in the origins of the country has left its profound mark in a general inability to make a principled distinction between nature and grace. One of two things happens. On the one hand, and this seems especially true of late-eighteenth-century America, reason and nature are abstracted from love and grace in a rationalist or mechanist manner, so that two (unclearly distinguished) orders are juxtaposed. Rationalists may ignore the sphere set aside for grace, and those who wish to be both rational

19. See my "American Culture and Liberal Ideology in the Thought of Christopher Dawson," *Communio* 22 (1995): 702–20, on this and my following discussion in the text.

and religious simply shift gears from one to the other, move from one compartment to another. The long-term logic here is on the side of compartmentalizing or privatizing religion as something subjective.[20] On the other hand, and this seems true especially of the various American religious awakenings, all may be seen to be grace. That is, a majority of Americans in all periods have probably instinctively thought of one's moral views and political principles, if not self-made, as coming from one's religion. By contrast, the notion of a philosophically grounded idea of the good distinct from revelation has been uncommon. One's political principles have been understood as not so much derived from a natural source by deduction from sense experience, as directly or intuitively, in a way similar to religious truth, from "the Laws of Nature and of Nature's God." A Protestant notion of religion as immediate relation to God has been extended to the political order in a language of self-evidency that must seem very strange to anyone familiar with Aristotle or the history of logic. The "we hold these truths to be self-evident" of the Declaration of Independence is not presented as a set of propositions self-evident in a philosophical sense, but as something any human "just knows."

To say that America has the soul of a church is to remark on this tendency to run together under the heading of grace what from a Catholic viewpoint may be formally distinguished as natural and supernatural. This "failure to note boundaries" accounts for much that is often taken as most distinctively good about America, her traditions of generosity and philanthropy, for instance, which have never much bothered about the exact reasons one could give for government compelling a generosity in its citizenry, say in foreign aid, in excess of any requirement of justice. The Enlightenment project itself, aimed at the creation of a better and more just world, melded Christian and philosophic goals.[21] But perhaps the best illustration of the confusion of natural and supernatural is the way America conducts foreign policy and war, forever wavering be-

20. Schindler, "Christological Aesthetics," 210.

21. Bernard Bailyn, "An American Tragedy," *NYRB,* October 5, 1995.

tween a *realpolitik* or pragmatism that would gladden the heart of the most hardened European exponent of self-interest, and a high moralism in the tradition of Woodrow Wilson and Jimmy Carter, which sees America as bound to pursue not just the "self-evident" truths of the founding documents, but, in a Christian way, to reach beyond obligations of justice in the direction of self-sacrifice.

The American national faith is well illustrated by a weekly collection envelope illustration used each year around Independence Day in my parish, which superimposes a *corpus*-less cross on the stars and stripes, and above these, quotes 2 Corinthians 3:17: "Where the spirit of the Lord is there is liberty." This is a perfect icon of Catholicism in America. This American faith is founded as much on the Declaration of Independence and the Constitution as on any holy book. Its nature is confusing to Americans themselves: its easy use of the language of scripture and belief leads some to think Americans pervasively religious, while others, noting for instance how unwilling many Americans are to consider effective checks on market capitalism coming from the side of morality, let alone theology, believe that theirs is a religion with a dead God.[22] This American faith has interpreted and refashioned religion itself.

The American national faith is formed of a generic Protestant Christianity, deeply influenced by a Deist bracketing of God in which God is kept at some distance from especially the economic order, so that a materialistic life of this world may enthusiastically be pursued. This religion of a deeply secular people, a people conformed to their age and lacking almost all categories of transcendence and contemplation, "excessively concerned with efficiency," again to use the words of *Evangelium Vitae* (no. 12; cf. no. 64), is epitomized in the success of the ideas of Adam Smith in America: the robust, world-interfering and awe-inspiring God of pre-Enlightenment Christianity has been remade into a safe God, the clockmaker God of Deism, set back from an economic order that, as a kind of *vestigium Dei,* has

22. Schindler, "Christological Aesthetics," as at 211n31. Robert Wuthnow, ed., *Rethinking Materialism: Perspectives on the Spiritual Dimension of Economic Behavior* (Grand Rapids, Mich.: Eerdmans, 1995), suggests means of reversing fixation on the material.

its own "invisible hand." Praised is precisely that interpretation of the quality of life in terms of "economic efficiency" that *Evangelium Vitae* (no. 23) warns against.[23]

Whatever pious things are said to the present about guiding the economy by moral principles, much American Catholic thought pretty much accepts the capitalist, technological world as it is. Indeed, commonly it rejoices in that world, and even bends the teachings of the Church to be in service to it. The admission that the logic of the market, brought into our houses in televisions that play the pimp not just for our children, but, with their constant lies about what is necessary for a happy human life, for us, never leads anywhere. It makes only those adjustments from the side of religion that do not seriously impede worldly success. It has great difficulty in seriously engaging in discussion of things that would protect our children, of censorship and the like, for then goodness would have to triumph over freedom as an ordering principle. This intertwining of piety or moralizing and secularity or busyness is "the American way of life."

I now wish to pose a problem. My argument has been that a deep pluralism of incompatible world views or moralities undermines social life, but that cultural variation short of this often enriches life. Two generations ago John Courtney Murray observed that, although America lacked much of a formal natural law tradition, it had been formed from groups that shared much common ground in the ideas of good, often rooted in religion, that they brought to America. I take it that an anxiety that broods in the background of

23. Donald Worster, most recently in *The Wealth of Nature: Environmental History and the Ecological Imagination* (New York: Oxford University Press, 1993), has been developing an analysis of the culture of capitalism and its commodification of nature. His goal in a frontal attack on the "progressive, secular, and materialist philosophy" of the West during the last three centuries is "material simplicity and spiritual richness" (143). Richard White, "Back to Nature," *Reviews in American History* 22 (1994): 1–6, has generally shrewd things to say about the strengths and limitations of Worster's views. David Brion Davis, "Southern Comfort," *NYRB,* October 5, 1995, surveys the views of one of the most astute critics of the commercialization of life, Eugene Genovese. David L. Schindler's "Economics and the Civilization of Love," *Chesterton Review* 22 (1994): 189–211, is a splendid exposition that argues that the deficiencies of liberalism, specifically of Adam Smith, are rooted in a misunderstanding of human freedom.

his work is the possibility of the disintegration of this consensus, and that, since he died, his fears have been realized in the spread of a deep pluralism in which the churches themselves no longer agree on the most basic issues of life and death.[24] I have suggested that indiscriminate praise of pluralism is a disservice to life in society, and that Americans, who constantly try to make virtues out of the necessities stemming from their sectarian origins, have failed to achieve any measured understanding of all the issues involved in the question of pluralism. Because their highest social value has been liberty, they tend to unreserved praise of such things as religious toleration, without showing much self-understanding of all the ways they and all political regimes try to limit the effects of pluralism. To help pose my problem let me take an event not from America, but from Germany. On August 10, 1995, Germany's highest court ordered Bavaria to remove crucifixes from its classrooms, saying they were in violation of freedom of religion. Minister President Edmund Stoiber correctly noted that "The mere presence of a cross doesn't force anyone to accept Christian beliefs," and then somewhat lamely added "It's a symbol of our Western culture and values."[25] This is a story that could have occurred any place the culture of liberalism exists. On the one side we have a religion with a certain long-standing position in public life; on the other hand we have the fact of increasing religious diversity, in this case especially the growing number of Muslims in German schools. The majority on the German Constitutional Court took a line very familiar to Americans—that the public schools must as the state itself be religiously neutral. The dissenting minority (three of eight) took the view that schools reflect the values their communities hold, and that a crucifix did not exert unreasonable pressure on non-Christians. The question that I wish to consider is whether posing the problem the way the American Supreme Court has treated parallel questions does not end in one

24. See Martin F. Larrey, "John Courtney Murray: A Reappraisal," *Triumph* 7, no. 10 (December 1972): 20–23, at 22.

25. "No Crosses Allowed on School Walls," *Deseret News,* August 10, 1995. See also Leon Mangasarian, "Ban on Crosses Fuels Firestorm of Protest," *Deseret News,* August 19, 1995, which reports that "only 24 percent of all Germans support the crucifix ban."

more form of the establishment of religion, and therefore whether it is possible to have a religiously neutral state. If it is not, then the whole question of pluralism needs further consideration.

My argument is that the logic of absolute religious freedom and its attendant pluralism leads not just to the disestablishment of religion, but logically to the removal of every trace of it from public life. But such logic is not possible unless, as the first step, liberalism establishes itself as the state religion under the guise of neutrality, i.e., by saying that all other forms of belief must be disestablished. On the first point, if either conscience or the unencumbered self trumps all other moral considerations, the logic of society is one of unending disintegration. If there is one person who does not assent to some publicly sanctioned religious practice, and religious freedom means to have no external pressures toward conformity placed on oneself, then inevitably absolute religious freedom has to involve both unlimited pluralism and the quest for a claimed religiously neutral public order. But this presents a major natural problem, and a major supernatural problem. An absolute religious freedom, with its ever-dissolving pluralism, tends to make any *unum* impossible, and thus presents a natural danger to any state. In America this is hidden by such practices as teaching civics in the public school—that is, against the logic of religious freedom, by using the schools to inculcate specific values. This is one of the ways in which pluralism is affirmed while a given view of the world is taught. Not much protest is received because the religion civics teaches is the founding religion, national faith, or American way of life. Now I personally think the public schools should teach a politically and morally virtuous life, but this is only possible on the basis of natural law—that is, shared rules of evidence and argument, common assent to universal truths. My point is that one can either have deep pluralism, or one can have civics and public instruction in morality, but one cannot logically have both. Unless there is common agreement about the good, an agreement rooted not in religious revelation but in reason, the quintessential American question inevitably arises, "Whose morality is to be taught?" Unless this question is understood to be as silly as asking, "Whose geometry is to be taught?" because not seeing that the good is open to public inspection rather than a matter of individual creativity, it always reveals the impossibility of reconciling pluralism with an *unum*. If I may speak provocatively, if we really believe in a Protestant fashion that one's values come from one's religion, and that religious freedom should be absolute, then pornography is as American as apple pie. That is, the logic of such a position is to make all shared values impossible, to prohibit the legislation of any of them.

The irony is that the proposal of the so-called religiously neutral state as the only way to deal with deep pluralism itself establishes a religion and set of values. This is the religion of liberalism. It legislates on the nature of God himself, saying in effect that anything stronger than a Deist notion of the presence of God is to be removed from public life. It also legislates on the nature of what must not be believed. For instance, any religion that believes that it is to form all of human life—and this in fact includes all the historic so-called high religions—is circumscribed. The so-called religiously neutral state limits the practice of any such religion to an essentially private sphere. Alexis de Tocqueville's distinction between government and society has not proved very serviceable here, for, as the logic of the allegedly religiously neutral state has worked itself out, the government increasingly has enlarged that which is defined as public and subject to the laws of liberalism. Only the purely private and voluntary, by being socially marginalized, can evade this logic. Again, all high religions are driven from public life, and liberalism under the guise of neutrality becomes the established religion.

I cannot take this conundrum further here. It has no resolution without a rejection or radical rethinking of the notions of religious freedom and of the liberal state bequeathed by the Enlightenment. It is, however, an example of how much a criticism coming from the side of a Catholicism not itself suborned to the age could reveal about the logic at work in an especially advanced form in American history. John Paul II paved the way here, and not just for America. What he aimed at was the use of the language and concerns of modern thought, either to correct from the inside its own most grievous errors, or from the outside by the introduction of a theological perspective to recast the issues. Thus, using the modern world's own language of human rights, John Paul showed the inadequacy of a notion of human freedom in which freedom does not exist for truth.[26] He showed that we may indeed use the language of rights, but only if we are more honest than a modern liberalism and legal positivism that retain the notion of inalienable rights while rejecting the ground out of which these rights historically developed, "a common shared notion of transcendent norms such as natural or divine laws."[27]

An admission is in order, though. Although the Church at its center has increasingly articulated a legitimate political sense of the many and of the one, it has, beginning with Vatican II, passed through a period of some uncertainty during which, arguably, it insufficiently pursued a project so magnificently begun in the age of Pius IX and Leo XIII: namely, the criticism of liberalism. *Dignitatis Humanae,* the Declaration on Religious Freedom, and all the discussion generated as to its meaning and continuity or lack of continuity with past teaching, symbolize this uncertainty. The same Church teaching that recently has been so full and satisfying in trying to reconnect freedom to truth has had less to say about the social means to such reconnection, especially when they are necessarily illiberal. *Evangelium Vitae,* for instance, in laying part of the blame for the decay of moral conscience on society itself and its toleration of the behavior of the culture of death (no. 24), comes just to the point at which it could have concluded to censorship as a social good, and then explored that subject. Instead it throws the reader back on the voice of God in the individual conscience. Even where censorship is addressed, as in the treatment of the Eighth Commandment in the *Catechism of the Catholic Church,* the treatment, though on the side

26. Kenneth L. Schmitz, *At the Center of the Human Drama: The Philosophical Anthropology of Karol Wojtyla/Pope John Paul II,* with an appendix by John M. Grondelski (Washington, D.C.: The Catholic University of America Press, 1993).

27. These are the words of Robert C. Figueira in a lucid review, *Speculum* 70 (1995): 667–71, of a book by Kenneth Pennington, *The Prince and the Law, 1200–1600: Sovereignty and Rights in the Western Legal Tradition.*

of the angels, is undeveloped. Thus, citing *Inter Mirifica,* the *Catechism* (no. 2498) states "by promulgating laws and overseeing their application, public authorities should ensure that 'public morality and social progress are not gravely endangered' through misuse of the media."[28] The sentences immediately following, however, deal with the defense of such individual rights as reputation and privacy.

Often in Church history, lack of clarity in ecclesiastical documents mirrors contemporary lack of philosophical clarity, and this may be the case here. Since Vatican II the Church has in some areas more asserted than shown the continuity of its teachings. In spite of many deepenings of insight and introductions of new considerations, it has not always been clear how these are developments of doctrine, rather than departures from earlier teachings. For instance, a person who has studied the encyclicals of Leo XIII in all their clarity might well be puzzled by some of the things said in *Dignitatis Humanae.* Sometimes one wonders whether certain passages of the Conciliar documents have been so well received because they have a false clarity about them, achieved by ignoring half of what a pope such as Leo took as relevant to the question.

An analysis of the failure of John Courtney Murray to place religious freedom on a secure foundation and to solve the church-state problem could at points be applied to the development of papal teaching itself. Keith J. Pavlischek suggests that a kind of halfway house in the transition from saying "error has no rights" to the exposition of religious freedom he believes characteristic of *Dignitatis Humanae* be named the *modus vivendi* approach.[29] This approach assumes that the members of any political community will have varying ideas of the good, but that a convergence of rational support for central institutions is a *sine qua non* for a shared life together. Granted this, people may agree to disagree. They can live together by the *modus vivendi* of religious toleration, which they do not see as a basic good, but as something necessary for each to pursue his view of reality without too much compromise. I will frankly say that, grant-

28. *Catechism of the Catholic Church* (Vatican City: Libreria Editrice Vaticana, 1994).
29. See note 18. I am using Craycraft's review in what follows.

ed everything I have already said about the impossibility of a religiously neutral state, I remain to be convinced that, without further clarification, the views of *Dignitatis Humanae* represent an advance on this position, which I would personally tie to an "accommodationist" approach to the church-state question.[30] Indeed Pavlischek's analysis of Murray concludes that in the end Murray tended to return to the *modus vivendi.*

Pavlischek calls the view of Vatican II the "moral Esperanto" approach. Though this label seems to have originated in Jeffrey Stout's conclusion that foundationalist positions are no longer viable, and may also reflect Presbyterian dislike for natural law positions on Pavlischek's part, it seems fair enough. The moral Esperanto approach seeks to ground religious freedom foundationally or transcendentally on a common and objectively true understanding of the good, and to see religious freedom as itself a basic good. Attractive as this may be, any application of it seems to me involved in the kind of problems I have been articulating throughout this chapter. Above all, to be more than an ideal, it needs a consensus that religious freedom is a basic good; more fundamentally, that there are basic goods on which there can be wide agreement. The principles of religious freedom and toleration must be themselves universal. Now, it is no argument against the universality of something that not all recognize it: Some people do not know that 2 and 2 equal 4. But the whole point of the "culture of death" is that in the last two centuries the kind of epistemological foundationalism that would make the moral Esperanto approach capable of wide implementation has largely disappeared. That is, while *Dignitatis Humanae* articulated religious freedom as a basic good, it insufficiently spoke to a fundamental fact of the contemporary world of which the encyclical tradition itself is fully cognizant—that natural law positions, positions that articulate basic goods, have long been in retreat and are in many quarters not understood. This retreat has been ever more marked in the years since the Conciliar document was written. This

30. See my "Separating Church and State," *Faith and Reason* 20 (1994): 403–25 (chapter 6 of this volume).

allowed, *Dignitatis Humanae* did not give very specific guidance to Christians living in political democracies of deep pluralism in which a majority of people are incapable of recognizing a common good. Such guidance would presumably of its nature have had to be illiberal, because insisting that all human dealings are bound by the moral law (no. 7), and aiming at the goal of reducing moral pluralism. Not only did *Dignitatis Humanae* not give such guidance, it did not implicate political democracy very directly in our inability to achieve general recognition of basic goods.[31] One could read *Veritatis Splendor* and *Evangelium Vitae* as having now been franker that, although there is no other alternative, a natural law position cannot work under these conditions. In an obvious sense this is everyone's problem, for part of the debate between the *Modus Vivendi* and Moral Esperanto positions is about the extent of the implicitly natural law ground that must exist in society, specifically whether this includes a basic right to freedom of religion. In sum, the moral Esperanto approach, as it had developed to the time of *Dignitatis Humanae,* does justify the part of natural law and/or true religion trying to educate and influence public life, but does not explain how, in any world at least an American can reasonably hope for, we can ever have more than a *modus vivendi.*

As has been suggested, *Evangelium Vitae,* with its strong condemnation of (1) majoritarian violations of the natural law (no. 20; cf. nos. 69–71); (2) the idea that the law should always express what the majority wills (nos. 68–69, 71); (3) a pluralism that holds that the government cannot impose any specific moral view (no. 68) and that

31. I use the expression "political democracy" in the way *Evangelium vitae* no. 70 speaks of democracy as a "system," as a means or mechanism to an end but not an end in itself. The worth of democracy in this sense is not intrinsic, but dependent on conformity to the moral law (see the following paragraph in my text). *Evangelium vitae* no. 101 offers a standard for "true democracy," namely respect for life, which America does not meet. Commonly for the popes, "democracy" refers to a constitutional order that recognizes universal human rights anterior to and above the state and the reason for treating all as equal before the law: this is similar to the founding American ideal of government as established to ensure natural rights. *Evangelium vitae* no. 57 takes the absolute equality of one human life to another as the basis, not just of the right to life, but of all social relationships. For obvious reasons, the encyclical tradition hardly attends to specific mechanisms of government.

democracy must be founded on moral relativism (nos. 70–71); and (4) a totalitarianism of the strong against the weak to which democracy is liable (nos. 12, 20, 70), seems, though accepting democracy as a "sign of the times" (no. 70), and despite an occasional pulling of punches, to be a considerable return to frankness. The encyclical raises a whole series of questions that reveal the incoherency of the radical liberal ideal of a society organized to facilitate moral pluralism. It also strongly denounces the logic that ends in the individual at least selectively renouncing the obligation to follow conscience when employed in public business (nos. 69, 71), the path routinely taken now in America by "personally opposed, but . . ." politicians.

Most directly (no. 70), *Evangelium Vitae* leaves no doubt that:

> If, as a result of a tragic obscuring of the collective conscience, an attitude of skepticism were to succeed in bringing into question even the fundamental principles of the moral law, the democratic system itself would be shaken in its foundations, and would be reduced to a mere mechanism for regulating different and opposing interests on a purely empirical basis. . . . Without an objective moral grounding . . . democracy easily becomes an empty word.

This of course has already occurred in the form of liberalism that I am calling radical liberalism, but is the outcome of any unrestricted pluralism. In the same encyclical Pope John Paul even addressed the means by which a society may legitimately defend itself from the dissolution of its grounding in objective good. He stated (no. 71) that "the legal toleration of abortion or of euthanasia can in no way claim to be based on respect for the conscience of others, precisely because society has the right and the duty to protect itself against the abuses which can occur in the name of conscience and under the pretext of freedom." We seem here to be back in Leonine territory, with illiberal principles again in place, and certain readings of *Dignitatis Humane* disallowed.

When Leo XIII began the tradition of the social encyclicals, he was unafraid to say very unpopular things about the measures a society needed to take to be as good as an earthly society can be. He was unafraid to address questions such as whether limitations may be placed on freedom of the press, whether society is obliged to practice censorship, and whether the historical goal where possible is the establishment of Catholicism as the truest religion. Like Pius IX, he was unafraid to come down, at least in some degree, on the illiberal side of these questions. Instinctively, at the center of his thought was not the liberal model of a rational citizenry choosing the best course of action through access to unlimited information and discussion, but the idea of a more wounded humankind, in which the average person simply is disinclined to pursue very far the duties of citizenship as defined by liberalism and political democracy. Since Leo XIII, liberalism in one or the other of its forms has become such a fact of life in the West that it has created a climate of opinion in which to attack risks one's credibility. It seems that John Paul as a man of hope took this risk.

Although Leo XIII saw freedom as a *sine qua non* without which goodness cannot exist, the whole direction of his thought, *contra* the liberal tradition and the American value system, ranked goodness higher than freedom. It was not that one could have the former without the latter, but that Leo had not been taken in by liberal notions of autonomy, and had a strong sense, as strong as Augustine's or Newman's, of the role of external circumstance in human formation. He understood that all human choices are made from within history and that the whole Cartesian or Enlightenment notion of a choice free from all determination was written in the language of mathematics, not of history and politics. The popes since Leo XIII have never failed to rank goodness above freedom, or to see the only proper freedom as one that aims at the good. Still, if I may indicate one more area that may need attention, there seems to me sometimes an unguarded or unintegrated quality in some of their more recent statements in which the majesty of man's origin and final end stand out to the neglect of full examination of man's present predicaments as a fallen being. Thus, while *Evangelium Vitae* (no. 38) notes that eternal life (only) begins to spring forth in our earthly state, and (nos. 50, 103–04) makes it clear that the struggle between light and darkness continues to the end, that is, fills history, it also (no. 29) speaks of man as capable of "'knowing' the *complete truth* concerning the value of human life" and having "the capacity to 'accomplish' this truth perfectly." These are true and precious statements about man's nature and destiny, but they leave unraised many questions about the here and now, where there is incompleteness of knowledge and imperfection of will. In some ways, the logic of openness to the world and of speaking a language the world understands, pursued since the Council (see *Veritatis Splendor* no. 29), has involved laying stress on the splendor of the Christian view of what man may be, something the modern mind can identify with, at the expense of the Christian memory of what man has been and of how the political order must cope with this, sobering thoughts many moderns wish to avoid or deny. It is not that documents such as *Veritatis Splendor* (no. 17) do not lay down Pauline and Augustinian perspectives in which perfect freedom is impossible in time, but that what follows from such perspectives is not fully developed.

However the question of the need for further development of the encyclical tradition itself is understood, one could wish that American exposition of it would catch up with what already has been said. Before Vatican II there was a tradition in America of, when publishing study editions of the papal encyclicals, underlining certain passages not underlined in the original. Upon examination, such passages commonly underwrote things in which Americans already believed. Presumably, Americans thus were encouraged to see the papal statements as sanctioning their way of life. Even the best American theologians sometimes still give us variations on this. Avery Dulles, for instance, wrote an exposition of the development of John Paul II's understanding of freedom, which, while very fine on the positive meaning of freedom, left out almost every hard question that John Paul II raised about how "freedom" actually functions today.[32] Were one to accept Dulles' survey of the pope's writ-

32. Avery Dulles, "John Paul II and the Truth about Freedom," *First Things,* no. 55 (August-September 1995): 36–41. Dulles did cite John Courtney Murray to the effect that any public consensus, understood as a doctrine that commands agreement because of its intrinsic merit, must be accepted by the people (40), and notes that Murray rejected a majoritarian notion of truth and, implicitly, deep pluralism as I have defined it.

ings on this subject as thorough, one would have little idea of how many reservations John Paul II himself raised about the working of "freedom" and democracy. In Dulles' exposition we seem still to have selective reading through American eyes.[33]

Few Americans seem capable of looking at the historical record and asking the simple question of when consensus of any form has flourished most, and when least. The Enlightenment myth is that unfettered access to information and freedom of discussion throughout society ferret out the truth and foster consensus based on this truth. Leaving aside the fact that this is a strange myth, for it implicitly acknowledges that the goal is agreement in the truth and not pluralism, it seems to go against observation. The study of American history should have led to the opposite conclusion, for in America there was the most agreement when churches were established and morals written into the law, and religious freedom was hedged about by considerations of what was thought the common good. The more open discussion has become and the more information has become available, the more disagreement and pluralism have appeared and the further we are from unanimity. In a general way, as in Athens long ago, unlimited discussion in America has tended to the breakdown of consensus, to a growing refusal to acknowledge "unwritten laws," to a Euripidean "anything goes." If we hold Murray to his idea that democracy depends on the virtue of its citizens, then it is sick indeed. The experiment seems to have failed, and pluralism daily to make this failure deeper and more irreversible.

One of the greatest tasks facing the Catholic in America is to find ways by which Catholicism can prod Americans to think about their own culture in ways they have not. I have tried to give some illustration here. The pope remains a lightning rod for the hopes and hostility of the world. He tries to mark a path forward, and thus disturbs all that is most comfortable and resistant to self-examination.

33. A fully annotated version of Dulles, "John Paul II and the Truth about Freedom," 36, and now titled *Truth as the Ground of Freedom: A Theme from John Paul II,* is available as an Acton Institute Occasional Paper (Grand Rapids, Mich.: Acton Institute, 1997).

The Catholic task in America is to be much more countercultural than previously, much more conscious of the ways in which assimilation has meant selling one's soul and birthright; if need be, to be as hated for telling the truth as is the pope. The Christian is told he must be in but not of the world, and we could do well to exclaim with the reformers through the ages, "Christ said, 'I am the truth.' He did not say, 'I am the custom,' but 'I am the Truth.'"[34]

AFTERWORD

This chapter perhaps most clearly announces the political and social aspects of the argument developed in my *The Turn to Transcendence: The Role of Religion in the Twenty-First Century.* This book also treats the growing claims in recent scholarship for the presence of natural law thinking in early Protestantism; see my "The Natural Law: The First Grace." J. Hoberman, "Orphan of History," tells the tale of twentieth-century disillusionment with progressive/utopian categories; see also William Pfaff, *The Irony of Manifest Destiny: The Tragedy of America's Foreign Policy.* One link in the ever-evolving history of definitions of "liberty" is treated in Quentin Skinner, *Hobbes and Republican Liberty,* on which see Blair Worden, "Hobbes and the Halo of Power." See also the discussion of the role of individualism and libertarianism in contemporary America by Mark Lilla, "The Tea Party Jacobins." Lilla rightly sees that trust in government is declining in all advanced democracies because mediating ideas and institutions are disappearing, but does not adequately see the role of pluralism in this. Walter Brandmüller, *Light and Shadows: Church History amid Faith, Fact and Legend, translated by Michael J. Miller,* notes that the revolutionary calendar of 1790

34. Glenn W. Olsen, "Cultural Dynamics: Secularization and Sacralization," *Christianity and Western Civilization,* ed. The Wethersfield Institute (San Francisco: Ignatius Press, 1995), 97–122, is a meditation on Philippians 2:5–16. The formula quoted goes back to Tertullian and was especially the cry of the Gregorian reformers: Gerhard B. Ladner, "Two Gregorian Letters on the Sources and Nature of Gregory VII's Reform Ideology," in his *Images and Ideas in the Middle Ages: Selected Studies in History and Art* (Rome: Edizioni di Storia e Letteratura, 1983), 2:665–86 at 669–86.

counted years of liberty rather than of salvation. There is a second edition of *The Catechism of the Catholic Church.* The discussion of the compatibility of democracy, rights theory, and Catholicism has become more pointed in the wake of Robert P. Kraynak, *Christian Faith and Modern Democracy,* discussed in especially chapter 6 of my *Turn to Transcendence;* see also Ian Linden, *Global Catholicism: Diversity and Change since Vatican II.* On the idea of "civil religion," see Ronald Weed and John von Heyking, eds., *Civil Religion in Political Thought: Its Perennial Questions and Enduring Relevance in North America.* On the illiberal aspects of study of identity, ethnic or otherwise, see Tony Judt, "Crossings."

8

AMERICA AS AN ENLIGHTENMENT CULTURE

THE UNITED STATES remains a puzzle to itself and to others. On the one hand, no country, not France itself, is so obviously the offspring of the Enlightenment and the revolutionary ideals of the late eighteenth century. On the other hand, America has not inaptly been described as "a nation with the soul of a church," and even today one will likely misperceive motives if one forgets how decisive the Calvinist heritage has been in forming American views of the world. Down to the present in the United States such Enlightenment values as individual autonomy, equality, and reason stand alongside religious patrimonies stressing community, authority, and the importance of tradition.[1] The two heritages were already entwined in the Colonial period, and have stood in a symbiotic relation ever since. The goal of this chapter is to examine the nature of this relationship: the way in which in America Enlightenment ideals and religion have related to and reshaped each other and have become locked in a perpetual dance, with the Enlightenment the leading partner.

In part because of what the polls say, namely that America remains the most religious industrialized modern country in the world, some are tempted to see religion as the dominant shaper of American history to the present, and the ideals of the Enlightenment as of lesser

1. William M. Shea and Peter A. Huff, eds., *Knowledge and Belief in American Enlightenment Traditions and Modern Religious Thought* (New York: publisher unknown, 1995), trace the interaction throughout American history.

importance.[2] One can not be dogmatic here, but the argument of this chapter is that the reverse is true. It is not just that in America Judaism and Christianity have been refashioned to the Enlightenment—that has happened everywhere. The argument is that the ideas that gave birth and form to America and are caught in her founding and defining documents, the Declaration of Independence and Constitution, with the Bill of Rights, more centrally express Enlightenment than earlier Christian or Jewish ideas, and place the Enlightenment at the birth and defining moment of America. The unity of most nations is found in a common language, culture, or religion, but America is founded on a proposition.[3]

The very idea of taking polls seriously, and of attempting to assess religion by them, is witness to the influence of the Enlightenment. One might state as an axiom that the more complex the subject matter, the more unlikely a poll will be able to gauge it. Only a son or daughter of the Enlightenment could think that polls measure anything of complexity and depth with any precision; that serious questions can be examined by polls. Anyone with a Christian sense of original sin and the mysteriousness of human life—that is, with a developed sense of human duplicity and of the complexity of all questions—is not likely to lay much weight on polls. They, with newspapers, are attended to by a type of human being the twentieth century perfected, and with television and cyberspace continues to perfect, what Georges Bernanos called the imbecile.[4]

2. Gary Wills, "A Tale of Three Leaders," *New York Review of Books,* September 19, 1996, in treating a number of themes relevant to the present essay, considers the abiding place of religion in America. When John Courtney Murray, *We Hold These Truths: Catholic Reflections on the American Proposition* (1960; repr. New York: Sheed and Ward, 1985), 39, writes "The American Bill of Rights is not a piece of eighteenth-century rationalist theory; it is far more the product of Christian history. Behind it one can see, not the philosophy of the Enlightenment but the older philosophy that had been the matrix of the common law," he seems to me to have gotten the accent wrong. Murray's analysis seems to me itself accommodated to Enlightenment principles, and has rightly been described (see notes 8 and 19 below) as itself an exercise in the liberal tradition.

3. This was suasively argued by Christopher Dawson, on whom see Glenn W. Olsen, "American Culture and Liberal Ideology in the Thought of Christopher Dawson," *Communio* 22 (1995): 702–20

4. Hans Urs von Balthasar, *Bernanos: An Ecclesial Existence*, trans. Erasmo Leiva-Merikakis (San Francisco: Ignatius Press, 1996), 358–68 at 358–49, 364–65: "To be sure,

Though both the Enlightenment and religion are powerful currents in American history, one better understands the arc of American history, what America has become, if one sees the social and political beliefs of the European Enlightenment as in America a grid to which all else must be adjusted.[5] In many Continental European countries, by contrast, especially countries in which there was once a strong Catholic presence at the center of national life, there continue to be what might be spoken of as two parties, two Frances or two Spains. The parties of the Enlightenment are in the ascendancy virtually everywhere, but the parties of tradition are not so broken or reconciled to modernity that they stop offering radical critique of modern mass consumer society. Things are hardly ever clear here, because the conflict between the two parties rarely translates into choice between Right and Left, and the parties of dissent typically speak from within modern technological society—that is, as themselves compromised. Still, even that very middle class and selective dissident Margaret Thatcher had enough sense of the issues, in an unwonted show of humor, to give François Mitterand a copy of Dickens' *A Tale of Two Cities* in commemoration of the Bicentennial

---

there have always been dumb people. But their dumbness was somehow sheltered and neutralized by being contained within a very broad sociological framework erected by the not-dumb, which imperceptibly communicated even to the existence of the dumb a certain rightness and reasonableness. But what if the imbeciles should gain the upper hand and become the ones who erect the framework for all? . . . this state of affairs . . . is in fact the modern development. . . . The infantile ideologies that have been substituted for an adult conception of the world, with all their 'right' and 'left' and other idiotic classifications, constitute the imbeciles' normal ersatz for thought. . . . They are one and all half-cultured individuals, at least at the level that is decisive for Bernanos: 'Experience has long since shown me that imbeciles are never simple and only rarely ignorant. Should the intellectual, then, by definition be suspect? For sure! . . . I am obviously not speaking of the scientist, the artist, or the writer, whose vocation is to create and for whom intelligence is not a profession but a vocation. . . . The intellectual is so frequently an imbecile that we should always take him to be such until he has proved to us the contrary.' He is particularly at home in the modern world of technology and numbers. In such a world he can climb to very high positions without giving away his half-culture. . . . Throughout his life Bernanos listened to the voice of the imbecile. Vallery-Radot tells us the following: 'He would knock at my door at about nine in the morning, his pockets stuffed with newspapers. He always had a passion for newspapers. . . . Newspapers were his connection with the hundred-mouthed voice of Stupidity, which the creators of the great Press can call 'public opinion' with a straight face."

5. For the most part, this chapter must concentrate on the social and political ideas of the Enlightenment rather than on its critical heritage in learning, literature, and science.

of the French Revolution. In America, in comparison, though there have long been populist movements of dissent from, say, big government seen as a threat to individual liberty, these overwhelmingly have believed in the founding documents and values of the country. The largest such present-day group in the United States, the so-called Religious Right, virtually never suggests that the Enlightenment values of the American founding documents are flawed, superficial, and time-bound. None but marginalized thinkers pursue the American equivalent of European discussion of whether the French Revolution was a bad thing: probably some homeschoolers come the closest. Rather, the American Religious Right commonly wishes to recover the values of the founding documents, just as the Left wishes to extend them. These are not seen by the Right as in conflict with their religious views, because their religious views have so long been placed in service of the American way of life."[6]

Our argument can be clarified by turning to definitions and a brief survey of the founding moment in the history of the United States. The religious component in American life from the beginning hardly needs remarking. America was founded by peoples coming from a European age of faith who brought to the New World the seventeenth-century assumption that they would practice true religion in a public manner shaping all of life. From the beginning the Calvinist tradition had a special prominence. The doctrine of election was strong, and Americans saw what they formed as a light set on a hill for the nations. Though such ideas were the special preserve of preachers and governors, and the level of actual religious practice in pre-Revolutionary America often indifferent, America was from the first a country molded by Protestantism. Reception of the Enlightenment emphases on individual autonomy and equality was prepared in America by the dominance of a form of Protestantism that had originated on the margins of English life and

6. For the origins of this expression in the mid-twentieth century to describe the American melding of Enlightenment and religion, see the still pertinent analysis of Will Herberg, *Protestant, Catholic, Jew: An Essay in American Religious Sociology,* with a new introduction by Martin G. Marty (Chicago: University of Chicago Press, 1983).

carried with it a certain instinctive anti-authoritarianism. While encouraging of respect for its own traditions and authority, the anti-episcopalism and anti-monarchism of Puritanism prepared the way for later American attitudes that burst out in the Revolutionary period, and remain in the common refusal to understand democratic man under the heading of the imbecile.

Today license plates in the state of New Hampshire still bear the motto "Live Free or Die," making Cadillacs the bearers of the Revolutionary sentiment famously associated with Patrick Henry and Ethan Allen. This sentiment did not simply stand at the heart of American Revolutionary consciousness in the later eighteenth century, but promoted the element of the Enlightenment inheritance that has remained most central to the American experience to the present: *liberté*—liberty or freedom. This above all Americans continue to invoke. Thus a very striking series of legal decisions, running from *Planned Parenthood v. Casey* through and beyond *Compassion in Dying v. State of Washington,* have asserted that each American has the right to make up his or her own morality and understanding of the universe. In the words of Casey: "At the heart of liberty is the right to define one's own concept of existence, of meaning, of the universe, and of the mystery of human life."[7] One may doubt that people of the late eighteenth century, who still believed in "nature and nature's laws," would fully assent to such "creative antirealism," which makes the human subject the central architect of the universe, of its structure and nature, but clearly liberty remains the central value of the tradition from which such a pronouncement could come.[8] In this sense Herman Melville's poetics of individualism or Walt

7. Quoted approvingly by Ronald Dworkin, "Sex, Death and the Courts," *New York Review of Books,* August 8, 1996, at 46, in an article that seems wholly unconscious of the problems caused for the law itself by the abandonment of any notion of objective good. Such abandonment is of course necessary to continue the liberal project of allowing mothers to define their "own concept of existence" by defining their unborn children out of existence, and Dworkin does see *Roe v. Wade* as the source of the latest campaign on behalf of "liberty."

8. "Creative antirealism" is an expression of Alvin Plantinga, taken up by David L. Schindler, *Heart of the World, Center of the Church: "Communio" Ecclesiology, Liberalism, and Liberation* (Grand Rapids, Mich.: Eerdmans, 1996), 158–59.

Whitman's "Song of Myself," with its placement of oneself above all institutions, expressed quintessential American sentiments.

The Enlightenment had stood for many things, reason, natural rights, and limited government among them. But in America, important as these other things were, special weight was and has always been assigned to the first member of the French revolutionary triad "liberty, equality, fraternity." Indeed, like the flattened Trinitarianism of Calvinism itself, with its conception of the relations between the divine persons as essentially extrinsic rather than circumincessive, "liberty," the goal of the Revolution, held pride of place from the first; "equality," a preoccupation from the 1790s expressed in the struggle between Federalists and Republicans capped by the victory of democratic views in Jefferson's election in 1800, came next, and could be invoked almost independently of liberty as well as in relation to it; and "fraternity" remained a rather indistinct idea.[9]

The Enlightenment refashioning of Christianity can be no better seen than in what God became for the Americans. In America the Augustinian "God and the soul" has been recast so that God, that is the Father, is taken out of his Trinitarian context and the soul—that is, the individual—out of its ecclesiological context. The Father does not so much exist within a Trinitarian life of love or communion, or the soul within the Body of Christ, as both exist in a kind of majestic isolation or autonomy, extrinsically related to one another.[10] The heart of religion is an uncontextualized and unmediated "God and the soul," eminently suited to a nation of individualists who above all prize their liberty, and are especially susceptible to the notion that religion can flourish without religious institutions—that is, is a direct noninstitutional, nonsacramental affair between "God and the soul." Calvinism and Deism prepared the way here, and we must turn to them to understand further aspects of the refashioning of God.

9. Gordon S. Wood. "The Would-Be Gentleman," *NYRB,* August 8, 1996, lays out the issues of the 1790s; see also Wood, *The Radicalism of the American Revoution* (New York: A. A. Knopf, 1991).

10. In classical theological language, the "immanent" Trinity is neglected in favor of the "economic" Trinity.

In America, as is evident in the greatest pre-Revolutionary American thinker, Jonathan Edwards, Calvinism stood in close alliance with the Newtonian view of the world, and as elsewhere took the form of what Max Weber called "ascetic rationalism."[11] The ancient and medieval Christian view had been that God is love, a love that fills and forms all things interiorly, so that nothing bodily can be adequately described as inanimate.[12] Soul, as Aristotle had said, is the form of the body. Causation, as Aristotle also had said, was not something merely exterior to effects (as material and, from a certain point of view, efficient causation are), but something also interior (as formal and final causation are). Teleology describes the fact that objects that lack will, such as acorns, nevertheless of their nature invariably become oaks if they become anything. Goal-seeking is built into them. Such a view had been swept away by Newton with the dogmatic fiat necessary to create a radically simplified and mechanized cosmos in which the central category was the mathematically measurable. God was retained, but not a God who works interiorly to all things, for matter is declared to have no "interior" in which to work. Every thing, humans themselves, is thought of "individualistically," or mechanistically—that is, as standing to other things primitively only by external relations. Matter is dead, suitable only to measurement and manipulation.

This was a development suitable to the Americans, who had a wilderness to tame. Thinking of the world as created by love and

11. This is well brought out in the classic, if in a number of aspects dated, studies of Perry Miller, *Jonathan Edwards* (New York: W. Skoane, 1949); and Miller, *The New England Mind,* 2 vols. (1953; 2nd ed. Boston: Beacon Press, 1965). For orientation to the newer scholarship on Edwards, see John E. Smith, "Puritanism and Enlightenment: Edwards and Franklin," in *Knowledge and Belief in American Enlightenment Traditions and Modern Religious Thought,* ed. William M. Shea and Peter A. Huff (New York: publisher unknown, 1995), at 197–211. See on both Weber and the interdependence of Puritanism and science, Robert K Merton, *Science, Technology and Society in Seventeenth Century England,* 2nd ed. (New York: H. Fertig, 1970), esp. ix–xxiv, and chaps. 4–6, and Merton, *The Sociology of Science: Theoretical and Empirical Investigations,* ed. Norman W. Storer (Chicago: University of Chicago Press, 1973), esp. 173–90, 223–53.

12. Schindler, *Heart of the World,* 14–16, 161–62, 165–66, 171–72, following Plantinga, contrasts naturalist and antirealist (see note 8) views of the world with the Christian view. Plantinga, a Calvinist, has in his own thought recovered the view that love is the structure of the universe.

filled with immeasurable mystery encourages awe, contemplation, and worship, not the attributes needed for success in America. Much more suitable was the Newtonian world in which, though an awe inspired by mathematics remained, power-seeking knowledge replaced contemplation. In spite of much language about atonement—that is, about the Second Person of the Trinity, the leading Calvinist image of God was of the Father, conceived under the attributes of Creator and Judge. Here, whether in Europe or America, an active culture, evermore stressing creativity rather than receptivity, received an appropriate God. The promise was that knowledge gives power, and for this nature was best conceived as something apart from God and man—"raw material." As Walt Whitman would proclaim in a passage uniting materialism, individualism, and quest for freedom:

> Hurrah for positive science! long live exact demonstration! . . .
> Gentlemen, to you the first honors always!
> Your facts are useful, and yet they are not my dwelling,
> I but enter by them to an area of my dwelling.
> Less the reminders of properties told my words,
> And more the reminders they of life untold, and of freedom.[13]

The Marian dimension of religion, spousal, receptive, and contemplative, almost disappeared from the busy world of the Calvinist and American God, though in a host of counterattacks—the Great Awakenings, Transcendentalism, Romanticism, the devotional life of Catholic immigrants, Theosophy, the Catholic Worker movement, environmentalism, the New Age cults—a plethora of correctives or alternatives continue to be offered for the narrow definitions of reason and man bequeathed by the Enlightenment.[14]

Calvinism and Deism share much in common. Calvinism had already made God "unitarian," effectively imaged under the head-

13. Walt Whitman, "Song of Myself," *Leaves of Grass,* introduction by Gay Wilson Allen (New York: publisher unknown, 1958), 67, line 23.

14. Many of the points made in this and the last paragraphs are in one way or another related to the most astute analysis of America ever made from the viewpoint of theology: Schindler, *Heart of the World,* esp. 166–69.

ing of Creator. What remained was to set him back from matter in a temporal as well as relational manner, to see Creation as "at the beginning" rather than, as in ancient or medieval theology, an ongoing process in which the world is dependent on God for its existence at every moment. Newton's view of matter greatly aided this "setting back" of God from the Creation, and we might almost say that in it the watchmaker God, and thus Deism, was born. Here we have "limited government" of the world, an analogue for the political order, and an attenuating of the medieval natural law tradition, formerly an expression of God's reason as it fills the universe and holds all to the "common good," into what by the time of the Bill of Rights became a short list of natural rights centered on the autonomous individual. Theology and politics suit the times, and, had not similar developments taken place in Europe, we could say that the American theology had been born. What this means—as Nietzsche so clearly saw—was that wherever this process took place, Christianity was placed less "at the heart of things," was partly removed from the world so that a profitable worldly life might be lived. People continued to go to church, but God was for them emaciated, if not quite dead. In America even fewer than in Europe noticed that Christianity had been refashioned. Perhaps ante bellum Southerners noticed in unusually large numbers: Eugene Genovese has a point when he says that Southerners perceived social relations in the North—what we describe as capitalism—as intrinsically revolutionary and undermining of traditional values.[15]

This said, almost all churches in America identified Christianity with the ideas promoted in the founding documents. Lacking a Catholic sense of belonging to a universal communion, which sometimes has fostered a certain reserve in viewing the claims and achievements of one's own country, the churches in America promoted the American way of life almost without reserve. While many in Europe stopped going to church, in nineteenth-century

15. Eugene Genovese in an interview by Bill Kauffman and Scott Walter, "Eugene Genovese and Elizabeth Fox-Genovese," *The American Enterprise* (September/October 1996): 21–25, at 23.

America fewer stopped going. Certainly neighborliness and other communitarian notions continued to be valued in America, but Christianity was understood to bless a world centered on liberty, the individual, and creativity, especially in the form of hard work.

In America there has never been an integralism of the European form—that is, a political life in which the juridical structures of Christianity have been extended to the state to give not just an established religion, but an institutional integration of religious and political life. However one reads the First Amendment to the Constitution, it does mandate a kind of dualism basic to American life, in which the political order and religion are envisaged as each having its own integrity or freedom. The two orders may talk to one another, but it is not foreseen that they will integrate. This said, the argument is that *de facto* there has been a form of integralism in America in which the union of religion and the Constitutional tradition around Enlightenment ideals has achieved a society as united in what it gives assent to as anything found in Europe. Indeed, whereas in Europe, precisely because there has been so much struggle between the parties of tradition and of Enlightenment, people generally are aware that there are choices to be made and sides to be taken, Americans, especially those whom Alasdair MacIntyre has called liberal liberals, have been quite unconscious of the ways in which America has a *de facto* integralism.[16]

In an Anglo-Saxon manner, in America liberal liberalism has presented itself as a neutral method or procedure, a level playing field, open to any democratically determined content, without acknowledging that things like the First Amendment foreclose America to the European forms of integralism while mandating an American or liberal form of integralism.[17] American integralism is

16. See the following two paragraphs and note 19.

17. The points made in this and the last paragraphs are a reflection on Schindler, *Heart of the World,* 153–54, 161–65, who, in studying another matter, the incoherency of the liberal understanding of the university, traces the ideal of methodological neutrality back to Descartes and argues, 154: "liberalism's purported pure form is already the expression of a definite content . . . there are no instances of purely formal, hence neutral, methodological procedures, in the way claimed by liberalism; . . . on the contrary, all methodological procedures, insofar as they claim to mean anything at all . . . imply and thus are shaped

not neutral, but favors liberty against other possible ordering values, such as goodness, and has the effect of privatizing whatever in religion goes beyond the Enlightenment heritage.[18] We might call it a cultural rather than institutional integralism but for the paradoxical fact that, by specifying that there may be no establishment of religion, the First Amendment walls off all institutions of government, and especially the law, from any significant transformation by religion. To explain a paradox with a paradox and in a European language, we may say that government is saved for the lay party, if we remember that in America the lay party includes virtually everyone, those who practice religion and those who do not. Virtually no one wants the inconvenience of actually reordering individual or institutional life by subjecting it in some way to God, of seriously questioning at the personal level a life of money-making or at the social level the designation of institutions as forever "secular." In Protestant and American fashion, many will allow religion an edifying or moral impact on government, but not a substantive role aimed at the transformation of institutions, along with all creation.[19] In sum, the American way of life is an integralism both cultural and institutional, the building of a shared life on a shared valuation of liberty.

This last point needs development. Liberalism has had many forms and traditions, all in some way linked to the Enlightenment emphasis on *liberté.* The argument has been that in America, founded in rebellion, the quest for freedom was central to national for-

internally (if often tacitly) by metaphysical and theological presuppositions." With Kenneth L. Schmitz, "Postmodern or Modern-plus?" *Communio* 17 (1990): 152–66, Schindler sees "post-liberalism" of the form held by Richard Rorty as logically linked to liberalism. Liberalism's self-understanding or claim to neutrality might be described as the last bastion of notions of a pure objectivity abandoned elsewhere: see Peter Novick, *That Noble Dream: The "Objectivity Question" and the American Historical Profession* (Cambridge: Cambridge University Press), 1988.

18. Harvey C. Mansfield, *Machiavelli's Virtue* (Chicago: University of Chicago Press), 1996, analyzes the larger story of modernity and its attendant attenuation of ancient understandings of virtue.

19. Space does not allow anticipation of and response to all the objections, well-grounded or misconceived, that might be made at this point. Schindler, *Heart of the World,* has anticipated most of them, and gives very detailed criticism of the assumptions of the forms of political dualism running from the Gelasian two powers to the "articles of peace" interpretation of the American founding documents; see esp. 4–6, 11–29, and part 1.

mation and definition. This was not the "freedom" of traditional Christian thought—that is, free will that exists only so that one may choose and cling to the truth, be bound by it. It was not "freedom for." But it was not exactly "freedom from," either, for the ideal, at least for the Federalists in the wake of the Constitution, was "ordered liberty," that is, a freedom that acknowledged certain limitations on itself, certain things written into the nature of things that could not be violated. We might say that while all valued liberty, different assessments were made of how it was best to be fostered and what form it should take, running from conservative to liberal. Thus Alasdair MacIntyre has ranged Americans according to how much weight they have given such things as tradition and order in interpreting the liberty they desire.[20] In the years immediately following the Revolution, in the 1790s, the aristocratic Federalists, classical republicans, saw the Revolution as having been necessary to protect liberty, while the more egalitarian Republicans saw it as needed to acquire liberty, but both agreed on liberty's value. This is MacIntyre's point. Belief in the rightness of the founding act unites virtually all Americans—those who had not agreed and could had fled to Canada—and Americans tolerate in one another a variety of religions or no religion at all so long as whatever is held affirms the rightness of the founding act and the resultant American experiment. David Schindler, who stresses that what is common to the traditions of liberalism is not one ideological content but the acceptance of an allegedly neutral, purely formal-juridical, liberal methodology—that is, a purely formal freedom—offers John Courtney Murray in an earlier generation and the neo-conservatives of the present generation as examples of conservative liberals, of people

20. Alasdair MacIntyre, *Three Rival Versions of Moral Inquiry: Encyclopaedia, Genealogy, and Tradition* (Notre Dame, Ind.: University of Notre Dame Press, 1990). Louis Hartz's partly similar claims about the tradition of liberal consensus are addressed by J. David Greenstone, *The Lincoln Persuasion: Remaking American Liberalism* (Princeton: Princeton University Press), 1993, who argues instead for a fundamental bipolarity between "humanist liberalism" and "reform liberalism," and sees Lincoln as a synthesizer of the two traditions, thereby giving the country a new foundation. Olsen, "American Culture and Liberal Ideology," esp. 709 ff., gives more historical detail, bibliography, and sense of the varieties of liberalism than I can give here.

who, while ordering life to liberty, wish this somehow developed in a way that fosters virtue.[21]

As we have said, nineteenth-century Americans, including a growing Catholic and Jewish immigrant population as eager for assimilation and acceptance into the American way of life as had been earlier generations of Protestants, still flocked to the churches and synagogues, but much of their religion was in approval of their national way of life.[22] It is sometimes hard for Europeans to understand the centrality of the Enlightenment to America, for they are accustomed to viewing the Enlightenment as an attack on religion and know that by quantitative measures in America the level of religious practice remains relatively high. They fail to see that in America the Enlightenment is virtually the national religion, that the values of the Enlightenment were set in place at the time of the founding, and that most Americans find acceptable only those forms of religion that support *liberté.* The Declaration of Independence and Constitution are as much scripture as the Bible. In the state in which I live, Utah, the Mormons have followed the American logic to its conclusion, and count the Constitution an inspired document. Whereas in Europe one has to choose between the Enlightenment and religion, or at least make the most excruciating assessment, point by point, of the relative merits of the two inheritances, in America one can have both because almost all religion has been remade in the mold of the Enlightenment. The Americans' ability to forge an *unum* may be the result of their dimness about history, philosophy, and theology, but it is a dimness that has made their experiment possible.

AFTERWORD

Minor changes have been made in this chapter. The original essay was based in part on my journal article "John Rawls and the Flight from Authority: The Quest for Equality as an Exercise in Primitiv-

21. Schindler, *Heart of the World,* 153–54, 159–61, 168–71.

22. Nicholas Lemann, "An Attack in Atlanta," *NYRB,* September 19, 1996, is a moving description of the Jewish drive for assimilation, built on unobtrusiveness and quest for approval, in the nineteenth- and early-twentieth-century American South. In the same

ism." I have expanded my idea that European countries are divided between a "party of the Enlightenment" and a "party of tradition" in "The Two Europes." There is very useful discussion of the persistence of the medieval and traditional into the modern, and of early modern concepts of the relations between medieval and modern, in Gordon McMullan and David Matthews, eds., *Reading the Medieval in Early Modern England.* For the history and criticism of "human rights," see Samuel Moyn, *The Last Utopia: Human Rights in History.* The relationship among the various forms of Christianity found in early America and the cultural patterns that they fostered is explored in both the text and introduction of Christopher Dawson, *The Crisis of Western Education,* introduction by Glenn W. Olsen. See also Francis Cardinal George, *The Difference God Makes: A Catholic Vision of Faith, Communion, and Culture.* The religion of the American founders continues to be much studied: Vincent Phillip Muñoz, *God and the Founders: Madison, Washington, and Jefferson.* David Sorkin, *The Religious Enlightenment: Protestants, Jews, and Catholics from London to Vienna,* marks new tendencies in the study of eighteenth-century religion. What I say about causation is expanded in "The Return of Purpose." Bradley Bateman and H. Spencer Banzhaf, eds., *Keeping Faith, Losing Faith: Religious Belief and Political Economy,* explore the historical relationship between religious and economic thought. Lorman A. Ratner, Paula T. Kaufman, and Dwight L. Teeter, Jr., *Paradoxes of Prosperity. Wealth-Seeking Versus Christian Values in Pre-Civil War America,* study American Christian criticism of Enlightenment values. On the relationship between the Enlightenment and the creation of the modern forms of Christianity, see Hermann Lübbe, *Religion nach der Aufklärung,* 3rd ed.; Michael Printy, *Enlightenment and the Creation of German Catholicism;* David Bentley Hart, *Atheist Delusions: The Christian Revolution and its Fashionable Enemies;* David Walsh, *The Modern Philosophical Revolution: The Luminosity of Existence;* and Bruce K. Ward, *Redeeming the Enlightenment: Christianity and the Liberal Virtues.*

---

issue, Wills, "A Tale of Three Leaders," analyzes the paths ranging from assimilation to separatism three American black leaders have taken, and the logic of their choices.

9

JOHN RAWLS AND THE FLIGHT FROM AUTHORITY

The Quest for Equality as an Exercise in Primitivism

JOHN RAWLS' *A Theory of Justice* has been at the center of discussion of justice in the United States for more than three decades, and has had a not negligible influence elsewhere. The book, along with Rawls' many second thoughts about its arguments, stands in a dominant stream of political theory, one of the Anglo-Saxon forms of liberalism, which self-consciously develops and refines the theory of the social contract. Rawls gives the contract its most influential contemporary form.[1] The extended discussion of Rawls' position

1. John Rawls, *A Theory of Justice,* rev. ed. (Cambridge, Mass.: Belknap Press of Harvard University Press, 1999). The criticism, defense, and modification of Rawls' ideas may be explored through Rawls, "Justice as Fairness: Political Not Metaphysical," *Philosophy and Public Affairs* 14 (1985): 223–51, and Rawls, "The Priority of the Right and Ideas of the Good," *Philosophy and Public Affairs* 17 (1988): 251–76; see also Thomas W. Pogge, *Realizing Rawls* (Ithaca: Cornell University Press, 1989); Patrick Neal, "Justice as Fairness: Political or Metaphysical?" *Political Theory* 18 (1990): 24–50; and Chandran Kukathas and Philip Pettit, *Rawls: "A Theory of Justice" and Its Critics* (Oxford: Polity Press, 1990), especially chap. 2, on contractarian positions. *Ethics* 99, no. 4 (July 1989), is entirely on Rawls. I wish to thank my colleague Bruce Landesman for calling some of the literature referred to in the present chapter to my attention, for allowing me to read three of his unpublished papers, and for making available to me Rawls' own unpublished commentary on his book "Guided Tour"; Rawls, "Justice as Fairness: A Guided Tour" (unpublished; but see Rawls, *Justice as Fairness: A Restatement,* ed. Erin Kelly (Cambridge, Mass.: Harvard University Press, 2001). The direction of Rawls' recent thought is to bring to the fore the "pragmatic" or "game" aspects of his earlier position, and thus to drop the truth claims found in his book. Against a position that makes no truth claims there can be no properly philosophic

has led him to modify it at many points, indeed to abandon many of his original assertions. Yet neither in his nor his critics' revisions has what I would call his mythical quest for equality been seen in sufficient historical context or subjected to the whole range of criticism to which it is vulnerable. This is the task of the present chapter, which for the most part addresses Rawls' position as originally formulated, because this center of his thought has survived his revisions, except insofar—an important qualification—as Rawls now offers his theory as suitable to the constitutional democracies, rather than as a universal theory of justice to which all societies should aspire.

I will have accomplished something if I am able to show the provincialism and arbitrariness of Rawls' thought. Every philosopher has to work within a received tradition, but the best philosophers challenge and probe their tradition at every point, read outside it, and in some way refashion it into something larger. In some ways Rawls does this in his laudable attempt to find a viable alternative to utilitarianism and intuitionism, yet he seems to me hedged in by, even content with, a kind of received canon taught in most English-speaking philosophy departments that, despite the occasional reference to Aristotle, does not go much beyond, first, the Anglo-American traditions, and second, northern European philosophy. Because many of his deepest assumptions embody a form of unexamined cultural imperialism, in some respects he is but one late example of a kind of secularized cultural Protestantism that still often dictates the agenda in Anglo-Saxon moral philosophy.[2] If by

criticism, and in this sense the present chapter *must* address the earlier Rawls, who thought he was doing something more than finding a theory of justice that would work for those who want a liberal democracy. Rawls, *Political Liberalism* (New York: Columbia University Press, 2005) was not yet available to me at the time of composition of the present chapter; see also Lloyd L. Weinreb, *Natural Law and Justice* (Cambridge: Harvard University Press, 1987). Ronald Steel draws out the sense in which the dream of equality is utopian: Steel, "Guest of the Age," *New York Review of Books* (hereafter *NYRB*), August 17, 1989.

2. See Jeffrey Stout, *The Flight from Authority: Religion, Morality, and the Quest for Autonomy* (Notre Dame, Ind.: University of Notre Dame Press, 1981), 71–72, for the argument that, with Romanticism in poetry, modern philosophy is a "continuation of Protestantism by other means" (71). Although the historical analyses of this book are very illuminating, they often oversimplify. In general the medieval ideas of authority were more varied, and Trent more complicated, than Stout suggests. As at 114, he seems overreliant on the not-always-reliable descriptions of Aquinas given by Ian Hacking, *The Emergence*

modern moral philosophy one means the traditions of the English-speaking schools, one can see the truth of some of his claims, such as that "During much of modern moral philosophy the predominant systematic theory has been some form of utilitarianism (vii)."[3] But such claims look exceedingly odd from the perspective of, say, Spanish, Italian, or Polish philosophy. Even where one is inclined to Rawls' conclusions, one must bridle at his unargued assimilation of terms like "person" and of ideas whose historical origins were in revealed theology into what is supposed to be a purely philosophical position. He tells us, in a passage full of the imprecision that mars his book, that "Each person possesses an inviolability founded on justice that even the welfare of society as a whole cannot override (3)."[4] As far as I know, every legal code in the Western tradition before or outside the influence of Judaism and Christianity held the opposite: this indeed was at the heart of the Roman law distinction between public and private law.

---

of Probability: A Philosophical Study of Early Ideas about Probability, Induction, and Statistical Inference (London: Cambridge University Press), 1975. Stout's quotation from Aquinas (107) contains ideas of authority and probability that do not square with the oversimplified position ascribed to Aquinas (7, 38–39). George Parkin Grant, *English-Speaking Justice* (Notre Dame, Ind.: University of Notre Dame Press, 1985), as at 58 ff., brilliantly portrays the interrelations between liberalism, Protestantism, and English-speaking philosophy.

3. Some of Rawls' descriptions of classical positions do not seem to me very accurate. Thus, in ascribing to Aristotle a teleological theory that directs society to the principle of perfection (Rawls, *A Theory of Justice,* 325), Rawls says slavery was justified as necessary for the culture to develop philosophy and science. Aristotle, rather, argues that by nature some are not suited to being citizens, and it would be unjust, for them and for society, to make them citizens. On 383, Rawls does not recognize the variety of historical "divine right" theories of government, and says that in them "subjects have only the rights of suppliants." This would be news to many medieval and natural-law forms of this position. Rawls presumably is aware of historical discussion of topics like regicide, but his further statement that subjects "cannot disobey" implies considerable ignorance of medieval, more generally Catholic, political thought. As too frequently, we are given some form of reduction of such positions to a type commonly found from the time of Luther.

4. George Grant, *English-Speaking Justice,* 33, shows the sentimental retention of "person" by Rawls. Rawls returns to this question in "Justice as Fairness: Political not Metaphysical," *Philosophy and Public Affairs* 14 (1985): 223–51. His distinction (245) between the person's public identity, defined by the free and equal individual, and the person's nonpublic identity, in which other than liberal ideals may be embraced, seems to replicate the schizophrenia of the privatization or isolation of religion from public life in America. For Rawls, one's public and nonpublic identities can hold quite different views of the good. Pogge, *Realizing Rawls,* chap. 2, rightly defends Rawls against common misreadings of his idea of the person, but without seeing that the deeper issue is his use of the idea at all.

His book seems to assume that, along with a few Continental thinkers like Kant, the English-speaking tradition should set the terms of discourse. Of course a philosopher of law, even more than most, must begin with and speak to his own tradition. Yet Rawls is also a political philosopher, and here there seems to me a special obligation never to assume the rightness of one's own traditions. I can only suspect that ignorance of the traditions in which, say, Georgio del Vecchio or Javier Zubirez stand makes possible the astounding praise Rawls lavishes on thinkers like J. S. Mill as a prelude to asserting that "we often seem forced to choose between utilitarianism and intuitionism" (viii, 3). That is a choice forced only on those who think the English-speaking tradition adequate.

I do not want to belabor the point or win arguments by citing authors outside the Anglo-Saxon canon. Yet I must insist on the arbitrariness of Rawls' point of departure. He writes, "What I have attempted to do is to generalize and carry to a higher order of abstraction the traditional theory of the social contract as represented by Locke, Rousseau, and Kant" (viii, 3, 11). As Jeffrey Stout has noted in a book from whose title I have appropriated the phrase "The Flight from Authority" for the present chapter's title, nowhere does Rawls show the truth of the theory of the social contract. He stands, rather, in a tradition of "flight from authority" that has fastened, largely for historical, political, or prudential reasons, on first this and then that strategy for undermining or replacing some traditional authority structure that has fallen into disfavor. This "flight from authority" has come to assert the autonomy of morality—a language of rational individualism.[5] Not just in his thought, the medi-

5. Stout, *The Flight from Authority,* 218–23, 226, 232–35, 238–41, on Rawls. Rawls' comments (*A Theory of Justice,* 389–90) on the kind of parallel authority found in the sciences and in a democratic society, while in my opinion describing neither accurately, reveal particularly well his idea of autonomy (see 513–20 for more detail), which is more a credo than anything else: "Equals accepting and applying reasonable principles need have no established superior. To the question, who is to decide? The answer is: all are to decide, everyone taking counsel with himself, and with reasonableness . . . it often works out well enough" (390). Here we have Rawls' strange and continuing shift from an opening theoretical, mythical, and unearthly equality, where by definition authority is not needed, to judgments about man in time ("it often works out well enough") that are no truer than their opposites ("it never works out very well," if I may coin my own phrase), and simply

eval "philosophy as a handmaid to theology" has been replaced by a modern "philosophy as a handmaid to politics." In the process primitivist modes of discourse, mythical points of departure for politics, which after more than a millennium of debate had been expelled from at least the Aristotelian branch of medieval Catholic thought, have reappeared at every step in the modern world.

In the larger flight from authority, the conclusion drawn from the appearance of Protestantism and the resulting conflict of authorities was that medieval ideas of authority were untenable. A new notion of politics had to be drawn in which the needs of the historical moment could shape a suitable notion and place for authority. In the manner of Descartes, one cast about for a rhetoric disconnected from traditional authority, in this sense secularized yet capable of establishing a new form of authority. If one had a specific cause to advance in the Glorious Revolution (Locke), or a program to recommend to replace the *ancien regime* (Rousseau), one redefined or relocated authority accordingly.[6] Of course it had always been so: the "handmaid" business had always been susceptible to politics and power. Political interest had had a perduring influence on political thought. Yet a shift from the category of "nature" to that of "history" clearly took place in the modern period. Machiavelli, the bellwether here, marks the shift from the political theory of the ancients and medievals, which had generally understood politics as the discovery of and submission to principles rooted in an order of nature, to the political science of the moderns, which has tended to see politics as the study of the exercise of power in a circumstance dictated by history.[7]

---

reveal the irrealism of stubborn belief in Enlightenment notions about human reasonableness; see also Thomas Nagel, "Rawls on Justice," *Philosophical Review* 82 (1973): 220–34. George Grant, *English-Speaking Justice,* as at 11 ff., on the aridity of the social contract, makes a number of criticisms of Rawls similar to those found in the present book.

6. Ruth W. Grant, *John Locke's Liberalism* (Chicago: University of Chicago Press, 1987), surveys the controverted literature on Locke and defends him as non-ideological against the kind of reading he receives from Stout. Also arguing for the coherency of Locke's thought is Andrzej Rapaczynski, *Nature and Politics: Liberalism in the Philosophies of Hobbes, Locke, and Rousseau* (Ithaca: Cornell University Press, 1987). Ian Shapiro, *The Evolution of Rights in Liberal Theory* (New York: Cambridge University Press, 1986), is much sharper in both his treatment of Locke as ideologue and of Rawls.

7. J. Budziszewski, *The Resurrection of Nature: Political Theory and the Human Charac-*

There is a difference between Plato's Myth of Er and Locke'social contract, which might otherwise be taken to be similar attempts to find a "useable myth" on which to ground society. In Plato's case the myth was offered for those not capable of understanding philosophy, of understanding that the observable inequalities of nature, the differences between people, dictate a hierarchy for society, and that each therefore should accept the place for which nature had fashioned him or her: those who used their reasons aright could conclude to the truths embodied for the less disciplined in the Myth of Er. Nowhere in Locke, that "story-teller,"[8] by comparison, are the notions captured in the social contract established independently by observation and argument. The attempt to find either a historical or ontological home for the contract has been notoriously difficult—thus Kant's abandonment of such claims. It now seems, so far as the unaided reason can determine, that there never was, chronologically or ontologically, a first state of nature for man to be in. Such an idea is essentially the bringing into politics, the secularizing, of Christianity's Eden or paganism's dream of a Golden Age or Age of Saturn. The contract seems neither true of any moment in the past, when egalitarian conditions actually prevailed, nor of some founding moment of political life, in which authority passed from the people to a state. Rather, as Edmund S. Morgan has shown, the contract, the whole movement toward popular sovereignty in England and America in the seventeenth and eighteenth centuries, was a device for making the political argument that authority no longer was what it once had been—rooted in God: it was now to be placed in a fiction called "the people." Ray Gunn has shown a similar process at work in the constant redefinition of liberalism in nineteenth-century America.[9]

---

ter (Ithaca: Cornell University Press, 1986), 11, attacks the "historical retreat from the idea that Nature—*human* nature—somehow provides the rule and measure for human life," engaging Rawls; and extends the analysis in Budziszewski, *The Nearest Coast of Darkness: A Vindication of the Politics of Virtue* (Ithaca: Cornell University Press, 1988).

8. Mary Ann Glendon, *Rights Talk: The Impoverishment of Political Discourse* (New York: Free Press, 1991).

9. Edmund S. Morgan, *Inventing the People: The Rise of Popular Sovereignty in England and America* (New York and London: Norton, 1988); Morgan, "The Fiction of 'The

Rawls is aware of the problems in determining the exact status of the seventeenth-century state of nature. Therefore, in redoing contract theory, he with Kant attempts to abandon nature and history for pure reason as the point of departure for thinking about justice.[10] He begins from a purely hypothetical point of "original position" or "original agreement" on the principles of justice (see esp. 11–22, 118–92, 251–57). Although he allows that in every actual society discord and dissent are present, when he speaks of the "original agreement" not only does human historicity fall away, he writes as one might imagine Descartes reborn as an economist (cf. 14): the principles of justice "are the principles that free and rational persons concerned to further their own interests would accept in an initial position of equality as defining the fundamental terms of their association (11)."[11] It is as if the ideals of the Enlightenment had never

---

People,'" *NYRB,* April 23, 1992; and L. Ray Gunn, *The Decline of Authority: Public Economic Policy and Political Development in New York State, 1800–1860* (Ithaca: Cornell University Press, 1988); see also J. P. Sommerville, *Politics and Ideology in England, 1603–1640* (London: Longman, 1986), 57–66. Jeffrey Reiman, *Justice and Modern Moral Philosophy* (New Haven: Yale University Press, 1990), 12–14 and throughout) makes a thoughtful attempt to defend the contractarian idea by providing foundations Rawls does not. Rawls, *A Theory of Justice,* 454n1, briefly considers the Myth of Er. With Alasdair MacIntyre, *Whose Justice? Which Rationality?* (Notre Dame, Ind.: University of Notre Dame Press, 1988), 392, on the pre-rational foundation of the liberal project, I am inclined to regard most American political debate as between various forms of liberalism.

10. Rawls, in spite of his denial of this, seems to me frequently to argue from nature. In a way common in the liberal tradition, he bases his ethics on natural inclinations, passions, or interests. In so doing, because he rejects an Aristotelian teleology, he opens himself up to the very thing he arguably is trying to avoid, the naturalistic fallacy (see notes 3 and 12). When he describes nature he refashions it at critical points by assumptions that come from the a priori of equality—thus the convoluted discussion of how general the capacity for a sense of justice is. Some of what is at issue here is laid bare by Rapaczynski, *Nature and Politics,* in his argument that a doctrine of human nature must undergird a liberal polity, and in the somewhat similar argument of Reiman, *Justice and Modern Moral Philosophy.* Ellis Sandoz, *A Government of Laws: Political Theory, Religion, and the American Founding* (Baton Rouge: Louisiana State University Press), 1990, who sees the centrality of discussion of human nature, weighs in on the side of a significantly classical, Christian, and liberal republicanism and of Locke, acutely criticized. Again, Rawls, *A Theory of Justice,* by making self-respect so central to a just society, and securing it (545) "by the public affirmation of the status of equal citizenship for all," does not confront the "natural" question of the likelihood that a country can long survive in which decisions requiring high expertise, as in the areas of foreign policy, economics, or ecology, are influenced by a general citizenry that will be underinformed.

11. In a highly original critique of the ideal of autonomy, Leon Kass, "Man and Woman: An Old Story," *First Things,* no. 17 (November 1991): 14–26, wonders in Augustine-like

been criticized, as if no one had noted that the liberal notion of rationality is impossibly neutral, presented under the pretense or delusion of being free from any specific tradition; and that the liberal sense of community is too narrowly political, or even economic.[12] As John Dewey, who is an example of an exceptional American rejecter of the social contract, observed in 1888, "The non-social individual is an abstraction arrived at by imagining what man would be if all his human qualities were taken away."[13]

Rawls does not clearly see that, as Stout (especially in chapters 2 and 3) puts it, the age begun by Descartes, originating in the attempt to overcome skepticism by some form of foundationalism, and ever since fluctuating between these two, has ended with each party inflicting mortal wounds on the other. According to Rawls, persons unqualifiedly free, that is, without historical determination or necessity, are nevertheless asked to act as if they had interests and could commit themselves to some specific act, some mode of historical existence. Beside this, God's decision to create the world seems small potatoes. As Stout queries in his discussion of what Rawls terms "the veil of ignorance" (see especially Rawls, *A Theory of Justice,* 136–42), "What language is spoken behind the veil of ignorance?"

---

fashion whether an isolated individual would be capable of self-knowledge. If John Paul II and at least one school of phenomenology (let alone Trinitarianism) are right that persons can only be defined in relations, Rawls' form of the liberal project collapses. For further criticisms see Alan Wolfe, *Whose Keeper? Social Science and Moral Obligation* (Berkeley: University of California Press, 1989).

12. William A. Galston, *Liberal Purposes: Goods, Virtues, and Diversity in the Liberal State* (New York: Cambridge University Press, 1991), pursues the question of neutrality, especially concerning individual definitions of the good; cf. the description of Georg Simmel's critique of Kant in Han Urs von Balthasar, *Theo-Drama: Theological Dramatic Theory,* vol. 1, *Prolegomena,* trans. Graham Harrison (San Francisco: Ignatius Press, 1988), especially 611–12, and the argument of Robert H. Frank, *Passions Within Reason: The Strategic Role of the Emotions* (New York: Norton, 1988), especially 146. Many of the criticisms Denis Donoghue, "Bewitched, Bothered, and Bewildered," *NYRB,* March 25, 1993, makes of the thought of J. Hillis Miller apply analogously to Rawls: "He wants to start the world over again and to act as if there were only the present tense and a future of his devising" (49–50). David Gauthier, *Morals by Agreement* (Oxford: Clarendon Press, 1986), has given a new form of the social contract, which departs from Rawls in significant ways. Ellen Frankel Paul, Fred D. Miller, Jr., Jeffrey Paul, and John Adams, eds., *The New Social Contract: Essays on Gauthier* (Oxford: Basil Blackwell, 1988), viii, note: "Gauthier's contract is an agreement between real and distinct people, whereas Rawls' is not."

13. Louis Menand, "The Real John Dewey," *NYRB,* June 25, 1992.

If they speak a language, the original contractors will already be determined by history—that is, will not be free and rational without qualification, and will be unable to achieve an agreement that is universal. For that a universal language would be necessary, but such a language, because "neutral with respect to belief, would be meaningless." As Stout dryly observes, the contractors would be under no small disadvantage.[14] In sum, Rawls, like Kant, is mistaken in thinking that reducing the "state of nature" of traditional theory to a "purely hypothetical situation" (121) leads to a conception of justice: it merely empties the traditional theory of what little meaning it had had. If Rawls is trying to discover what principles ought to apply to all irrespective of natural differences, this is not a thought experiment of likely success.

If we grant Rawls "the traditional theory of the social contract" in his updated version, it is clear that he has much of importance to say. But why grant the theory? It is clear that there are historical reasons for using the theory, but what are the philosophical reasons for granting it? One can see many historical reasons for the grounding myth of his system, but, as with many modern points of depar-

14. The quotations are from Stout, *The Flight from Authority,* 220–21). Stout's point is that because, with David A. J. Richards, Rawls accepts that "meaning and substance cannot be separated," a *universal language* . . . would be meaningless" (Rawls, *Theory of Justice,* 221). The goal of Stout is to show that "the quest for autonomy was . . . an attempt to deny the historical reality of having been influenced by tradition" (Stout, 3). Along this line I would observe that, because all languages are used in a specific historical form (Old English, Middle English), if people behind the veil are speaking at all, they cannot satisfy such of Rawls' conditions as not knowing their stage of civilization (Rawls, 287) or where they stand in the generations. The earlier one stands—that is, the more primitive one's language, the more Rawls' conditions would be approximated. Rawls expresses his ideal as "a kind of moral geometry" (Rawls, 121). Rawls' idea of community is developed in his *Theory of Justice* on 258–65 and 395–587. Clearly he holds that "justice as fairness has a central place for the value of community," and that an individualistic conception of justice leads to valuing associative activities (Rawls, 264). Here the question is what kind of community results from an Enlightenment idea of the individual. What seems decisive is the way Rawls contrasts the right and the good (Rawls, 446–52), holding all to the right but not to the same good; see further 520–29. It is clear that Rawls holds for the complementariness of human society: this commonly is not at issue between "conventional" and "natural" positions. Cf. George Grant, *English-Speaking Justice,* 16 ff., for a somewhat different account of the significance of the state of nature for Locke, and the suggestion that Rawls' position is generated by the desire to avoid the "naturalistic fallacy." For criticism of the fallacy, see Henry B. Veatch, *Swimming Against the Current in Contemporary Philosophy: Occasional Essays and Papers* (Washington, D.C.: The Catholic University of America Press, 1990).

ture, not reasons for valuing the system except in the historical situation that generated its grounding myth. For instance, so sure is Rawls that a theory of justice is to be raised on the supposition of equal persons, rather than, say, on an idea of the common good, that he holds that some questions can only "be answered in a certain way": he says, as an example, that religious intolerance is assuredly unjust (19). I would merely observe that, whether we are talking of inquisitorial Spain, socialism with a human face, or Walter Lippmann's quest for a "public philosophy," the desire to live a public life of shared values in human solidarity is very deep-rooted, and by definition not possible without some form of "religious intolerance." Current debate about "political correctness" and "multiculturalism" centers on the fact that "Even free and open societies devise something akin to an 'official' knowledge."[15] As I have argued elsewhere, the First Amendment to the American Constitution, directed initially against above all the Puritan tradition, is intolerant of any form of religion that sees its fullness to lie in expression in a public order manifesting the beliefs of that religion.[16] Rawls justi-

15. Andrew Hacker, "Playing the Racial Card," *NYRB,* October 24, 1991; see page 18 in regard to Arthur Schlesinger, Jr., *The Disuniting of America* (New York: Norton, 1992). I have considered multiculturalism in "The Ethics of Conquest: The European Background of Spain's Mission in the New World," *Communio* 19 (1992): 619–34, and "1492 in the Judgment of the Nations," in *Actas del II Congreso "Cultura Europea,"* ed. Enrique Banús (Pamplona: Aranzadi, 1994), 175–81.

16. Olsen, "The Meaning of Christian Culture: A Historical View," in *Catholicism and Secularization in America,* ed. David L. Schindler (Notre Dame, Ind.: Communio, 1990), 98–130; Olsen, *Deconstructing the University,* the 52nd Annual Frederick William Reynolds Lecture (Salt Lake City, 1991), republished in a slightly revised version in *Communio* 19 (1992): 226–53; and Olsen, "'You Can't Legislate Morality': Reflections on a Bromide," *Communio* 2 (1975): 148–62. Olsen, "The Catholic Moment?" *Communio* 15 (1988): 474–87, also contains an attack on the Enlightenment model of community, found throughout Rawls, as a kind of "debating society." Christopher Lasch, "Orestes Brownson's Christian Radicalism," *New Oxford Review* 56, no. 7 (September 1989): 4–8 describes an earlier criticism of both church-state separation and civil religion. Gordon S. Wood, "Struggle Over the Puritans," *NYRB,* November 9, 1989, esp. 26, describes the manner in which liberal democratic historians even wrote the Puritans out of American History. Eugene D. Genovese, "Religious Foundations of the Constitution," *Reviews in American History* 19 (1991): 338–46, contains an amusing attack on the left from the left for excluding the scholarship of conservatives on the place of religion in the American founding: "However much some of us may wince, the conservatives who our profession is treating as nonpersons . . . are publishing much of the work that promises to provide the basis for an intellectually and politically honest reassessment of our constitutional history" (338).

fies the use of force by the tolerant against the intolerant when the latter threaten the liberty of all (219), and this makes good sense on his principles. Yet he does not seem to realize that, unless there are no shared or public values, any tradition to be a tradition must set up some form of intolerance.[17] Religious bigotry certainly has been part and parcel of the liberal tradition itself, with its various forms of *Kulturkampf* and May Laws that have been used, for instance, to pressure Catholics to accommodate to Protestant majorities. I think more than forcing the intolerant to play by liberal rules is involved here: Rawls only makes sense on the premise of an individualism or atomism of individual ends limited in its radical pluralism solely by the preservation of liberty itself. He robs us of most of our humanity in the name of an impossibly abstract, mathematical, and procedural view of what life in society, what community, is about. Or to speak more sharply, he is blind to the intolerance of his own position, hidden by its starting point in the myth of equality, "the shattering of the 'givenness' of existence as symbolized in the hierarchical representation of being." (Sandoz uses this phrase in an attack on moral relativism.)[18]

17. One wonders whether in spite of Rawls' tolerance of "religion," what he really aims at is a Kantian "religion within the limits of reason alone." Is this not the force of "If a religion is denied its full expression, it is presumably because it is in violation of the equal liberties of others"? (Rawls, *A Theory of Justice,* 370). Rawls hopes for some forms of moral unanimity (263–64) natural-law societies have hoped for, but seems to lay the burden of the achievement of such on persons acting rationally, rather than on all the force of tradition that natural theories of society have tended to assume necessary to shape "thinking reeds." This is particularly evident in chapter 8, where the "morality of authority" is the lowest form of a sense of justice. Rawls' whole schematic movement from a morality of authority to the higher senses of justice again embodies an "Enlightenment" ideal. Wolfe, *Whose Keeper?* (123–24, 222) notes the influence of Lawrence Kohlberg here, on whom see Olsen, *Deconstructing the University,* 15. It seems to me that societies as a whole never rise above a preponderant morality of authority. Sometimes, as in the following quotation, Rawls strikes me as touchingly naive and ignorant of "man in history," as well as retaining some traces of a progressive (culturally Protestant) view of history: "Eventually there comes a time in the history of a well-ordered society beyond which the special form of the two principles [of justice] takes over and holds from then on." I can see why Rawls has to say, "One must suppose [that individuals have] . . . equal capacity for the activities and interests of men as progressive beings" (Rawls, *A Theory of Justice,* 210), but what if such a position goes against observation? If "equal justice is owed to those who have the capacity to take part in and act in accordance with the public understanding of the initial situation" (505), would it even be owed to a majority?

18. Sandoz, *A Government of Laws,* 29.

It has been observed that one aspect of the collapse of the Communist states is the inability of a state ordered to a specific notion of good, attempting in the modern world a "communitarian Age of Faith," to stand up to modernity, that is to the dissolving ideas of freedom and democracy."[19] Some of us may even have some sympathy for the more spiritually inclined of the former subject peoples, somewhat reluctant to join politically with the West, and wondering whether what glitters in Berlin is anything more than gold. However benighted one might think this or that quest for a shared public life ordered to a specific view of the world, there are serious questions involved here. Rawls' kind of liberalism seems incapable of dealing with these. It does not clearly see that, because its point of departure is itself theological, lying in the idea of equality, it outlaws all forms of religion that are not "Protestant." Ruled out is all religion that is unwilling to restrict itself to the private and individual, that sees itself as about more than God and the soul. I am not referring to classical Protestantism here, but to that remade Protestantism of the Enlightenment, which, classical Protestantism having failed roughly as much as Catholicism in its practice of intolerance (215–16), adjusted itself to the "pluralism" necessary for there to be, for instance, an American republic. As Will Herberg showed fifty years ago, this was at a tremendous price paid by Judaism and Christianity, which in the United States abandoned most of their prophetic dimension and, instead of criticizing the American way of life, became its prime boosters.[20]

Rawls emphasizes "equal liberty" and "the priority of liberty" (viii, with 195–257, 541–48). Such liberal preferences are perfectly intelligible within the context of a modern "pluralist" society. In such we protect ourselves from each other's orthodoxy by (on the

19. Dale Vree, "Communism: From Modernity's Vanguard to History's Rearguard," *New Oxford Review* 56, no. 19 (December 1989): 2–4; see also Buruma, "Heimat," *NYRB,* December 20, 1990. Cf. on the retreat of the state, Neal Ascherson, "About the European House," *NYRB,* September 28, 1989.

20. Will Herberg, *Protestant-Catholic-Jew: An Essay in American Religious Sociology,* with a new introduction by Martin G. Marty (Chicago: University of Chicago Press, 1983), 271; cf. Robert N. Bellah and Robert Neely, *Habits of the Heart: Individualism and Commitment in American Life* (New York: Harper and Row, 1985).

surface, it turns out) disestablishing all orthodoxies and displacing the ancient ends of politics, education, and goodness—above all, what was called the "common good." Emphasis shifts from truth and virtue to liberty, itself a new kind of orthodoxy hidden from careful identification by the terms "pluralism" and "liberalism." Just as Locke refashioned natural-law theory into natural-rights theory without abandoning all the language and commitments of the past, so Rawls has refashioned the "common good" to reorient authority around justice, liberty, and the individual. If in Rawls we miss convincing arguments justifying such a shift, this is because they hardly exist. Rawls may in fact sometimes argue from nature, but this he formally impugns. The shift is better explained as dictated by a new historical circumstance.[21] One can see how in a modern atomist society justice moves to the fore as that which protects each of us from notions of virtue with which we do not agree, but why should a philosopher accept the liceity of this development, in a sense become the (somewhat flatfooted) Virgil of the American experiment, without any proper grounding of the priority of liberty or justice? My argument is that such notions embody an ancient and mythical pattern of thought and set of ideas still living in Rawls' thinking. The Kantian bath may have cleansed this thought from its grosser

21. Rawls (*A Theory of Justice,* 528) specifically rules out the idea of a society having a dominant end. I agree with him that dominant-end views are vague and do not give much information on how precisely to rank social activities, but I do not see that this should be called a weakness if the purpose of the dominant end, say to know God, is a way of announcing that man's final ends lie beyond politics and philosophy, but have some implications for both. Because what Rawls says in criticism of teleological theories (560) might be taken to apply to natural-law moral theories, demur from his analysis is in order. He believes teleological theories are misconceived because they first try arrive at the good independently (of the right), and then try "to give form to our life" by the good. This, if intended also as a criticism of natural-law theories, seems to me to confuse two issues. Such theories only attempt to decide how to act in each choice by reference to an objective definition of good: the sum of such choices does not give a "plan of life" in Rawls' sense. The only "form" that natural-law moral theories give to life is that which comes from accumulated choices of the good (character or habit). The discussion of liberty on 201–05 is inadequate, even refusing to define the meaning of the term. In saying "The controversy between the proponents of negative and positive liberty as to how freedom should be defined . . . is not concerned with definitions at all, but with the relative values of the several liberties" (201), Rawls shows little sense of the difference between, say, the Augustinian *liberum arbitrium* and *libertas* (this despite his discussion on 202).

historical claims to be an actual account of the race's first condition, but in the now abstract or hypothetical "original position," almost point for point, the age-old claims reappear. This thinking indeed is circular or merely re-expresses the myth. To show this, and to connect it with what has already been said of the social contract, background is needed.

If what writers like Mircea Eliade have said is true, there is hardly a culture or religion in the world without a myth of a "once upon a time," a primordial state of life, now lost, with conditions radically different from the present. To stay with the Western tradition, in the 1930s and '40s, Arthur O. Lovejoy and George Boas massively documented the ubiquity of the idea of the Golden Age in ancient and medieval thought.[22] I am inclined to call this in all its variations the central myth (imaginative representation of reality) of our culture, if not of the race. Hundreds of times we find either cultural primitivism, an early form of the idea of the noble savage, in which the first state of the race is seen as morally pure and harmonious, or of chronological primitivism, in which the best is seen at the beginning. The Christian myth of Eden is an example of the common combination of elements from both forms of primitivism. Although few pictures of the Golden Age were identical, very commonly the "once upon a time" was seen as a time of unity; harmony both between human beings and between God or the gods, the animals, and humans; and of the absence of hierarchy, law, and the state—people naturally did the right thing.

The Christians, heirs to both the Eden story and the manifold Golden Ages of classical literature, conflated these two traditions, and writer after writer of the first centuries argued that in man's first state, before the Fall, there was no private property, government, or law. All were equal and no one dominated. Peter Brown's

22. Arthur O. Lovejoy and George Boas, *Primitivism and Related Ideas in Antiquity* (Baltimore: The Johns Hopkins University Press, 1935); see also Alison Goddard Elliott, *Roads to Paradise: Reading the Lives of the Saints* (Hanover, N.H.: University Press of New England, 1987); Olsen, "Recovering the Homeland: Acts 4:32 and the *Ecclesia Primitiva* in St. Bernard's Sermons on the Song of Songs," *Word and Spirit: A Monastic Review* 12 (1990): 104-07; and Olsen, "The City in Christian Thought," *Thought* 66 (1991): 259–78.

splendid *The Body and Society*[23] shows us that the greatest of the Latin thinkers, Augustine, no longer fits as neatly into this tradition as he did for the brothers Carlyle (volumes 1 and 3). In part this is because Augustine was one of those relatively rare persons Lovejoy and Boas had labeled antiprimitivist.[24] But Augustine was an exception among Christians, more generally among ancients. Most saw the race as God-descended and as having lost the unity of an earlier and better life. Rare was the Aristotle, the thinker with no myth of man's origins to tell, no outrunning of the historical record, no myth of a better state or original society on which to erect his political thought. Or rather, rare in the ancient world, for from the twelfth century Aristotle came to enjoy an influence he had never had in the ancient world. In a Christendom largely still embracing notions of an original equality and absence of human authority (God's authority in Eden was presumed), Aristotle's counterproposal that political society is rooted in nature, and should reflect the nature of people as we find them in the historical record and not as they allegedly were in some mythical first state, made deep inroads. Ultimately this counterproposal was to lie at the basis of much political thought in Catholic culture. The earlier notions of the Church Fathers, on this point discredited or at least partly abandoned in medieval Aristotelian university circles, would have a new life with the Reformation, along with a general revival of much that was chiliastic. In time they would find their way into the social contract of the seventeenth-century thinkers, a reversion, as I have observed, to a primitivist or mythical mode of departure for political thought: this is part of what I meant when I said that philosophy in the north of Europe maintained Protestantism at the cultural level, just as in the south it maintained Catholicism.

Once again we must drop back to the beginning, this time to the origins of the alternative of conceiving society as natural or conven-

23. Peter Brown, *The Body and Society: Men, Women, and Sexual Renunciation in Early Christianity,* rev. ed (New York: Columbia University Press, 2008).

24. George Boas, *Essays on Primitivism and Related Ideas in the Middle Ages* (Baltimore: The Johns Hopkins University Press, 1948).

tional. Although the brothers Carlyle, in the first of their six-volume history of medieval political thought, only saw this antithesis as appearing with Cicero, it clearly was a commonly understood contrast centuries earlier, and is described in Book 2 of Plato's *Republic*.[25] Here Glaucon, in puzzling over whether Socrates had really vanquished Thrasymachos in the previous book, touches on one of the great alternative ways of conceiving political life. Plato-Socrates himself rejects what Glaucon says "countless others" hold. Yet at least some scholars have noted the distinct resemblance of the ideas Glaucon describes to the social contract of the seventeenth century, as well as to other aspects of what has come to be termed a liberal politics and theory of rights.[26] Glaucon gives the argument that justice is mere social convention. For those who hold this, the customary rules of morality are not discovered in "nature," but are forged by human intelligence and rest on tacit consent. They are neither laws of nature nor divine enactments, but conventions that man made and can alter. Listen to Glaucon describe this position he takes to be common:

> when people do and suffer injustice in dealing with one another, and taste both, those who cannot both escape the one and take the other think it profitable to make an agreement neither to do nor to suffer injustice; from this they begin to make laws and compacts among themselves, and they name the injunction of the law lawful and just.
>
> This, they say, is the origin of justice.[27]

A few lines later, after an account of the self-seeking of both the so-called just and unjust of which Hobbes could have been proud, the story of Gyges is recounted.

25. R. W. Carlyle and A. J. Carlyle, *A History of Mediaeval Political Theory in the West* (Edinburgh and London: W. Blackwood and Sons, 1903–62), 1:17, 63, shows that the Carlyles knew that the idea of the social contract went back to Plato. Arguably, although I do not know that anyone has pointed this out, Herodotus' story of Dioces (*Histories*, bk. I, chaps. 96 ff.) is also an early example of the formation of a "social contract."

26. Plato, *The Republic of Plato*, trans. Francis Cornford (New York: Oxford University Press, 1945), 41–42; see also Plato, *Great Dialogues of Plato*, ed. Eric H. Warmington and Philip G. Rouse (New York: New American Library, 1956; repr.: New York: Mentor, 1984).

27. Plato, *The Republic of Plato*, ed. Cornford, 2:358–59; *Great Dialogues of Plato*, ed. Warmington and Rouse, 156).

In chapter 2 Socrates responds in a manner that associates nature with inequality. Men, he argues, are born neither self-sufficient nor alike. Therefore organized society, in which people are interdependent and specialize according to innate aptitudes, is both natural and advantageous to all. Aristotle of course later works out more thoroughly the observation that men are by nature unequal, but the basic insight that the inequalities of nature lead to the inequalities or complementariness of society is shared with his teacher. As Aristotle has it, the race cannot continue without the union of male and female. The individual cannot survive infancy without a "family"—that is, a stable association to supply its wants. The family cannot go much beyond the satisfaction of daily needs, and hence the village is born to develop the more distinctively human capacities of the individual and the family. Finally, the limitations of all lesser forms of natural association are overcome by the polis, a community large and diverse enough to perfect all human possibilities. As I will note in a moment, we can readily acknowledge the time-boundedness of what Aristotle takes to be natural here without undermining his main point—that whatever the historical progress, the smallest viable social unit is the family, not the individual, which left to itself literally dies. No society was ever formed of autonomous individuals who came together. Moreover, the individual's full humanity is only revealed in a differentiated society that allows for leisure and thus for the highest human pursuits, above all philosophy. That is, man is by nature, rather than by convention, a social animal.

Let me, by way of contrast to the egalitarianism and individualism of the conventional tradition, which we might call theological, ideological, or counterfactual, call this a scientific politics. By this I mean that Plato and Aristotle see the observable differences found in nature and history as replicated in and the basis of social and political life. This is one of the things Aristotle means when he says man is by nature a political animal. Society perfects what is incomplete or potential in the individual, and is necessary and natural to that completion. On the one side, then, we have the natural or scientific politics of Aristotle, on the other the conventional or counterfactual politics of Glaucon's unnamed "many," of most of the Church Fathers, of the social contract, and of Rawls and his kind of liberalism. The one assumes that politics works from and respects the natural inequalities between human beings, the other that politics exists to diminish or eliminate these natural differences. Rawls actually writes of looking for "a conception of justice that nullifies the accidents of natural endowment" (*A Theory of Justice,* 15, 102). The natural or scientific approach has no myth of human origins or human ends to tell; the conventional or liberal approach is commonly rooted in both—first in a myth of an original equality. Thus Rawls explains that he carries the social contract "to a higher level of abstraction" by replacing "the compact of society . . . by an initial situation that incorporates certain procedural constraints on arguments designed to lead to an original agreement on principles of justice" (3). The "initial situation" and the "original agreement" have, as has been suggested, a greater bloodlessness than the seventeenth-century form of the contract, but encourage in turn a myth of human ends, the use of politics to attain a state like that of the original hypothetical situation. This seems one more example of Eric Voegelin's claim that most modern politics is Gnostic (chaps. 4–6).[28]

Again, I do not want to be misunderstood. Aristotle is not the last word in politics. We can understand but deplore a certain ahis-

28. For a disapproving view of Voegelin's use of "gnosticism," see Louis Dupré, "A Conservative Anarchist: Eric Voegelin, 1901–85," *Clio* 14 (1985): 423–31; cf. Eric Voegelin, *The New Science of Politics: An Introduction* (Chicago: University of Chicago Press, 1952). I thank Professor Dupré for calling this article to my attention. The contrast between the natural and conventional is a contrast between tendencies or models, and especially in conventional positions we find fragments of the opposite tendency. Rawls (*A Theory of Justice,* 108–17, 333–91), for instance, retains the notion of natural duties, such as not being cruel, while deriving notions of obligation from the contract or the principle of fairness. The idea of beginning with an order of nature is retained to a certain (unclear) point, although the nature is already one of "equal moral persons" (115). Rawls fairly clearly understands what is at issue between a natural and a conventional view, but of course, as at 328–31, can reject the natural because it leads to a drastic alteration of the original position. See in addition to note 9 above, Joseph Raz, *The Morality of Freedom* (New York: Clarendon Press, 1986). Thomas Aquinas, *Summa Theologiae* II-II, 66, 2, reads the patristic and canonistic association of common property with the natural law in such a way as to avoid speculation about man's first state: he holds that community of goods in the natural law does not mean common possession, but the absence of distinction of possessions—that is regulation of property, which is in the province of positive law.

torical nature to his thought, in which he does not grasp that we have no cases of "pure nature"—that is, a nature unconditioned by history. He has little to say on the vexing question of whether what we find in history can ever be called "natural" in anything but a qualified sense—that is, as qualified by some particular set of antecedents and some particular context. Like the confusion still found in, say, Gerda Lerner's feminism,[29] he assumes that by looking at the historical record from its beginnings we can discover a "natural" innate human relations, a *gener purus* that has been overridden by history.[30] I do not think he was completely mistaken in his turn to what he calls the natural, but I do not think he clearly saw that reason cannot recover or discover any unhistorically qualified "natural."

Similarly, there is an issue treated too superficially in virtually all classical philosophy that is almost exactly matched by what seems to me a lack of thoughtfulness in Rawls' position. Plato and Aristotle clearly believed that the actual hierarchy of their societies was not just, that some were shoemakers who should be soldiers, and some slaves who should be citizens. That is, they understood that the inequalities of actual society were not necessarily built on natural inequalities, but on things such as different social positions at birth. Plato clearly had a mechanism for dealing with this by force—the reassignment of people to the class to which they were suited—but the more historically minded Aristotle, more willing to work with inherited institutions, glosses over how the polity is to sift natural inequalities from "accidental" ones like the family one is born into. Rawls would be right to criticize classical philosophy for not giving more attention to this problem. Yet, presumably because his thought is built on contract, convention, and the individual, he seems to me unsatisfactory at the heart of his own position

29. Gerda Lerner, *The Creation of Patriarchy* (New York: Oxford University Press, 1986).

30. I am in sympathy with Stout's attempt to overcome the tradition of Descartes and Kant without falling into an unqualified historicism (Stout, *The Flight from Authority,* 3 ff.). Stephen R. L. Clark's work *Civil Peace and Sacred Order: Limits and Renewals,* vol. 1 (Oxford: Oxford University Press, 1989) is an important challenge not only to views like that of Rawls, but implicitly to the historical argument of Stout.

in the treatment of what he calls the "deep inequalities" (7), those rooted in people having different starting places in life that have nothing to do with personal merit. I can only make one observation about Rawls' treatment of this most vexing question here. Because he sees society as composed of individuals, rather than, as in the scientific or Aristotelian tradition, of families, or more fully, of various levels of social incompleteness, like the family or village for the completion of which the polis exists, Rawls is willing to attack nature in a new way. He renders problematic all labor of families to provide for offspring. The family, for him, stands in the way of equality.[31] The criticism of Plato by Aristotle in the *Politics*, that finally he forgets that the state exists to perfect rather than destroy the lesser forms of society of which it is composed, is a criticism not without relevance to Rawls' liberal individualism. On this issue, then, one can be unhappy with the incompleteness of ancient thought but see Rawls as no remedy.

Let me summarize my argument. A primitivist mode of affirming an original state of the race very different from anything found in history is found across the cultures. Such a point of departure is replicated in hundreds of forms as we pass through our own history, in for instance the Renaissance attempt to overcome the Middle Ages in order to recover the classical Golden Age, or in the Reformation attempt to recover an original form of Christianity. It lies behind the social contract, even when purified of any explicitly chron-

31. On 73–75 of *A Theory of Justice,* Rawls attacks the Aristotelian idea of the family, but I cannot discover a coherent position (see index under "Family"). Families by definition limit autonomy and embody the irrationalities of history, and especially from the child's point of view, cannot be viewed as contractual. Liberalism of Rawls' kind tends to avert its eyes from them. Locke of course had already attacked the patriarchal family: see Robert N. Bellah, "The Church in Tension with a Lockean Culture," *New Oxford Review* 57, no. 10 (December 1990): 10–16; and Wolfe, *Whose Keeper?* 101, 109–09,123–26, 193. Rawls suggests that his whole theory of justice as fairness might have to be revised if one should attempt a more complete "metaphysics" (512). (Like many modern philosophers, Rawls uses such words with virtually no regard for their original meanings, and very little meaning at all. Whatever it means in this context—"view of the world"?—it has little to do with ontology.) I could not agree more. In regard to his statement "I assume that a stage of near justice requires a democratic regime" (363), one might ask if there are ever "near just" regimes in history.

ological claim, and runs in myriad ways through European and American history to the present.[32] I do not think that in some Comteian way the race or the individual passes from a mythical through a theological to a scientific stage. Rather, one role of reason is to reflect on myth, on the function of primitivist and similar modes of thought, which are always with us. Thus we may discover a proper boundary between the unifying visions that myth attempts and the sense of human limitation that reason produces.[33] It is always the myths that provide some sense of the whole, some sense of a place in being and perhaps of a direction in which to move. At the level at which reason examines them they are expressions of inchoate desire, of something in our nature yearning for more than reason and history can provide, a harmony perhaps between all beings. The myths cannot validate themselves and they cannot be validated by reason, although reason can perform the very important function of pointing out conflict between myth and what observation can discover, and thus help to hedge our imaginations into proper limits. Because

32. The world of scholarship on primitivism in American history may be entered through Theodore Dwight Bozeman, *To Live Ancient Lives: The Primitivist Dimension in Puritanism* (Chapel Hill: University of North Carolina Press, 1988); Wood, "Struggle Over the Puritans"; Richard T. Hughes, ed., *The American Quest for the Primitive Church* (Urbana: University of Illinois Press), 1988; and Richard T. Hughes and C. Leonard Allen, *Illusions of Innocence: Protestant Primitivism in America* (Chicago: University of Chicago Press, 1988). Bellah describes the "ontological individualism" of Americans by writing that "the individual has a primary reality whereas society is a second-order, derived or artificial construct" ("The Church in Tension with a Lockean Culture," 234). This is pursued, especially in regard to Locke, in a successor book by Bellah, et al, The *Good Society* (New York: Knopf, 1991) (see note 20). For primitivism and "misguided utopianism" in European history, see Ian Buruma, "From Hirohito to Heimat," *NYRB,* October 26, 1989); and for a ferocious attack on primitivism and the social contract, see Isaiah Berlin, "Joseph de Maistre and the Origins of Fascism: II," *NYRB,* October 11, 1990, an essay marred by the author's uneven historical knowledge.

33. What Eugene Garver, *Machiavelli and the History of Prudence* (Madison: University of Wisconsin Press, 1987), 161, remarks of the relation between reflection and action in society might also be said of reason's critique of myth: "The possibility of being a part and yet apart from a society, of recognizing that one cannot stand outside society yet can still be critical, depends on the ability of a system to recognize its own incompleteness." On myth as always with us, see Hans Blumenberg, *Work on Myth,* trans. Robert M. Wallace (Cambridge, Mass.: MIT Press, 1985), and Leszek Kolakowski, *The Presence of Myth,* trans. Adam Czerniawski (Chicago: University of Chicago Press, 1989). In addition to what Blumenberg has to say of Freud, von Balthasar, *Theo-Drama: Theological Dramatic Theory,* vol. 1, *Prolegomena,* trans. Graham Harrison (San Francisco: Ignatius Press, 1988), 508–13, lays bare the primitivist core of Freud's thought.

the desire for wholeness and unity seems to lie within our nature, the myths may perform a utopian or paradigmatic function, not unlike that of political theory. Held in check by reason, they may suggest not that our world can become radically different from what it has been, but somewhat different. The myths are not clear enough, the natural desires too imprecise, for a political system to be built on them. If they have more than an imaginative function, that lies beyond reason and history.

AFTERWORD

After I published this essay, Rawls continued to reconsider some of the issues about which I and various writers had criticized him, and published, for instance, *Justice as Fairness: A Restatement,* and *Political Liberalism.* To avoid confusion, I have published my original essay almost completely without change, because it seems to me that the positions discussed in it persisted through Rawl's later writings (see the beginning of this chapter). My comments about Rawls' position being a kind of secularized Protestantism are reinforced by his posthumous *A Brief Inquiry into the Meaning of Sin and Faith: With "On My Religion."* For criticism of Rawls from another angle, see Amartya Sen, *The Idea of Justice,* with Samuel Freeman, "A New Theory of Justice." On the viability of democracy, see Jodi Dean, *Democracy and Other Neoliberal Fantasies: Communicative Capitalism and Left Politics.* I develop what I say about religious tolerance at greater length in "Setting Boundaries: Early Medieval Reflections on Religious Toleration and their Jewish Roots"; "The Middle Ages in the History of Toleration: A Prolegomena"; and *The Turn to Transcendence: The Role of Religion in the Twenty-First Century,* the latter of which also expands on what is said here about utopianism. Peter H. Wilson, *The Thirty Years War: Europe's Tragedy,* challenges interpretations that see the Thirty Years War as primarily religious, but traces the rise of sovereign states and a secular order to it; see also William T. Cavanaugh, *The Myth of Religious Violence: Secular Ideology and the Roots of Modern Conflict.*

My comments on multiculturalism are developed in the latter and in "The Ethics of Conquest: The European Background of Spain's Mission in the New World" and "1492 in the Judgment of the Nations." I explore the question of teleology further in "The Return of Purpose," and of the natural law in "The Natural Law: The First Grace." For contrast between the contractual theories of Protestant-formed countries and the natural-law theories of Catholic countries, see Juan Fernando Segovia, *Orden Natural de la Política y Orden artificial del Estado: Refleciones sobre el Derecho Natural Católico y la Política.* Philippe Buc, *The Dangers of Ritual: Between Early Medieval Texts and Social Scientific Theory*, shows the anticipation of some of my criticisms in counter-Enlightenment thought. I have retained the format specific to the journal in which this chapter was originally published.

10

THE QUEST FOR A PUBLIC PHILOSOPHY IN TWENTIETH-CENTURY AMERICAN POLITICAL THOUGHT

THOUGH THE SUBJECT is the United States, the background is France, Alexis de Tocqueville, and the late François Furet, de Tocqueville's most influential recent interpreter. The one thing Furet thought de Tocqueville had missed in his analysis of *The Old Regime and the French Revolution* was the Revolution's dynamic. During the five years from 1789 to 1794, Furet argued, a new political theory or experience of the political came to flourish in France. This held that the traditional conflicting interests of French society were not forever to set the terms of political discourse. A new politics was to be based on "the concept of a unitary 'people' and of the 'general will'—a seamless aggregate of 'right' wills."[1] In this the idea of public opinion found its origins. Furet did not put it this way, but effectively the idea of public opinion privileged the views of one faction, identified these with right thinking, and then claimed that a general will affirming these views existed throughout society. Arguably this was no more than the old politics with a popular front. The fiction of a populace in agreement had been marshaled to override or bludgeon those of unacceptable opinions. But, to return to Furet's anal-

1. P. N. Furbank, "Tocqueville's Lament," *New York Review of Books* (hereafter *NYRB*), April 8, 1999, for this and the following.

ysis, this itself was new. From 1789, "the people" and their opinion had a striking visibility.[2]

This form of politics, Jacobinism, required a specific form of leader. Hitherto, under the old monarchy, the monarch represented but did not embody the people.[3] "The people" hardly existed. It was the nation that the king embodied. In Jacobinism, by contrast, the leader did not represent, but embodied, the people. Power was transferred from the monarchy to the people/leader and expressed through his/their voice, "opinion." Since Furet, some scholars have tried to antedate the appearance of "the people," perhaps to the 1760s, and clearly there are precedents for the developments following 1789.[4] Earlier centuries had known various attempts to influence either the thinking of all or, more typically, of some elite. Constantine had placed political messages on his coins, and there had been a propaganda war to win minds during the so-called "investiture contest" of the eleventh century. However, the "people" involved, those at whom the message had been aimed, had commonly been some minority, aristocratic or clerical. Even in the Reformation and the so-called "wars of religion," though popular passions flared in a more sustained fashion, there was no concerted attempt to develop a language in which representations about power became a new linguistic common coin.[5] In many ways, traditional patterns of lay theocracy were simply placed in service to the nation, and vice versa. The nation-state aggrandized power especially at the expense of the Church, but kings continued to embody nations, not the people. Public discourse might be of divine right—that is, about claims

2. For parallel developments in the United States, see Richard Buel, Jr., "Public Opinion," in *Securing the Revolution: Ideology in American Politics, 1789–1815* (Ithaca, N.Y.: Cornell University Press, 1972), part 3.

3. When the present chapter speaks of Jacobinism in its original form, it follows François Furet, *Interpreting the French Revolution,* trans. Elborg Forster (Cambridge: Cambridge University Press, 1981), 173–74.

4. See note 7.

5. For an introduction to the new scholarship challenging traditional thought about the wars of religion, see William T. Cavanaugh, "'A Fire Strong Enough to Consume the House': The Wars of Religion and the Rise of the State," *Modern Theology* 11 (1995): 397–420. More generally see John Milbank, Catherine Pickstock, and Graham Ward, eds., *Radical Orthodoxy: A New Theology* (New York: Routledge, 1999).

to power—yet it was about much else, as well. The Revolution, in Furet's words, "ushered in a world where mental representations of power governed all actions, and where a network of signs completely dominated political life."[6]

Thus, Furet argued, language came to center on the exercise of power. The centralized bureaucracy of the Old Regime, its patterns of thought and behavior, survived, but now it spoke the language of public opinion. The linguistic break was sharp. In the 1740s bureaucrats spoke of concrete matters, of maintaining order and of taxes. By the 1780s "their heads were filled with public and philanthropic projects: roads, canals, manufactures, charity organizations, and agronomy."[7] "Public opinion"—so Furet develops de Tocqueville's analysis—the ideas of the *philosophes,* first became the language of the king's own letters and then, with the Revolution, the language of "the people." The linguistic turn was away from the past and toward the radical, abstract, rational, and utopian. This involved a turn from practice, from the practical wisdom formed by experience in dealing with intractable realities, and a loss of skepticism about the likelihood of achieving even the most desirable of reforms. It "brought all the habits of literature into politics."[8]

According to P. N. Furbank, the Jacobins, following that side of Rousseau they understood, gave a special meaning to democracy. In an extraordinary passage of *The Social Contract,* Rousseau had declared that representation has no place in a democracy: "The moment a people provides itself with representatives, it is no longer free."[9] Here Rousseau had introduced the paradox that the purer the democracy, the more impossible its existence. "In a strict sense, there has never been a true democracy, and there never will be one. It is against the natural order of things that the many govern and the few are governed. . . . If there were a people of gods, it would govern itself democratically, but so perfect a government is not for

6. Furet, *Interpreting the French Revolution,* 48.

7. Furbank, "Tocqueville's Lament," 49–50.

8. De Tocqueville, cited in Furbank, "Tocqueville's Lament," 50.

9. J. Rousseau, *Du Contrat Social,* book 3, chap. 15, translated by and cited in Furbank, "Tocqueville's Lament," 51. See also Furet, *Interpreting the French Revolution,* 30–32.

men."[10] Therefore a democracy of any size should not govern itself through representatives, but "be governed autocratically by all-powerful magistrates."[11] This is the original Jacobin idea.

An argument of the present chapter is that, though Jacobinism in its original form was specific to a time and place, the term may analogously name a family of ideas that has occurred since ancient times. These center on three beliefs placed in service of a specific way of defining democracy: (1) that good government is only possible through expertise; (2) that the general populace always falls short of the expertise needed for self-government; and (3) since the end of government is the good of the people, about the nature of which unanimity is necessary, government must be by some form of magistracy on the people's behalf that brooks no opposition. To use contemporary terminology, the argument is that, though the two forms of democracy, Jacobin and representative, each embrace a type of "public reason" in quest of a public philosophy, each theory has problems specific to it. Analyzed as forms—in history they are of course mixed with each other in unending variety—each involves internal contradictions. Hence the agony of the quest for a public philosophy in our own times, but also anywhere "democracy" labels a form of government, and not simply the idea of equal treatment before the law.

The Jacobins, Furet noted, agreed that representation has no place in a democracy. Their *urtyp* was the philosophical society, which aimed at producing a unanimous opinion intended to permeate society.[12] They have had many heirs, and another argument of the present chapter is that because of the Jacobin belief that unanimity is more important than the content of what is agreed on, their model of public reason has fostered a deep irrationalism in subse-

10. J. Rousseau, *Du Contrat Social,* book 3, chap. 4; translated by and cited in Furbank, "Tocqueville's Lament," 51.

11. Rousseau, *Du Contrat Social,* book 3, chap. 1; translated by and cited in Furbank, "Tocqueville's Lament," 51.

12. Furet, *Interpreting the French Revolution,* 174: "A philosophical society . . . served as a tool designed to produce unanimous opinion, regardless of the content of that unanimity."

quent public life, nowhere more clearly than in the mode of deliberation of Communist regimes.[13] The paradox is that, though the model seems eminently rational, it ends in the deepest irrationalism. Its need for unanimity at each stage overrides its need for expertise and truth, both of which typically lead to dissent and inability to achieve unanimity.[14] When the American pragmatists or Jürgen Habermas embrace "discourse ethics," making participation in continuing public discourse more important than truth itself, if indeed truth has not become an impugned category, this continues the Jacobin project.[15]

The Jacobins have had successors to the present who have understood Rousseau's point that representation has no place in a democracy, but probably more common has been a basic confusion that simultaneously speaks the language of Jacobin and of representative democracy. Especially the latter language fails to grasp the "Rousseauian paradox": that pure democracy is impossible. Here the obvious question is, "how . . . can an impossible system be regarded as a model?"[16] The "paradox" Rousseau set forth has always confronted democracy. Thucydides clearly understood it. He found the alternative models of democratic leadership, "Jacobin" and "representative," already in fifth-century Athens. Thucydides admired the "Jacobin" Pericles—"in what was nominally a democracy, power was really in the hands of the first citizen"[17]—because he understood that the people are inexpert actually to govern and

13. Aileen Kelly places Communist Russia firmly in the neo-Enlightenment tradition ("The Russian Sphinx," *NYRB,* May 20, 1999).

14. For a study regarding the importance of reasoned dissent, see Stephen L. Carter, *The Dissent of the Governed: A Meditation on Law, Religion, and Loyalty* (Cambridge, Mass.: Harvard University Press, 1998). Bernard of Clairvaux makes the classic rejoinder of the truth-lover: "better that scandal erupt than that the truth be abandoned" ("Apologia for Abbot William," trans. Pauline Matarasso, *The Cistercian World: Monastic Writings of the Twelfth Century* [London: Penguin Books, 1993], 48).

15. See notes 34–39 below.

16. Furbank, "Tocqueville's Lament," 51, directed against what he regards as the misconceived proposal that Jacobinism "can still be a model for modern democrats" made by Patrice Higonnet in *Goodness Beyond Virtue: Jacobins During the French Revolution* (Cambridge, Mass.: Harvard University Press, 1998). Furbank speaks of a "Rousseauian paradox," but Rousseau's goal is to bring to the surface the latent contradictions of democratic theory.

17. Thucydides, *The History of the Peloponnesian War,* trans. Rex Warner (Harmondsworth: Penguin Books, 1986), bk. 2, chap. 6.

must be led.[18] Among other things, the people fight wars stupidly. Pericles' genius was that he did not follow or represent public opinion, but constantly formed it, sometimes through honest argument, but if necessary through duplicitous manipulation when the *demos* were too slow to see their own best interests (bk. 2, chap. 3). The radical ("representative") democrats of the generation after Pericles, above all Cleon and Alcibiades, led Athens to disaster, Thucydides thought, because they were only party leaders, representing the opinion of their faction more than forming it (see especially bk. 2, chap. 6 and bk. 4, chap. 15 ff.).

Thucydides, as Plato a little later, understood that because good government involves actually mastering a world of fact in a way that the people are disinclined to do, what is desirable is not democracy as rule by the people, but democracy as rule by a magistracy on behalf of the people. This was only partly Jacobin, because, though it continued the idea that rule ought to be "for" rather than "by" the people, it valued expertise more highly than the goal of convincing every last citizen of the correctness of magisterial action. That is what Plato and Aristotle meant when they defined democracy (rule by the many for the interests of the many) as a bad form of government, but insisted that all good forms of government must have as their goal the good of everyone (whether they recognize this good or not), what the Romans called the common good. Representative democracy, especially when great numbers of people are involved, inevitably leads to miscalculation and the following of irrational enthusiasms.[19] By contrast, a Jacobin form of democracy, democracy from above on behalf of the people, though of course vulnerable to all the forms of human weakness and malice that afflict every form of government, at least in principle is capable of competence, especially if it neglects that part of the Jacobin tradition that insists on

18. Thucydides, *History of the Peloponnesian War,* bk. 1, chap. 11 ff.

19. A special issue of *Critical Review,* devoted to "Public Ignorance and Democracy," takes seriously studies that confirm the abysmal level of public ignorance of everything political, and the resultant manipulation of opinion, that draw into question the coherence of democratic theory (*Critical Review* 12, no. 4 [1998]).

unanimity. Rousseau and late-eighteenth-century thought thus continued ancient discussion regarding the profound ambiguity in the meaning of democracy: discussion of whether the good of the people is best obtained by or for them. In America the two sides of a similar debate subsequently formed around Jeffersonian and Jacksonian alternatives. In Europe, always more reluctant to embrace democracy in a representative sense, the two parties formed around all the successors of enlightened monarchy from Republicanism to Communism, on the one side, and on the other, around all the tendencies to more radical forms of direct rule by the people, from the Revolutions of 1848 to the Greens today.

It is a commonplace that the European Union continues the patterns of French and Jacobin thought, albeit in a soft form. Under the banner of strengthening democracy in countries such as Greece, Spain, and Portugal, it has worked to extend the hegemony of liberal democratic institutions, and it has made the acceptance of these institutions the condition of membership for countries such as Slovakia. However, the democracy that has thus achieved hegemony is much more Jacobin than representative:

> The EU's own institutions and functioning are only minimally democratic in character. Ideas are hatched within an isolated policy elite at the Commission, or in private discussion among national leaders, and often passed into law with much of the European public scarcely noticing. But this is in large measure the secret of the EU's success. It has progressed through bold and sweeping initiatives (internal free trade, open borders, admission of new members, and a single currency) which might never have found majority support in public opinion had public opinion been allowed a determining say on any of these issues.[20]

20. Robert Cottrell, "Europe: So Far, It Flies," *NYRB,* April 8, 1999. Cottrell goes on to discuss various problems facing the EU, such as that "seen from the elitist perspective of Brussels, the question is how to increase the weight of democracy in the EU, so that it becomes more popular and more legitimate, without at the same time making its deliberations more of a hostage to the sort of populism and national chauvinism that could block further integration" (69). He admits "the Euroskeptical view of Europe as an 'elite project,' not willingly exposed to public debate, does have an awkward amount of truth in it" (71). In a follow-up piece, written after the resignation on March 16, 1999, of all the commissioners of the European Commission in the face of accusations of "fraud, mismanagement,

Wherever the European liberal and democratic tradition has spread, typically in a Jacobin form, it has continued the project of the nation-state, the direction and control of all life within its borders. Using the language of tolerance that, especially since John Locke and John Stuart Mill, has been its chief intellectual weapon against the single most important obstacle to its seizing of control—i.e., the continued influence of religion—it has been a powerful engine of secularization.[21] Thus, in a replay of earlier controversies involving the wearing of the Muslim veil in French public schools, when Merve Kavaki tried to take her oath of office on May 2, 1999, in the newly elected Turkish Parliament wearing a head scarf, she was greeted with shouts of "Out! Out! The prime minister, Bulent Ecevit, representing a strongly secular tradition that fiercely resists religious influence in public matters, declared: "No one may interfere with the private life of individuals, but this [the Parliament] is not a private space. This is the supreme foundation of the state. It is not a place in which to challenge the state."[22]

Such words—which around the world play out the history of the quest for hegemony of the nation-state and of the kind of secular universalist values embraced for India by Mohandas K. Gandhi and Jawaharal Nehru—reveal the continuing vitality of Jacobinism. That what the French call the lay tradition does not often understand itself in such matters to epitomize the intolerance it constantly ascribes to the Church and religion shows a remarkable lack of self-

---

and nepotism," Cottrell suggested that the resignation might encourage greater (representative) democracy and a shift in power from the Commission "toward national governments acting collectively" ("It Still Flies," *NYRB,* April 22, 1999).

21. For a treatment regarding the definition of liberalism, toleration, and religious freedom, see Glenn W. Olsen, "Religion, Politics, and America at the Millennium," *Faith and Reason* 22 (1996): 285–315 at 286–91, 303–14 (chapter 7 of this volume). See also Roy A. Clouser, *The Myth of Religious Neutrality: An Essay on the Hidden Role of Religious Belief in Theories* (Notre Dame, Ind.: University of Notre Dame Press, 1991). For a treatment of secularization, see Olsen, "The Meaning of Christian Culture: A Historical View," in *Catholicism and Secularization in America: Essays on Nature, Grace, and Culture*, ed. David L. Schindler (Notre Dame, Ind.: Communio, 1990), 98–130; and Olsen, "Cultural Dynamics: Secularization and Sacralization," in *Christianity and Western Civilization,* ed. the Wethersfield Institute (San Francisco: Ignatius Press, 1995), 97–122. For Mill, see note 48.

22. New York Times News Service, "Scarf Angers Lawmakers in Turkey," *Deseret News*, May 3, 1999, A4.

understanding.[23] A further argument of the present chapter is that until liberal democracy and secularism become self-conscious about the assumptions underlying their own agendas, it is difficult to see how a comprehensive public reason will be possible. The lay tradition is strongly inclined to rule out of court all arguments or points of view not rooted in its own secular tradition. Its public reason is that of the Enlightenment: abstract, quantitative, and set against tradition understood as adherence to religion and the acquired wisdom of one's fathers. Unless other languages, say that of Pascal, are also allowed into the public space, and some way is found of comparing the Cartesian or Enlightenment language of reason with, say, the much more critically aware understanding of reason found in the thought of Augusto del Noce (1910–89), public reason will embody no more than the victory of one party over another within the state.[24] John Paul II took the initiative here, and a particular project of his pontificate was the translation of traditional natural law language into the Enlightenment language of rights.[25]

It would seem that, in an obvious sense, Jacobin democracy, the totalizing state, and public opinion were made for each other. As the American anarchist Randolph Bourne put it toward the end of the First World War, the goal of the (modern national) state, its ideal, is to control everything within itself.[26] Much in the way Furet

23. Owen Chadwick chronicles the illiberalism and cynicism in regard to freedom of religion of the liberal state as represented by men such as Cavour; Chadwick, *A History of the Popes, 1830–1914* (Oxford: Oxford University Press, 1998); see note 21.

24. Giuseppe Riconda has written a stunning essay on the significance of Pascal's inability to gain entrance into the philosophical "canon," and on his critique of rationalism, with its intrinsic logic of secularization; Riconda, "Augusto Del Noce: Between Thomism and Religious Existentialism," *Communio* 25 (Winter 1998): 716–31.

25. For a treatment of both the nature and limitations of such translation in regard to political language, see Olsen, "Religion, Politics, and America," 306–15; and Peter Toon, "Christianity and Subjective Human Rights," *Touchstone* 11, no. 6 (November–December 1998): 31–35. David Novak brilliantly explains how many Enlightenment thinkers advanced an idea of natural law that little reflects human nature; Novak, *Natural Law in Judaism* (New York: Cambridge University Press, 1998). Novak's final chapter explains how natural-law theory can be used by religious people, or any minority, to make rights claims without accepting the logic of secularism that has commonly accompanied a Kantian account of universal human rights.

26. This and the following are much indebted to Michael J. Baxter, "Peter Maurin Blows the Dynamite," *Houston Catholic Worker* 19, no. 2 (March–April 1999): 7–11, here at

later described the origins of public opinion, Bourne revealed the state as aiming at a system of conformity through the construction of an elaborate complex of symbols and attitudes aiming at "state-feeling" or "state-enthusiasm": "Public opinion, as expressed in the newspapers, and the pulpits, and the schools, becomes one solid block."[27] This has been described for America in another context as "Americanism": the civil religion of America, founded on the Declaration of Independence and the Constitution as holy documents.[28] Though Jacobinism has had a role in its dissemination, this civil religion has been genuinely popular, rooted in America's founding events. Americanism is the worship of America, of American exceptionalism, of the American experience, of America the light of the nations. Although called into question and eroded in the disenchantment following the Vietnam War, it has provided the closest thing in America to a common ground of belief on which most could unite.[29]

The deep irony, rarely explored, is that the premises on which public debate is founded in America are a melding of religion and Enlightenment as they stood in the late eighteenth century.[30] That is, in this "nation with the soul of a church," public reason has always had religious roots. Nothing more clearly illustrates this than

10. For Bourne, see "The State," in *War and the Intellectuals: Collected Essays by Randolph S. Bourne, 1915–1919,* ed. Carl Resek (New York: publisher unknown, 1964), 65–104. Over the course of its history, the European state has of course taken many forms, with varying degrees of single-mindedness in pursuit of control: for a good introduction, see Thomas Ertmann, *Birth of the Leviathan: Building States and Regimes in Medieval and Early Modern Europe* (New York: Cambridge University Press, 1997).

27. Bourne, "The State," 70, 77–78; Baxter, "Peter Maurin," 10.

28. Olsen, "American Culture and Liberal Ideology in the Thought of Christopher Dawson," *Communio* 22 (1995): 702–20, at 705 ff.; Olsen, "Religion, Politics, and America," 288 ff.; and Olsen, "America as an Enlightenment Culture," in *Actas del IV Congreso "Cultura Europea,"* ed. Enrique Banús and Beatriz Elío (Pamplona: Arazandi, 1998), 121–28 (chapter 8 of this volume).

29. There have, of course, always been dissenters: Mark Y. Hanley, *Beyond a Christian Commonwealth: The Protestant Quarrel with the American Republic, 1830–60* (Chapel Hill: University of North Carolina Press, 1994). Mary P. Ryan presents the nineteenth-century background of many concerns of the present essay; Ryan, *Civic Wars: Democracy and Public Life in the American City During the Nineteenth Century* (Berkeley: University of California Press, 1997).

30. See note 28.

the assumption, still today, of putatively secular thinkers of a culturally Protestant way of defining moral questions. The American Civil Liberties Union takes it for granted that one's position on an issue such as abortion comes from one's religion, because that is how Protestantism understands moral questions. If bigotry involves refusal to describe the views of one's opposition correctly, the putatively liberal and secular ACLU every day on this question practices anti-Catholic bigotry, for Catholicism understands the morality of abortion in the first instance to center on questions of natural justice.[31]

In America, though there have always been traditions of republican virtue, the understanding of democracy generally and increasingly, at least on the face of it, has been representative rather than Jacobin. If indeed it is now common to dismiss Jacobin democracy as no more a "real" democracy than the democracy of the former German Democratic Republic, this has only increased the poignancy of the Rousseauian paradox. By whatever definition, democracy, whether in Europe or America, seems implicated in dilemmas it cannot resolve. These become particularly acute in America because of a values pluralism that, especially at the present, unendingly complicates any attempt at the long-term and broad-based public discussion necessary to a representative form of democracy.[32] In response, many ostensible believers in representative democracy make proposals that in fact embody a Jacobin vision of public reason. Public discussion of a representative form seems by definition to require agreement on terms, continuity of debate over time, and some consensus as to the goods to be pursued—that is, about the aims of national life. Historically, the civil religion of Americanism has provided some degree of such things, but in an age of multiculturalism

31. Olsen, "Separating Church and State," *Faith and Reason* 20 (1994): 403–25 (chapter 6 of this volume). On "the inherent illiberalism of liberal ideology," see Mary Frances Berry, "Review," *American Historical Review* 103 (1998): 1677–78, at 1678.

32. In addition to note 21 above, see Olsen, "The Catholic Moment?" *Communio* 15 (1988): 474–87, and "The 'Catholic Moment' and the Question of Inculturation," in *Catholicity and the New Evangelization,* Proceedings from the Seventeenth Convention of the Fellowship of Catholic Scholars, Corpus Christi, Texas, 1994, ed. Anthony J. Mastroeni (Steubenville, Ohio: Franciscan University Press, 1995), 17–54, esp. 36–41 (chapter 1 of this volume).

involving not just different cultural styles but incommensurate values, this religion is finding it harder to be the "tie that binds."

Thus in America the quest for a public philosophy has increasingly a tragic dimension that perhaps even de Tocqueville, with his belief that democracy was the future providence intended, did not fully anticipate. In Europe, at least some, the Burckhardts, Nietzsches, and Unamunos, have always seen this tragic dimension. In America, with some exception for thinkers such as H. Richard and Reinhold Niebuhr, it is mostly in recent decades that debate between liberals and communitarians has begun adequately to reveal the depths of the American dilemmas and has begun to assess the possibility of a shared philosophy or public reason in a culturally diverse democracy of the representative form.[33] If de Tocqueville was right—that democracy is the future—the question now is whether that future can ever be anything but obscurantist and irrational, caught between incompatible affirmations and premises, always ideological, forever the realm of a public opinion so embarrassing as to merit caricature of the order the Greek stage regularly reserved to its choruses: the voice of the people, fluctuating, cowardly, and addled.

The lines of a very influential form of twentieth-century American quest for a public philosophy were laid down by John Dewey in his *The Public and its Problems.*[34] This work stands in a tradition of American liberal pragmatism that has argued that legislation should not advance any particular moral view, but should simply facilitate the smooth functioning of society. Dewey conceived of public authority as justified by its ascertaining and satisfying public needs. His public was the area in which the consequences of the

33. For orientation to this debate, see Olsen, "John Rawls and the Flight from Authority: The Quest for Equality as an Exercise in Primitivism," *Interpretation: A Journal of Political Philosophy* 21 (1994): 419–36 (chapter 9 of this volume); Stephen Mulhall and Adam Swift, *Liberals and Communitarians,* 2nd ed. (Cambridge, Mass: Blackwell, 1996); and Michael J. Sandel, *Democracy's Discontent: America in Search of a Public Philosophy* (Cambridge, Mass.: Harvard University Press, 1996).

34. John Dewey, *The Public and Its Problems* (New York: Henry Holt, 1927); cf. Olsen, "'You Can't Legislate Morality': Reflections on a Bromide," *Communio* 2 (1975): 148–62, at 150–53.

actions of individual citizens are felt by others and regulated by the state. Dewey saw questions of truth and value as not applying to this public, and he eschewed traditional discussion of "the best form of government." Inconsistently, he wrote of the "good" state as well-organized for the care of the public interest. For Dewey, law and morality are to be disjunct, the one regulating public interests, the other calculating the relation of means to ends in private life. This is a naive view that, like the claim that the liberal state is capable of providing a value-neutral playing field for all citizens, fails to recognize that it is impossible for legislation not to embody some moral viewpoint. Dewey's view thus fails to understand that "the smooth functioning of society" cannot be defined without introducing moral questions.

Though disliking nineteenth-century individualism and *laissez-faire* ideals, Dewey developed an implied social model that was atomistic. He stood within a long tradition of English-American liberalism and the social contract, which saw the individual as prior to the state and, then, the state as the regulator of individuals, rather than as engaged in the classical project of making good citizens and men. Virtually everything Dewey advocated has remained central to American liberalism and pragmatism—witness the thought of John Rawls.[35] Similarly, Dewey's internal contradictions have remained the internal contradictions of the liberal and pragmatic traditions: again witness Rawls.[36] Of course there has been refinement and, to stay with Rawls as an example, Rawls's theory of justice tried to answer some of the most embarrassingly unanswered questions in Dewey's thought, above all the question of whether there are felt individual interests that ought to be denied by the state, and on what grounds.[37] One of the more striking things about Dewey's thought

35. Olsen, "John Rawls and the Flight from Authority."

36. John Kekes offers a devastating analysis of the incoherence of Anglo-American liberal theory in his *Against Liberalism* (Ithaca, N.Y.: Cornell University Press, 1997). His subsequent *A Case for Conservatism* (Ithaca, N.Y.: Cornell University Press, 1998) is a case for a post-religious conservatism that is almost as secularist as the liberalism he earlier critiqued.

37. My last-cited article (note 35 above) argues for Rawls's failure here.

is that, though his typically American caricatures of non-democratic forms of governments and his prejudices on behalf of (representative) democracy are everywhere visible, his ruling out of arguments about "the best state" and his belief that public authority should be morally neutral make it impossible to judge between political systems, except by the criterion of their efficiency in addressing felt interests. The logic of such a criterion, a logic Dewey never saw, was if anything on the side of a Jacobin conception of democracy.

Probably the most influential of twentieth-century American attempts to develop a public philosophy was Walter Lippmann's *Essays in the Public Philosophy,* published in 1955, twenty-eight years after Dewey's *Public and Its Problems.* Lippmann (1889–1974) represented a kind of qualified liberalism that, while not wanting to destroy the pluralism of American society, saw the need for a common core of values and goals, as well as of an agreement to pursue these through rational public debate. This was a rather academic view of what actually happens in public life, but is not, on that account, to be scorned. Its educational equivalent and parallel were the many Great Books and Western Civilization courses of mid-century, which tried to do for education what Lippmann proposed for public life: to provide a canon or core of required readings that the educated would have read as the basis on which public discussion could go forward.[38] By a method not wholly unlike that sketched out in the matter of religion in Thomas More's *Utopia,* people of differing traditions were to take up at least some of the great questions of human life and through prolonged and thorough analysis and discussion construct a common core any rational man could accept as the basis for public life.

Lippmann, like the larger liberal tradition in which he stood, never confronted very directly or in a principled way the brute fact that pluralism of values and the ideal of a shared public discourse work against one another. Each gains at the expense of the other. If the form of pluralism under discussion is value or deep pluralism, and not simply cultural pluralism, by definition the more plu-

38. Olsen, "The University as Community: Community of What?" in *Ideas for the University,* ed. Ed Block, Jr. (Milwaukee: Marquette University Press, 1995), 29–60, at 31–33.

ralism reigns, the more impossible it is even to find a common language for discourse. A shared view of life will always be gained at the expense of deep pluralism. With Dewey, Lippmann's reasons for limiting deep pluralism tended to be pragmatic rather than philosophical. This remained the situation to the end of the twentieth century, when, though under attack, the ideals of Lippmann were still alive, as in the thought of Arthur Schlesinger, Jr. In some ways Schlesinger was a man of Lippmann's generation, of the "Old Left," who lived into grimmer times. He realized that the ideals of community and multiculturalism (here meaning pluralism of values) are incompatible. He saw the need for a common core of values and experience—the cultural equivalent of a canon—if any nation is to survive. Like Gore Vidal in his famous comparisons of Lincoln to Bismarck, he saw that "the *unum* comes at the expense of the *pluribus*."[39] But he was unable to see that the social dissolution he lamented was, in its intellectual aspects, the working out of the thin ideals of community that are at the core of the liberal tradition.[40]

The liberal tradition has historically been a great solvent. Beginning in its English form in a self-assured culture with a broad base of accepted truths, liberalism has always represented a "flight from authority" in the sense that it has been ordered to "freedom from" rather than "freedom for."[41] Just as Protestantism from the beginning defined itself in opposition to Catholicism, liberalism has been able to define itself negatively, as wishing to increase "freedom." In America, liberalism has defined itself, again negatively, against especially the religious traditions of Calvinism and Puritanism, but also of the Protestant ascendancy as embodied in a man like John Pierpont Morgan (c. 1913), with his insistence that trust and character, not property, money, or competitive markets, are the basis of a sound economy.[42] His was a view that rooted the public philos-

39. Christopher Hitchens, "The Cosmopolitan Man," *NYRB,* April 22, 1999.

40. Arthur Schlesinger, Jr., *The Disuniting of America* (New York: Norton, 1992); cf. Olsen, "University as Community," 43–44.

41. See notes 21 and 32.

42. Jean Strouse, *Morgan: American Financier* (New York: Random House, 1999); cf. Richard Skidelsky, "Giant," *NYRB,* May 6, 1999.

ophy in a Protestant ascendancy. Arguably, commercial and mercantile traditions always tend toward the cosmopolitan and tolerant: that is, what is good for business. Morgan represented a moment in time when the logic of *laissez-faire* economics, what Elizabeth Fox-Genovese and Eugene Genovese subsequently excoriated as the developing capitalism of the North of the United States, was becoming pervasive.[43] As a rather old-fashioned banker who believed in character, Morgan turned his energies to protecting the American economy from itself, intervening in the money market to stop various panics—not without benefiting in the process himself.

Schlesinger, a secularized Jew, had the misfortune to live through the collapse of the Protestant ascendancy represented by men such as Morgan. This collapse further revealed, for those with the eyes to see, the symbiotic relationship liberalism had always had to some "thicker" community against which it defined itself. Schlesinger could not see with all clarity that it was his own liberalism that was implicated in the social dissolution of America. All he could do was wish for the recovery of an earlier time in which it had not yet been declared that nothing could stand in the way of the individual's definition of his own existence (the latter view is epitomized in the decision of the Supreme Court in *Planned Parenthood v. Casey,* which, abandoning earlier Supreme Court appeals to a right to privacy, grounds the right to abortion on the right to construct one's own meaning of life).[44] Because, like More's Utopians, Schlesinger took his own position as the only one that enlightened people would embrace, he was unable to see that what he wanted by way of a shared life was in fact the victory of his own liberal position. Liberalism should be the public philosophy.

At the present, T. M. Scanlon continues the tradition of atom-

43. Elizabeth Fox-Genovese and Eugene Genovese, *Fruits of Merchant Capital: Slavery and Bourgeois Property in the Rise and Expansion of Capitalism* (New York: Oxford University Press, 1983); and Eugene Genovese, *The Southern Tradition: the Achievement and Limitations of an American Conservatism* (Cambridge, Mass.: Harvard University Press, 1994).

44. According to *Casey,* the right to abortion is necessary "to define one's own concept of existence, of meaning, of the universe, and of the mystery of human life"; cited in "Abortion and a Nation at War," an editorial in *First Things,* no. 26 (October, 1992): 9–13, at 9.

ism and the social contract that runs from Dewey through Rawls. Extending the notion of an implied social contract, Scanlon in some ways gives an Anglo-Saxon version of Jürgen Habermas's "communicative interaction" and "discourse ethics," in which social integration is seen as obtained by struggle between points of view.[45] As with Habermas, this integration is not through a "common good," suited to all human beings and universally true, but through assent to public discourse envisioned as a continuing discussion. This discussion is intelligible within its own tradition, but incapable of transcendence or of being true in any absolute sense. It is a game in which one finds oneself, and by the rules of which one agrees to play. All that is normative is the ever-shifting configuration of an unending debate. We might call this deeply irrational view, which gives no reason beyond self-interest and survival for participating in such a game, a kind of "democratic fascism," for lacking any objective standards of truth, social integration is obtained by subjection to the rules of the game and the soft fascism of majority rule.[46] Its discourse is that of a novel by George Eliot, Charles Dickens, or Salman Rushdie, "a loose journalistic epic, documentary or possibly even didactic in inspiration, offering a commentary on current institutions."[47] "*Middlemarch* and *Bleak House* simply *are* the philosophical discourse of Liberalism, which is constitutionally unamenable to dialectical defense. . . . The novel is Liberalism's true and proper genre."[48]

45. For Habermas and the following criticisms, see my "Religion, Politics, and America," 294. For Michael Oakeshott's attacks on political rationalism and his theory that civil association is a continuous conversation with no goal, see Robert Grant, *Oakeshott* (London: Claridge Press, 1990).

46. Barbara Herrnstein Smith offers a very able analysis of the fate of law and justice when truth, reason, and objectivity are rejected, in her *Belief and Resistance: Dynamics of Contemporary Intellectual Controversy* (Cambridge, Mass.: Harvard University Press, 1997); cf. William E. Connolly, *Why I Am Not a Secularist* (Minneapolis: University of Minnesota Press, 1999).

47. Iris Murdoch, *Existentialists and Mystics: Writings on Philosophy and Literature* (New York: Allen Lane, 1998), as quoted by the amusing Alan Jacobs, "The Liberal Neoplatonist?" *First Things,* no. 89 (January 1999): 57–61, at 59. Tim Parks makes parallel comments on Rushdie's multicultural or multiform aesthetic, developed as an anesthetic against or solvent of fundamentalism, but incapable of more than random comment and storytelling; Parks, "Gods and Monsters," *NYRB,* May 6, 1999.

48. Jacobs, "The Liberal Neoplatonist?" 60.

For Scanlon, all political community is a community of persons who have made a contract of reasonableness to respect shared deliberative processes for making important decisions. Each society has an implied contract of consensual reasoning that makes public deliberation possible. There is no question of truth here in the sense of a claim that the content of this public deliberation corresponds to anything universal.[49] Harmony and cooperation, playing by the rules of the game, are privileged, as they always are in liberal and pragmatic positions, and it is unclear on what grounds one could dissent from the practices or habits of a given society; on what grounds one could refuse to play the game. In sum, there appears to be no place for Socrates in this world. Again, one can wonder whether once more we have anything more than a very academic view of political life, which presents everything as too peaceful and rational (the latter defined by society's conventions). Wrongdoing in Scanlon's position is no more than miscalculation or lapse of judgment, and there is no mention of the demonic or acknowledgment that history, whatever else it is, is a continuing story (also) of hate, lying, and *libido dominandi.* There is also no explanation of how, if every people has its own tradition-bound discourse, there ever could be communication, let alone peace, between traditions.

To turn to Catholic thinkers, in the twentieth century the most influential Catholic to explore the nature of America's public philosophy was John Courtney Murray. Murray took as a given the pluralistic nature of American society, which he viewed primarily as a pluralism of religion. He then set out to form a "public philosophy" that could be the ground of common action, a philosophy that would appeal to and could be used by all, of whatever or of no religion. Such a philosophy obviously could not be grounded in the beliefs of any one religion. It could, however, be based on the distinction between the natural and the supernatural that the neo-

49. In his review of T. M. Scanlon's *What We Owe to Each Other* (Cambridge, Mass.: Harvard University Press, 1998), which I am following, Stuart Hampshire criticizes Scanlon for stopping short of claiming that the processes of moral reasoning, but not the content, are universal; Hampshire, "The Reason Why Not," *NYRB,* April 22, 1999.

Scholasticism of his day affirmed. Here, the claim was that there was a natural law, autonomous from the supernatural and revelation and capable of being known by reason alone. Any human, whatever his religion or lack of religion, could use unaided reason to discover the universally good. Public philosophy could proceed as discussion and analysis of this good, and prudential judgment as to what portion of it should become the legislated basis of common life.[50] Although the doctrine of natural law played a larger role in Murray's thought than in that of Dewey or Lippmann, and while he saw American pluralism more clearly as grounded in religion and therefore necessarily religious, in many ways Murray's views were a kind of Catholicized liberalism.

Murray failed to perceive that his position accepted without examination the claim of the liberal state to be religiously neutral. He was here in the majority, for it was even more uncommon in his day than now to understand that the First Amendment to the Bill of Rights is not religiously neutral, but privileges the state over all religions, and then "protestant" forms of religion over those religions that do not accept the privatization of religion implicit in a strict separationist view of the relation of church and state.[51] Neo-Scholasticism, the Thomism of the years before the Second Vatican Council, though clearly right in thinking that natural-law theory provides the most obvious ground for a doctrine of public reason, had given a historically inaccurate account of thinkers such as Thomas Aquinas, attributing to them the theory that humans have two separate (extrinsically related) ends, one natural and one supernatural, and then seeing natural law as capable of articulating man's natural end without reference to revelation.[52] Murray accepted such neo-Scholastic views.

The Murray project is by no means dead, and it continues to be advocated by both Catholic progressives and by a group of writers

50. Baxter, "Peter Maurin," 8.

51. See notes 21–23, 26–31.

52. The essays gathered in *Radical Orthodoxy* show the limitations of this tradition. In *Fides et Ratio* 104, Pope John Paul II continued to insist that philosophical thought is often the only common ground for dialogue between different faith traditions.

sometimes called neoconservative and sometimes neoliberal. The latter is probably the better label for describing such thinkers as Michael Novak, George Weigel, and Richard John Neuhaus. But all through the twentieth century a partially distinct project, both standing alongside and intertwining with the Murray project, has appealed to American Christian thinkers. This is descendant from Max Weber, and ultimately from classical Protestantism, of which Weber expounded a worldly form.[53] This "neo-orthodox" project in one way or another continues the Lutheran distinction or disjunction between two kingdoms, one of this world and one of the next, one of politics and pragmatism, and one of religion and ideals. Two generations ago its exponents were the Niebuhrs, and in the last generation James Gustafson, but now it influences American Catholics as much as it does Protestants. In this view, religion deals with ultimate ends, "the vision thing," and politics with means. Each has its own laws, but above all politics is about compromise and not realizing ideals. One of its jobs is to make sure that the Sermon on the Mount, with its unrealistic demands, does not intrude on the political order. In its own way, as much as liberalism, this view allows politics its own autonomous life.

American Catholic thinkers such as David L. Schindler and Michael J. Baxter have shown that twentieth-century neo-Scholasticism inherited a debased understanding of the natural law, which had spread in the seventeenth and eighteenth centuries: "the neo-Scholastic enclosure of the natural within an autonomous sphere precluded a fundamental theological critique of the modern liberal state."[54] It had the effect of making religious people think they had done their duty as citizens when they had pursued concepts of the public good understood as a lowest common denominator on which people coming from any tradition could agree. It led Catholics to accept the idea that if the state could not be challenged on the

53. See especially John Milbank, *Theology and Social Theory: Beyond Secular Reason* (Malden, Mass.: Blackwell, 1991), 84.

54. On both the foregoing and the following, see Baxter, "Peter Maurin," 8, and David L. Schindler, *Heart of the World, Center of the Church: "Communio" Ecclesiology, Liberalism, and Liberation* (Grand Rapids, Mich.: Eerdmans, 1996).

basis of right reason, it could not be challenged at all—that is, from the viewpoint of revelation. By not conceiving the natural law as ordered to a supernatural end from which it could never be separated, it left Christians with no resources other than the political with which to challenge the state. Thus the lives of most religious people, in America or elsewhere, could be characterized as assimilationist, as conformed to the nation's expectations. The civil religion of Americanism became the true religion of most Catholics (or Jews, etc.), placing almost beyond imagination a vibrant Catholicism in which life in all things was ordered by the supernatural. In America, if the intense patriotism of the Catholic Church at mid-twentieth century has perhaps slightly abated, unwillingness to challenge the culture in fundamental ways continues.

Criticism of the idea of "pure nature" had been the centerpiece of the thought of French *nouvelle théologie* thinkers such as Henri de Lubac (1896–1991), but for the most part, American Catholics are only now and sometimes under the influence of non-American thinkers such as John Milbank, coming to criticize a "disenchanted" politics in favor of a "supernaturalized" politics.[55] One of the most desired goals of such an approach is to break the lock of liberalism on the political order in favor of something more generous and modest. Typically, liberalism portrays religion as the bogey, which, if allowed into the political order, will cause countless Kosovos. Thus its own control is maintained, all of which follows from the nation-state's earlier driving of religion from the political arena, beginning with that great coup of smart-labeling, "the Wars of Religion," in which in fact the nation used war and the existence of religious animosity to increase its hegemony.[56]

55. For a summary of neo-Scholastic understanding of the natural and supernatural, and of de Lubac's criticisms thereof, see Paul McPartlan, *Sacrament of Salvation: An Introduction to Eucharistic Ecclesiology* (Edinburgh: T and T Clark, 1995), chap. 4. John Montag deepens this criticism in his "Revelation: The False Legacy of Suarez," in *Radical Orthodoxy,* 38–63. Central to current discussion is Milbank, *Theology and Social Theory,* 206–55. The reference to disenchantment of course is to Max Weber, on whom see Frederick C. Bauerschmidt, "The Politics of the Little Way: Dorothy Day Reads Thérèse of Lisieux," in *American Catholic Traditions: Resources for Renewal,* ed. Sandra Yocum Mize and William L. Portier (Maryknoll, N.Y.: Orbis Books, 1997), 77–95, at 77–79.

56. In addition to note 5 above, see the introduction to *Radical Orthodoxy,* 14; and, in

What the supernaturalization of politics involves, by contrast, is the claim that religious people do not have to "leave their religion at the door," but can try to form the political order according to their full view of the truth (not just their "natural" views). One should no more expect religious people to abide by the lowest-common-denominator rules of liberalism than liberals expect to be held to a supernatural view of life. Once one has admitted that the "tolerance" liberals typically practice is an exercise in bigotry that excludes supernatural religion from the political order so that secular people can feel comfortable in it, it has to be acknowledged that we all make each other uncomfortable and that, short of war and compulsion, the principal means we have for mediating our differences is public argument. From the viewpoint of any revealed religion self-conscious enough to make a distinction between faith and reason, nature must intrinsically be ordered to the supernatural. Because God is the Creator of both nature and that which is above nature, the natural or political cannot be simply autonomous and self-enclosed. It is much more human for a liberalism become self-conscious to confront a self-conscious Catholicism in a battle of ideas than for one or both sides to practice either a Jacobin or a populist manipulation of language and subterfuge. The goal here is *convivencia,* living beside one another, allowing all religions that do not attack nature a place in public life.[57] That is, the ideal is not the privatization of religion, but a political life in which the religions have a place as public actors. This *convivencia* is not a static toleration, but argument and evangelization, each trying to win over the other.

The Christian claim, more generally the claim of religion, is that since everything in fact is oriented to God, whether a given person recognizes it or not, nothing separated from revelation, politics included, is as intelligible as it could be if considered in relation to God. This is by definition an affirmation only available to the believer, but

the same volume, William T. Cavanaugh, "The City: Beyond Secular Parodies," 182–200, at 190–91.

57. Olsen, "Separating Church and State," 424–25, argues that religion does not need to be respected when it attacks nature.

the insight it provides seems very salutary after a century of asphyxiating self-enclosed political orders. The Christian claim is that, since nature always points to something beyond itself, politics conceived as simply natural is necessarily incomplete. No merely political description of reality can be adequate; life at simply the level of the political must necessarily be in some way unfulfilling. Rather than conceive of the political as an enclosed or autonomous framework that exhausts the meaning of life in some form of wholism, whether fascist, totalitarian, or liberal, the religious man suggests that politics is meant to be "open at the top" to something greater than itself. No culture is in fact self-contained, and the Christian aims at the most profound form of cultural criticism, the exploration of the limits of all existing cultures to the goal of their self-transcendence.[58]

The not-so-modest proposal of American Catholic radicals in the tradition of Dorothy Day is that it is the Church, not the state or nation, in which the Christian finds his life and being. From within the Church the Christian often must resist the order/disorder imposed by the nation-state. This is not a resistance to government *per se,* but to government in its totalizing, national-state forms, which leave no public space for the Church and religion. It should not be expected that the Christian can produce supra-political—that is, ecclesial—principles that could be the base of a public philosophy shared with nonbelievers. Rather, the Christian challenges others' claims to have produced such a "public theology," challenges the notion of public reason as it now exists, and challenges the perversion of Christianity involved in even making available to the state a justification or legitimization of its totalizing claims. In this a radical Catholicism agrees with the Old European Left in its attack on Christianity placed in service to the nation-state. The public opinion of the Jacobin tradition is revealed commonly not to be about every man, not about the common good, but about the needs of the state and those who profit from it. The poor, typically, are excluded from this public. What the Christian seeks of the political order, to repeat,

58. This is a theme of John Paul II's encyclicals *Veritatis Splendor* (see especially nos. 36 and 53) and *Fides et Ratio.*

is *convivencia,* what sometimes in America is called accommodationism, an ordering of public life so that believer and unbeliever can "share space," both to argue about differences and to manifest to each other public forms of the lives they have chosen.[59] At base, the life of a Christian is ecclesial, not national: "true society is rooted in the supernatural life of Christ and cannot be abstracted from the beliefs and practices of the Church."[60] Arguably this life takes a localist flavor and hopes and works for that day in which the principle of subsidiarity is honored.[61]

Such a point of view may be summarized in the words of John Paul II:

> There is sometime an unwillingness to challenge cultural assumptions as the Gospel demands. . . . This attitude embodies a too optimistic view of modernity, together with an uneasiness about the cross and its implications for Christian living. . . . All this causes uncertainty about the distinctive contribution which the Church is called to make in the world.[62]

In speaking of the Church's dialogue with the world, Pope Paul VI used the phrase *colloquium salutis;* not just dialogue for its own sake, but a dialogue that has its source in the Truth and seeks to communicate the Truth that frees and saves. The *colloquium salutis*

59. I argue for a prudential, but not final, accommodationism in "Separating Church and State" (see note 57).

60. Baxter, "Peter Maurin," 9. Baxter goes on, "the modern nation-state is a fundamentally unjust and corrupt set of institutions whose primary function is to preserve the interests of the ruling class, by coercive and violent means if necessary—and there will always come a time when it is necessary." Though I have considerable sympathy with his views, this does not seem to me quite right, unless the "ruling class" be extended to include all the "haves" of society. Baxter does not observe sharply enough the tendency of democracy to extend the vices of the former aristocracy to most of society.

61. Olsen, "Unity, Plurality, and Subsidiarity in Twentieth-Century Context," in *Actas del III Congreso "Cultura Europea,* 311–17 (chapter 11 of this volume). Immanuel Wallerstein traces the failures of liberal ideology and the breakdown of the nation-state system, arguing that the first quarter or half of the twenty-first century will be characterized by the breakdown of the modern world system, conflict, and disorder; Wallerstein, *Utopistics: Or, Historical Choices of the Twenty-first Century* (New York: New Press, 1998). For the argument that what rather is occurring is "globalization," the development of international laws, regulations, and economic arrangements in a way that inevitably limits the autonomy of any single state, see Tony Judt, "On Kosovo: The Reason Why," *NYRB,* May 20, 1999.

62. John Paul II, "Ad Limina Address to Australian Bishops," *Adoremus Bulletin* 4, no. 9 (February 1999): 6–8, at 6.

requires that the Church be different precisely for the sake of dialogue.

AFTERWORD

This chapter is a revision of a paper presented at the Third International Symposium on Philosophy and the Social Sciences, Pamplona and San Sebastiàn, Spain, October 29–31, 1999; I have made minor changes. Aziz Al-Azmeh and János M. Bak, eds., *Monotheistic Kingship: The Medieval Variants,* in noting how common monotheistic kingship was in the ancient world and into modern times, present this as "a vast perspective in which the primitive republican image of Rome or of Athens seems aberrant, paltry and inconsequential, if indeed this image of republican purity, of the splendid childhood of rational political man, has any credibility apart from Jacobin and proto-Jacobin imaginings." Some of the themes of the present chapter are pursued further in my *The Turn to Transcendence: The Role of Religion in the Twenty-First Century.* See the various books of Ephraim Radner on Christianity and modernity. See also J. Budziszewski, "To Lose Man: What 'Public Reason' Can Learn from Public Faith," and on the larger question of the quest for community, Robert Nisbet, *The Quest for Community: A Study in the Ethics of Order and Freedom,* with a new introduction by Ross Douthat. I have elaborated on the use of the Great Books curriculum to give cultural cohesiveness in "Christopher Dawson and the Renewal of Catholic Education: The Proposal that Catholic Culture and History, not Philosophy, should Order the Catholic Curriculum." See also on both the use of education in the U.S. to foster civic ideals, and on the child-centered educational ideals of Dewey and his successors, E. D. Hirsch, Jr., "How to Save the Schools." Jonathan Zimmerman, "What Are Schools For?" treats the importance of collective goals in education. My comments on the relation of grace to nature are expanded in "The Natural Law: The First Grace," *Communio* 35 (2008): 354–73, an issue devoted to natural law. See on Rousseau, Francis Oakley, *The Emergence of Western Po-*

litical Thought in the Latin Middle Ages, vol. 1, *Empty Bottles of Gentilism: Kingship and the Divine in Late Antiquity and the Early Middle Age (to 1050)*. John Dewey and progressive ideology are well treated by Michael D. Aeschliman, "The Catholic Authority of Reason," in *The Idea of the Catholic University,* ed. Kenneth D. Whitehead; see also Michael Hampe, ed., *John Dewey,* 2 vols. On Jürgen Habermas, see David Ingram, *Habermas: Introduction and Analysis.* There is a second edition of John Milbank, *Theology and Social Theory: Beyond Secular Reason.*

PART 3

THE ENCOUNTER WITH EUROPE, NATIVE AMERICANS, AND MODERNITY

11

UNITY, PLURALITY, AND SUBSIDIARITY IN TWENTIETH-CENTURY CONTEXT

A DEBATE ABOUT THE RELATIONSHIP between unity, plurality, and subsidiarity runs through European culture and history. "Unity" indicates the degree to which any culture possesses or forms a consensus and has shared values or a common world view. "Plurality" marks the existence, persistence, or development of subcultures within a culture, views of the world distinct from and not easily assimilable to the preponderant culture. "Subsidiarity" designates a cultural form of the political principle that in any society each human activity should be accomplished at the lowest possible social level compatible with survival and effectiveness: culturally this means the toleration of diverse subcultures within a larger culture as long as the shared existence of all is not seriously imperiled or rendered unacceptably inefficient. Put another way, subsidiarity as a cultural principle involves decisions about what degree of plurality is to be tolerated or fostered "in the middle," in between a destructive overunification and a dissolving, unending pluralism. Being "in the middle" can designate either organic and intermediate institutions in a single state, regions or peoples within some larger political entity, or small countries. Since the Middle Ages, questions of the relationship of unity, plurality, and subsidiarity have most commonly been asked at the national level, but increasingly these questions are being posed at the level of Europe itself. Historically composed of some shared elements, the very definition of "Europe," as well as its future, increasingly is the subject of debate and contention. What is or should be common ("unity"); what is or should be the expression of difference ("plurality"); at what level of social organization can regional, religious, or ethnic variation within a culture be tolerated or encouraged ("subsidiarity")?

Rather than deal in a single chapter with the unending social and historical detail relevant to this topic, I would like to articulate what is involved in principle if we stress one or the other of the polar terms "unity" and "plurality," and I wish to argue for the wisdom of a cultural emphasis on the principle of subsidiarity. For this some historical background is necessary. First it should be said that the terms "principle of subsidiarity" and "principle of subsidiary function" are of twentieth-century invention, going back no further, so far as I have been able to determine, than the papal encyclical *Quadragesimo Anno*, published by Pope Pius XI in 1931.[1] This said, the debate between unity and plurality goes back at least as far as Aristotle's criticism in book II of the *Politics* of Plato's proposals in the *Republic* concerning community of goods. In discussing the impracticability of Socrates' proposals in regard to the community of women, Aristotle observed that Socrates worked from the mistaken supposition "that it is best for the whole state to be as unified as possible."[2] This was a criticism of the argument of the *Republic* as a whole, in which, from Aristotle's point of view, Socrates' vision of justice as the preeminent virtue of the state led to an overunification in which the state ended up destroying things, such as property and the family, that it exists in fact to nurture. Unity destroys plurality and in the process all "middling" institutions, such as the family. Although Aristotle does not use the work "subsidiarity" to describe his

1. See note 9. Pope John XXIII, referring back to and quoting this encyclical in *Mater et Magistra* 53 (see also 65, 117, 152), trans. H. E. Winstone, *New Light on Social Problems* (London: Catholic Truth Society, 1963), 53, used the expression "principle of subsidiary function."

2. *The Complete Works of Aristotle*, vol. 2, ed. Jonathan Barnes (Princeton: Princeton University Press, 1984), 2001, for this and the following.

argument that society is an organic or hierarchic whole of which the parts must each have their appropriate level of self-determination, he is the fount of consideration of subsidiarity in Western tradition. His is not an autonomy that is absolute and thus disallows all unity, but a self-determination limited by such natural authority as that of parents and by what the Romans were to call the common good. Such relative autonomy allows individuals, families, and villages each to work toward their own perfection by making choices for themselves, but choices not destructive of forms of human society more complete than themselves. Aristotle asked "Is it not obvious that a state may at length attain such a degree of unity as to be no longer a state?" and then answered his own question with a *reductio ad absurdum* of Plato's position. Since a family is more unified than a state, and an individual than a family, if unity truly is Socrates' goal the state should try to eliminate all plurality within itself until, as a limit, it stands forth as an individual. This of course is a formula for tyranny, an anticipation of the formula "L'État, c'est moi." For Aristotle it completely missed the fact that "the nature of a state is to be plurality." That is, according to Aristotle's analysis or counterproposal, in the order of nature the family perfects the individual, and the state the family, so that the state exists to complete, not destroy, the parts or plurality, the "subcultures," of which it is composed. Both plurality and subsidiarity are features of a healthy state. Were the state to attempt a level of unity in which, for instance, the family was destroyed, it would effectively have destroyed itself, for its very *raison d'être* is to lead toward perfection the various things of which it is composed, the things less complete than itself.

Aristotle seems to me to have gotten it exactly right, to have explained the nature of the state as a plurality. Unity and plurality cannot exist without each other, because unity itself, that is, the state, is a kind of ordered plurality. The function of the state is to allow each kind of thing within it to flourish at its appropriate level. Although here I can only make the observation, I would note that Aristotle's analysis is not available to anyone who denies the idea of "the natural." Most twentieth-century political positions are ideological—that is, begin with an *a priori* such as that all people by nature are equal, rather than attending to a natural order in which, so far as empirical observation is concerned, all people are by nature unequal. That is, most twentieth-century positions begin with what from Aristotle's point of view is an attack on nature, by asserting something counterfactual: namely, that people are equal. In all observable and measurable ways, people are not. Therefore, a scientific politics such as Aristotle's, which begins with the observation of nature and assumes that the inequalities observed in nature will be replicated in the political order, can hardly be placed in the service of the denials of a natural order that dot the twentieth-century political landscape. So far as I can see, if the denial of nature is taken seriously, say as in the thought of John Rawls, all that remains is plurality or individualism—Anglo-Saxon liberalism.[3] Without an analysis that leads from the incompletenesses of natural entities such as the family to the desirability of such instruments of their perfection as the state, we can have no principled discussion of the question of unity, plurality, and subsidiarity itself. The very idea of subsidiarity implies the hierarchical, rather than egalitarian, nature of human society. If the only reality is the individual, and then perhaps as in the myth of the social contract, a state erected above individuals as a matter of convenience, there is no natural hierarchy of entities within the state, nothing ontologically "in the middle," to be ordered between unity and plurality. The existence of intermediary associations becomes as arbitrary as the existence of the state itself. As I have said, I cannot deal with this question in all its ramifications here, but the point is that it is doubtful that a modern politics of an individualist, utilitarian, or liberal form can have any principled resolution of the relations between unity, plurality, and subsidiarity.

Although scattered further discussion of the question of subsidiarity can be found later in the ancient world, Aristotle's ideas had only limited influence in the Latin West before the high Middle

3. Of my various writings on this subject, see "John Rawls and the Flight from Authority: The Quest for Equality as an Exercise in Primitivism," *Interpretation: A Journal of Political Philosophy* 21 (1994): 419–36 (chapter 9 in this volume).

Ages. When the *Politics* was recovered in the thirteenth century and translated into Latin, the discussion of subsidiarity proceeded, notably in the thought of Aquinas and Dante. The specifically theological ideas of the former immensely deepened the understanding of what was philosophically at issue in any discussion of unity, plurality, and subsidiarity. I will leave aside Aquinas' observations about mankind's natural desire for good and therefore for unity, and, to illustrate the advance in understanding he represents, restrict myself to his remarks on "secondary causation" and the possibility of the human sciences.[4] In discussing God's providence, Aquinas observed that at any level of government "it is a greater perfection for a thing to be good in itself and also the cause of goodness in others, than only to be good in itself."[5] He drew an analogy between God and a schoolmaster. The ideal schoolmaster is not one who simply imparts knowledge, but one who forms a pupil to one day be a master. That is, the ideal is a form of self-possessed knowledge, in which knowledge is not merely held in a rote way, but is understood in itself in a manner that could be passed on to another. Whether we wish to follow Aquinas further in his argument that this is the way in which God rules the universe, both directly and indirectly through laws that are part of the natural order, the point is that he proposed a view of human life in which each person is, so far as possible, to achieve his or her full human potential not as an imposed perfection, but as something achieved by him- or herself. Here, although the discussion is not formally about subsidiarity at all, we see the reason for subsidiarity. Granted a natural and hierarchical order of being, the goal of subsidiarity is to foster at each level of human society self-possession and mastery of one's immediate world.

There is an ideal running through Spanish history beginning in the Middle Ages that illustrates this rather well.[6] Without getting into discussion of the adequacy of this or that particular historical

4. See, for instance, Thomas Aquinas, *Summa Theologica* (hereafter *ST*), Part I, q. 103, a. 3.

5. *ST* I, q. 103, a. 6, in *Basic Writings of Saint Thomas Aquinas,* vol. 1, ed. Anton C. Pegis (New York: Random House, 1945), 958.

6. Miguel Ayuso Torres, *La Filosofía Juridica y Política de Francisco Elías de Tejada*

expression of this traditional ideal, I simply refer to the idea that every level of society should deal with those aspects of life immediate to itself, in which reasonably it can be expert: at the level of the city, there is to be self-government over the affairs of daily life; the province is to deal with more regional questions; and the monarch or state is above all responsible for foreign and military affairs. In such a view the creation of culture, the environment in which one lives, is the means by which humans perfect themselves, and for this each needs an appropriate stage on which to work out his or her destiny. For many purposes, that which is local or regional, perhaps that which is the expression of a linguistic frontier, will be on a scale more appropriate to the development of the capacities of most people than that which is national or international.

To understand is to move toward unity, to order more and more phenomena by fewer and fewer principles. The political correlative of this observation historically has been the quest for a universal political institution, an empire, monarchy, or United Nations. Until the eighteenth century such a quest most commonly took the form of argument for monarchy as the best form of human government, and thus we are not surprised to find development of the principle of subsidiarity in Dante's essay *On World-Government.* That is, precisely because he felt the power of arguments for unity and world government while also being a Florentine Republican, Dante reflected on the place and dignity of the regional. He observed that in arguing for one supreme prince to govern the entire race he did not mean that every decision of every municipality was to issue directly from the world monarch: "For nations, kingdoms, and cities have their special conditions which ought to be regulated by different laws."[7] Dante went on to give examples of these special con-

(Madrid: Fundación Francisco Elías Tejada y Erasmo Pèrcopo, 1994), esp. 286 ff., treats both Spanish and European traditionalism.

7. *Dante* Alighieri, *De Monarchia,* book I, 14, trans. Philip Wicksteed, *A Translation of the Latin Works of Dante Alighieri* (London 1904; repr. New York: Greenwood Press, 1969), reprinted in *The Intellectual Tradition of the West,* vol. 1, ed. Morton Donner, Kenneth Eble, and Robert Helbling (Salt Lake City, Utah: no publisher given, 1982), 378. For orientation, see Joan M. Ferrante, *The Political Vision of the Divine Comedy* (Princeton: Princeton University Press, 1984).

ditions, all of which involved what today would be called cultural variation. The Scythians must be governed differently than the Garamantes because of difference in climate and geography. "But it must be . . . understood that the human race in those things which are common, and are inherent in all, should be ruled by . . . [the one supreme prince], and guided by his common rule to peace."

Here Dante brought to center stage the Roman ideal of jurisprudence. As perhaps the most self-conscious of ancient imperialists, the Romans gave much attention to the possibility that there was a best law for all mankind, and that this law should aim at peace. In the territories they conquered they found in fact unending legal variation, which they tended to tolerate, but their legal thinkers wondered whether in principle, if man is a rational animal, it did not follow that the working out of human reason should express itself in a law most suited to perfecting humans. Was it possible with time for regional variation to decline in favor of a more philosophical conception of law, a *ius naturale* or a *ius gentium?* Such an idea of law has remained the ideal in the Latin countries of Europe, and stands in stark contrast to the Anglo-Saxon notion of law as precedent, a much more historical and much less philosophical or jurisprudential idea. Although presumably a united Europe would leave these very different conceptions at the national level, the proposal that all states apply the same norms of international law perhaps continues the Roman project of a best legal code. I say perhaps, because especially in the North of Europe, there are strongly utilitarian, positivist, and pragmatic conceptions of law that envision international law as no more than a problem-solving device. One must admit that, even in this case, international law does provide a principle of unity for a plurality of what, on one account, would remain the sovereign states of a European commonwealth.[8] Still, this unity is quite superficial, and does not express agreement even over the nature of the law, let alone a very long list of shared values.

8. Tony Judt, "How the East Was Won," and Eric Hobsbawm, "The New Threat to History," *New York Review of Books* (hereafter *NYRB*), December 16, 1993, and Michael

The most sustained development of the principle of subsidiarity is found in the papal social encyclicals of the last hundred and some years, beginning with Leo XIII's *Rerum novarum* of 1891 and especially prominent in John Paul II's commemoration of the centennial of Leo's document. The earlier encyclical began (3) with a lament on the eighteenth-century destruction of the guilds and other intermediary social institutions that had shielded the working man from the callousness of employers and the quasi-slavery of unrestrained competition. In a line of argument descendant from Aquinas, Leo then observed (6–7) that the remedy for such problems lies in man himself, for by possessing reason man chooses regarding the future. The family is a true society having "at least" equal rights with the state (13) in regard to preservation and liberty. "At least" means that, because the family is anterior to the state, both in fact and in the kind of analysis of the relation of the kinds of levels of society to one another Aristotle already had pursued (i.e., logically prior), it is the more primordial social unit: should the state attack the rights of the family, it itself is to be repudiated. The reason that socialism—understood here by Leo as a doctrine that teaches the community of goods—is to be rejected, is that by this doctrine the state (15) penetrates the family, disturbing its role in the preparation of the child for "civil society." With Leo this latter term, like "subsidiarity" itself later in the writings of Pius XI, became part of a papal vocabulary intended to find a proper autonomy for each level of society. The socialist state in Leo's understanding sets aside the providence of the family in favor of the providence of the state, thus making for a kind of immaturity or stunted growth in which both parents and child are deprived of the opportunity to collaborate in the child's mastery of free will. It is precisely the natural differences between people, Leo continues (17), that makes possible the variety of roles that constitutes social life. Such natural differences exist not to cause class conflict, but as an opportunity for harmony and agreement—as many before him, Leo makes recourse to the organic metaphor

---

Ignatieff, "Homage to Russia," *NYRB,* April 21, 1994, survey recent understandings of Europe and European union.

of the body. In sum, although Leo's Catholicism probes the reasons for the need of every human to develop through participating in the creation and mastering of a world of culture immediate to him or her, the issues remain very much those articulated by Aristotle.

Forty years after Leo's encyclical, Pius XI in *Quadragesimo Anno* recalled Leo's teaching. From the perspective of 1931, Pius acknowledged that in his day large corporations had taken over much that earlier had been done by small bodies. Yet, he maintained (79): "it is a fundamental principle of social philosophy, fixed and unchangeable, that one should not withdraw from individuals and commit to the community what they can accomplish by their own enterprise and industry."[9] Leo then used the term "subsidiarity" to designate the principle we have been tracing: "The State authorities should leave to other bodies the care and expediting of business and activities of lesser moment, which otherwise become for it a source of great distraction " In 1961 John XXIII in turn in *Mater et Magistra* took up Pius' thought, laying special stress on the idea that what was at issue in discussing subsidiarity was the "social conditions which favor the full development of human personality."[10] He saw these to lie with intermediary bodies and corporate enterprises, which were simultaneously to look to their own interests and the common good. This latter theme was in turn developed by Pope John Paul II in *Laborem Exercens* (1981), which (14) presented as a kind of ideal "a wide range of intermediate bodies with economic, social, and cultural purposes."[11] These were envisioned as autonomous with regard to the public powers, but subordinated to the demands of the common good. Throughout this and John Paul's later pronouncements, there is a constant stress on the link, already present in Leo XIII's thought, between personality and property. To be brief, property, intermediary institutions, culture, all are the expression of personality, the results of the creativity, the properly human work, of man the worker.

9. Pius XI, *Quadragesimo Anno,* in *Seven Great Encyclicals,* ed. William J. Gibbons (Glen Rock, N.J.: Paulist Press, 1963), 147, for this and 147–48, for the following quotation.

10. John XXIII, *Mater et Magistra* 65, trans. Winstone, 21.

11. John Paul II, *Laborem Exercens,* Vatican translation, *On Human Work* (Boston: St. Paul's Editions, 1982), 37.

John Paul filled out the meaning of subsidiarity most fully in *Centesimus Annus.* Here government was seen as the coordinator, aiming at the common good, of the spontaneous initiatives of intermediary institutions: (48) "A community of a higher order should not interfere in the internal life of a community of a lower order, depriving the latter of its functions, but rather should support it in case of need and help to coordinate its activity with the activities of the rest of society, always with a view to the common good."[12] The political order is servant to civil society. John Paul continued the pragmatic justification of subsidiarity found in much traditionalist European thought: (48) "it would appear that needs are best understood and satisfied by people who are closest to them and who act as neighbors to those in need."[13] But the ultimate justification is found in the social nature of man, which, so far as the average human being is concerned, realizes itself most in intermediary institutions.

I briefly suggested above that on all sides it is assumed that greater philosophical agreement about the nature of law is most unlikely in Europe today. To see this is to see the difficulty in giving the term "Europe" much content. The lack of agreement on substantive matters, both between countries and within each country, seems to be one of the most important things standing in the way of a European form of what in America is called a "public philosophy." That is, perceiving that a shared life is not possible without shared values, throughout the twentieth century certain American political thinkers have sought a "public philosophy." Of course by other names such a quest is as old in Europe as Thomas More's attempt in *Utopia,* in the midst of growing religious divisions, to imagine into existence a natural religion, one to which, revelation aside, any rational person would assent. Even without agreement upon revealed religion, this could continue to foster public life. While probably most would agree that American pluralism makes such a public philosophy even more unlikely than in Europe, certain American thinkers

12. John Paul II, *Centesimus Annus,* trans. in Richard John Neuhaus, *Doing Well and Doing Good: The Challenge to the Christian Capitalist* (New York: Doubleday, 1992), 243.

13. John Paul II, *Centesimus Annus* 259; see also 242–45, 249–55.

have come to the conclusion that only something like the historic "natural law" could provide a neutral ground on which people from different cultures and religions could rationally construct shared values. But to say that only with such agreement could such a project proceed is to say that there will be no public philosophy. Such a solution to the problem of shared values is not much more likely of success in Europe than in America. Among other things, such an approach would basically represent the victory of the legal ideals of the South of Europe, earlier delineated. This is beyond imagination. The conclusion is that, while the idea of "Europe" can carry considerable historical freight, it cannot carry much contemporary meaning. Of course in each of the separate countries of Europe we can, in spite of all ideological divisions, still have a considerable sense of community, if nothing else founded on some great historical accommodation, as over religion in Germany or Holland. But pluralism of world views, what elsewhere I have called deep pluralism, is far too advanced in Europe for "Europe" to mean much.[14]

What presumably will continue to happen is two movements working in opposite directions. On the one hand we will have the mass culture of TV, which already in a country such as Italy has replaced local dialects with Italian as the current speech of most Italians. This mass culture, which, despite the *lottizzazione* or allocation of power over public TV practiced by RAI or the BBC, seems increasingly to be creating a common culture, both national and European, works in the direction of a kind of cultural leveling. On the other hand, within every country parties of dissent foster various forms of regionalism and tribalism: when I first began visiting Spain in the 1970s during the *dictablanda,* although there was longstanding resistance to Castile in a number of parts of the country, there was nothing like the regionalism that popped up all over after the death of Franco. One may expect that, as in America, the tug between a common mass culture and a profound pluralism of irrec-

14. I have discussed "public philosophy," the comparative experience of community in America and Europe, and deep pluralism in "The University as Community: Community of What?" *Communio* 21 (1994): 344–62.

oncilable world views among subcultures will continue. Whereas in certain countries, as France, historically the culture has been open to all those willing to Frenchify, to adopt French and assimilate at least somebody's idea of French values, there will be nothing so unifying about "Europe." Europe historically was composed of many inheritances, but the most important, the most defining, was Christianity. Above all, this defining characteristic has been the subject of contention now for centuries, and it is hard to imagine a Europe actually willing to endure the discomfort self-definition in regard to such historic inheritances would entail.[15] This will continue to encourage the liberal, technocratic, or bureaucratic option, which is to abstain from such definition as not worth the trouble: life is to be built around individual life strategies rather than a shared life or view of the world. Such liberalism is itself the victory of a world view, one in which public life is largely viewed under procedural rather than philosophical or religious categories. Of course, as a world view that encourages any form of individualism or plurality that does not challenge its own hegemony, this is an agreement gained by demeaning the life of the mind. In the degree it dominates, one will hardly be able to speak of a public philosophy. To stay with our Italian example, already the true civil religion of Italy is football.[16]

Deep pluralism involves disagreement about right and wrong, about the meaning of life, incompatible views of the world. This grows daily. On present evidence, what lies in the cards for a united Europe is not simply the kind of cultural pluralism that enriches life, but a deep pluralism that makes a significant shared life as Europeans impossible. Even the separate nations, where greater levels of

15. See however, Joseph Cardinal Ratzinger, *Turning Point for Europe? The Church in the Modern World—Assessment and Forecast,* trans. Brian McNeil (San Francisco: Ignatius Press, 1994).

16. Adrian Lyttelton, "Italy: The Triumph of TV," *NYRB,* August 11, 1994, gives examples used in this paragraph. Robert Hughes, "The Medium Inquisitor," *NYRB,* October 21, 1993), describes the grim prognosis of the American critic Clement Greenberg in regard to the future of "high culture." Joseph Brodsky seems to me much more clear-headed than Václav Havel about the nature of the mass society of the future, in their exchange, "'The Post-Communist Night': An Exchange," *NYRB,* February 17, 1994. Brodsky takes the Communist and post-Communist catastrophe as, on 29, "the first cry of mass society: a cry as it were from the world's future."

community still exist, usually have within them incompatible views of the world. The historiography speaks of the Two Spains, which have now struggled with one another since especially the Bourbon reforms of the early eighteenth century.[17] Here, in the matter of nations composed of antagonistic subgroups with irreconcilable world views, perhaps Europe's future is being written in the United States, with its increasing crime, alienation, and decline of education and the family attendant on the breakdown of shared values.

Presumably the lesson here is that cultural subsidiarity will remain a way of defending a greater degree of shared values and culture on a relatively local or regional level than is possible on either a national or European level. A common general European culture, to the extent that this ever existed, seems already significantly diminished. Witness to this is the vagueness of writers such as Václav Havel when they speak of Europe. On examination, the things viewed as "European" usually come down to little more than the ideals of some one of the subcultures that make up Europe, in this case the party of the Enlightenment.[18] Those who value a shared public life and shared works of cultural creation may in certain places still look to the nation or state for a public stage, but increasingly the most one will be able to hope for by way of a shared life will be at a more local level. Here the Germans, for instance, have often been very intelligent, fostering cities that combine modern life with tradition, and allowing the state in certain ways to support the practice of religion without establishing any one religion.

Today Europe stands caught between two options. On the one

17. Ramón Menendez Pidal, *The Spaniards in Their History,* trans. Walter Starkie (New York: Norton, 1950), chap. 5, is a classic discussion.

18. The exchange mentioned in note 16 was in response to Havel's "The Post-Communist Nightmare," *NYRB,* May 27, 1993. In the exchange, the continuing insipidness, albeit decency, of Havel's response contrasts with Brodsky's sharp "maybe somebody should admit that man isn't that good . . . maybe they should start by recognizing themselves and their history for the better part of this century as a reminder of Original Sin"; cf. Adam Krzeminski, "'More Humility, Fewer Illusions': A Talk between Adam Michnik and Jürgen Habermas," *NYRB,* March 24, 1994. Michnik's despising of the ethically pure state, praise for cultural heterogeneity, and realization of the ambivalence of all traditions contrast strikingly with Habermas' utopian advocacy of radical democracy, positivism, and secularity—that is, the intolerance borne of the Enlightenment.

hand we have "thin" or liberal notions of unity and the common good, which are intended to allow for the flourishing of cultural diversity of "plurality," but commonly cause deep pluralism. I observed above that it is doubtful that a modern politics of an individualist, utilitarian, or liberal form can have any principled resolution of the relations between unity, plurality, and subsidiarity. Since one can reasonably take such forms of politics to be in the ascendancy, the conclusion must be that there will be no principled resolution of the questions we have been considering, but rather the mandates of *ad hoc* technocratic responses. Put this way, the secular party in Europe may find this path not altogether attractive. So far as I can see, the alternative, the "on the other hand," is a "thicker" or more communitarian notion of Europe and the common good that seeks relatively greater "unity" in life. For such, the party of the Enlightenment is going to have to be willing to reconsider its most basic commitments: for instance, its beliefs in egalitarianism and human goodness and its antagonism to a place for religion in public life. I assume such a conclusion is no more palatable in Europe than in the United States, but that does not make it wrong. In the words of the poet Joseph Brodsky's sharp response to Václav Havel:[19]

> Maybe the real civility, Mr. President, is not to create illusions. "New understanding," "global responsibilities," "pluralistic metaculture" are not much better at the core than the retrospective utopias of the latter-day nationalists or the entrepreneurial fantasies of the *nouveaux riches.* This sort of stuff is still predicated on the promise, however qualified, of man's goodness. . . . This sort of diction befits, perhaps, the innocents, or demagogues, running the affairs of industrial democracies, but not you, who ought to know the truth about the condition of the human heart.

AFTERWORD

Minor changes have been made in this chapter from the original essay. See further on subsidiarity, Patrick A. Jones and Robert L. Waller, "A Model of Catholic Social Teaching: Assessing Policy

19. Brodsky and Havel, "'The Post-Communist Nightmare.'"

Proposals." I discuss public philosophy and deep pluralism further in "The Quest for a Public Philosophy in Twentieth-Century American Political Thought" (chapter 10 in this volume); see Tim Parks, "America First?" on the phenomenon of an international liberal body of readers, ever more homogeneous in such things as commitment to the use of literature to construct a better future and hostile to anything that curbs individual freedom, whose prejudices may be appealed to in presenting anything as "provincial." I pursue the definition of "Europe" further in "The Changing Understanding of the Making of Europe from Christopher Dawson to Robert Bartlett," and in "The Two Europes." See also Jason Byassee and L. Gregory Jones, "Methodists and Microcredit"; and Charles J. Chaput, "A Charitable Endeavor." See also John L. Allen, Jr., in *The Future Church: How Ten Trends Are Revolutionizing the Catholic Church*, who describes attempts to practice and update the idea of subsidiarity. Benedict XVI, *Deus Caritas Est,* continues the papal exposition of subsidiarity.

12

THE ETHICS OF CONQUEST

The European Background of Spain's Mission in the New World

CHRISTOPHER COLUMBUS was no Spaniard, but rather brought to the employ of the Catholic monarchs a specifically Italian experience of the larger world. An avid reader of Marco Polo, who had traveled many of the shipping routes used by Europeans, Columbus, like any Italian merchant, knew the implications of the conquest of the Byzantine Empire by the Ottoman Turks in the mid-fifteenth century.[1] The Italians had been cut off from their customary trade relations, especially to the spices of the East, and were having to either adjust their hopes for future prosperity downward or turn to alternative ways of reconnecting with the East. This was a European-wide problem: "In many directions the fifteenth century was for Western Europe a period of contraction, not of expansion."[2] The quest for solutions to the problems of contraction lies behind much fifteenth-century exploration, Portuguese or otherwise. In one way or another, Europeans were looking for new prospects: thus, for instance, the seeking for direct trade, especially in gold, with central Africa. Columbus's proposal was merely the bold-

1. Felipe Fernández-Armesto, *Before Columbus: Exploration and Colonization from the Mediterranean to the Atlantic, 1229–1492* (Philadelphia: University of Pennsylvania Press, 1987).

2. J. H. Parry, *The Establishment of the European Hegemony 1415–1715: Trade and Exploration in the Age of the Renaissance*, 3rd ed. (New York: Harper Torchbooks, 1966), 7.

est in the ongoing quest for new routes to compensate for what had been lost.

The debate on Columbus's religious views continues. As part of a more general historiographical tendency to emphasize his medieval background, many see him as a visionary Catholic. Pauline Moffitt Watts argued that religion was central to all he did, and not a cloak for greed.[3] Djelal Kadir, to the contrary, held that his religious rhetoric was itself a conquering ideology.[4] Clearly, the role of religion in what happened is most complex. First, we must remember the diversity of "Spain," which term in our period still named a geographical rather than political entity. Only with the Reglamento of 1716 by Philip V, two centuries in the future, did "Spain" designate a political entity. Politically, in the age of conquest as in the Middle Ages, we must speak of "the Spains." In the eyes of other Spaniards, the New World enterprises of the sixteenth and seventeenth centuries were quintessentially Castilian. Indeed, into the seventeenth century, the administrative documents speak of Castile in relation to the New World kingdoms. The juridical ties of New Spain—that is, Mexico—or New Castile—that is, Peru—were with the Crown of Castile exclusively.[5] But to stay with Columbus, the place of religion in Spanish life varied a good deal in his day. In tone of life, the long-commercial and cosmopolitan Catalonia had more in common with the French or Italian Riviera than with the Spanish interior. Rural, anti-commercial, and sometimes fanatic Castile, which was the motivating force behind the conquest and which,

3. Pauline Moffitt Watts, "Prophecy and Discovery: On the Spiritual Origins of Christopher Columbus's 'Enterprise of the Indies,'" *American Historical Review* 90 (1985): 73–102.

4. Djelal Kadir, *Columbus and the Ends of the Earth: Europe's Prophetic Rhetoric as Conquering Ideology* (Berkeley: University of California Press, 1992); and Tzvetan Todorov, *The Conquest of America: The Question of the Other,* trans. Richard Howard (New York: Harper and Row, 1984). James Muldoon, "Columbus's First Voyage and the Medieval Legal Tradition," *Medievalia et Humanistica* n.s. 19 (1992): 11–26, kindly made available to me in typescript, notes "There was no priest on Columbus's first voyage, suggesting that missionary work was not a prime consideration at the time." Muldoon also suggests that Columbus's interests shifted from trade to colonization, and thence to missionary work, and that his explanation of what he was doing shifted accordingly. Missionaries were taken on the second voyage.

5. Martin Larrey has given me careful criticism on this paper as a whole, here as elsewhere sharpening the argument.

especially in the time of the Catholic monarchs, set its religious character upon the conquest, tended to be much more sober. For instance, in addition to the various activities more commonly associated with that often misunderstood institution, the Spanish Inquisition, such as centralization and dealing with *conversos,* in Columbus's day, the Catholic monarchs were systematically reforming the Spanish Church through the Inquisition by careful examination of the moral life of the clergy.[6]

Spain in Columbus's day had traditions of both religious tolerance and of intolerance. On the one hand, its history for centuries had revolved around a relatively small number of conquerors of one religion ruling over a much larger conquered population of some other religion. Before their own conversion to Catholicism, the Visigothic Arian Christian rulers had ruled a much larger subject Catholic population, with some enclaves of Jews. The Muslims, who themselves were composed of many different peoples and historical experiences, and who practiced Islam with strikingly different levels of seriousness, in turn had ruled a subject Christian and Jewish population. Now, in Columbus's day, when in the recent drive for national unity and uniformity arguably more intense animosity had been turned against minority groups than in any earlier period, the Christians ruled over substantial numbers of Muslims. The point is that there had never been uniform policy on any side toward members of other religions. Sometimes Christians had persecuted Jews, sometimes they had protected them and given them certain forms of preference. Sometimes Muslims had persecuted Christians, sometimes Christians had been substantially left to live their own lives. Many Christians had become Muslims, many Jews—in terms of the apparently small Jewish population—had become Christians. On all sides many conversions had been opportunistic, some serious, some

6. Edward Peters, *Inquisition* (New York: Free Press, 1988), chap. 3, is excellent, as is Felipe Fernández-Armesto, *Ferdinand and Isabella* (London: Weidenfeld and Nicolson, 1975), chap. 9. See also Stephen Haliczer, *Inquisition and Society in the Kingdom of Valencia, 1478–1834* (Berkeley: University of California Press, 1990); and William Monter, *Frontiers of Heresy: The Spanish Inquisition from the Basque Lands to Sicily* (New York: Cambridge University Press, 1990).

made under a degree of compulsion, some freely. In sum, if in the late fifteenth century intolerance grew hand in hand with the drive for national unity, and was certainly not to be defused by the imminent European-wide split over Protestantism, the Spanish religious reality was very complex.

Just as, in important senses, Iberia in the Middle Ages had not been one society, and we cannot assume that what one Spaniard held was held by another, some basic differentiation must be made in turning to the Spanish in the New World. J. H. Parry has divided the early period into three distinct stages, and has noted a kind of three-cornered tug-of-war. The first period was that of Columbus and the professional explorers, and extended to about 1520.[7] From 1520 to 1550 was the age of the *conquistador,* by the end of which individual Spaniards had seized the chief sedentary centers of population. However, by the end of the same period private armies had been superseded by the initiative of the Spanish government, which was successfully intervening to give some order, and replacing the *conquistadores* with its own nominees.[8] Until this large-scale intervention by the government, the quest for gold and glory arguably dominated, although many also felt strongly about religion. This was a time of free-booters, of an unusual number of men coming out of the forbidding Extremadura of the west of Spain, men seeking in one blow radically to change their lots in life. This was a time of conquest before the giving of public order to what had been conquered. The desire to extend Christianity certainly was present in the calculations of Columbus himself, but for some it took second place. From a moral point of view, much was done that few later would want to justify. From the viewpoint of the crown, there was the great danger that the feudalism of late medieval European society, which had just been turned back in Spain, would gain a second life in the New World.

Clearly Parry's chronology, while useful, is overly simplified.[9]

7. Parry, *Establishment,* 54 ff.
8. Parry, *Establishment,* 54, 57.
9. A more recent overview is given by J. H. Elliot, "The Spanish Conquest and

For instance, although there was an evolution of the Castilian government toward greater royal control over all kinds of matters, the crown already tried to control the treatment of the native peoples in the Laws of Burgos of 1512–13. Again, a royal governor had been appointed as early as 1500 to replace Columbus. Thus, rather than stress discrete states of development in the degree Parry does, we are advised to see conquest and settlement as part of the same process. As Parry himself shows, those participating in conquest usually became the first settlers, and in turn royal control was quick to follow. This pattern was fairly constant, but followed different timelines in different regions.

Parry may very well be right that, after 1550, while of course greed and cruelty continued, the position of religion somewhat changed. An increasing number of members of religious orders came with conversion of the native population as their first priority. Many were shocked at seeing what had already happened, and reported home to Castile on what Spanish citizens had been doing. Yet we should remember that this was not new. The most famous of Spain's critics in later memory, the Dominican Bartolomé de Las Casas (1484–1566), initially took up his pen to record what he had witnessed in the Caribbean or had heard about well before 1550, and wrote to awaken a more general European populace to the tragedy that was unfolding. Here we have a very complicated inheritance. De Las Casas at once pointed out true abuse, lied or exaggerated about the situation in the New World, quickened Spain's conscience, and through all became an important source of the Black Legend—that is, the blackening of Spanish culture and history in the histori-

---

Settlement of America," in *The Cambridge History of Latin America,* vol. 1, ed. Leslie Bethell (New York: Cambridge University Press, 1984), 149–206. Elliot's "The World After Columbus," *The New York Review of Books* (hereafter *NYRB*), October 10, 1991, is better at showing the shortcomings of Europeans, as in relating the puzzlement of the king of the Tartars over European greed (12) than the lack of self-understanding of their own activities among some of the victims of the Europeans. The introductions of editors James Lockhart and Enrique Otte in *Letters and People of the Spanish Indies: Sixteenth Century* (New York: Cambridge University Press, 1976) also add precision to Parry's general schema. I thank Rebecca Horn for suggestions, embodied in the following, about the need to modify Parry's views, and for a helpful reading of the present essay; see further J. H. Parry, *The Spanish Seaborne Empire* (New York: Knopf, 1966).

cal memory of the rest of Europe.[10] From almost the first, some of the more scholarly-minded tried to get down on paper the nature of the world they had entered, and in the process became our sources for a good deal of what we know of the native cultures at this moment of encounter. Others, again, began to figure out strategies for protecting especially their converts, "their Indians" in the paternalistic language that had been transferred from Iberia. Undoubtedly, such activities became more pronounced as we approach mid-century.

The growth in the African slave trade seems to have been not so much, as an older scholarship had it, the result of the religious orders' struggle to protect the Indian population. Rather, it was a hardheaded attempt to bring in slaves to areas where the indigenous population had largely died out and a new work force was needed. Such introduction was not in itself remarkable. Slavery had been a part of each of the civilizations that had contributed to Spanish history: Roman, Visigothic, and, above all, Arabic. Jews and Christians had long practiced various forms of slavery in the peninsula. It was also a part of the native cultures the Spanish found in the New World, and for that matter, of the cultures of Black Africa from which the new slaves came.[11] Yet on both sides of 1550, certain religious figures did succeed in convincing the Spanish government that things were

10. To add to her earlier publications, Helen Rand Parish has edited Bartolomé de Las Casas's *The Only Way,* trans. Francis P. Sullivan (New York: Paulist Press, 1992). See also de las Casas's *The Devastation of the Indies: A Brief Account,* trans. Herma Briffault, introduction by Bill Donovan (Baltimore: Johns Hopkins University Press, 1992). On the Black Legend, see Philip Powell, *Tree of Hate: Propaganda and Prejudices Affecting United States Relations with the Hispanic World* (New York: Basic Books, 1971; repr. Vallecito, Calif.: 1985). Powell traces the story down through *indigenismo,* the exaltation of things Indian and depreciation of Spanish culture, which intensifies as we near the present. David Henige, *In Search of Columbus: The Sources for the First Voyage* (Tucson: University of Arizona Press, 1971), considers the role of de Las Casas in the convoluted history of the *Journal* of Columbus's first voyage. See also note 26, ff., for further literature on de Las Casas, the Black Legend, and Lewis Hanke's views; James Muldoon, "Solórzano's *De indiarum iure:* Applying a Medieval Theory of World Order in the Seventeenth Century," *Journal of World History* 2 (1991): 29–43 at 30 ff.; and Antonio García y García, "La découverte du Nouveau Monde et les prédécesseurs de F. de Vitoria," *Revue catholique international: Communio* 17, no. 4 (1992): 58–75.

11. Roger Collins, *Early Medieval Spain: Unity in Diversity, 400–1000* (New York: St. Martin's Press, 1983), index under "slaves"; and see the article by García y García cited above.

seriously amiss, and Spain responded in an increasingly concerted manner to bring law and order to the conquered areas.

In tracing the place of Christianity in the New World, we should make some distinctions in speaking of what are sometimes indifferently called missionaries. The word "missionary" is best reserved for those like the Jesuits in Paraguay or the Franciscans in Northern Mexico who ran missions—that is, who commonly addressed something short of a fully sedentary population. The clergy sent to already sedentary peoples, who functioned much as the parish clergy did in Europe, were not normally called missionaries. Like European clergymen, these *doctrineros* might in fact be the source of cultural instruction, but they understood themselves as ministering to an established culture, and as having as their main goal religious instruction rather than the civilizing of peoples who needed civilizing.[12] Either group, missionaries or clergy, might call abuse to the attention of the government. The government in turn intervened to try to check the rapaciousness of its citizens, but also itself to profit in a more organized and efficient manner from the constellation of kingdoms that composed the empire. This could in turn set the missionaries against the government, but here too the patterns varied. We must remember that the King of Spain late in the century was the austere Philip II (1556–98). Philip, while interested in gold, was utterly sincere about placing the economic and political interests of his government second both to stopping the advance of Protestantism and to Christianizing the New World. Especially in the light of his need to finance wars in France and the Netherlands, he could hardly be king without an interest in continually increasing the profits coming in from the New World. In 1557,

12. Colin Morris, *The Papal Monarchy: The Western Church from 1050 to 1250* (Oxford: Clarendon Press, 1989), 263–68, 478–89, 616–17, 643–44, describes the high medieval idea of mission; and see Odilo Engels, "Mission und Friede an der Reichsgrenze im Hochmittelalter," in *Aus Kirche und Reich: Studien zu Theologie, Politik und Recht im Mittelalter*, Festschrift für Friedrich Kempf (Sigmaringen: Thorbecke, 1983), 201–24, with 218 ff., a well-informed history of medieval natural law theory, and note 16. Antony Pagden, *The Fall of Natural Man: The American Indian and the Origins of Comparative Ethnology*, reprinted with corrections and additions (Cambridge: Cambridge University Press, 1986), 15–24, discusses how civilized and barbarian societies were defined.

1575, and 1595 he faced bankruptcies following from his spending to try to turn back Protestantism. Still, Philip was famous for his devotion to the missions. It is said that in a time of financial crisis in Castile itself, he put the palace on a diet of bread and water, but kept the candles going to the missions. The point is that, in the question of religion, we can find everything from the most selfless devotion to the newly discovered peoples by Spaniards whose first motive was the spread of what seemed to them the truth to people who had not yet heard it, to the cynical use of religious position in the New World as just one more form of expropriation.

Before we consider, on the basis of this briefest of sketches, how we are to judge the ethics of conquest, we should note that the moral criticism of what Spain, or at least some Spaniards, had done, which was written about by other Spaniards, was in time eagerly received elsewhere in Europe: this came to be one element of what has been titled the Black Legend. Briefly, the European countries, first Italy and Germany, but later especially England and Holland, came to hate and resent Spain for a host of reasons—religious and commercial—above all, for having gotten so much of the New World first. In the English language tradition we do not normally call the northern privateers and people licensed as colonialists by the English government *conquistadores,* but, language aside, that is because our historical literature is written from the point of view of the Protestant north. To a Spaniard, Sir Walter Raleigh is but the English version of the Spanish freebooters. To someone in the English or American tradition, he is usually presented as a hero. To put the point sharply, Spanish historical literature was aware of Spanish moral failure in the sixteenth century in a way that English and American literature only came to see in its own past in the twentieth century.

If we are to speak of the *conquistadores* of the north, there are of course differences between them and those of the south. In England almost up to the time of the American Revolution, the government practiced a kind of *laissez-faire* almost the reverse of the Spanish policy. That is, whereas Spain had intervened against the *conquistadores,* the English, interested in colonization on the cheap, pretty much gave license to individuals to do what they wanted in the New World. The point is that the received picture of Spain in English-language countries has been written by Spain's historical archenemies selectively using Spanish self-criticism. The European countries that J. H. Parry argued were the most brutal in the treatment of native peoples, Holland and England, composed the Black Legend as their reading of Spanish history, thus legitimating their own record of horror.[13] I do not want to get into the quagmire of comparative European brutality, but the point is that with time one can find the most grotesque distortion of the historical record. This is perhaps summed up nowhere better than in Dostoyevsky's portrait of the Grand Inquisitor in *The Brothers Karamazov.* Here a picture that developed in deep historical ignorance and disdain for Latin Christianity and Europe comes to summarize all that is dark in the South of Europe.[14]

THE CONQUEST AS A MORAL QUESTION

One large question that must be faced concerns the sense in which Western civilization is a universal civilization—that is, not only a civilization that historically produced ideals such as universal human rights and a universal science, but also a civilization that has become self-conscious enough to be capable of understanding others, and imparting to them new understandings of what is (universally) true and good and the like.

The Romans as imperialists were the first to go in quest of some jurisprudence, some universal best law most suited to human nature. If they did not see the individual as of infinite value, this did not prevent them from seeing the individual as nevertheless of considerable value. They could ask what idea of good was most suited to being human. Like the Spaniards later, their empire had taken

13. The record of Holland into the twentieth century was particularly horrible: see on Bali, Robert Craft, "Bali H'ai," *NYRB,* October 24, 1991. Powell, *Tree of Hate,* in portraying the formation of the Black Legend, discusses later images of the Inquisition.

14. Edward Peters, *Inquisition* (New York: Free Press, 1988), 254–62; chaps. 5–8 gives a history of the creation of the myth of the Inquisition.

into itself many peoples, many religions, many kinds of law. Also like the Spaniards, they tended in the practical order to accept this variety, but wondered whether nevertheless human reason could not discover certain rights anyone possessed by the fact of being human: their minds moved toward a best law code that would articulate the best laws for any human being.

Such considerations must lie in the distant background behind the famous late-sixth-century letter of Pope Gregory the Great to Abbot Mellitus and Augustine of Canterbury. Gregory's insistence that the introduction of Christianity must disturb the native culture as little as possible became archetypical for subsequent Catholic missionizing. Where there was no way of reconciling Christianity to the already existing culture, Christianity could replace it: the pagan holy places were to be deconsecrated. But so far as possible, Christianity was to build on or continue the old culture: the Christian altar could arise at the very spot just deconsecrated, for that was the customary place of worship. Such teaching merely updated the ancient Christian inculturation into Roman culture, as in placing the day of the weekly rest on the day of the sun. The goal was to introduce a fuller truth while disorienting people as little as possible. This instinct to inculturation of religion remained through the Middle Ages, and thence was transmitted by the religious orders to the New World.

The quest for a law of nations, moored in the idea of natural law, was continued by the medieval papacy.[15] The Crusades, for instance, raised the question of whether, whatever one's religion, any human had certain intrinsic rights. The Christians were generally in agreement that in some sense the Islamic world had to be undermined, but was this by conversion, extermination, or some combination thereof?[16] By the thirteenth century, Pope Innocent IV

15. James Muldoon has traced some of the shifting meaning of these terms (see note 4).

16. A work critical of Church and Crusade initiates serious twentieth-century discussion: Carl Erdmann, *The Origin of the Idea of the Crusade,* trans. Marshall W. Baldwin and Walter Goffart (Princeton: Princeton University Press, 1977). See then Benjamin Z. Kedar, *Crusade and Mission: European Approaches Toward the Muslims* (Princeton: Princeton University Press, 1984), esp. chap. 5; Morris, *Papal Monarchy,* 277–78, 282; and note 17 in this chapter; cf. Robert Chazan, *Daggers of Faith: Thirteenth-Century Christian Missionizing and Jewish Responses* (Berkeley: University of California Press, 1989).

(1243–54) declared, with Muslims in mind, that Christians could not initiate war for the purpose of conversion, although they could if the right to preach was denied. All men had the right to organize society and govern themselves by their own lights. Institutions like property and marriage were natural to man, and natural goods that must be respected were found in non-Christian societies.[17]

The Christians could defend themselves from unjust aggression or take back that which had been unjustly seized, but they could not "convert by the sword."[18] At almost the same time, Thomas Aquinas at the University of Paris began to articulate, on the basis of the received Roman natural law ideas, a short list of natural rights that must be defended against injustice for all humans: this began with the right of self-defense against unjust aggression, but also included the right of organization and self-government.[19]

As the great imperialists of the sixteenth century, the Spaniards continued the articulation of natural law ideas, the law of nations, and a theory of empire. As Parry has written: "The conquest of America touched not only the royal authority, but the royal conscience and the tradition of royal justice."[20] Ideas varied, but there was general retention of the medieval idea that the law of God, whether natural or revealed, was above human law and authority, and also that the customs of conquered peoples must in some

17. James Muldoon, *Popes, Lawyers and Infidels* (Philadelphia: University of Pennsylvania Press, 1979), 3–48, with Elliott, "World After Columbus," 13. Muldoon, "Solórzano's *De indiarum iure,*" considers other aspects of Innocent's thought. Alberto Melloni, *Innocenzo IV: La concezione e l'esperienza della cristianità come "regimen unius persona"* (Genoa: Marietti, 1990), is a fine work.

18. For the treatment of forced conversion and the position of baptized Jews in canon law from the seventh century on, see note 12; Morris, *Papal Monarchy,* 143–47, 267–68, 355; and John Van Engen, "Faith as a Concept of Order in Medieval Christendom," in *Belief in History: Innovative Approaches to European and American Religion,* ed. Thomas Kselman (Notre Dame: University of Notre Dame Press, 1991), 19–67, at 29.

19. James Muldoon, "The Conquest of the Americas: The Spanish Search for Global Order," in *Religion and Global Order,* ed. Roland Robertson and William Garrett (New York: Paragon House, 1991), 65–85, at 68.

20. *Parry, European Hegemony,* 58, with 57–60, on which the following is closely based. For orientation, see Colin M. MacLachlan, *Spain's Empire in the New World: The Role of Ideas in Institutional and Social Change* (Berkeley: University of California Press, 1988), and Robert A. Williams, Jr., *The American Indian in Western Legal Thought: The Discourses of Conquest* (New York: Oxford University Press, 1990).

way be respected. At Salamanca, Francisco de Vitoria (1486–1546), a Dominican friend of de Las Casas and critic of what seemed to him Alexander VI's (1492–1503) overstepping of papal authority in the Treaty of Tordesillas of 1494, maintained an essentially medieval view: peaceful conversion was the only legitimate justification for the presence of the Spaniards in the New World.[21] Yet arguably, in some quarters there was a retreat from thirteenth-century ideas. Here, for instance, the declaration by Pope Alexander VI that the Spanish kings had the duty of converting the Indians was understood to mean that force was appropriate where conversion was resisted. Presumably in 1537 Pius III in *Sublimis Deus* had such an interpretation in mind when, in prohibiting slavery and dispossession of native property, he stated that conversion was to be achieved by preaching and the example of good living.

Conversion itself was commonly seen in the larger context of a duty of civilizing what non-learned Europeans often indiscriminately perceived as barbarous peoples, in spite of reports of urban wonders coming from the New World. Columbus had remarked on desirable moral qualities he had found in some of the native peoples, but Europeans, partly from ignorance and partly because the differences were real, had to be struck with the chasms between the cultures of Europe and the New World, beginning with obvious things like technology.[22] Some things in some of the native religions,

21. Morris, *Papal Monarchy,* 442–43, describes the thirteenth-century ideal of persuasion of heretics. James Muldoon, "Papal Responsibility for the Infidel: Another Look at Alexander VI's *Inter Caetera,*" *Catholic Historical Review* 64 (1978): 168–84, shows that Alexander did not claim to be able to deprive infidels of their lands, but only to authorize a division of royal support of missionary labor; cf. García y García, "La découverte du Nouveau Monde."

22. Robert Royal, "Consequences of Columbus," *First Things,* no. 20 (February 1992): 9–11, criticizes a number of statements, such as the 1990 "A Faithful Response to the 500th Anniversary of the Arrival of Christopher Columbus" of the National Council of Churches, for their failure to assess the advances, as well as the evils, caused by encounter with Europe; see also Royal, "Apologizing for the Faith" in *First Things,* no. 17 (November 1991): 69–70. Frances Berdan, *The Aztecs of Central Mexico: An Imperial Society* (New York: Holt, Rinehart, and Winston, 1982), especially at chap. 7, is an attempt to assess the achievements of one New World society; see also David Carrasco, *Religions of Mesoamerica: Cosmovision and Ceremonial Centers* (New York: Harper and Row, 1990), and Miguel León-Portilla, *Aztec Image of Self and Society: An Introduction to Nahua Culture,* ed. J. Jorge Klor de Alva (Salt Lake City: University of Utah Press, 1991).

such as human sacrifice, appeared deeply benighted. Presumably, the question, which would occur to a modern and did occur to some of the learned as to why the Europeans could not simply engage in some form of discussion or cultural encounter short of the use of force, would not have appeared very realistic to many Europeans when faced with this kind of "heart of darkness." Theirs was not the medieval legal and theological tradition that stressed the common humanity of all people, and thus the need to convert through argument.[23] They saw their conquest as just.

Still the question remained, what rights did the native peoples have? Naturally the *conquistadores* emphasized what they called their own rights, but also claimed that some form of paternalism was in the Indians' own interest. Columbus himself had contrasted the peaceful Indians he met with the fierce Caribs, who preyed on them. Subsequently, just-war theory could be and was invoked to justify protection of the peaceful people and pacification of the Caribs.[24] Especially some members of the religious orders tended, rather, to the view that the contact between the two worlds was not so much of the order of physical conquest as of a kind of spiritual enterprise—some kind of joint membership of each people, Indian or Castilian, in something larger than any one kingdom or people, namely the empire itself. This view was but an elaboration of Isabella's continuation of the medieval practice of expanding the laws of Castile to new peoples, who were to have the same legal rights as any Spaniard. We can glimpse it in the words of the first viceroy of New Spain, Antonio de Mendoza: "Treat the Indians like any other people and do not make special rules and regulations for them. There are few persons in these parts who are not motivated in their opinions of the Indians by some interest, good or bad."[25] Undoubtedly the most famous exponent of this view of empire was de Las

23. James Muldoon, "The Nature of the Infidel: The Anthropology of the Canon Lawyers," in *Discovering New Worlds: Essays on Medieval Exploration and Imagination,* ed. Scott Westrem (New York: Garland, 1991), 115–24, studies this tradition in its thirteenth-century form.

24. Muldoon, "Columbus's First Voyage."

25. Quoted in Royal, "Consequences of Columbus," 10.

Casas. Robert Royal has commented on Las Casas's famous debate with Juan Ginés Sepúlveda at Valladolid before the imperial court in 1550 after the crown's decision to halt military activity in the New World until a commission had examined Castile's behavior there: "No other growing empire in history has ever similarly interrupted itself to take up moral issues."[26] De Las Casas saw no essential difference between Indian and Spaniard, and believed the former to possess all the human talents necessary for Castilian citizenship. In a variation on Roman practices, he hoped the Indians could follow their traditional institutions of political life under the watchful eye of royal officials. Slowly they would become Hispanized. Except for the officials and missionaries themselves, who were to be peaceful instructors in a better way of life, Europeans in the New World were to be kept separate from Indian culture and could not live off of it. Parry's conclusion was: "Spanish methods of government, as distinct from methods of conquest, were cautious, legalistic, slow, above all conscientious."[27] In the words of the greatest student of *The Spanish Struggle for Justice in the Conquest of America* in the twentieth century, the conquest of the New World called forth "one of the greatest attempts the world has seen to make Christian precepts prevail in the relations between peoples."[28]

Las Casas's was only one, extreme, position among many, but by 1550 there existed an official theory of empire. The New World was composed of kingdoms separate from those of Spain and under their own royal council, but like the kingdoms of Spain under the crown of Castile. The Indians were free people whose land and property was their own; they were subjects of the crown who could sue and be sued by other Spaniards; they were not to be enslaved except in cases of rebellion; and they could follow their own laws ex-

26. "Royal, "Consequences of Columbus," for translation. The debate is described by Lewis Hanke, *The Spanish Struggle for Justice in the Conquest of America* (Philadelphia: University of Pennsylvania Press, 1949; repr. Boston: Little, Brown, 1965), 117–32. De las Casas's *In Defense of the Indians*, trans. Stafford Poole (Dekalb, Ill.: Northern Illinois University Press, 1974), is a response to Sepúlveda's arguments.

27. Parry, *European Hegemony,* 59. On de Las Casas see Hanke, *Spanish Struggle,* and Elliott, "World After Columbus," 14.

28. Hanke, *Spanish Struggle,* 1.

cept when deemed barbarous by the crown. Their traditional leaders were to be counted minor officials of the crown. Conversion to Christianity was the goal, but was not to be forced—here the high medieval tradition reasserted itself. Lapse into heresy was to be dealt with by the local bishop rather than the Inquisition. Certain colonists, who were of course already in place, could draw tribute or pension, *encomienda,* from specified villages. Such grants could not involve either jurisdiction or forced labor, but could involve the obligation to give military service and parish tithes. The crown, however, could and did itself require forced labor.

Such was the situation in the second half of the sixteenth century. As in any large historical enterprise, there often was a gap between theory and practice, although Parry concluded, presumably with the Black Legend in mind: "The enforcement of the policy . . . though incomplete, was by no means as incompetent as the enemies of Spain pretended."[29] Here I have been able to give the barest sense of what happened, and only an indication of the moral issues involved. By way of conclusion I would stress that no more than of Native Americans can we speak of Europeans or Spaniards as one thing. We must differentiate between many Spains, many periods, many different goals, and many different degrees of uprightness and sensitivity. Like the native cultures, the Spaniards were in history and were always changing. Unless we adopt some anachronistic or ahistorical point of judgment, which itself may be subject to many criticisms, and hold for instance that cultures are somehow frozen out of time and compartmentalized one from the other, we must begin with the fact that contact between two areas of the world that had traveled substantially different paths was inevitable.[30] That,

29. Parry, *European Hegemony,* 60.

30. This is the point of Octavio Paz, whose essays stress the isolation of pre-Columbian Mexican civilization. Paz, fully cognizant of the great artistic and cultural achievements of the Mesoamerican past, sees contact with Europe—that is, the end of isolation—as inevitable, along with the tragedies that flowed from meeting in profound inequality: Paz, *The Labyrinth of Solitude, The Other Mexico,* trans. Lysander Kemp, et al. (New York: Grove Press, 1985), 89–116, 284–325; Paz, *Los privilegios de la vista: Arte de México* (Mexico City: Fondo de Cultura Económica, 1987), 39–144; and Paz, "The Power of Ancient Mexican Art," *NYRB,* December 6, 1990. What Christopher Dawson, *Religion and the Rise of*

for many reasons, many advantages should lie with the Europeans when contact was made was also virtually inevitable. Much was done on all sides that was indefensible. But what is striking in the encounter is that certain decent men struggled with the problem of massive cultural contact to channel it in a way that, in spite of the large-scale destruction and resultant centuries-long disorientation caused by this collision of worlds, arguably was more a "quest for justice" than any such earlier historical experience had been.[31]

AFTERWORD

Minor changes have been made in this chapter from the original essay. The bibliography on inquisition and missionizing continues to grow: see for orientation Robin Vose, *Dominicans, Muslims and Jews in the Medieval Crown of Aragon*. Similarly the history of tolerance continually expands: see my "Setting Boundaries: Early Medieval Reflections on Religious Toleration and their Jewish Roots" and "The Middle Ages in the History of Toleration: A Prolegomena." I have now considered the nature and history of natural law more fully in "The Natural Law: The First Grace." Recent treatment of sixteenth-century natural law theory is also found in Joachim Stüben, ed., *Politische Philosophie und Rechtstheorie des Mittelalters und der Neuzeit,* Abteilung I, *Texte, Francisco de Vitoria: De lege*. On international law see Chantal Delsol, *Unjust Justice: Against the Tyranny of International Law,* trans. Paul Seaton. For orienta-

Western Culture (Garden City, N.Y.: Image Books, 1985), says of the "energy of spiritual unrest . . . to change the world" that runs through European history is important here.

31. This is a reference to Hanke, *Spanish Struggle*. Eugene Genovese, "Religious Foundations of the Constitution," *Reviews in American History* 19 (1991): 338–46, at 46, makes the general comment, "contrary to current lying, Western civilization has been distinguished not by racism, sexism, and imperialism, which have disfigured all civilizations, but by its extraordinary and partially successful movements of opposition to those enormities." Earlier versions or parts of the present chapter of this volume were given in lectures in Salt Lake City sponsored by the Utah Humanities Council and the Utah State Office of Education and by the Fifth Annual Madeleine Festival of the Arts and Humanities. A related paper, Olsen, "1492 in the Judgment of the Nations," was given at the Second Congress on European Culture, Universidad de Navarra, Pamplona, October 1992, and has been published in *Actas del II Congreso "Cultura Europea,"* ed. Enrique Banús (Pamplona: Aranzadi, 1994), 175–81.

tion to the very large recent literature on the nature of the Crusades, see Jonathan Riley-Smith, *What Were the Crusades?* For additional materials on Columbus' voyages see the thirteen volumes of the *Repertorium Columbanium* under the general editorship of Geoffrey Symcox, specifically vols. 7 and 11, De *Las Casas;* see also Felipe Fernández-Armesto, *Columbus on Himself.* Frances Berdan, *The Aztecs of Central Mexico: An Imperial Society,* has been published in a second edition.

BIBLIOGRAPHY

Abbot, Walter, ed. "Pastoral Constitution on the Church in the Modern World." In *The Documents of Vatican II,* chap. 4. New York: Guild Press, 1966.

"Abortion and a Nation at War." *First Things,* no. 26 (October, 1992): 9–13.

Aeschliman, Michael D. "The Catholic Authority of Reason." In *The Idea of the Catholic University,* edited by Kenneth D. Whitehead, 117–24. Scranton, Penn.: University of Scranton Press, 2009.

Akeroyd, Richard H. *Reason and Revelation from Paul to Pascal.* Macon, Ga.: Mercer University Press, 1991.

Allen, John L., Jr. *The Future Church: How Ten Trends Are Revolutionizing the Catholic Church.* New York: Doubleday, 2009.

Alley, Robert S. *The Supreme Court on Church and State.* New York: Oxford University Press, 1988.

Andre, Jean-Marie. *L'Otium dans la vie morale et intellectuelle romaine.* Paris: Presses universitaires de France, 1966.

Aquinas, Thomas. *Summa Theologica.* In *Basic Writings of Saint Thomas Aquinas.* Vol. 1. Edited by Anton C. Pegis. New York: Random House, 1945.

Arias, David. *Spanish Roots of America.* Huntington, Ind.: Our Sunday Visitor, 1992.

Aristotle. *The Complete Works of Aristotle.* Vol. 2. Edited by Jonathan Barnes. Princeton: Princeton University Press, 1984.

Ascherson, Neal. "About the European House." *New York Review of Books,* September 28, 1989.

Ash, Timothy Garton. "1989!" *New York Review of Books,* November 8, 2009.

———. "Velvet Revolution: The Prospects." *New York Review of Books,* December 3, 2009.

Assmann, Jan, and Harald Strohm, eds. *Herrscherkult und Heilserwartung.* Munich: Wilhelm Fink, 2010.

Athanasius. *Vita di Antonio.* Edited by G. J. M. Bartelink. Translated by Pietro Citati and Salvatore Lilla. Verona: Arnaldo Mondadori, 1974.

Attarian, John. "Good Intentions and Bad Economics." *Crisis* 12, no. 7 (July–August 1994): 48–50.

Auerbach, Erich. *Mimesis: The Representation of Reality in Western Literature.* Translated by Willard R. Trask. Princeton: Princeton University Press, 1968.

Augustine. *Sermones.* In *Patrologiae cursus completes.* Series Latina. Edited by J.-P. Migne. 221 vols. Paris: Migne, 1844–64), vol. 38.

———. *The City of God.* Translated by Henry Bettenson. Edited by David Knowles. Harmondsworth: Penguin, 1972.

Azmeh, Aziz Al, and János M. Bak, eds. *Monotheistic Kingship: The Medieval Variants.* Budapest: Central European University Press, 2004.

Bailyn, Bernard. "An American Tragedy." *New York Review of Books,* October 5, 1995.

———. "How England Became Modern: A Revolutionary View." *New York Review of Books,* November 19, 2009.

"Ban on Teaching Abstinence in Louisiana Baffles Utahns." *Deseret News,* March 28, 1993.

Bateman, Bradley, and H. Spencer Banzhaf, eds. *Keeping Faith, Losing Faith: Religious Belief and Political Economy.* Durham, N.C.: Duke University Press, 2008.

Bauerschmidt, Frederick C. "The Politics of the Little Way: Dorothy Day Reads Thérèse of Lisieux." In *American Catholic Traditions: Resources for Renewal,* edited by Sandra Yocum Mize and William L. Portier, 77–95. Maryknoll, N.Y.: Orbis Books, 1997.

Baxter, Michael J. "Peter Maurin Blows the Dynamite." *Houston Catholic Worker* 19, no. 2 (March–April 1999): 7–11.

Becker, Ernest. *The Denial of Death.* New York: Free Press, 1973.

Bede. *Historia Ecclesiastica Gentis Anglorum.* Edited by E. B. Colgrave and R. A. B. Mynors. Oxford: Oxford University Press, 1969.

Bell, Madison Smartt. "Blood on the Border." *New York Review of Books,* October 8, 2009.

Bellah, Robert N., and Robert Neely. *Habits of the Heart: Individualism and Commitment in American Life.* New York: Harper and Row, 1985.

———, et al. "The Church in Tension with a Lockean Culture." *New Oxford Review* 57, no. 10 (December 1990): 10–16.

———, et al. *The Good Society.* New York: Knopf, 1991.

Benedict XVI. "Europe and Its Discontents." *First Things,* no. 159 (January 2006): 16–22.

Benestad, J. Brian. "On Richard John Neuhaus's *The Catholic Moment.*" *Communio* 15 (1988): 488–96.

———. "In reply to Richard John Neuhaus." *Communio* 16 (1989): 559–60.

Benson, Robert L. *The Bishop-Elect: A Study in Medieval Ecclesiastical Office.* Princeton: Princeton University Press, 1968.

Berdan, Frances. *The Aztecs of Central Mexico: An Imperial Society.* New York:

Holt, Rinehart, and Winston, 1982. 2nd ed. Belmont, Calif.: Thomson Wadsworth, 2005.

Berlin, Isaiah. *The Crooked Timber of Humanity: Chapters in The History of Ideas.* London: J. Murray, 1990.

———. "Joseph de Maistre and the Origins of Fascism: II." *New York Review of Books,* October 11, 1990.

Bernardi, Peter J. *Maurice Blondel, Social Catholicism, and Action Française: The Clash over the Church's Role in Society during the Modernist Era.* Washington, D.C.: The Catholic University of America Press, 2009.

Bisson,Thomas N. *The Crisis of the Twelfth Century: Power, Lordship, and the Origins of European Government.* Princeton: Princeton University Press, 2009.

Bloch, Marc. *Feudal Society.* Translated by L. A. Manyon. Chicago: University of Chicago Press, 1961.

Blodgett, Edward D. "The Unquiet Heart: Time and the Poetry of Antiquity in the Middle Ages." *Filolski Pregled* 1–4 (1971): 55–83.

———. "Chaucerian Pryvetee and the Opposition to Time." *Speculum* 51 (1976): 477–93.

Blum, John D. "Ontario Health Care: A Model to Be Emulated or Avoided?" *National Forum: The Phi Kappa Phi Journal* 73, no. 3 (Summer 1993): 41–44.

Blumenberg, Hans. *Work on Myth.* Translated by Robert M. Wallace. Cambridge, Mass.: MIT Press, 1985.

Boas, George. *Essays on Primitivism and Related Ideas in the Middle Ages.* Baltimore: The Johns Hopkins University Press, 1948.

Bonino, Serge-Thomas, ed. *Surnaturel: A Controversy at the Heart of the Twentieth-Century Thomistic Thought.* Translated by Robert Williams. Revised translation by Matthew Levering. Ave Maria, Fla.: Sapientia Press, 2009.

Borst, Arno. *Medieval Worlds: Barbarians, Heretics and Artists in the Middle Ages.* Translated by Eric Hansen. Chicago: University of Chicago Press, 1991.

Bottum, Joseph. "The Death of Protestant America: A Political Theory of the Protestant Mainline." *First Things,* no. 185 (August–September 2008): 23–33.

———. "American Exceptionalism and American Religion." *First Things,* no. 199 (January 2010): 63–67.

Bourne, Randolph S. "The State." In *War and the Intellectuals: Collected Essays by Randolph S. Bourne, 1915–1919,* edited by Carl Resek, 65–104. New York: publisher unknown, 1964.

Bouyer, Louis. *Introduction to Spirituality.* Translated by Mary Perkins Ryan. New York: Desclee, 1961.

———. *A History of Christian Spirituality.* Vol. 1, *The Spirituality of the New Testament and the Fathers.* Translated by Mary Perkins Ryan. New York: Desclee, 1963.

Boyd, Catherine. *Tithes and Parishes in Medieval Italy: The Historical Roots of a Modern Problem.* Ithaca, N.Y.: Cornell University Press, 1952.

Bozeman, Theodore Dwight. *To Live Ancient Lives: The Primitivist Dimension in Puritanism.* Chapel Hill: University of North Carolina Press, 1988.

Braaten, Carl E. "Protestants and Natural Law." *First Things,* no. 19 (January 1992): 20–26.

Brandmüller, Walter. *Light and Shadows: Church History amid Faith, Fact and Legend.* Translated by Michael J. Miller. San Francisco: Ignatius Press, 2009.

Braun, Harald E. *Juan de Mariana and Early Modern Spanish Political Thought.* Aldershot, U.K.: Ashgate, 2007.

Bray, Alan. *The Friend.* Chicago: University of Chicago Press, 2003.

Briggs, David. "A New Generation Is Heeding Pope's Call to Serve the Lord." *Deseret News,* October 7, 1995.

Broda, Johanna, David Carrosco, and Eduarado Matos Moctezuma. *The Great Temple of Tenochitilan: Center and Periphery in the Aztec World.* Berkeley: University of California Press, 1987.

Brodsky, Joseph, and Václav Havel. "'The Post-Communist Night': An Exchange." *New York Review of Books,* February 17, 1994.

Bromwich, David. *Politics by Other Means: Higher Education and Group Thinking.* New Haven, Conn.: Yale University Press, 1992.

Broudéhoux, Jean-Paul. *Mariage et Famile chez Clément d'Alexandrie.* Théologie historique 2. Paris: Buchesne, 1970.

Brown, Peter. *Augustine of Hippo: A Biography.* Berkeley and Los Angeles: University of California Press, 1969. Rev. ed. 2000.

———. *The Body and Society: Men, Women, and Sexual Renunciation in Early Christianity.* Rev. ed. New York: Columbia University Press, 2008.

———. "A Surprise from Saint Augustine." *New York Review of Books,* June 11, 2009.

Buc, Philippe. *The Dangers of Ritual: Between Early Medieval Texts and Social Scientific Theory.* Princeton: Princeton University Press, 2001.

Budziszewski, J., *The Resurrection of Nature: Political Theory and the Human Character.* Ithaca: Cornell University Press, 1986.

———. *The Nearest Coast of Darkness: A Vindication of the Politics of Virtue.* Ithaca: Cornell University Press, 1988.

———. *The Line Through the Heart: Natural Law as Fact, Theory, and Sign of Contradiction.* Wilmington, Del.: ISI Books, 2009.

———. "To Lose Man: What 'Public Reason' Can Learn from Public Faith." *The Catholic Social Science Review* 15 (2010): 35–46.

Buel, Richard, Jr. "Public Opinion." In *Securing the Revolution: Ideology in American Politics, 1789–1815.* Part 3. Ithaca, N.Y.: Cornell University Press, 1972.

Burridge, Kenelm. *In the Way: A Study of Christian Missionary Endeavours.* Vancouver, B.C.: University of British Columbia Press, 1991.

Buruma, Ian. "From Hirohito to Heimat." *New York Review of Books,* October 26, 1989.

———. "There's No Place Like Heimat." *New York Review of Books,* December 20, 1990.

Busse, Heribert, and Georg Kretschmar. *Jerusalemer Heiligtumstradition in altkirchlicher und frühislamischer Zeit.* Wiesbaden: Otto Harrassowitz, 1987.

Butterfield, Andrew. "The Fierce Emotions of Siena." *New York Review of Books,* October 14, 2010.

Butterfield, Fox. *All God's Children: The Bosket Family and the American Tradition of Violence.* New York: Knopf, 1995.

Buttiglione, Rocco. "Christian Economics 101." *Crisis* 10, no. 7 (July–August 1992): 32–36.

Byassee, Jason, and L. Gregory Jones. "Methodists and Microcredit." *First Things,* no. 197 (October 2009): 20–22.

Callahan, Daniel. *Setting Limits: Medical Goals in an Aging Society.* New York: Simon and Schuster, 1987.

Canavan, Francis. "The Popes and the Economy." *First Things,* no.16 (October 1991): 35–41.

Carlyle, R. W., and A. J. Carlyle. *A History of Mediaeval Political Theory in the West.* 6 vols. Edinburgh and London: W. Blackwood and Sons, 1903–62.

Carrard, Philippe. *Poetics of the New History: French Historical Discourse from Braudel to Chartier* Baltimore: Johns Hopkins University Press, 1992.

Carrasco, David. "Star Gatherers and Wobbling Suns: Astral Symbolism in the Aztec Tradition." *History of Religions* 26 (1987): 279–94.

———. *Religions of Mesoamerica: Cosmovision and Ceremonial Centers.* New York: Harper and Row, 1990.

Carter, Mike. "Prayer Debate Heightens Religious Tension in Utah." *Deseret News,* January 27, 1993.

Carter, Stephen L. *The Dissent of the Governed: A Meditation on Law, Religion, and Loyalty.* Cambridge, Mass.: Harvard University Press, 1998.

Casanova, José. *Public Religions in the Modern World.* Chicago: University of Chicago Press, 1994.

The Catechism of the Catholic Church. Vatican City: Libreria Editrice Vaticana, 1994. 2nd ed. 2000.

Catholic Bishops of Texas. *Mission Texas: A Pastoral Letter on Evangelization.* Lubbock: Catholic Bishops of Texas, 1989.

Cavanaugh, William T. "'A Fire Strong Enough to Consume the House': The Wars of Religion and the Rise of the State." *Modern Theology* 11 (1995): 397–420.

———. "The City: Beyond Secular Parodies." In *Radical Orthodoxy: A New Theology,* edited by John Milbank, Catherine Pickstock, and Graham Ward, 182–200. New York: Routledge, 1999.

———. *The Myth of Religious Violence: Secular Ideology and the Roots of Modern Conflict.* Oxford: Oxford University Press, 2009.

Chadwick, Owen. *A History of the Popes, 1830–1914.* Oxford: Oxford University Press, 1998.

Chaput, Charles J. "A Charitable Endeavor." *First Things,* no. 197 (October 2009): 25–29.

Chazan, Robert. *Daggers of Faith: Thirteenth-Century Christian Missionizing and Jewish Responses.* Berkeley: University of California Press, 1989.

Christian, William A, Jr. "Priests, Mountains, and 'Sacred Space' in Early Modern Europe." *The Catholic Historical Review* 93 (2007): 84–103.

Cicero. *De republica, De legibus.* Translated by Clinton Keyes. Loeb Classical Library. Cambridge: Harvard University Press, 1961.

Clark, Stephen R. L. *Civil Peace and Sacred Order: Limits and Renewals.* Vol. 1. Oxford: Oxford University Press, 1989.

Clouser, Roy A. *The Myth of Religious Neutrality: An Essay on the Hidden Role of Religious Belief in Theories.* Notre Dame, Ind.: University of Notre Dame Press, 1991.

Cochrane, Charles N. *Christianity and Classical Culture: A Study of Thought and Action from Augustus to Augustine.* London: Oxford University Press, 1974.

Cohen, Naomi. *Jews in Christian America: The Pursuit of Religious Equality.* New York: Oxford University Press, 1992.

Collins, Roger. *Early Medieval Spain: Unity in Diversity, 400–1000.* New York: St. Martin's Press, 1983.

Colombas, Garcia. *Paraiso y vida angelica.* Montserrat: Abadía de Montserrat, 1958.

Comblin, Joseph. *Théologie de la ville.* Paris: Editions universitaires, 1968.

"Commonweal Editor Accuses *New York Times* of Anti-Catholic Bias." *Intermountain Catholic,* March 26, 1993.

Congar, Yves. *Lay People in the Church: A Study for a Theology of Laity.* Translated by Donald Attwater. Westminster, Md.: Newman Press, 1967.

Connolly, William E. *Why I Am Not a Secularist.* Minneapolis: University of Minnesota Press, 1999.

Cottrell, Robert. "Europe: So Far, It Flies." *New York Review of Books,* April 8, 1999.

———. "It Still Flies." *New York Review of Books,* April 22, 1999.

Craft, Robert. "Bali H'ai." *New York Review of Books,* October 24, 1991.

Craycraft, Kenneth R., Jr. "Church-State Problems." *Crisis* 13, no. 6 (June, 1995): 47–48.

———. *The American Myth of Religious Freedom.* Dallas: Spence, 1999.

Crosby, John F. "How the Gospel Encounters the Culture in the Catholic University: Some Lessons from John Henry Newman." In *The Idea of the Catholic University,* edited by Kenneth D. Whitehead, 13–24. Scranton, Pa.: University of Scranton Press, 2009.

Cunningham, Lawrence S., ed. *Intractable Disputes about the Natural Law: Alas-*

dair MacIntyre and Critics. Notre Dame, Ind.: University of Notre Dame Press, 2009.

Curry, Thomas J. *The First Freedoms: Church and State in America to the Passage of the First Amendment.* New York: Oxford University Press, 1986.

Dalin, David G. "Still Strangers." *First Things,* no. 37 (November 1993): 32–35.

———, ed. *American Jews and the Separationist Faith: The New Debate on Religion in Public Life*. Washington, D.C.: Ethics and Public Policy Center, 1992.

Daniélou, Jean. *The Lord of History: Reflections on the Inner Meaning of History.* Translated by Nigel Abercrombie. Cleveland and New York: World Publishing, 1958.

———. *From Glory to Glory: Texts From Gregory of Nyssa's Mystical Writings.* Translated by Herbert Musurillo. New York: Scribner, 1961.

———. *Prayer as a Political Problem.* Translated by J. R. Kirwan. New York: Sheed and Ward, 1967.

Dante Alighieri. *De Monarchia.* Translated by Philip Wicksteed. *A Translation of the Latin Works of Dante Alighieri.* London, 1904. Reprinted New York: Greenwood Press, 1969. Reprinted in *The Intellectual Tradition of the West,* vol. 1. Edited by Morton Donner, Kenneth Eble, and Robert Helbling, 272–87. Salt Lake City, Utah: no publisher given, 1982.

Davidson, James. *The Greeks and Greek Love.* New York: Random House, 2007.

Davis, David Brion. "The Triumph of the Country." *New York Review of Books,* May 12, 1994.

———. "Southern Comfort." *New York Review of Books,* October 5, 1995.

Dawson, Christopher. *The Judgment of the Nations.* New York: Sheed and Ward, 1942.

———. *The Making of Europe: An Introduction to the History of European Unity.* New York: Sheed and Ward, 1952. Reprinted Washington, D.C.: The Catholic University of America Press, 2002.

———. *The Dynamics of World History.* Edited by John J. Mulloy. New York: Sheed and Ward, 1956.

———. *Religion and the Rise of Western Culture.* Garden City, N.Y.: Image Books, 1958.

———. *Christianity and the New Age.* Manchester, N.H.: Sophia Institute Press, 1985.

———. "Natural Law in the Protestant and in the Catholic World." *The Dawson Newsletter* 10, (Fall 1992): 4–5.

———. *The Crisis of Western Education.* Introduction by Glenn W. Olsen. Washington, D.C.: The Catholic University of America Press, 2010.

De Jong, Mayke. *The Penitential State: Authority and Atonement in the Age of Louis the Pious, 814–840.* Cambridge: Cambridge University Press, 2009.

De Las Casas, Bartolomé. *In Defense of the Indians.* Translated by Stafford Poole. Dekalb, Ill.: Northern Illinois University Press, 1974.

———. *The Devastation of the Indies: A Brief Account.* Translated by Herma

Briffault. Introduction by Bill Donovan. Baltimore: Johns Hopkins University Press, 1992.

———. *The Only Way.* Edited by Helen Rand Parish. Translated by Francis P. Sullivan. New York: Paulist Press, 1992.

De Lubac, Henri. *Catholicism: A Study of Dogma in Relation to the Corporate Destiny of Mankind.* Translated from the 4th French edition by Lancelot C. Sheppard. New York: Sheed and Ward, 1964.

———. *The Mystery of the Supernatural.* Translated by Rosemary Sheed. New York: Herder and Herder, 1967.

Dean, Jodi. *Democracy and Other Neoliberal Fantasies: Communicative Capitalism and Left Politics.* Durham, N.C.: Duke University Press, 2009.

Delbanco, Andrew. "Dreams of Better Schools." *New York Review of Books,* November 19, 2009.

Delsol, Chantal. *Unjust Justice: Against the Tyranny of International Law.* Translated by Paul Seaton. Wilmington, Del.: ISI Books, 2008.

De Tocqueville, Alexis. *Democracy in America.* Edited by Richard Heffner. New York: Penguin, 1956.

Dewey, John. *The Public and its Problems.* New York: Henry Holt, 1927.

"The Difference a Child Makes." *Crisis* 10, no. 7 (July–August 1992): 4–5.

Dirda, Michael. "The Treasure Hunter." *New York Review of Books,* August 14, 2008.

Donoghue, Denis. "Bewitched, Bothered, and Bewildered." *New York Review of Books,* March 25, 1993.

Donoso Cortés, Juan. *Ensayo Sobre el Catolicismo, el Liberalismo y el Socialismo.* 2nd ed. Buenos Aires: Espasa-Carpe Argentina, 1949.

Dronke, Peter. *Women Writers of the Middle Ages: A Critical Study of Texts from Perpetua (c. 203) to Marguerite Porete (c. 1310).* Cambridge: Cambridge University Press, 1984.

Duffy, Eamon. *The Stripping of the Altars: Traditional Religion in England c. 1400–1580.* 2nd ed. New Haven: Yale University Press, 2005.

Dulles, Avery. "John Paul II and the Truth about Freedom." *First Things,* no. 55 (August-September 1995): 36–41. Published in an annotated version as *Truth as the Ground of Freedom: A Theme from John Paul II.* Available as an Acton Institute Occasional Paper. Grand Rapids, Mich.: Acton Institute, 1997.

Dupré, Louis. "The Religious Crisis of our Culture." *Analecta Husselriana* 5 (1976): 205–18.

———. "A Conservative Anarchist: Eric Voegelin, 1901–85." *Clio* 14 (1985): 423–31.

———. *Passage to Modernity: An Essay in the Hermeneutics of Nature and Culture.* New Haven: Yale University Press, 1993.

Dworkin, Ronald. *Life's Dominion: An Argument about Abortion, Euthanasia, and Individual Freedom.* New York: Knopf, 1993.

———. "Sex, Death and the Courts." *New York Review of Books,* August 8, 1996.

Eagleton, Terry. *Reason, Faith, and Revolution: Reflections on the God Debate.* New Haven: Yale University Press, 2009.

Eastland, Terry, ed. *Religious Liberty in the Supreme Court: The Cases That Define the Debate Over Church and State.* Washington, D.C.: Ethics and Public Policy Center, 1993.

Eliade, Mircea. *Cosmos and History: The Myth of the Eternal Return.* 2nd pbk ed. Translated by Willard R. Trask. New York: Harper, 1954. Reprinted as *The Myth of the Eternal Return: Cosmos and History.* Princeton: Princeton University Press, 2005.

Elizondo, Virgilio. *The Future is Mestizo: Life where Cultures Meet.* New York: Crossroad, 1988; University Press of Colorado, 2000.

Elliot, J. H. "The Spanish Conquest and Settlement of America." In *The Cambridge History of Latin America,* vol. 1, edited by Leslie Bethell, 149–206. New York: Cambridge University Press, 1984.

———. "The World after Columbus." *New York Review of Books,* October 10, 1991.

Elliott, Alison Goddard. *Roads to Paradise: Reading the Lives of the Saints.* Hanover, N.H.: University Press of New England, 1987.

Engels, Odilo. "Mission und Friede an der Reichsgrenze im Hochmittelalter." In *Aus Kirche und Reich: Studien zu Theologie, Politik und Recht im Mittelalter.* Festschrift für Friedrich Kempf, 201–24. Sigmaringen: Thorbecke, 1983.

Erdmann, Carl. *The Origin of the Idea of the Crusade.* Translated by Marshall W. Baldwin and Walter Goffart. Princeton: Princeton University Press, 1977.

Ertmann, Thomas. *Birth of the Leviathan: Building States and Regimes in Medieval and Early Modern Europe.* New York: Cambridge University Press, 1997.

Ethics 99, no. 4 (July 1989).

Evennet, H. Outram. *The Spirit of the Counter-Reformation.* Notre Dame, Ind.: University of Notre Dame Press, 1970.

Fallows, James. "What Can Save the Economy?" *New York Review of Books,* April 23, 1992.

Fedoryka, Damian P. "'Dworking' the Abortion Issue." *Crisis* 11, no. 1 (December 1993): 50–54.

Fedwick, Paul. *The Church and the Charisma of Leadership in Basil of Caesarea.* Toronto: Pontifical Institute of Mediaeval Studies, 1979.

Feingold, Lawrence. *The Natural Desire to See God According to St. Thomas Aquinas and His Interpreters.* Ave Maria, Fla.: Sapientia Press, 2010.

Fernández-Armesto, Felipe. *Ferdinand and Isabella.* London: Weidenfeld and Nicolson, 1975.

———. *Before Columbus: Exploration and Colonization from the Mediterranean to the Atlantic, 1229–1492.* Philadelphia: University of Pennsylvania Press, 1987.

———. *Columbus on Himself.* Indianapolis: Hackett, 2010.

Ferrante, Joan M. *The Political Vision of the Divine Comedy.* Princeton: Princeton University Press, 1984.

Fichtenau, Heinrich. *The Carolingian Empire: The Age of Charlemagne.* Translated by Peter Munz. New York and Evanston: Harper Torchbooks, 1964.

Finley, Moses I. *Economy and Society in Ancient Greece.* Edited by Brent D. Shaw and Richard P. Saller. Harmondsworth: Penguin, 1982.

Fischer, David Hackett. *Albion's Seed: Four British Folkways in America.* New York: Oxford University Press, 1989.

Foley, Patrick. "Catholics of the South." *The Catholic Social Science Review* 13 (2008): 77–90.

Forte, David. "Children No Longer Taught with 'Grace.'" *Casper Star-Tribune,* July 9, 1992.

Fowler, Robert Booth. *The Dance with Community: the Contemporary Debate in American Political Thought.* Lawrence, Kan.: University Press of Kansas, 1991.

Fox, Robin Lane. *Pagans and Christians.* New York: Knopf, 1987.

Fox-Genovese, Elizabeth, and Eugene Genovese. *Fruits of Merchant Capital: Slavery and Bourgeois Property in the Rise and Expansion of Capitalism.* New York: Oxford University Press, 1983.

Frank, Karl Suso. *Aggelikos Bios, Begriffsanalytische und begriffsgeschichtliche Untersuchung zum "engelgleichen Leben."* Beiträge zur Geschichte des alten Mönchtums und des Benediktinerordens 26. Münster: Aschendorff, 1964.

Frank, Robert H. *Passions Within Reason: The Strategic Role of the Emotions.* New York: Norton, 1988.

Freeman, Samuel. "A New Theory of Justice." *New York Review of Books,* October 14, 2010.

Friedman, Benjamin M. "Two Roads to Our Financial Catastrophe." *New York Review of Books,* April 29, 2009.

Furbank, P. N. "Tocqueville's Lament." *New York Review of Books,* April 8, 1999.

Furet, François. *Interpreting the French Revolution.* Translated by Elborg Forster. Cambridge: Cambridge University Press, 1981.

Galston, William A. *Liberal Purposes: Goods, Virtues, and Diversity in the Liberal State.* New York: Cambridge University Press, 1991.

García y García, Antonio. "La découverte du Nouveau Monde et les prédécesseurs de F. de Vitoria." *Revue catholique international: Communio* 17, no. 4 (1992): 58–75.

Garver, Eugene. *Machiavelli and the History of Prudence.* Madison: University of Wisconsin Press, 1987.

Gauthier, David. *Morals by Agreement.* Oxford: Clarendon Press, 1986.

Gawantka, Wilfried. *Die sogenannte Polis: Entstehung, Geschichte und Kritik der modernen althistorischen Grundbegriffe der griechische Staatsidee, die Polis.* Stuttgart: Steiner, 1985.

Gay, Peter. *The Enlightenment: An Interpretation*. Vol. 1, *The Rise of Modern Paganism*. New York: Knopf, 1966.

Genovese, Eugene D. "Religious Foundations of the Constitution." *Reviews in American History* 19 (1991): 338–46.

———. *The Southern Tradition: The Achievement and Limitations of an American Conservatism*. Cambridge, Mass.: Harvard University Press, 1994.

George, Francis Cardinal. *Inculturation and Ecclesial Communion: Culture and Church in the Teaching of Pope John Paul II*. Rome: Urbaniana University Press, 1990.

———. *The Difference God Makes: A Catholic Vision of Faith, Communion, and Culture*. New York: Crossroad, 2009.

George, Robert P. *Making Men Moral: Civil Liberties and Public Morality*. New York: Clarendon Press, 1993.

Georgi, Dieter. *The Opponents of Paul in Second Corinthians*. Translated by Harold Attridge, et al Philadelphia: Fortress Press, 1986.

Gibbons, William, ed. *Seven Great Encyclicals*. Glen Rock, N.J.: Paulist Press, 1963.

Gilkey, Langdon. *On Niebuhr: A Theological Study*. Chicago: University of Chicago Press, 2001.

Gilson, Étienne. *Reason and Revelation in the Middle Ages*. New York: Scribner, 1938.

———. *The Christian Philosophy of Saint Augustine*. New York: Random House, 1960.

Glendon, Mary Ann. *Rights Talk: The Impoverishment of Political Discourse*. New York: Free Press, 1991.

———. "Religion and the Court: A New Beginning?" *First Things*, no. 21 (March 1992): 21–26.

Golding, M. P., ed. *The Nature of Law: Readings in Legal Philosophy*. New York: Random House, 1966.

Gould, William J., Jr. "The Challenge of Liberal Political Culture in the Thought of John Courtney Murray." *Communio* 19 (1992): 113–44.

Grafton, Anthony "'A Jewel of a Thousand Facets.'" *New York Review of Books*, June 24, 2010.

Grant, George Parkin. *English-Speaking Justice*. Notre Dame, Ind.: University of Notre Dame Press, 1985.

Grant, Robert. *Oakeshott*. London: Claridge Press, 1990.

Grant, Ruth W. *John Locke's Liberalism*. Chicago: University of Chicago Press, 1987.

Grasso, Kenneth L. "John Paul II on Modernity, Freedom, and the Metaphysics of the Person." *The Catholic Social Science Review* 15 (2010): 15–34.

Greenberg, Ben. "The Orthodox Moment." *First Things*, no. 200 (February 2010): 39–43.

Greenstone, J. David. *The Lincoln Persuasion: Remaking American Liberalism.* Princeton: Princeton University Press, 1993.

Grendler, Paul F. *The Jesuits: Cultures, Sciences, and the Arts, 1540–1773.* Edited by John W. O'Malley, et al. Toronto: University of Toronto Press, 1999.

Guardini, Romano. *The End of the Modern World.* Translated by Joseph Theman and Herbert Burke. Edited with an introduction by Frederick Wilhelmsen. Chicago: H. Regnery, 1968.

Gunn, L. Ray. *The Decline of Authority: Public Economic Policy and Political Development in New York State, 1800–1860.* Ithaca: Cornell University Press, 1988.

Gurevich, A. J. "Time as a Problem of Cultural History." In *Cultures and Time,* edited by Louis Gardet, et al., 229–45. Paris: UNESCO Press, 1976.

Hacker, Andrew. "Playing the Racial Card." *New York Review of Books,* October 24, 1991.

———. "'Diversity' and Its Danger." *New York Review of Books,* October 7, 1993.

Hacking, Ian. *The Emergence of Probability: A Philosophical Study of Early Ideas about Probability, Induction, and Statistical Inference.* London: Cambridge University Press, 1975.

Haliczer, Stephen. *Inquisition and Society in the Kingdom of Valencia, 1478–1834.* Berkeley: University of California Press, 1990.

Hammann, Louis L., and Harry M. Buck, eds. *Religious Traditions and the Limits of Tolerance.* With Michael McTighe. Chambersburg, Pa.: publisher unknown, 1988.

Hampe, Michael. *John Dewey.* 2 vols. Stuttgart: Frommann-Holzboog, 2009–10.

Hampe, Michael, ed. *Wege der Philosophie ins 21. Jahrhundert.* Heft 3/2009, *John Dewey.* Stuttgart: Frommann-Holzboog, 2009.

Hampshire, Stuart. "The Reason Why Not." *New York Review of Books,* April 22, 1999.

Hanke, Lewis. *The Spanish Struggle for Justice in the Conquest of America.* Philadelphia: University of Pennsylvania Press, 1949. Reprinted Boston: Little, Brown, 1965.

Hanley, Mark Y. *Beyond a Christian Commonwealth: The Protestant Quarrel with the American Republic, 1830–60.* Chapel Hill: University of North Carolina Press, 1994.

Hanning, Robert W. *The Vision of History in Early Britain: From Gildas to Geoffrey of Monmouth.* New York: Columbia University Press, 1966.

Hart, David Bentley. *Atheist Delusions: The Christian Revolution and its Fashionable Enemies.* New Haven: Yale University Press, 2009.

Hauerwas, Stanley, and Michael Baxter. "The Kingship of Christ: Why Freedom of 'Belief' is not Enough." *DePaul Law Review* 42 (1992): 107–27.

Havel, Václav. "The Post-Communist Nightmare." *New York Review of Books,* May 27, 1993.

Heer, Friedrich. *The Intellectual History of Europe.* 2 vols. Translated by Jonathan Steinberg. Garden City, N.Y.: Image Books, 1968.

Henige, David. *In Search of Columbus: The Sources for the First Voyage.* Tucson: University of Arizona Press, 1971.

Herberg, Will. *Protestant, Catholic, Jew: An Essay in American Religious Sociology.* With a new introduction by Martin G. Marty. Chicago: University of Chicago Press, 1983.

Hertz, Deborah. *How Jews Became Germans: A History of Conversion and Assimilation in Berlin.* New Haven: Yale University Press, 2007.

Higonnet, Patrice. *Goodness Beyond Virtue: Jacobins During the French Revolution.* Cambridge, Mass.: Harvard University Press, 1998.

Hirsch, E. D., Jr. "How to Save the Schools." *New York Review of Books,* May 13, 2010.

Hitchcock, James. *The Recovery of the Sacred.* New York: Seabury Press, 1974.

Hitchens, Christopher. "The Cosmopolitan Man." *New York Review of Books,* April 22, 1999.

Hittinger, Russell. *The First Grace: Rediscovering the Natural Law in a Post-Christian World.* Wilmington, Del.: ISI Books, 2003.

Hoberman, J. "Orphan of History." *New York Review of Books,* October 22, 2009.

Hobsbawm, Eric. "The New Threat to History." *New York Review of Books,* December 16, 1993.

Hogan, Richard M., and John M. LeVoir. *Covenant of Love: Pope John Paul II on Sexuality, Marriage, and Family in the Modern World.* San Francisco: Ignatius Press, 1985. 2nd ed., 1992.

Holland, Tom. *The Forge of Christendom: The End of Days and the Epic Rise of the West.* New York: Doubleday, 2008.

Horton, John, and Susan Mendus, eds. *After MacIntrye: Critical Perspectives on the Work of Alasdair MacIntyre.* Notre Dame, Ind.: University of Notre Dame Press, 1994.

Hughes, Richard T., ed. *The American Quest for the Primitive Church.* Urbana: University of Illinois Press, 1988.

Hughes, Richard T., and C. Leonard Allen. *Illusions of Innocence: Protestant Primitivism in America.* Chicago: University of Chicago Press, 1988.

Hughes, Robert. *Culture of Complaint: The Fraying of America.* New York: Oxford University Press, 1993.

———. "The Medium Inquisitor." *New York Review of Books,* October 21, 1993.

Hunt, Robert P., and Kenneth L. Grasso, eds. *John Courtney Murray and the American Civil Conversation.* Grand Rapids, Mich.: Eerdmans, 1992.

Hürten, Heinz. "'Libertas' in der Patristik: 'Libertas episcopalis' im Frühmittelâter." *Archiv für Kulturgeschichte* 45 (1963): 1–14.

Ignatieff, Michael. "Homage to Russia." *New York Review of Books,* April 21, 1994.

Ingram, David. *Habermas: Introduction and Analysis.* Ithaca, N.Y.: Cornell University Press, 2010.

Jacobs, Alan. "The Liberal Neoplatonist?" *First Things,* no. 89 (January 1999): 57–61.

Jacobsen, Douglas G. *An Unprov'd Experiment: Religious Pluralism in Colonial New Jersey.* Brooklyn: publisher unknown, 1991.

Jacobsohn, Gary. *Apple of Gold: Constitutionalism in Israel and the United States.* Princeton: Princeton University Press, 1993.

Jaeger, Werner. *Early Christianity and Greek Paideia.* Cambridge, Mass.: Belknap Press, 1985.

Jencks, Christopher. *Rethinking Social Policy: Race, Poverty, and the Underclass.* Cambridge, Mass.: Harvard University Press, 1992.

Jenson, Robert W. "Hauerwas Examined." *First Things,* no. 25 (August–September 1992): 49–51.

Jerome. *Epistulae.* Edited by Isidorus Hilberg. *Corpus Scriptorum Ecclesiasticorum Latinorum (CSEL).* Vol. 54. Vienna: F. Tempsky, 1910. Translated in *A Select Library of Nicene and Post-Nicene Fathers,* edited by Philip Schaff. 2nd series. Vol. 6. Reprint Grand Rapids, Mich.: Eerdmans, 1954.

The Jerusalem Bible. Garden City, New York: Doubleday, 1966.

Joas, Hans, and Klaus Wiegandt, eds. *Secularization and the World Religions.* Liverpool: Liverpool University Press, 2009.

John XXIII. *Mater et Magistra.* Translated by H. E. Winstone. *New Light on Social Problems.* London: Catholic Truth Society, 1963.

John Paul II. *Laborem Exercens.* Vatican translation, *On Human Work.* Boston: St. Paul's Editions, 1982.

———. *Centesimus Annus.* In *Doing Well and Doing Good: The Challenge to the Christian Capitalist,* by Richard John Neuhaus. New York: Doubleday, 1992.

———. "The Economics of Human Freedom." *First Things,* no. 15 (August/September 1991): 36–45.

———. *Crossing the Threshold of Hope.* Edited by Vittorio Mesori. New York: Knopf, 1994.

———. *Evangelium vitae.* Translation *The Gospel of Life.* Special Supplement to *Inside the Vatican*, April, 1995. New Hope, Ky.: New Hope Publications, 1995.

———. "Ad Limina Address to Australian Bishops." *Adoremus Bulletin* 4, no. 9 (February 1999): 6–8.

Johnson, Rheta Grimsley. "Is America Spinning Out of Control?" *Deseret News*, April 18, 1993.

Jones, Patrick A., and Robert L. Waller. "A Model of Catholic Social Teaching: Assessing Policy Proposals." *The Catholic Social Science Review* 15 (2010): 283–96.

Jonsson, Jeffrey D., and Sean McBride. "Critic's Book Exposes Hollywood's Three Big Lies." *Utah Daily Chronicle,* March 5, 1993.

Judt, Tony. "How the East Was Won." *New York Review of Books,* December 16, 1993.

———. "On Kosovo: The Reason Why." *New York Review of Books,* May 20, 1999.

———. "Ill Fares the Land." *New York Review of Books,* April 29, 2009.

———. "Crossings." *New York Review of Books,* March 25, 2010.

Juergensmeyer, Mark. *Global Rebellion: Religious Challenges to the Secular State, from Christian Militias to al Quaeda.* Berkeley: University of California Press, 2008.

Kadir, Djelal. *Columbus and the Ends of the Earth: Europe's Prophetic Rhetoric as Conquering Ideology.* Berkeley: University of California Press, 1992.

Kaeuper, Richard W. *Holy Warrior: The Religious Ideology of Chivalry.* Philadelphia: University of Pennsylvania Press, 2009.

Kantorowicz, Ernst H. *The King's Two Bodies: A Study in Mediaeval Political Theology.* Princeton: Princeton University Press, 1957.

Kasper, Walter. *Jesus the Christ.* Translated by V. Green. Mahwah, N.J.: Paulist Press, 1976.

———. *Theology and Church.* Translated by Margaret Kohl. New York: Crossroad, 1989.

Kass, Leon R. "Man and Woman: An Old Story." *First Things,* no. 17 (November 1991): 14–26.

Kateb, George. *The Inner Ocean: Individualism and Democratic Culture.* Ithaca, N.Y.: Cornell University Press, 1992.

Kauffman, Bill, and Scott Walter. "Eugene Genovese and Elizabeth Fox-Genovese." *The American Enterprise* (September–October 1996): 21–25.

Kavanaugh, John F *Following Christ in a Consumer Society: The Spirituality of Cultural Resistance.* Maryknoll, N.Y.: Orbis Books, 1991.

Kazin, Alfred. "The Way We Live Now." *New York Revew of Books,* April 22, 1993.

Kearney, Richard. *Anatheism: Returning to God after God.* New York: Columbia University Press, 2010.

Kedar, Benjamin Z. *Crusade and Mission: European Approaches Toward the Muslims.* Princeton: Princeton University Press, 1984.

Kekes, John. *Against Liberalism.* Ithaca, N.Y.: Cornell University Press, 1997.

———. *A Case for Conservatism.* Ithaca, N.Y.: Cornell University Press, 1998.

Kelly, Aileen. "The Russian Sphinx." *New York Review of Books,* May 20, 1999.

Kelly, George A. *The Battle for the American Church.* Garden City, N.Y.: Doubleday, 1979.

———. "Let's Stop Kidding Ourselves About Catholic Higher Education." *Fellowship of Catholic Scholars Newsletter,* 16, no. 4 (September 1993): 15–24.

Kelly, J. N. D. *Jerome: His Life, Writings, and Controversies.* New York: Harper, 1975.

Kennan, George F. *Around the Cragged Hill: A Personal and Political Philosophy.* New York: W. Norton, 1993.

———. "The Balkan Crisis: 1913 and 1993." *New York Review of Books,* July 15, 1993.

Kennedy, Paul. "The American Prospect." *New York Review of Books,* March 4, 1993.

Kerr, Sarah. "A Tale of Two Cities." *New York Review of Books,* December 16, 1993.

Kidd, Thomas S. *God of Liberty: A Religious History of the American Revolution.* New York: Basic Books, 2010.

Kitto, H. D. F. *The Greeks.* Baltimore: Penguin Books, 1954.

Kolakowski, Leszek. *The Presence of Myth.* Translated by Adam Czerniawski. Chicago: University of Chicago Press, 1989.

Kozinski, Thaddeus J. *The Political Problem of Religious Pluralism: And Why Philosophers Can't Solve It.* Foreword by James V. Schall. Lanham, Md.: Lexington Books, 2010.

Kraynak, Robert P. *Christian Faith and Modern Democracy.* Notre Dame, Ind.: University of Notre Dame Press, 2001.

Krom, Michael P. "Transcendence and Human Freedom: Modernity and the Right to Truth." *The Catholic Social Science Review* 15 (2010): 153–73.

Krzeminski, Adam. "'More Humility, Fewer Illusions': A Talk between Adam Michnik and Jürgen Habermas," *New York Review of Books.* March 24, 1994.

Kukathas, Chandran, and Philip Pettit. *Rawls: "A Theory of Justice" and Its Critics.* Oxford: Polity Press, 1990.

Ladner, Gerhart. *The Idea of Reform: Its Impact on Christian Thought and Action in the Age of the Fathers.* Rev. ed. New York: Harper and Row, 1967.

———. "Two Gregorian Letters on the Sources and Nature of Gregory VII's Reform Ideology." In *Images and Ideas in the Middle Ages: Selected Studies in History and Art,* 2:665–86. Rome: Edizioni di Storia e Letteratura, 1983.

Lamb, Matthew. "Inculturation and Western Culture: The Dialogical Experience Between Gospel and Culture." *Communio* 21 (1994): 124–44.

Langer-Kaneko, Christiane. *Das reine Land: Zur Begegnung von Amida-Buddhismus und Christentum.* Zeitschrift für Religions-und Geistesgeschichte, Beiheft 29. Leiden: E. J. Brill, 1986.

Larrey, Martin F. "John Courtney Murray: A Reappraisal." *Triumph* 7, no. 10 (December 1972): 20–23.

Lasch, Christopher. "Orestes Brownson's Christian Radicalism." *New Oxford Review* 56, no. 7 (September 1989): 4–8.

———. "Communitarianism or Populism?" *New Oxford Review* 59, no. 4 (May 1992): 5–12.

Le Goff, Jacques. *The Medieval Imagination.* Translated by Arthur Goldhammer. Chicago and London: University of Chicago Press, 1988.

Lemann, Nicholas. "An Attack in Atlanta." *New York Review of Books,* September 19, 1996.

Leo XIII. *Diuturnum.* In *The Church Speaks to the Modern World,* edited by Étienne Gilson. Garden City, N.Y.: Image Books, 1954.

———. *Immortale Dei.* In *The Church Speaks to the Modern World,* edited by Étienne Gilson. Garden City, N.Y.: Image Books, 1954.

———. *Rerum novarum.* In *The Church Speaks to the Modern World,* edited by Étienne Gilson. Garden City, N.Y.: Image Books, 1954.

———. *Sapientiae Christianae.* In *The Church Speaks to the Modern World,* edited by Étienne Gilson. Garden City, N.Y.: Image Books, 1954.

León-Portilla, Miguel. *Aztec Image of Self and Society: An Introduction to Nahua Culture.* Edited by J. Jorge Klor de Alva. Salt Lake City: University of Utah Press, 1991.

Lerner, Gerda. *The Creation of Patriarchy.* New York: Oxford University Press, 1986.

Lienhard, Joseph. *Paulinus of Nola and Early Western Monasticism.* Theophaneia 28. Cologne- Bonn: P. Hanstein, 1977.

Lilla, Mark. "The Tea Party Jacobins." *New York Review of Books,* May 27, 2010.

Lind, Michael. *The Next American Nation: The New Nationalism and the Fourth American Revolution.* New York: Free Press, 1995.

Linden, Ian. *Global Catholicism: Diversity and Change since Vatican II.* New York: Columbia University Press, 2009.

Lippmann, Walter. *Essays in the Public Philosophy.* Boston: Little, Brown, 1955.

Little, Joyce A. "Naming Good and Evil." *First Things,* no. 23 (May 1992): 23–30.

Lockhart, James, and Enrique Otte, eds. *Letters and People of the Spanish Indies: Sixteenth Century.* New York: Cambridge University Press, 1976.

Lonergan, Bernard. *A Third Collection: Papers.* New York: Paulist Press, 1985.

Louth, Andrew. *The Origins of the Christian Mystical Tradition: From Plato to Denys.* Oxford: Clarendon Press, 1981.

———. *Discerning the Mystery: An Essay on the Nature of Theology.* Oxford: Clarendon Press, 1983.

Lovejoy, Arthur O., and George Boas. *Primitivism and Related Ideas in Antiquity.* Baltimore: Johns Hopkins University Press, 1935.

Löwith, Karl. *Meaning in History.* Chicago: University of Chicago Press, 1949.

Lübbe, Hermann. *Religion nach der Aufklärung.* 3rd ed. Munich: Wilhelm Fink, 2004.

Lucas, Joseph S. "Montesquieu, the Modern West, and Democracy's Drift: An

Interview with Paul A. Rahe." *Historically Speaking* 11, no. 4 (September 2010): 25–27.

Lukacs, John. "Bare Ruined Choirs (Ample Parking in Church Yard)." *Triumph* 8, no. 4 (April 1973): 22–24.

———. "Christians and the Temptations of Nationalism." *New Oxford Review* 59 (Nov. 1992): 12–18.

Lutz, David W. "Can Notre Dame Be Saved?" *First Things,* no. 19 (January 1992): 35–40.

Lyttelton, Adrian. "Italy: The Triumph of TV." *New York Review of Books,* August 11, 1994.

MacCarthy, Fiona. "A Hero of the Gothic." *New York Review of Books,* September 24, 2009.

MacFarquhar, Roderick. "The Pride of Empire." *New York Review of Books,* September 24, 2009.

MacIntyre, Alasdair. *Whose Justice? Which Rationality?* Notre Dame, Ind.: University of Notre Dame Press, 1988.

———. *Three Rival Versions of Moral Inquiry: Encyclopaedia, Genealogy, and Tradition*. Notre Dame, Ind.: University of Notre Dame Press, 1984, 1990.

———. *After Virtue: A Study in Moral Theory.* Notre Dame, Ind.: University of Notre Dame Press, 1988. 3rd ed., 2007.

MacLachlan, Colin M. *Spain's Empire in the New World: The Role of Ideas in Institutional and Social Change.* Berkeley: University of California Press, 1988.

Mahony, Cardinal Roger. "*FOCA:* No 'Freedom of Choice' for Catholic Hospitals." *National Right to Life News,* January 1993.

Mangasarian, Leon. "Ban on Crosses Fuels Firestorm of Protest." *Deseret News,* August 19, 1995.

Mannion, M. Francis. "Liturgy and the Present Crisis of Culture." *Worship* 62 (1988): 98–123.

Mansfield, Harvey C. *Machiavelli's Virtue.* Chicago: University of Chicago Press, 1996.

Mantel, Hilary. "Dreams and Duels of England." *New York Review of Books,* October 22, 2009.

Margalit, Avishai. *On Compromise and Rotten Compromises.* Princeton: Princeton University Press, 2010.

Maritain, Jacques. *Integral Humanism: Temporal and Spiritual Problems of a New Christendom.* Translated by Joseph W. Evans. New York: Scribner, 1968.

———. *Christianity and Democracy and the Rights of Man and Natural Law.* Translated by Doris C. Anson. Introduction by Donald Arthur Gallagher. San Francisco: Ignatius Press, 1986.

Markus, R. A. *Saeculum: History and Society in the Theology of St. Augustine.* Cambridge: Cambridge University Press, 1970.

Marrou, Henri-Irené. *Saint Augustin et la fin de la culture antique.* 4th ed. Bibliothèque des Ecoles Françaises d'Athènes et de Rome, fasc. 145 and 146 bis. Paris: E. de Boccard, 1938, 1949.

———. *A History of Education in Antiquity.* 3rd ed. Translated by George Lamb. London: Sheed and Ward, 1956.

———. *Histoire de l'éducation dans l'antiquité.* 6th ed. Paris: Éditions du Seuil, 1965.

Matarasso, Pauline, trans. *The Cistercian World: Monastic Writings of the Twelfth Century.* London: Penguin Books, 1993.

May, William. *Marriage: The Rock on Which the Family Is Built.* Rev. ed. San Francisco: Ignatius Press, 2009.

McFadyen, Alistair I. *The Call to Personhood: A Christian Theory of the Individual in Social Relationships.* New York: Cambridge University Press, 1990.

McLaughlin, Terence P., ed. *The Church and the Reconstruction of the Modern World: The Social Encyclicals of Pope Pius XI.* Garden City, N.Y.: Image Books, 1957.

McLeod, Hugh. *The Religious Crisis of the 1960s.* New York: Oxford University Press, 2007.

McMullan, Gordon, and David Matthews, eds. *Reading the Medieval in Early Modern England.* Cambridge: Cambridge University Press, 2007.

McPartlan, Paul. *Sacrament of Salvation: An Introduction to Eucharistic Ecclesiology.* Edinburgh: T and T Clark, 1995.

McPherson, James. "Lincoln Off His Pedestal." *New York Review of Books,* September 24, 2009.

Meconi, David Vincent. "Traveling without Moving: Love as Ecstatic Union in Plotinus, Augustine, and Dante." *Mediterranean Studies* 18 (2009): 1–23.

Medved, Michael. *Hollywood vs. America: Popular Culture and the War on Traditional Values.* New York: HarperCollins, 1992.

Meilaender, Gilbert. "Marriage in Counterpoint and Harmony." *First Things,* no. 4 (June–July 1992): 30–36.

Melloni, Alberto. *Innocenzo IV: La concezione e l'esperienza della cristianità come "regimen unius persona."* Genoa: Marietti, 1990.

Menand, Louis. "The Real John Dewey." *New York Review of Books,* June 25, 1992.

Mendelsohn, Daniel. "A Wild Night in the Park," *New York Review of Books,* Oct. 22, 2009.

Menendez Pidal, Ramón. *The Spaniards in Their History.* Translated by Walter Starkie. New York: Norton, 1950.

Merton, Robert K. *Science, Technology and Society in Seventeenth Century England.* 2nd ed. New York: H. Fertig, 1970.

———. *The Sociology of Science: Theoretical and Empirical Investigations.* Edited by Norman W. Storer. Chicago: University of Chicago Press, 1973.

Metaxas, Eric. *Bonhoeffer: Pastor, Martyr, Prophet, Spy.* Nashville: Thomas Nelson, 2010.

Mews, Constant J. *The Lost Love Letters of Heloise and Abelard: Perceptions of Dialogue in Twelfth-Century France.* 2nd ed. Translated by Neville Chiavaroli and Constant J. Mews. New York: Palgrave MacMillan, 2008.

Milbank, John. *Theology and Social Theory: Beyond Secular Reason.* Malden, Mass.: Blackwell, 1991; 2nd ed. 2006.

Milbank, John, Catherine Pickstock, and Graham Ward, eds. *Radical Orthodoxy: A New Theology.* New York: Routledge, 1999.

"The Midwestern Historical Imagination." *Historically Speaking: The Bulletin of the Historical Society* 11, no. 1 (January 2010): 28–33.

Miller, Julia I., and Laurie Taylor-Mitchell. "The *Ognissanti Madonna* and the Humiliati Order in Florence." In *The Cambridge Companion to Giotto,* edited by Anne Derbes and Mark Sandona, 157–75. Cambridge: Cambridge University Press, 2004.

Miller, Perry, *Jonathan Edwards.* New York: W. Skoane, 1949.

———. *The New England Mind.* 2nd ed. 2 vols. Boston: Beacon Press, 1953, 1965.

Montag, John. "Revelation: The False Legacy of Suarez." In *Radical Orthodoxy: A New Theology,* edited by John Milbank, Catherine Pickstock, and Graham Ward, 38–63. New York: Routledge, 1999.

Monter, William. *Frontiers of Heresy: The Spanish Inquisition from the Basque Lands to Sicily.* New York: Cambridge University Press, 1990.

Morgan, Edmund S. *Inventing the People: The Rise of Popular Sovereignty in England and America.* New York and London: Norton, 1988.

———. "The Fiction of 'The People.'" *New York Review of Books,* April 23, 1992.

———. "Power to the People?" *New York Review of Books,* December 2, 1991.

Morris, Colin. *The Papal Monarchy: The Western Church from 1050 to 1250.* Oxford: Clarendon Press, 1989.

Morrison, Karl F. *The Mimetic Tradition of Reform in the West.* Princeton: Princeton University Press, 1982.

Moyn, Samuel. *The Last Utopia: Human Rights in History.* Cambridge, Mass.: Harvard University Press, 2010.

Muldoon, James. "Papal Responsibility for the Infidel: Another Look at Alexander VI's *Inter Caetera.*" *Catholic Historical Review* 64 (1978): 168–84.

———. *Popes, Lawyers and Infidels.* Philadelphia: University of Pennsylvania Press, 1979.

———. "The Conquest of the Americas: The Spanish Search for Global Order." In *Religion and Global Order,* edited by Roland Robertson and William Garrett, 65–85. New York: Paragon House, 1991.

———. "The Nature of the Infidel: The Anthropology of the Canon Lawyers." In *Discovering New Worlds: Essays on Medieval Exploration and Imagination,* edited by Scott Westrem, 115–24. New York: Garland, 1991.

———. "Solórzano's *De indiarum iure:* Applying a Medieval Theory of World

Order in the Seventeenth Century." *Journal of World History* 2 (1991): 29–43.

———. "Columbus's First Voyage and the Medieval Legal Tradition." *Medievalia et Humanistica,* no. 19 (1992): 11–26.

Mulhall, Stephen, and Adam Swift. *Liberals and Communitarians.* 2nd ed. Cambridge, Mass: Blackwell, 1996.

Müller, W. *Die heilige Stadt: Roma quadrata, himmlisches Jerusalem und Mythe von Weltnabel.* Stuttgart: W. Kohlhammer, 1969.

Muñoz, Vincent Phillip. *God and the Founders: Madison, Washington, and Jefferson.* Cambridge: Cambridge University Press, 2009.

Murdoch, Iris. *Existentialists and Mystics: Writings on Philosophy and Literature.* New York: Allen Lane, 1998.

Murray, John Courtney. *We Hold These Truths: Catholic Reflections on the American Proposition.* New York: Sheed and Ward, 1960, 1985.

———. "A Common Enemy, A Common Cause." *First Things,* no. 26 (October 1992): 29–37.

———. *Religious Liberty: Catholic Struggles with Pluralism.* Edited by J. Leon Hooper. Louisville, Ky.: Westminster/John Knox Press, 1993.

Nagel, Thomas. "Rawls on Justice." *Philosophical Review* 82 (1973): 220–34.

Neal, Patrick. "Justice as Fairness: Political or Metaphysical?" *Political Theory* 18 (1990): 24–50.

Nelson, Robert H. *The New Holy Wars: Economic Religion Versus Environmental Religion in America Today.* University Park: Pennsylvania State University Press, 2010.

Neuhaus, Richard John. *The Catholic Moment: The Paradox of the Church in the Postmodern World.* San Francisco: Harper and Row, 1987.

———. "In response to Glenn W. Olsen and J. Brian Benestad." *Communio* 16 (1989): 552–57.

———. *America Against Itself: Moral Vision and the Public Order.* Notre Dame, Ind.: University of Notre Dame Press, 1992.

———. *Doing Well and Doing Good: The Challenge to the Christian Capitalist.* New York: Doubleday, 1992.

———. *Catholic Matters: Confusion, Controversy, and the Splendor of Truth.* New York: Basic Books, 2006.

———. *American Babylon: Notes of a Christian Exile.* New York: Basic Books, 2009.

———, ed. *Unsecular America.* Grand Rapids, Mich.; Eerdmans, 1986.

Neuhaus, Richard John, and George Weigel, eds. *Being Christian Today: An American Conversation.* Washington, D.C.: Ethics and Public Policy Center, 1992.

New York Times News Service. "Scarf Angers Lawmakers in Turkey." *Deseret News,* May 3, 1999, A4.

Newman, Barbara. *Sister of Wisdom: St. Hildegard's Theology of the Feminine.* Berkeley: University of California Press, 1987.

Newman, John Henry. *A Grammar of Assent.* Garden City, N.Y.: Image Books, 1955.

Nichols, Aidan. *The Realm: An Unfashionable Essay on the Conversion of England.* Oxford: Family Publications, 2008.

Nisbet, Robert. *The Quest for Community: A Study in the Ethics of Order and Freedom.* With a new introduction by Ross Douthat. Wilmington, Del: ISI Books, 2010.

"No Crosses Allowed on School Walls." *Deseret News,* August 10, 1995.

Novak, David. *Natural Law in Judaism.* New York: Cambridge University Press, 1998.

———. *Freedom for Faith, Freedom for All: In Defense of Religious Liberty.* Wilmington, Del.: ISI Books, 2009.

———. *In Defense of Religious Liberty.* Wilmington, Del.: ISI Books, 2009.

Novak, Michael. "Seven plus Seven—The Responsibilities of Business Corporations." *Crisis* 12, no. 7 (July-August 1994): 5–9.

Novick, Peter. *That Noble Dream: the "Objectivity Question" and the American Historical Profession.* Cambridge: Cambridge University Press, 1988.

Oakley, Francis. *The Medieval Experience: Foundations of Western Cultural Singularity.* New York: Charles Scribner's Sons, 1974.

———. *The Emergence of Western Political Thought in the Latin Middle Ages. Vol. 1, Empty Bottles of Gentilism: Kingship and the Divine in Late Antiquity and the Early Middle Age (to 1050).* New Haven: Yale University Press, 2010.

O'Donovan, Oliver. *The Desire of the Nations: Rediscovering the Roots of Political Theology.* New York: Cambridge University Press, 1996.

Olsen, Glenn W. "The Idea of the *Ecclesia Primitiva* in the Writings of the Twelfth-Century Canonists." *Traditio* 25 (1969): 61–86.

———. "The Investiture Contest." In *Religion in the Making of Western Man.* Edited by Frank J. Coppa, 79–93. New York: St. John's University Press, 1974.

———. "'You Can't Legislate Morality': Reflections on a Bromide." *Communio* 2 (1975): 148–62.

———. "Allegory, Typology and Symbol: The Sensus Spiritalis." Part 1, "Definitions and Earliest History." Part 2, "Early Church through Origen." *Communio* 4 (1977): 161–79, 357–83.

———. "Lay Spirituality *ad majorem Dei gloriam.*" *Communio* 6 (1979): 405–12.

———. "Reference to the *Ecclesia Primitiva* in Eighth-Century Irish Gospel Exegesis." *Thought* 54 (1979): 303–12.

———. "Transcendental Truth and Cultural Relativism: An Historian's View." In *Historicism and Faith,* edited by Paul L. Williams, 49–61. Proceedings of the Third Convention of the Fellowship of Catholic Scholars. Scranton, Pa: Northeast Books, 1980.

———. "Christian Faith in a Neo-Pagan Society." In *Christian Faith in a Neo-Pagan Society,* edited by Paul Williams, 16–34. Scranton: Northeast Books, 1981.

———. "The Gay Middle Ages: A Response to Professor Boswell." *Communio* 8 (Summer 1981) 119–38.
———. "Hans Urs von Balthasar and the Rehabilitation of St. Anselm's Doctrine of the Atonement." *Scottish Journal of Theology* 34 (1981): 49–61.
———. "Reference to the Primitive Church in the Thought of Salvian of Marseilles." *The Catholic Historical Review* 68 (1982): 1–12.
———. "The Benedictine Way of Life: Yesterday, Today, Tomorrow." *Communio* 11 (1984): 35–45.
———. "St. Augustine and the Problem of the Medieval Discovery of the Individual." *Word and Spirit* 9 (1987): 129–56.
———. "The Catholic Moment?" *Communio* 15 (1988): 474–87.
———. "In Reply to Richard John Neuhaus." *Communio* 16 (1989): 558–59.
———. "The Meaning of Christian Culture: A Historical View." In *Catholicism and Secularization in America: Essays on Nature, Grace, and Culture,* edited by David L. Schindler, 98–130. Notre Dame, Ind.: Communio, 1990.
———. "Recovering the Homeland: Acts 4:32 and the *Ecclesia Primitiva* in St. Bernard's Sermons on the Song of Songs." *Word and Spirit: A Monastic Review* 12 (1990): 92–117.
———. "Twelfth-Century Humanism Reconsidered: The Case of St. Bernard." *Studi Medievali,* 3a Serie, XXXI, I, 1990: 27–53.
———. "The City in Christian Thought." *Thought* 66 (1991): 259–78.
———. *Deconstructing the University.* The 52nd Annual Frederick William Reynolds Lecture. Salt Lake City, 1991. Republished in a slightly revised version in *Communio* 19 (1992): 226–53.
———. "The Ethics of Conquest: The European Background of Spain's Mission in the New World." *Communio* 19 (1992): 619–34.
———. "One Heart and One Soul (Acts 4:32 and 34) in Dhuoda's *Manual.*" *Church History* 61 (1992): 23–33.
———. "Thy Kingdom Come on Earth as in Heaven: The Place of the Family in Creation." In *"And You Will Be My Witnesses,"* 1–28. 2nd ed. Irving, Tex.: University of Dallas Center for Christianity and the Common Good, 1993.
———. "1492 in the Judgment of the Nations." In *Actas del II Congreso "Cultura Europea,"* edited by Enrique Banús, 175–81. Pamplona: Aranzadi, 1994.
———. "The 'Catholic Moment' and the Question of Inculturation." In *Catholicity and the New Evangelization,* Proceedings from the Seventeenth Convention of the Fellowship of Catholic Scholars, Corpus Christi, Texas, 1994, 17–54. Steubenville, Ohio: Franciscan University Press, 1995.
———. "John Rawls and the Flight from Authority: The Quest for Equality as an Exercise in Primitivism." *Interpretation: A Journal of Political Philosophy* 21 (1994): 419–36.
———. "Separating Church and State." *Faith and Reason* 20 (1994): 403–25.
———. "The University as Community: Community of What?" *Communio* 21

(1994): 344–62. Published in a longer form in *Ideas for the University,* edited by Ed Block, Jr., 29–60. Milwaukee: Marquette University Press, 1995.

———. "American Culture and Liberal Ideology in the Thought of Christopher Dawson." *Communio* 22 (1995): 702–20.

———. "Cultural Dynamics: Secularization and Sacralization." In *Christianity and Western Civilization,* edited by the Wethersfield Institute, 97–122. San Francisco: Ignatius Press, 1995.

———. "Marriage, Feminism, Theology, and the New Social History: Dyan Elliott's *Spiritual Marriage.*" *Communio* 22 (1995): 343–56.

———. "Religion, Politics, and America at the Millennium." *Faith and Reason* 22 (1996): 285–315.

———. "Unity, Plurality, and Subsidiarity in Twentieth-Century Context." In *Actas del III Congreso "Cultura Europea,"* edited by Enrique Banús, 311–17. Pamplona: Arazandi, 1996.

———. "Christian Philosophy, Christian History: Parallel Ideas?" In *Eternity in Time: Christopher Dawson and the Catholic Idea of History,* edited by Stratford Caldecott and John Morrill, 131–50. Edinburgh: T. and T. Clark, 1997. A slightly different version is found in *The Catholic as Historian,* edited by Donald J. D'Elia and Patrick Foley, 81–96, 225–26. Naples, Fla.: Sapientia Press, 2006.

———. "America as an Enlightenment Culture." In *Actas del IV Congreso "Cultura Europea."* Edited by Enrique Banús and Beatriz Elío, 121–28. Pamplona: Aranzadi, 1998.

———. "John of Salisbury's Humanism." In *Gli Umanesimi Medievali,* edited by Claudio Leonardi, 447–68. Florence: SISMEL edizioni del Galluzzo, 1998.

———. "On the Frontiers of Eroticism: The Romanesque Monastery of San Pedro de Cervatos." *Mediterranean Studies* 8 (1999): 89–104.

———. "The Changing Understanding of the Making of Europe from Christopher Dawson to Robert Bartlett." In *Actas del V Congreso "Cultura Europea,"* edited by Enrique Banús and Beatriz Elío, 203–10. Pamplona: Aranzadi, 2000.

———. "The Influence of Europe in America: Religion and Enlightenment." In *Actas del V Congreso "Cultura Europea,"* edited by Enrique Banús and Beatriz Elîo, 1155–57. Pamplona: Aranzadi, 2000.

———. "The Quest for a Public Philosophy in Twentieth-Century American Political Thought." *Communio* 27 (2000): 340–62.

———. "Problems with the Contrast between Circular and Linear Views of Time in the Interpretation of Ancient and Early Medieval History." *Fides quaerens intellectum* 1 (2001): 41–65.

———. *Beginning at Jerusalem: Five Reflections on the History of the Church.* San Francisco: Ignatius Press, 2004.

———. "Humanism: The Struggle to Possess a Word." *Logos: A Journal of Catholic Thought and Culture* 7 (2004): 97–116.

———. "The Sodomitic Lions of Granada." *Journal of the History of Sexuality* 13 (2004): 1–25.

———. "The *Ecclesia Primitiua* in John Cassian, the Ps. Jerome *Commentary* on Mark, and Bede." In *Biblical Studies in the Early Middle Ages,* edited by Claudio Leonardi and Giovanni Orlandi, 5–27. Florence: SISMEL Edizioni del Galluzzo, 2005.

———. "The Return of Purpose." *Communio* 33 (2006): 666–81.

———. "Setting Boundaries: Early Medieval Reflections on Religious Toleration and their Jewish Roots." *Hebraic Political Studies* 2 (2007): 164–92.

———. "The Middle Ages in the History of Toleration: A Prolegomena." *Mediterranean Studies* 16 (2008): 1–20.

———. "The Natural Law: The First Grace." *Communio* 35 (2008): 354–73.

———. "Why We Need Christopher Dawson." *Communio* 35 (2008): 115–44.

———. "The Death of Liberal Education: Its Implications for the University, Democracy, and the American Polity." In *The Democratic Discourse of Liberal Education,* edited by Lee Trepanier, 1–17. Cedar City, Utah: Southern Utah University Press, 2009.

———. "The Two Europes." *The European Legacy: Toward New Paradigms* 14, no. 2 (2009): 133–48.

———. "Christopher Dawson and the Renewal of Catholic Education: The Proposal that Catholic Culture and History, not Philosophy, should Order the Catholic Curriculum." *Logos* 13, no. 3 (Summer 2010): 13–35.

———. "Introduction." In Christopher Dawson. *The Crisis of Western Education.* Washington, D.C.: The Catholic University of America Press, 2010.

———. *The Turn to Transcendence: The Role of Religion in the Twenty-First Century.* Washington, D.C.: The Catholic University of America Press, 2010.

———. "History in Its Relation to Theology and the Catholic Intellectual Tradition." In *Teaching the Tradition: A Disciplinary Approach to the Catholic Intellectual Tradition*, edited by John Piderit and Melanie Morey. Oxford: Oxford University Press. Forthcoming.

———, ed. *Christian Marriage: A Historical Study.* New York: Herder and Herder, 2001.

O'Malley, John W., et al, eds. *The Jesuits: Cultures, Sciences, and the Arts, 1540–1773.* Toronto: University of Toronto Press, 1999.

Pagden, Antony. *The Fall of Natural Man: The American Indian and the Origins of Comparative Ethnology,* reprinted with corrections and additions. Cambridge: Cambridge University Press, 1986.

Pagels, Elaine. *Adam, Eve, and the Serpent.* New York: Random House, 1988.

———. "The Politics of Paradise." *New York Review of Books.* May 12, 1988.

Parks, Tim. "Gods and Monsters." *New York Review of Books,* May 6, 1999.

———. "America First?" *New York Revew of Books,* July 15, 2010.

Parry, J. H. *The Establishment of the European Hegemony 1415–1715: Trade and*

Exploration in the Age of the Renaissance. 3rd ed. New York: Harper Torchbooks, 1966.

———. *The Spanish Seaborne Empire.* New York: Knopf, 1966.

Pasewark, Kyle A. *A Theology of Power: Being Beyond Domination.* Minneapolis: Fortress Press, 1993.

Paul, Ellen Frankel, Fred D. Miller, Jr., Jeffrey Paul, and John Adams, eds. *The New Social Contract: Essays on Gauthier.* Oxford: Basil Blackwell, 1988.

Pavlischek, Keith J. *John Courtney Murray and the Dilemma of Religious Toleration.* Kirksville, Mo.: Thomas Jefferson University Press, 1994.

Paz, Octavio. *The Labyrinth of Solitude, The Other Mexico.* Translated by Lysander Kemp, et al. New York: Grove Press, 1985.

———. "The Power of Ancient Mexican Art." *New York Review of Books,* December 6, 1990.

———. *Los privilegios de la vista: Arte de México.* Mexico City: Fondo de Cultura Económica, 1987.

Pennington, Kenneth. *The Prince and the Law, 1200–1600: Sovereignty and Rights in the Western Legal Tradition.* Berkeley: University of California Press, 1993.

Perry, Michael J. *Love and Power: The Role of Religion and Morality in American Politics.* New York: Oxford University Press, 1991.

Peter, Val J. "Divorce and Remarriage." *Communio* 1 (Fall, 1974): 261–74.

Peters, Edward. *Inquisition.* New York: Free Press, 1988.

Pfaff, William. *The Irony of Manifest Destiny: The Tragedy of America's Foreign Policy.* New York: Walker, 2010.

Pius XI. *Quadragesimo Anno.* In *Seven Great Encyclicals,* edited by William Gibbons. Glen Rock, N.J.: Paulist Press, 1963.

Plato. *Great Dialogues of Plato.* Edited by Eric H. Warmington and Philip G. Rouse. New York: New American Library, 1956. Reprint: New York: Mentor, 1984.

———. *The Republic of Plato.* Translated by Francis Cornford. New York: Oxford University Press, 1945.

Pogge, Thomas W. *Realizing Rawls.* Ithaca: Cornell University Press, 1989.

Posner, Richard A. *The Crisis of Capitalist Democracy.* Cambridge, Mass: Harvard University Press, 2010.

Powell, Philip. *Tree of Hate: Propaganda and Prejudices Affecting United States Relations with the Hispanic World.* New York: Basic Books, 1971. Reprint Vallecito, Calif.: 1985.

Printy, Michael. *Enlightenment and the Creation of German Catholicism.* Cambridge: Cambridge University Press, 2009.

"Public Ignorance and Democracy." Special issue of *Critical Review* 12, no. 4 (1998).

Pursell, Brennan C. "God in History: An Augustinian Approach to Narratives of Western Civilization." *The Catholic Social Science Review* 15 (2010): 125–35.

Rahner, Karl. "The Hermeneutics of Eschatological Assertions." In *Theological Investigations*. Vol. 4. Translated by Kevin Smyth, 323–46. Baltimore: Helicon Press, 1966.

Ramb, Martin, and Joachim Valentin, eds. *Natürlich Kultur: Postsäkulare Positionierungen zwischen Kirche und Welt.* Paderborn: Ferdinand Schöningh, 2010.

Rapaczynski, Andrzej. *Nature and Politics: Liberalism in the Philosophies of Hobbes, Locke, and Rousseau.* Ithaca: Cornell University Press, 1987.

Ratner, Lorman A., Paula T. Kaufman, and Dwight L. Teeter, Jr. *Paradoxes of Prosperity: Wealth-Seeking Versus Christian Values in Pre-Civil War America.* Champaign, Ill.: University of Illinois Press, 2009.

Ratzinger, Joseph Cardinal. *Behold the Pierced One: An Approach to Spiritual Christology.* Translated by Graham Harrison. San Francisco: Ignatius Press, 1986.

———. *Turning Point for Europe? The Church in the Modern World—Assessment and Forecast.* Translated by Brian McNeil. San Francisco: Ignatius Press, 1994.

Ratzinger, Joseph, and Jürgen Habermas. *The Dialectics of Secularization: On Reason and Religion.* San Francisco: Ignatius Press, 2006.

Rawls, John. "Justice as Fairness: Political Not Metaphysical." *Philosophy and Public Affairs* 14 (1985): 223–51.

———. "The Priority of the Right and Ideas of the Good." *Philosophy and Public Affairs* 17 (1988): 251–76.

———. *A Theory of Justice*. Rev. ed. Cambridge, Mass.: Belknap Press of Harvard University Press, 1999.

———. "Justice as Fairness: A Guided Tour." Unpublished.

———. *Justice as Fairness: A Restatement.* Edited by Erin Kelly. Cambridge, Mass.: Harvard University Press, 2001.

———. *Political Liberalism.* New York: Columbia University Press, 2005.

———. *A Brief Inquiry into the Meaning of Sin and Faith: With "On My Religion."* Edited by Thomas Nagel. Cambridge, Mass.: Harvard University Press, 2009.

Raz, Joseph. *The Morality of Freedom.* New York: Clarendon Press, 1986.

Reiman, Jeffrey. *Justice and Modern Moral Philosophy.* New Haven: Yale University Press, 1990.

Riché, Pierre. *Daily Life in the World of Charlemagne.* Translated by Jo Ann McNamara. Philadelphia: University of Pennsylvania Press, 1978.

Riconda, Giuseppe. "Augusto Del Noce: Between Thomism and Religious Existentialism." *Communio* 25 (Winter 1998): 716–31.

Riley-Smith, Jonathan. "Crusading as an Act of Love." *History* 65 (1980): 177–92.

———. *What Were the Crusades?* San Francisco: Ignatius Press, 2002.

Rouche, Michel. *A History of Private Life.* Edited by Philippe Ariès and Georges Duby. Vol. 1, "The Early Middle Ages in the West." In *From Pagan Rome to*

Byzantium, edited by Paul Veyne, translated by Arthur Goldhammer. Cambridge, Mass: Harvard University Press, 1987.

Rouner, Leroy S., ed. *Civil Religion and Political Theology.* Notre Dame, Ind.: University of Notre Dame Press, 1994.

Rouselle, Aline. *Porneia: On Desire and the Body in Antiquity.* Translated by Felicia Pheasant. Oxford: Basil Blackwell, 1988.

Rousseau, Philip. *Ascetics, Authority, and the Church in the Age of Jerome and Cassian.* Oxford: Oxford University Press, 1978.

Rowland, Tracey. *Culture and the Thomist Tradition after Vatican II.* New York: Routledge, 2003.

Royal, Robert. "Apologizing for the Faith." *First Things,* no. 17 (November 1991): 69–70.

———. "Consequences of Columbus." *First Things,* no. 20 (February 1992): 9–11.

Rush, Norman. "Naipaul's Mysterious Africa." *New York Review of Books,* November 11, 2010.

Ruthven, Malise. "The Big Muslim Problem!" In *New York Review of Books,* December 17, 2009.

Ryan, Alan. "Invasion of the Mind Snatchers." *New York Review of Books,* February 11, 1993.

———. "It Takes All Kinds." *New York Review of Books,* October 5, 1995.

Ryan, Mary P. *Civic Wars: Democracy and Public Life in the American City During the Nineteenth Century.* Berkeley: University of California Press, 1997.

Sale, Kirkpatrick. *The Conquest of Paradise: Christopher Columbus and the Columbian Legacy.* New York: Plume, 1990.

Sandel, Michael J. *Liberalism and the Limits of Justice.* New York: Cambridge University Press, 1982.

———. *Liberalism and Its Critics.* New York: New York University Press, 1984.

———. *Democracy's Discontent: America in Search of a Public Philosophy.* Cambridge, Mass.: Harvard University Press, 1996.

Sandoz, Ellis. *A Government of Laws: Political Theory, Religion, and the American Founding.* Baton Rouge: Louisiana State University Press, 1990.

Sante, Luc. "The Possessed." *New York Review of Books,* July 16, 1992.

———. "American Pie." *New York Review of Books,* January 28, 1993.

Savage, David G. "Supreme Court Taking 'Neutral' Tack on Religion." *Deseret News,* June 20, 1993.

Scanlon, T. M. "Partisan for Life." *New York Review of Books,* July 15, 1993.

———. *What We Owe to Each Other.* Cambridge, Mass.: Harvard University Press, 1998.

Schindler, David L. "Is America Bourgeois?" *Communio* 14 (1987): 263–90.

———. "The Church's 'Worldly' Mission: Neoconservatism and American Culture." *Communio* 18 (1991): 365–97.

———. "Christology and the Church's 'Worldly' Mission: Response to Michael Novak." *Communio* 19 (1992): 164–78.

———. "Towards a Eucharistic Evangelization." *Communio* 19 (1992): 549–75.

———. "Economics and the Civilization of Love." *The Chesterton Review* 22 (1994): 189–211.

———. "Religious Freedom, Truth, and American Liberalism: Another Look at John Courtney Murray." *Communio* 21 (1994): 696–741.

———. "Christological Aesthetics and *Evangelium Vitae:* Toward a Definition of Liberalism." *Communio* 22 (1995): 193–224.

———. *Heart of the World, Center of the Church: "Communio" Ecclesiology, Liberalism, and Liberation.* Grand Rapids, Mich.: Eerdmans, 1996.

Schlesinger, Arthur, Jr. *The Disuniting of America.* New York: Norton, 1992.

———. "The Radical." *New York Review of Books,* February 11, 1993.

Schmitz, Kenneth L. *The Gift: Creation.* Milwaukee: Marquette University Press, 1982.

———. "Postmodern or Modern-plus?" *Communio* 17 (1990): 152–66.

———. *At the Center of the Human Drama: The Philosophical Anthropology of Karol Wojtyla/Pope John Paul II. Appendix* by John M. Grondelski. Washington, D.C.: The Catholic University of America Press, 1993.

Schwartz, Stephen. "Broken Promises." *First Things* 162 (April 2006): 11–13.

Searle, John R. "Why Should You Believe It?" *New York Review of Books,* September 24, 2009.

———. "'Fear of Knowledge': An Exchange," *New York Review of Books,* December 17, 2009.

Segovia, Juan Fernando. *Orden Natural de la Política y Orden artificial del Estado: Refleciones sobre el Derecho Natural Católico y la Política.* Barcelona: Scire, 2010.

Sen, Amartya. *The Idea of Justice.* Cambridge, Mass: Harvard University Press, 2009.

Shannon, Christopher. *Conspicuous Criticism: Tradition, the Individual, and Culture in American Social Thought.* Baltimore: The Johns Hopkins University Press, 1996.

Shapiro, Ian. *The Evolution of Rights in Liberal Theory.* New York: Cambridge University Press, 1986.

Shea, William M., and Peter A. Huff. *Knowledge and Belief in American Enlightenment Traditions and Modern Religious Thought.* New York: publisher unknown, 1995.

Sheehy, Gail. *Passages: Predictable Crises of Adult Life.* New York: Bantam, 1976.

Shipps, Jan. *Mormonism: The Story of a New Religious Tradition.* Urbana and Chicago: University of Illinois Press, 1985.

Shulman, David. "Living in India's Spirit World." *New York Review of Books,* October 28, 2010.

Skidelsky, Richard. "Giant." *New York Review of Books,* May 6, 1999.

Skinner, Quentin. *Hobbes and Republican Liberty.* Cambridge: Cambridge University Press, 2008.

Smith, Barbara Herrnstein. *Belief and Resistance: Dynamics of Contemporary Intellectual Controversy.* Cambridge, Mass.: Harvard University Press, 1997.

Smith, John E. "Puritanism and Enlightenment: Edwards and Franklin." In *Knowledge and Belief in American Enlightenment Traditions and Modern Religious Thought,* edited by William M. Shea and Peter A. Huff. New York: publisher unknown, 1995.

Sommerville, J. P. *Politics and Ideology in England, 1603–1640.* London: Longman, 1986.

Sorkin, David. *The Religious Enlightenment: Protestants, Jews, and Catholics from London to Vienna.* Princeton: Princeton University Press, 2008.

Steel, Ronald. "Guest of the Age." *New York Review of Books,* August 17, 1989.

Stolinsky, David C. "America: A Christian Country?" *The New Oxford Review* 61, no. 6 (July-August 1994): 16–21.

Stout, Jeffrey. *The Flight from Authority: Religion, Morality, and the Quest for Autonomy.* Notre Dame, Ind.: University of Notre Dame Press, 1981.

Straub, Johannes. *Regeneratio Imperii: Aufsatze Über Roms Kaisertum und Reich im Spiegel der heidnischen und christlichen Publizistik.* Darmstadt: Wissenschaftliche Buchgesellschaft, 1972.

Strouse, Jean. *Morgan: American Financier.* New York: Random House, 1999.

Stüben, Joachim, ed. *Politische Philosophie und Rechtstheorie des Mittelalters und der Neuzeit.* Abteilung I, *Texte, Francisco de Vitoria: De lege.* Stuttgart: Frommann-Holzboog, 2009.

Swetland, Stuart W. "Radiating Jesus in Word and Sacrament: The Role of Catholic Campus Ministry at a Non-Catholic University." In *The Idea of the Catholic University*, edited by Kenneth D. Whitehead, 125–42. Scranton, Pa.: University of Scranton Press, 2009.

Symcox, Geoffrey, ed. *Repertorium Columbanium.* 13 vols. Turnhout: Brepols, 1998–2004.

Taylor, Charles. *Sources of the Self: The Making of the Modern Identity.* Cambridge, Mass.: Harvard University Press, 1989.

Tellenbach, Gerd. *Church, State and Christian Society at the Time of the Investiture Contest.* Translated by R. F. Bennett. Oxford: Blackwell, 1959.

———. *The Church in Western Europe from the Tenth to the Early Twelfth Century*. Translated by Timothy Reuter. Cambridge: Cambridge University Press, 1993.

Thucydides. *The History of the Peloponnesian War.* Translated by Rex Warner. Harmondsworth: Penguin Books, 1986.

Tierney, Brian. *The Crisis of Church and State 1050–1300.* Englewood Cliffs, N.J.: Prentice-Hall, 1964.

Todorov, Tzvetan. *The Conquest of America: The Question of the Other.* Translated by Richard Howard. New York: Harper and Row, 1984.

Tomkins, Calvin. "The Piano Principle." *The New Yorker* (August 22 and 29, 1994): 52–65.

Toon, Peter. "Christianity and Subjective Human Rights." *Touchstone* 11, no. 6 (November–December 1998): 31–35.

Torres, Miguel Ayuso. *La Filosofía Juridica y Política de Francisco Elías de Tejada.* Madrid: Fundación Francisco Elías Tejada y Erasmo Pèrcopo, 1994.

Uglione, Renato, ed. *Atti del Convegno Nazionale di Studi su la Città ideale nella Tradizione Classica e Biblico-Cristiana.* Turin: Regione Piemone/Assessorato alla Cultura, 1986

Van Anglen, Kevin P. "The Latest Form of Infidelity." *Crisis* 12, no. 7 (July–August 1994): 55–57.

Van Engen, John. "The Christian Middle Ages as an Historiographical Problem." *The American Historical Review* 91 (1986): 519–52.

———. "Faith as a Concept of Order in Medieval Christendom." In *Belief in History: Innovative Approaches to European and American Religion,* edited by Thomas Kselman, 19–67. Notre Dame, Ind.: University of Notre Dame Press, 1991.

Vauchez, André. *La spiritualité du Moyen Age occidental: VIIIe–XIIe siécles.* Paris: Presses universitaires de France, 1975.

———. *The Spirituality of the Medieval West: From the Eighth to the Twelfth Century*. Kalamazoo, Mich.: Cistercian Publications, 1993.

Veatch, Henry B. *Swimming Against the Current in Contemporary Philosophy: Occasional Essays and Papers.* Washington, D.C.: The Catholic University of America Press, 1990.

Voegelin, Eric. *The New Science of Politics: An Introduction.* Chicago: University of Chicago Press, 1952.

———. *Order and History*. 5 vols. Baton Rouge: Louisiana State University Press, 1974–87.

von Balthasar, Hans Urs. *A Theology of History.* New York: Sheed and Ward, 1963.

———. "The Meaning of Celibacy." *Communio* 3 (1976): 319–29.

———. *The Christian State of Life.* Translated by Mary Frances McCarthy. San Francisco: Ignatius Press, 1983.

———. *Theo-Drama: Theological Dramatic Theory.* Vol. 1, *Prolegomena.* Translated by Graham Harrison. San Francisco: Ignatius Press, 1988.

———. *The Theology of Henri de Lubac: An Overview.* Translated by Joseph Fessio and Michael Waldstein. San Francisco: Ignatius Press, 1991.

———. *Bernanos: An Ecclesial Existence.* Translated by Erasmo Leiva-Merikakis. San Francisco: Ignatius Press, 1996.

Vose, Robin. *Dominicans, Muslims and Jews in the Medieval Crown of Aragon.* Cambridge: Cambridge University Press, 2009.

Vree, Dale. "Communism: From Modernity's Vanguard to History's Rearguard." *New Oxford Review* 56, no. 19 (December 1989): 2–4.

Waddell, Helen. *Beasts and Saints.* London: Constable, 1945.

Wade, Nicolas. *The Faith Instinct: How Religion Evolved and Why It Endures.* New York: Penguin Press, 2009.

Walker, Adrian J. "Love Alone: Hans Urs von Balthasar as a Master of Theological Renewal." *Communio* 32 (2005): 517–40.

———. "*El don de la simplicidad.* Reflexiones sobre el significado esistencial de la obediencia en Adrienne von Speyr." In *Adrienne von Speyr a los cuarenta años de su muerte:* Actas del segundo Congreso Fe cristiana y servicio al mundo. Madrid, 9 y 10 de marzo de 2007. Madrid: Fundación Maior, 2007.

Wallerstein, Immanuel. *Utopistics: Or, Historical Choices of the Twenty-first Century.* New York: New Press, 1998.

Walsh, David. *The Modern Philosophical Revolution: The Luminosity of Existence.* Cambridge: Cambridge University Press, 2008.

Walzer, Michael. "Are there Limits to Liberalism?" *New York Review of Books,* October 19, 1995.

Ward, Bruce K. *Redeeming the Enlightenment: Christianity and the Liberal Virtues.* Grand Rapids, Mich.: Eerdmans, 2010.

Watts, Pauline Moffitt. "Prophecy and Discovery: On the Spiritual Origins of Christopher Columbus's 'Enterprise of the Indies.'" *American Historical Review* 90 (1985): 73–102.

Weed, Ronald, and John von Heyking, eds. *Civil Religion in Political Thought: Its Perennial Questions and Enduring Relevance in North America.* Washington, D.C.: The Catholic University of America Press, 2010.

Weigel, George. *The End and the Beginning: Pope John Paul II—The Victory of Freedom, the Last Years, the Legacy.* New York: Doubleday, 2010.

———. "Truths Still Held?" *First Things,* no. 203 (May 2010): 41–47.

Weinreb, Lloyd L. *Natural Law and Justice.* Cambridge: Harvard University Press, 1987.

Westbrook, Robert B. *John Dewey and American Democracy.* Ithaca, N.Y.: Cornell University Press, 1991.

Wheatcroft, Geoffrey. "The Voice of Unconventional Wisdom." *New York Review of Books,* November 11, 2010.

White, Richard. "Back to Nature." *Reviews in American History* 22 (1994): 1–6.

Whitehead, Barbara Dafoe, and David Blankenhorn. "What the Bishops Don't Know About Families." *First Things,* no. 23 (May 1992): 20–22.

Whitman, Walt. "Song of Myself." In *Leaves of Grass.* Introduction by Gay Wilson Allen. New York: publisher unknown, 1958.

Wilber, Charles, and Laura Grimes. "On Michael Novak's Democratic Capitalism." *New Oxford Review* 59, no. 4 (May 1992): 18–25.

Williams, George H. *Wilderness and Paradise in Christian Thought: The Biblical*

Experience of the Desert in the History of Christianity and the Paradise Theme in the Theological Idea of the University. New York: Harper, 1962.

Williams, Oliver F., and John W. Houck, eds. *Catholic Social Thought and the New World Order: Building on One Hundred Years.* Notre Dame, Ind.: University of Notre Dame Press, 1993.

Williams, Robert A., Jr. *The American Indian in Western Legal Thought: The Discourses of Conquest.* New York: Oxford University Press, 1990.

Wills, Gary. "A Tale of Three Leaders." *New York Review of Books,* September 19, 1996.

Wilson, Peter H. *The Thirty Years War: Europe's Tragedy.* Cambridge, Mass.: Harvard University Press, 2009.

Wojtyla, Karol (John Paul II). *The Acting Person.* Translated by Andrzej Potocki. *Analecta Husserliana* 10. Boston: D. Reidel, 1979.

Wolfe, Alan. *Whose Keeper? Social Science and Moral Obligation.* Berkeley: University of California Press, 1989.

Wolfe, Christopher, ed. *The Naked Public Square Reconsidered: Religion and Politics in the Twenty-First Century.* Wilmington, Del.: ISI Books, 2009.

Wood, Alan T. "Fire, Water, Earth, and Sky: Global Systems History and the Human Prospect." *Journal of the Historical Society* 10, no. 3 (September 2010): 287–318.

Wood, Gordon S. "Struggle Over the Puritans." *New York Review of Books,* November 9, 1989.

———. *The Radicalism of the American Revoution.* New York: A. A. Knopf, 1991.

———. "Not So Poor Richard." *New York Review of Books,* June 6, 1996.

———. "The Would be Gentleman." *New York Review of Books,* August 8, 1996.

Worden, Blair. "Hobbes and the Halo of Power." *New York Review of Books,* July 16, 2009.

Worster, Donald. *The Wealth of Nature: Environmental History and the Ecological Imagination.* New York: Oxford University Press, 1993.

Wuthnow, Robert, ed. *Rethinking Materialism: Perspectives on the Spiritual Dimension of Economic Behavior.* Grand Rapids, Mich.: Eerdmans, 1995.

Yanes, Raul F., and Mary Ann Glendon. "Religion and the Court 1993." *First Things,* no. 37 (Nov. 1993): 28–30.

Zaborowski, Holger ed. *Natural Moral Law in Contemporary Society.* Washington, D.C.: The Catholic University of America Press, 2010.

Zieba, Maciej. "The Monk and the Market: What Does a Priest Need Economics For?" *Crisis* 12, no. 7 (July–August 1994): 23–27.

Zimmerman, Jonathan. "What Are Schools For?" *New York Review of Books,* October 14, 2010.

INDEX

On the Road to Emmaus: The Catholic Dialogue with America and Modernity was designed in Granjon with Requiem display type and typeset by Kachergis Book Design of Pittsboro, North Carolina. It was printed on 60-pound Natures Book Natural and bound by Thomson-Shore of Dexter, Michigan.